It Happened 'Round North Bend

A HISTORY OF MIAMI TOWNSHIP AND ITS BORDERS

MARJORIE BYRNSIDE BURRESS

It Happened 'Round North Bend

A HISTORY OF MIAMI TOWNSHIP AND ITS BORDERS

MARJORIE BYRNSIDE BURRESS

Commonwealth Book Company
ST. MARTIN, OHIO

Copyright © 1970 by Marjorie Byrnside Burress.
Copyright © 2015 by Commonwealth Book Company, Inc.
All rights reserved. Printed in the United States of America.

ISBN: 978-1-948986-05-2

FOREWORD

Tell me a tale of the timber-lands,
Of the old-time pioneers;
Somepin' a pore man understands
With his feelin's well as ears.
Tell of the old log house-about
The loft and the puncheon flore,
The old fi-er-place, with its crane swung out,
And the latch string through the door.
                              James Whitcomb Riley

It is a mark of human nature to want to know something about our beginnings, who our forefathers were, where they lived, how they faced life, and what occupations they pursued. What child does not, at some time, say, "Tell me about the olden days, grandpa," or "How was it when you were a little boy?"

"History is the written record of all that man has ever hoped, thought, felt or done." This statement, oft quoted by the late Dr. William E. Smith to his students at Miami University, inspired me to set down something of the little told history of early-day life 'round North Bend, Miami Township and its borders. True, much has been recorded of this place concerning the acts and times of John Cleves Symmes and the Harrisons. However there are many accounts, from ledger and legend, of fact and fantasy, from lesser known men and matters, yet waiting to be told.

Woodrow Wilson, scholar, historian and President, had the following to say about the value of local history:

"A spot of local history is like an inn upon a highway; it is a stage upon a far journey; it is a place the national history has passed through. There mankind has stopped and lodged by the way. Local history is thus less than national history only as the part is less than the whole. Local history is subordinate to national only in the sense in which each leaf of a book is subordinate to the volume itself."

In the belief that men of the future will ever want to acquaint themselves with what has gone before, I have attempted in this book to record some everyday aspects of the history of the local region. I have tried particularly to tell of its story of transportation--from the flatboat to the diesel bus; of the progress of its schools and of the teachers who guided them; of its founders and their accomplishments; of its citizens and their deeds; of its villages and their growth; of its societies; of its legends and of its sites that hold memorable links to the past. I have hoped to capture the spirit of earlier times and to show the main forces at work in the community.

The chief problem in assembling this material was in knowing where to end, not in knowing where to begin. There is no end. The community holds a wealth of historical data waiting to be brought to light. Innumerable residents of this area count themselves among descendants of earliest settlers, some of those named herewith in the 1820 and 1830 census records. Biographical sketches and narratives should be written of more of these pioneer families who have left their marks on this Three Rivers region.

No work can be compiled without the help of the public, libraries, newspapers and collections of private citizens. Countless persons have aided me, in some way, in this endeavor; I have tried to acknowledge personally each source of help. Special credit must go to the staff of the Register Printing Company. My greatest debt is to early writers of history, newspaper journalists and delineators of maps. Without their works much of North Bend and Miami Township's past might long since have been forgotten. Upon their foundations this account has been built. To them I am grateful.

Judge Jacob Burnet, early Cincinnati historian, gave the following advice for recorders of history. I have tried to abide by it:

"It should ever be borne in mind that the office of an historian is one of immense responsibility; that it always tells for good or evil; and that he will be held responsible for the consequences of a want of fidelity."

This account must be judged for its historical worth; it was not undertaken as a literary endeavor. The book is meant to serve as a supplement to what has been recorded in the past and a guide to learning more of the history of the area. It is directed to the townspeople, the local citizenry, to all whose ancestry lies in the region and to those who have made it their home by adoption. May this account help them to feel a closer tie to the past and a deeper pride in their local heritage.

                              Marjorie Byrnside Burress
                              Cincinnati, Ohio
                              November, 1969

Marjorie Burress

CONTENTS

Chapter

1. It Happened 'Round North Bend
2. North Bend's Favorite Son, Harrison Memorial Park And Congress Green
3. Pioneers: Their Trials And Occupations
4. It Happened 'Round The Point
5. The Story Of Mt. Nebo, From Ledger And Legend
6. Grist And Sawmills
7. Miami And Whitewater Valley Pioneer Association
8. Sketch Of The Early Life And Times Of Bailey Guard, Esq., By Rev. B. W. Chidlaw
9. The Role Of The River In Early Life And Settlement: Its Place In Travel And Trade
10. Early Roads, With Emphasis On The River Road
11. Ferries
12. The Cincinnati And Whitewater Canal; Brick Making At North Bend
13. Railroads Come To Miami Township And Its Borders
14. Bridges And Floods
15. Trolleys, Street Cars And Buses Along River Road
16. The Harrison Family In Fact And Fantasy; Cold Springs And Cold Spring Houses
17. Growth Of North Bend As A Village
18. Indian Creek
19. Short's Station, Sekitan And Addyston
20. Burr Oak And Addyston Schools
21. New Life At The Point
22. Schools At The Point And Finney
23. Early Schools Of Miami Township And The Teachers Who Guided Them
24. History Of Mt. Nebo School: An Account Of A Rural School
25. John Aston Warder: Physician, Naturalist And Horticulturist
26. John James Piatt: North Bend Poet
27. The West End Of Cincinnati, By J. J. Piatt
28. Recollections Of The Campaign Of 1840, From **The Hesperian Tree,** By Bettie Harrison Eaton
29. John King: Pharmacologist, Medical Writer And Teacher
30. William Colby Cooper: Physician And Writer
31. The Legend Of The Wamsley Mad Stone
32. Cleves: A Page From The Past
33. John O. And Emma Stumpp Speed: Cleves Poets
34. Downriver Communities
35. Fernbank's Points Of Interest
36. Women And Their Activities In The Community: The Women's Fortnightly Reading Club
37. Legend Of A River Lady
38. Census Records Of Miami Township And Cleves, For 1820 And 1830; Representative Occupations In 1850

Bibliography

Index

Chapter 1

IT HAPPENED 'ROUND NORTH BEND

A story basic to all others in the history and legend of this region is the account of John Cleves Symmes and his settlement. No chronicle of North Bend and Miami Township would be complete without it. It must be told first.

It happened that in the year 1786, Major Benjamin Stites, while trading in Kentucky, came upon a beautiful valley along the Ohio River opposite the mouth of the Licking. On return to his home in New Jersey, Major Stites informed John Cleves Symmes, a man of wide influence, of this new country.

In 1787, Symmes made an exploratory trip down the Ohio. The following year he petitioned Congress for a million acre grant of land to border the north shore of the Ohio River between the two Miamis. Coincidentally, about the same time, he was appointed, in February, 1788, a judge--one of nine--of the Northwest Territory.

Even before he had the assurance of approval to purchase the tract, Judge Symmes began to advertise lots for sale in the new country. As an inducement to prospective settlers, he offered the land in this Miami Purchase for sale at 66 2/3 cents an acre until November, 1788, after which time the price would rise to one dollar.

Tracts were subsequently sold to Major Stites and Matthias Denman, who, with their parties, made initial settlements at Columbia and Losantiville before the year's end.

Judge Symmes made an expedition to the region surrounding the western boundary near the mouth of the Great Miami in September, 1788. At that time plans to build a city began to take shape in his mind and he had a plat drawn for its proposed establishment.

Prior to this time, in October, 1785, under General Richard Butler, Major Walter Finney had established fortifications and quarters along the Ohio one mile upstream from the Great Miami's juncture. This was the first place of habitation by white men in the area. It was named Fort Finney. The United States flag was hoisted and a store set up and stocked with provisions and goods having special appeal to the Indians. Here, it was hoped to negotiate a lasting treaty with the Shawnees. General George Rogers Clark, up from his headquarters at Louisville, was present for a treaty in November, at which six chiefs from the Shawnee, Wyandot and Delaware nations attended. Those chiefs were: Captain Johnny--or Red Pole, Half King, Crane, Pipe, Wingman, and White-Eyes. After several precarious assemblies, a treaty was formulated and signed January 31, 1786, at which five Shawnees were left as hostages. Lieutenant Ebenezer Denny acted as secretary during the negotiations, and it was in his journal that the events of Fort Finney were recorded. Lieutenant Denny was ordered to Fort Harmar, July, 1786, at which time his diary ended. Some months thereafter, severe weather conditions, ice and flood, caused the troops to be withdrawn and Fort Finney abandoned. The exact time is not known.

(In his historical narrative The Frontiersmen, based on fact, Allan W. Eckert on pages 294 to 296 related the account of the building of Fort Finney and the purpose of the treaty. He stated that the blockhouse was inundated and the fortification wiped out in April, 1786, by a flood and that Major Finney and his troops moved on down to Louisville. According to the author, the men did not realize that the flood which had destroyed their fort had saved their lives, for at that very moment Chief Blue Jacket of the Shawnees was leading a force of five hundred warriors to wipe out the fort and its garrison.)

When Judge Symmes and his pioneer party made its first encampment at North Bend, February 2, 1789, the river was in flood. Captain William Kearsey, and a few soldiers who had accompanied the settlers, urged them to continue downstream a few miles to the site of old Fort Finney, but the Judge refused. He had learned that the point there was easily overrun by floods; moreover, it would not adapt suitably for laying out his city. The location at the bend of the river seemed best. Captain Kearsey, who had hoped to make use of the facilities at Fort Finney, soon withdrew his troops from North Bend, to the Judge's extreme displeasure.

Ensign Francis Luce and eighteen men replaced Captain Kearsey at North Bend in March, 1789. They built a good blockhouse. With protection now at hand, settlers began to arrive and the Judge's hopes that his city might be realized were renewed.

However, to his disappointment, this small band of troops was soon withdrawn. Continued uprisings and incidents with the Indians caused many of the settlers to leave. Without an offer of protection, others could not be easily induced to settle there. The Judge sent a steady flow of correspondence to General Josiah Harmar, pleading for troops for his settlement, but to no avail. He needed guards, he wrote, "in defense of this Slaughterhouse, as some are pleased to call the Miami Purchase."

After floods at Columbia and North Bend, Losantiville was later determined to be the most advantageous and strategic site at which to erect a stronghold. Under General Harmar, Fort Washington was built.

The Judge was resigned to abandon the original plat he had proposed for his city. The village he named "Northbend-- as it was situated in the most northerly bend of the Ohio River between the Muskingum and Mississippi."

It is interesting to note that in a letter to his old associate, General Jonathan Dayton, Judge Symmes stated that some of the land nearby was "positively worth a silver dollar per acre."

Early in 1790, Governor Arthur St. Clair arrived at Fort Washington. He organized this section of the Miami Purchase into a county, giving Judge Symmes the honor of naming it. Symmes chose to call it Hamilton County, after the new Secretary of the Treasury.

When the Governor, a member of the "Order of Cincinnatus"--a society of Revolutionary officers--suggested Cincinnati as a better name than Losantiville, it was adopted. (Cincinnatus had been a model of patriotism in the legends of the Roman Republic.)

With the stationing of a fine garrison at Cincinnati, little hope remained for Judge Symmes and the growth of his city. The settlers naturally located where protection was afforded.

A romantic legend tells of a different version as to why North Bend lost its bid to become a city. It might be entitled "To Be or Not to Be Symmes City."

The story goes that within a very short time after the North Bend settlement was made, another called the "Sugar Camp" was established several miles downstream between the Bend and old Fort Finney. A commanding officer of the garrison, assembled at Judge Symmes' request to erect an army post, was charmed by the lovely wife of one of the "Sugar Camp" settlers. The officer's obvious attraction did not go unheeded by the damsel's husband, who, without hesitation, decided that the location at upstream Losantiville was more suitable and offered better protection on several grounds. He and his lady departed from the Bend by the next canoe. The officer, said to have been Ensign Francis Luce, not one to give up so easily, issued a communique stating that perhaps the site at Losantiville should be further considered as a military post. To that place he pursued the object of his affection. Soon after his departure a conclusion was reached that the garrison would be established at Losantiville. The troops were then transferred to that site, and North Bend, without a promise of protection, lost in the race to become "Symmes City."

In his book, Cincinnati Beginnings, Francis W. Miller wrote of the above event:

"That movement, produced by a cause whimsical and apparently trivial in itself, was attended with results of incalculable importance. It settled the question whether North Bend or Cincinnati was to be the great commercial town of the Miami country. If this captivating matron had continued at the Bend, the garrison would have been erected there, population, capital and business would have centered there, and there would have been the Queen City of the West."

According to Major Samuel S. Forman, in Forman's Journey Down the Ohio, 1789-90, Ensign Luce resigned from the Army, May 1, 1790. General Harmar forwarded his resignation to the War office. Captain Brice Virgin probably succeeded Ensign Luce at North Bend. Virgin's militia appointment was among the first made by Gov. St. Clair in the newly organized Hamilton County. Captain Virgin's name appears frequently in historical accounts of Noth Bend in that period.

Among original pioneers who settled at North Bend with Judge Symmes was Capt. John Matson, Revolutionary soldier, who, with his family, in time acquired hundreds of acres of land north of Cleves along the Big Miami, in the general region now known as East Miami River Road, where they operated a saw and grist mill for at least 75 years. Legend tells that the family originated from Maryland (one source says Pennsylvania) and descended the Ohio by flatboat. There were four Matson brothers. These appear to have been Thomas, John, Jr., Isaac and James (1766-1831), the latter having been the great-great grandfather of Mr. James E. Matson, lifetime resident of Cleves. Members of the Matson family, in addition to holding land north of Cleves, also acquired large tracts along the Ohio above Muddy Creek in what became the Fernbank-Home City locale, and along the Big Miami in the region of Lost Bridge. (See "Grist and Saw Mills".)

At CHS Library is a record stating that Pvt. John Matson and Pvt. Thomas Matson served in Capt. Brice Virgin's Co. of Militia Volunteers at North Bend. Recollections of his pioneer and military experiences were written by John Matson, Jr., under the name of Judge Matson, and recorded by Charles Cist, Cincinnati historian, around 1845.

That the pioneers in Symmes' settlement suffered great losses at the hands of the Indians is a recorded fact. Judge Matson recalled some of these encounters. In one account, he told of a Mr. Fuller who with his sixteen-year old son, William, worked for Capt. Matson at the mouth of the Great Miami, August, 1791. While building a fish dam there, young William Fuller was taken by Indians. Concerning another experience in January, 1792, Matson stated that he was among a group of volunteers of North Bend, under command of Capt. Brice Virgin, who were assigned to bury the dead at the scene of an Indian battle nearby. A complete account of the Indian attack at downriver Tanner's Creek was also included in Judge Matson's narratives.

Judge John Matson was an outstanding citizen in the early history of Hamilton County. Among offices that he held were: Hamilton County Commissioner, 1805-1808; Associate Judge of the Court of Common Pleas, 1808-1810; and vice-president, along with Major Daniel Gano, of the Hamilton County Agricultural Society during the same period when General Wm. H. Harrison was president of the organization.

Death notices of Judge Matson, found in old newspapers, give some interesting information about him:

Judge John Matson died in his 78th year, Jan. 10, 1847. Funeral from his residence at Pleasant Run near North Bend.

Another Pioneer Gone: The death of Judge Matson is announced. One of the earliest settlers in this county. He came here as early as 1793, (probably earlier), and located on a farm at North Bend on which he resided until his death. He was of highest reputation. (Cincinnati Gazette, Jan. 12, 1847.)

Death of Judge Matson; died at his residence near North Bend; the friends of Anti-Slavery have cause to regret his death, the loss of one of the pioneers in reform, and the citizens generally. One of the earliest inhabitants of the country. His funeral at his residence. (Cincinnati Morning Herald, Jan. 12, 1847)

Although it is a recorded fact that the North Bend settlement was the scene of numerous Indian attacks, it is likewise recorded that Judge Symmes' purpose in dealing with the Indians was to treat them kindly and justly, in hopes of thereby preventing outbreaks between them and his settlers. In this respect he has been likened to William Penn. With the defeat of the Indians by General Anthony Wayne in 1794, peace at last descended upon the Miami country and the inflow of settlers began.

A notice, which might be interpreted as evidence of North Bend's growth and progress, and probable cessation of Indian troubles, appeared November 9, 1793, in the first issue of Centinel of the Northwest Territory, Cincinnati newspaper. (This paper was printed by William Maxwell at the corner of Front and Sycamore Streets.) A news item, therein, stated: "Subscriptions (for this paper) will be received in North Bend by Aaron Cadwell, Esquire."

John Cleves Symmes, a most important figure in the history of the North Bend settlement, built his first home, a log cabin, about 1794. This house, so legend tells, was given to his daughter, Anna, and her husband, William Henry Harrison, about 1797. With later improvements and sprawling additions it came to be known as the "Big House" by townspeople. This was the same "log cabin" later to become famous in the Presidential campaign of 1840. It stood near the intersection of the present Symmes and Washington Avenues in North Bend.

Judge Symmes built another home, quite grand for the times, at the foot of Mt. Nebo, near the intersection of Mt. Nebo Road and Symmes Street, in what is now the incorporation of Cleves. This mansion, which cost $8,000 to construct, was built for his third wife, Susan Livingston Symmes, daughter of Gov. William Livingston of New Jersey. The place was called "The Chimneys." The brick for the house was said to have been brought all the way from Philadelphia. Mrs. Symmes never adjusted to life in this wilderness country, preferring her home in the east. Judge Symmes' fine home burned in 1811, and with it hundreds of important papers and documents. As a result of the disaster, it took many years to settle land disputes and transactions and to clear property rights. In the matter of financial accounts, Judge Symmes was found to have been most careless.

In a letter to his daughter and son-in-law, Maria (Polly) and Peyton Short, April 22, 1798, Symmes stated that his new house was nearly finished. It was perhaps then, or earlier, that the town of Cleves began to be called "Cleves" or "Clevestown." Another letter written to the Shorts was headed "Cleves," December 25th, 1799. (A good description of the Symmes home in Cleves is found in Ford's History, page 330. Some historians believe the account exaggerated.)

The town patriarch died in 1814 in Cincinnati. General Harrison had retired from the army in that year and he had moved his family from the North Bend farm, for a short time, to a rented house in the city, in order to facilitate the winding up of his public affairs. It was there that Judge Symmes passed away. At his request he was buried in the little pioneer cemetery at North Bend, which came to be called "Congress Green." His remains were brought back to the Bend by way of the river, the same pathway which had first carried him there.

An early pioneer, Henry Applegate, was quoted in Pioneer Annals of Green Township as telling of attending the funeral of Judge Symmes in the city, after which the mourners traveled by keelboat with his body to North Bend.

The inscription on his tomb at Congress Green reads:

"Here rest the remains of John Cleves Symmes who, at the foot of these hills, made the first settlement between the Miami Rivers. Born on Long Island, in the state of New York, July 21, 1742, Died at Cincinnati, February 26, AD 1814."

An iron picket fence for many years inclosed the plot. Around his tomb lie the remains of a number of his descendants, as well as many early-day pioneers.

By the will of John Cleves Symmes, son-in-law William H. Harrison and grandson John Cleves Short, then an attorney in Cincinnati, were appointed administrators of his affairs.

Some years ago, descendants of the family presented several mementoes to the Hamilton County Court House. These included a sword and scabbard carried by Col. John Cleves Symmes in the Revolutionary War and later owned, for a time, by General Harrison; an original land warrant for 160 acres of ground in the famous "Symmes Purchase;" and an oil painting of Col. Symmes.

A portrait of Symmes, painted by Charles Willson Peale, outstanding colonial artist, who also portrayed Washington, Jefferson and Franklin, hangs today at Miami University in the dining room of Symmes Hall. It is appropriate that the picture should be displayed there. Symmes and George Washington had an agreement that if the so-called "Miami Purchase" was approved, Symmes would set aside a tract of land for a seminary devoted to education. The land grant was made and Miami University chartered in 1809.

It is interesting to know that Dr. Stephen Wood, an intimate associate of Judge Symmes, a physician and storekeeper who resided at North Bend, served as a member of the very first board of trustees of the newly chartered college.

To the institution later went a number of persons who were to figure in the history and life of Miami Township and its borders. Among these were Carter Bassett Harrison, son of General Harrison, Benjamin W. Chidlaw, Abram Brower, David W. McClung, and Benjamin Harrison, future President and great-grandson of Miami University's first "sponsor," John Cleves Symmes.

It was William Henry Harrison who, back in 1818, laid out the town of Cleves, the name for which had been chosen many years earlier by his father-in-law, Judge Symmes. The town soon surpassed North Bend in population and for many years served as the post office for both villages.

Cleves post office was established Jan. 12, 1819, shortly after the town was platted. Postmasters and the dates of their appointments were:

Daniel Bailey, Jan. 12, 1819; John L. Watkins, July 17, 1826; Andrew Porter, Feb. 6, 1830; Joseph M. Runyan, Feb. 24, 1835; William T. Young, July 11, 1848; William Finkbine, Mar. 29, 1849; David I. Brown, Oct. 15, 1851; Amos B. Dunn, Dec. 1, 1852; Andrew Porter, Apr. 6, 1853; George Cassady, Oct. 27, 1854; James Carlin, Apr. 4, 1859; Joseph D. Brown, Apr. 14, 1860; Thomas Archer, Feb. 4, 1862; Charles K. Ruffin, Apr. 29, 1869; Rosalvo W. Crofoot, Jan. 31, 1871; George Cassady, June 20, 1871; James Carlin, Dec. 17, 1885; Fred A. Grossman, Apr. 3, 1889; James Carlin, July 26, 1893; William Argo, Aug. 7, 1897; Melissa Argo, June 30, 1899; Frank M. Carlin, July 15, 1913; Robert E. Carlin (Acting), Aug. 5, 1920; Emmert H. Crim (Acting), Sept. 23, 1920; G. B. Henderson (Acting), Jan. 1, 1921; Effie L. Moore, Nov. 2, 1921; E. H. Crim; Mabel A. Merrilees; Alex C. Franz, Jr.; Mabel A. Merrilees; Mary C. Dick; Robert W. Meyers; Conrad A. Bayer.

William H. Harrison and J. H. Howell were bondsmen for the post office at Cleves in 1826, according to information from the Post Office Department in Washington, D. C. (See "Growth of North Bend as a Village" for further information on postal service.)

Today the villages of Cleves and North Bend, lying side by side, share with pride the heritage left by their first settlers, those borne down the Ohio aboard flatboats. Such a heritage has motivated this writer to recount subsequent happenings around North Bend and its borders.

(Reliable accounts concerning John Cleves Symmes and his settlement at North Bend are found in the books of Beverley W. Bond, Jr., namely The Correspondence of John Cleves Symmes, 1926, and The Intimate Letters of John Cleves Symmes and His Family, 1956. These books were published by the Historical and Philosophical Society of Ohio, now-- since 1963--called the Cincinnati Historical Society (CHS). They were a great source of help to this writer.)

(The following item is inserted to set an oft erroneous record straight. Judge Symmes, through the years, has repeatedly been confused by writers with his nephew of the same name. That nephew, Capt. John Cleves Symmes (1780-1829), who lived his later life at Hamilton, Ohio, was the author of what he called the "Theory of Concentric Spheres." He believed that there were holes at the North and South poles through which an explorer might enter the interior world. These polar openings came to be known as "Symmes' Hole." Capt. Symmes influenced Kentucky Congressman Richard M. Johnson to present his case in Washington. Johnson, who was to become vice-president of U.S., a nephew of Cave Johnson who resided in Boone County, Ky., in a large home directly opposite North Bend, requested Congress to finance an expedition into the center of the earth. Although there was wide interest in the project, the petition was defeated in 1823. In later years a monument to the memory of Symmes was placed at Hamilton by his son Americus Vespucius Symmes. This stone marker, which may yet be seen, features a replica of Symmes' hollow earth. Jules Verne, in 1864, published his classic novel, Journey to the Center of the Earth, which owed its inspiration to some of the ideas advanced by Capt. Symmes, the Judge's nephew.)

(Three other towns in the United States bear the name of North Bend, each of them having received the name from their geographic location on a body of water. North Bend, Nebraska, stands beside the Platte River; North Bend, Washington, is located on a fork of the Snoqualmie River; and North Bend, Oregon, sits along Coos Bay, a salt water estuary formed by Coos River.)

Chapter 2

NORTH BEND'S FAVORITE SON HARRISON MEMORIAL PARK AND CONGRESS GREEN

In writing of this community's illustrious heritage, the pen literally needs no guide. It follows, as the day the night, that the story of North Bend's favorite son, "Old Tippecanoe," must next be told.

In turning back history's pages to the settlement of the Northwest Territory, we find on the staff of General Anthony Wayne a young lieutenant named William Henry Harrison, who had achieved marked success as an Indian fighter. Promoted, in 1795, to the role of commander of Fort Washington, young Harrison achieved still further success by winning the hand of Anna Symmes, the Judge's daughter.

After serving as Secretary of the Northwest Territory, first Governor of the Indiana Territory, victorious General at the Battle of Tippecanoe, Senator to Congress and Minister to Colombia, William Henry Harrison retired, about 1830, to his farm facing the peaceful river at North Bend.

Although he was best known for his military achievements, one of his most outstanding accomplishments was made while serving in Congress. As chairman of the committee on public lands, he brought about passage of the Land Act of 1800. Prior to that time western lands were sold only in tracts of a section (640 acres) or more. General Harrison saw that this law did not favor the poorer settler for he could not afford to purchase such sizeable sections. The new bill made it possible for lands to be divided and sold in smaller tracts. This act truly opened up the west.

Throughout his life General Harrison participated in numerous business ventures, although these were not always financially successful. He encouraged home industry and was a strong promoter of the building of the Miami and Whitewater Canals.

Harrison maintained an interest in civic affairs and was a frequent speaker at such functions. He was elected president of the newly organized Hamilton County Agricultural Society in 1819. When General Lafayette stopped in Cincinnati on May 19, 1825, Harrison was chosen to be chairman of the reception committee.

Before entering the army he had studied medicine and this subject continued, all of his life, to hold his interest. He served for a time on the board of the Medical College of Ohio and it was undoubtedly his influence that led one of his sons to study medicine.

The Harrisons had a large family and with it came much sickness and sorrow. There were endless debts and tragedies of every kind. Money being so scarce led the General, in 1835, to come out of semi-retirement and accept the position of clerk of the Common Pleas Court of Hamilton County. While working in this capacity, he was tapped by his political friends to re-enter the national scene, to run for the highest office in the land.

So it was that in 1836 and again in 1840, William Henry Harrison ran as Whig candidate for the United States Presidency.

North Bend became the hub of the now famous 1840 campaign. It was the first in history to be carried on with such fanfare, singing processions and mass meetings. History records Harrison's words: "When you come to North Bend you will always find the latch-string out."

His opponents referred to him as a backwoodsman, content with his log cabin, barrel of cider and pension for life. Log cabins, buckeye branches and coon skin caps became glaring symbols.

These campaign cries of the opponent worked to the Whigs' advantage. The log cabin was representative of many homes of the West in that day. This reference to Harrison pleased the cabin dwellers and won for him many followers who pictured their candidate as one of them. From his wilderness experience, Harrison knew, first hand, the problems of the West.

Among the songs credited with singing him into office was one called "The Tippecanoe or Log Cabin Quick Step." Other folksy tunes hailed him as "the farmer of North Bend."

Harrison's home at North Bend was not a log cabin; neither was he a backwoodsman. In reality he was an educated gentleman whose father, Benjamin Harrison, had been a signer of the Declaration of Independence.

The political opposition's own campaign cries unwittingly brought about victory for Harrison and his running mate, John Tyler.

When it came time for the President-elect to travel to Washington to be inaugurated, Anna Harrison was ill. Daughter-in-law Jane Irwin Harrison, widow of William H. Harrison, Jr., went with the General to serve as official hostess until the new First Lady would be able to join her husband in the White House. Also in attendance with the young Mrs. Harrison at the White House was her aunt, Mrs. James Findlay, widow of President Harrison's old friend, General Findlay.

Few members of the President's immediate family were present for the inauguration, March 4, 1841. Montgomery Pike Harrison, son of John Cleves Symmes and Clarissa Pike Harrison, was among those in attendance.

Original Tomb Of William Henry Harrison, 1841

William Henry Harrison's Presidential victory was short-lived. He died one month after his inauguration. In July, 1841, his remains were transported overland to Pittsburgh and there placed aboard the Steamer RARITAN, on which they were carried downstream for burial. At Cincinnati, the body lay in state at the home of the Harrison's daughter and son-in-law, Anna and William H. H. Taylor, on Sixth Street. A memorial service was conducted at old Wesley Chapel. The funeral procession then marched to the river where the President's body was placed aboard the RARITAN. Two other steamers traveling along side and loaded with mourners slowly moved to North Bend. Upon reaching the Bend, the funeral party gathered at the selected burial site where a service was led by Rev. John T. Brooke. Cincinnati undertaker Samuel Cobb gave the use of an elegant new hearse. Dr. John A. Warder, D. E. Strong and J. J. Stratton served on the committee which provided music for the ceremony. The remains of the President were then placed in a simple mausoleum of brick work.

Harrison's Tomb, About 1890

The burial spot overlooked the beautiful Ohio. Grandson Benjamin Harrison, future President, himself, later remarked that the loveliness of the place alone was monument enough for his grandfather because he had especially favored this view of the river.

As time passed the subject of the inadequacy and neglect of President Harrison's tomb began to recur again and again. The following lines gleaned from newspaper accounts through the years shed light on this matter:

March, 1855. Cincinnati Gazette. "This paper was informed by Col. Taylor, son-in-law of the late General Harrison, who with his family occupies the old homestead at North Bend, that within a few weeks the family will have caused an iron door to be made to the entrance to the tomb and which has been fitted that it will require a crow-bar to remove it. We are glad of this, although it is hard to think it was necessary in order to prevent strangers from violating the sanctuary of the illustrious dead."

Nov. 10, 1879. Cincinnati Daily Gazette. "Capt. Carter Harrison of Point Farm and his brother, Gen. Benjamin Harrison, have repaired the tomb of their honored grandfather. The work has been done in a thorough manner. It is warranted to last for 50 years. The remains of their honored father (John Scott Harrison) will be placed in the tomb shortly."

(Following the horrible grave robbery of John Scott Harrison, May, 1878, and the recovery of his body in a Cincinnati medical college, his remains were temporarily placed in the Strader vault at Spring Grove Cemetery.)

The original tomb of General Harrison had an arched roof which was sodded on top. When it was repaired in 1879, a flat roof replaced the arched one, and the brick work was covered with a thick cement coating set in squares. As time passed, grass began to grow in the seams.

Sometime during the early 1880's, a group of local citizens organized the North Bend Harrison Memorial Association for the care of the mound at North Bend, wherein Gen. Harrison was buried, and to assist in the erection of a monument thereon. Judge John S. Conner, whose home was just across the road from the tomb, next to Congress Green, was president of the memorial association. Keeping the underbrush and weeds down had been the most the organization had ever accomplished. After numerous efforts to secure an appropriation from Congress, the memorial association, by 1894, was virtually dead. The pathway leading to the tomb had been lined with cedar trees many years earlier, and although these were yet thriving, the general appearance and condition of the grounds at the tomb and in the pioneer cemetery, Congress Green, was depressing to see.

Around this time Anna A. Warder, daughter of Dr. John A. Warder, wrote a short history of North Bend, at the request of a Cincinnati newspaper which had just introduced a column of local history to its readers. In this article Miss Warder noted the neglect of the Harrison burial site. She stated:

"Until the interruption of navigation during the late war, steamboats generally tolled their bells in passing this place, then as now only marked by some cedar trees planted by Andrew Ernst, one of the pioneer nursery men of Cincinnati.

"Republics are said to be ungrateful, and although the subject of a fitting monument has been agitated, again and again, and pilgrimages have visited this spot, no stone has yet been erected to the memory of this servant of his country.

"A little further from the river, on a higher hill, is the old graveyard, where a flat stone bears the name and covers the grave of John Cleves Symmes, who purchased the land from the United States Government, and made the first settlement of North Bend in 1789.

"Symmes had expected to lay out a city at North Bend, which was to extend from the Ohio a mile back to the Miami...

"Congress Green still retains its name, though it never became the public grounds of the city, as had been intended, for the city has never been..."

Harrison's Tomb Rebuilt In 1897. Entrance Changed

The name Congress Green was originally applied to a reserved section of land in the village of North Bend, set aside by Judge Symmes and meant to be the public grounds, or village commons, of the "city of his vision." Among the writings of Charles Cist, Cincinnati historian, is a letter written by Judge Symmes at North Bend and dated Dec. 28, 1792, in which Congress Green is mentioned. The letter, addressed to Cincinnati officials, concerned the proposed location for the erection of a county jail. Among his suggestion, Judge Symmes cautioned that the jail be built on the second bank, rather than on the Cincinnati bottoms, to insure that prisoners might not drown in the event of a flash flood. (Cincinnati had had a devastating flood in that year, 1792.) Judge Symmes, in his letter, went so far as to suggest on behalf of North Bend inhabitants that the "prison be built on Congress Green, a most elegant situation." In a footnote, written in 1844, Cist explained that Congress Green was the public ground in front of the village of North Bend.

The Judge's city never came into being. The name Congress Green was eventually given to the pioneer burying ground, across from the Harrison Memorial, but when it was so named has not been learned. Legend says that the old graveyard was first established after a soldier was killed in a tavern brawl. Since no government cemetery existed, the soldier was buried on the hillside overlooking North Bend, in a spot of the Judge's reserved "Congress Green" section, which legend tells extended on up into Mount Nebo Hill. Later North Bend's patriarch, Judge Symmes, himself, chose to be buried there. After that time members of the Harrison family and other pioneers of the region were laid to rest in the old burying place. Apparently there was an eastern section of the grounds set aside for the burial of paupers. The following items from the Lawrenceburg Press tell of Congress Green:

May 16, 1872. "A mystery man, 'Mr. Hettlick,' earlier found in an insensible condition, possibly drugged, by Mr. Stephen Hayes in North Bend, died. He bore no other identification and was buried in a rough box at Congress Green."
May 27, 1875. "Judge John S. Conner is building an elegant residence near Congress Green."
June 3, 1875. "John S. Conner brought an action of ejection against the trustees of Miami Township to recover the eastern portion of Congress Green known as Potter's Field."
Aug. 26, 1875. "A. C. Bonham has the contract and has gone to work to make the fill at the new county bridge across the Whitewater Valley Railroad at Congress Green."

Congress Green was used as a burial ground at least until around 1884, at which time Maple Grove Cemetery was officially opened. According to dates on the headstones, Mary Buckingham, lifetime resident around North Bend, was buried there in 1883, and W. H. H. Thornton, son of Dr. John H. F. and Mary S. Harrison Thornton, was interred there as late as 1903. Undoubtedly many burials without benefit of markers were made there. Several soldiers who died in the Civil War are said to have been first buried at Congress Green but later re-interred at Maple Grove in the "Soldier's Ring."

(It is interesting to note that an act of the Ohio Legislature was required to allow trustees of Miami Township to purchase land for a cemetery in the adjoining Whitewater Township, known as Maple Grove Cemetery. The trustees purchased the land April 11, 1884. Prior to that time most burials were made in private family grounds. Other pioneer burying places, nearby, inclued Berea Cemetery, opened in 1804, Zion U. B. Church cemetery, and the township cemetery at Hunt's Grove.)

The shocking state of the Harrison burial site and the pioneer cemetery closeby was described at length in the Commercial Gazette, May 13, 1894. Prior to that time a bronze statue of General Harrison seated on a horse was cast and brought to Cincinnati, in July, 1892. An argument ensued as to where to place it. Burnet Woods Park was among the suggestions. The Harrison Monument Commission, organized in 1887, responsible for securing the memorial, was forced to store the statue until a site was selected. Subscriptions for a pedestal--a base for the statue--were collected. Finally, on May 30, 1896, with ex-President Benjamin Harrison in attendance, the monument was dedicated at Garfield Park (now Piatt Park) in the city. The statue was fittingly placed on the original site of old Fort Washington, where Harrison had first entered the service of his country as an aid to Gov. St. Clair. The unveiling of the marker, in the city, was commended.

However, Gen. Sam F. Cary, speaker at the dedication, who had known Harrison personally and had actively participated in the campaigns of 1836 and 1840, closed his address with this statement:

"This Republic will not do its full duty until it has erected at North Bend a monument which the tooth of time can not gnaw down."

Shortly thereafter, the residents of Cleves and North Bend raised $1,000 to repair the old tomb. Further excavation was made in the hillside, the burial space was enlarged to hold 16 crypts, and the entrance to the tomb was changed from the west to the south side. Col. D. W. McClung, whose wife was a granddaughter of General Harrison, took an active part in the rebuilding of the tomb, which was completed in 1897. Many visitors came to see the improvements. Until then even the last resting place of "Old Tippecanoe" had gone unmarked.

In spite of the improvements, no plan was established to care for the grounds. The property on which the Harrison monument and Congress Green lay was yet in the hands of the Harrison heirs. So it was that the deplorable conditions of the Harrison grave were again drawn into the spotlight following a ghostly episode in December, 1911. As it happened, the tomb and cemetery grounds surrounding it had become a playground for local boys. On this specific occasion, young George Smedley, on a dare from his playmates, had gone inside the door of the tomb. His friends quickly closed the heavy iron door, set the hasp over the staple, locking George inside, and scampered off home. Time passed during which the frightened boy called and called and cried out to anyone who might hear him. It happened that at dusk Mrs. Della Gabriel got off the traction car at the foot of the tomb and proceeded to her home on Cliff Road. On ascending the hill, she was shocked to hear cries coming from the tomb. She bravely investigated, found it was her neighbor-boy, George, and immediately opened the gate for him. The event caused quite a bit of excitement around North Bend and stirred up some sensational publicity. The neglect of the tomb was once more headlined. (The late John Zapf, Jr., who grew up in North Bend not far from the tomb, enjoyed reminiscing about the part he had played in this mischievous episode.) The publicity did, however, set some wheels in motion as seen in the following news items:

March 6, 1912. Lawrenceburg Press. "To arouse interest in the tomb, a patriotic society, through the Cincinnati Chamber of Commerce, launched a movement to have steamboats once more toll their bells as they pass the tomb of President Harrison at North Bend."
July 10, 1912. Lawrenceburg Press. "The Cincinnati Business Men's Club organized a William H. Harrison Memorial Association to facilitate the transfer to the government the property embracing Harrison's tomb at North Bend. The neglect of the tomb was deplored."
Nov. 12, 1912. The Cincinnati Enquirer devoted a full page to the subject of the tomb. Writer of this account was James B. Hendryx, great-grandson of President Harrison, who in time became known for his books of adventure stories for boys. Hendryx listed, in 1912, the burials within the tomb, eleven in number. These were, in addition to President Harrison; Anna Symmes Harrison, his wife; Mary S. Harrison Thornton, daughter; John Scott Harrison, son, (the father of President Benjamin Harrison); Mary Sutherland Harrison, daughter-in-law, wife of Carter Bassett Harrison; Bettie Harrison Eaton, granddaughter, (daughter of J. Scott); Anna Thornton Fitzhugh, granddaughter; George Eaton, great-grandson; Archibald Eaton, great-grandson; Anna Eaton, great-great-granddaughter; George Coleman Eaton, great-great grandson.
Jan. 1, 1921. The Cincinnati Enquirer reported that the Harrison Memorial Commission, authorized by the State of Ohio, had at last obtained title to the tomb from the heirs of John Scott Harrison. Horace Bonser was listed as chairman

of the Memorial Commission. This act, it was stated, would pave the way for a permanent memorial. Ground totaling 13 acres and including old Congress Green cemetery was secured for the project. Heirs of Abram Brower had donated one acre.

Feb. 20, 1921. The Cincinnati Commercial Tribune devoted a full page to the General Harrison memorial. It stated that at last action was to be taken by the Ohio Legislature to erect a worthy monument. The first step taken by the tomb improvement committee was to secure a caretaker for the park.

Sept. 22, 1921. Lawrenceburg Press. "By appropriation of the General Assembly of Ohio a fund is now available for the Harrison Memorial Park at North Bend. Plans call for an impressive entrance, well kept trees and suitable monument."

A beautiful entrance to the park was completed in 1922, and a tall monument erected in 1924. Hallie Stephens Caine, sister of Congressman A.E.B. Stephens of North Bend, served on the Harrison Memorial Commission under the chairmanship of Horace Bonser. Much credit goes to Hallie Caine for her efforts in securing this monument to North Bend's "favorite son."

Harrison Memorial, Built In 1924

It is interesting to note that a descendant of the pioneer Hughes family played on a cornet at the dedication ceremonies of the new entrance in 1922, which had also been played at the same site by an earlier family member at the funeral service of President Harrison in 1841.

Since that year, 1841, thousands of persons from far and near have visited the historic shrine, paying homage to the Ninth President. Steamboat bells have been rung, bands have played, school children have sung, soldiers and sailors--bearing floral wreaths--have marched, and eloquent words have been spoken in tribute to William Henry Harrison.

A "Sacred Pilgrimage" to the tomb took place Oct. 5, 1887. The occasion commemorated the Battle of Tippecanoe (Nov. 7, 1811) and the Battle of the Thames (Oct. 5, 1813). Advance publicity in a Cincinnati newspaper urged citizens "to do honor to the memory of the hero of Tippecanoe and at the same time spend a day in the country."

Special trains, carriages and chartered steamboats brought 2,500 "pilgrims" to North Bend. A log cabin was erected near the monument; souvenir ribbon-badges, depicting William H. Harrison and the log cabin, were sold and worn; and photographs were taken on that grand day.

Prominent persons and noted speakers mingled with the crowds. Rev. B. W. Chidlaw, old friend of the hero, opened the ceremonies with prayer. Congressman Charles E. Brown, presiding, delivered the welcome. Hon. W. C. P. Breckinridge of Kentucky spoke. The local G.A.R. unit assembled; Cleves Cornet Band, led by John R. Hughes, furnished music; pupils of Cleves Public School sang; and a choir and glee club, directed by Harry L. Cooper, Cleves attorney, performed.

North Bend's talented schoolmaster, Maximilian Braam, composed a number entitled "Tippecanoe" for his scholars to sing on this grand and patriotic occasion. The words of the composition extolled General Harrison. (See more of Max Braam in "North Bend Schools.")

Joining the never-ending procession of those who have paid honor to President Harrison was North Bend's Thomas J. Truitt (1845-1906). Unlike Max Braam who had praised "Old Trippecanoe" in song, Tom Truitt, public-spirited citizen, in 1902, gave tribute in the form of a flagpole.

Aware that no flag waved at the Harrison Tomb, and deploring that fact, Truitt set himself the task of calling on friends and asking their support in purchasing a flagpole. He collected $96 from persons who lived around North Bend--walking the area from Valley Junction to Fernbank, ordered, painted and installed a 63-foot pole. In response to the project, Mr. and Mrs. C. W. Caine donated a flag in the name of John S. Conner School pupils. Tom Truitt then had handbills printed and distributed, announcing to all that "the 'Star Spangled Banner' now waves o'er Harrison's Tomb."

Twenty-two years later, the new 60-foot monument constructed at the Harrison burial site was deemed too tall for the "little" 63-foot flagpole, placed there in 1902. Of necessity the old staff was replaced by a new one, 100 feet tall. However, the life of the old flagpole was not over.

On January 10, 1926, the new Taylor High School, of Cleves-North Bend School District, was the scene of a flag raising ceremony. The old Harrison's Tomb flagpole was transplanted at the site. A flag presentation program was given at which Edna Truitt Hayes appropriately told the history of the pole. That flagpole yet stands, today.

On the occasion of the 158th anniversary of the birthday of Harrison, Feb. 9, 1931, the 8th grade civics club of Cleves-North Bend schools placed a wreath at the tomb and presented an interesting program. Joseph W. Garrison of North Bend carved a gavel from wood of a pear tree from the original orchard of General Harrison to be awarded the president of the civics club. Supt. of Schools Charles T. Young presented the gavel to William Argo. J. Atkins of U.S. Grant Camp No. 100, Sons of Civil War Veterans, participated in the ceremony. Featured on the program were: Selections by Taylor High School Band; "The Whig Party" by Raymond Sisson; "The Log Cabin Campaign" by Willard Hayes; "Life of Wm. H. Harrison" by Miriam Moreland; "Harrison's Tomb, 1876-1931" by Hallie S. Caine; "Community Interests" by O. H. Bennett. The wreath was carried by Scouts J. Frank Wolcott and Bob

Campbell. Teacher of the civics class was Anna Gillespie. (Times-Star, Feb. 11, 1931)

On June 3, 1941, General Harrison was honored in still another way. That year marked the centennial of his Inauguration and death. Commencement exercises of Taylor High School were focused on this event. Graduate Huey R. Coward's oration saluted General Harrison's public service and military achievements.

The year 1941 will be remembered in North Bend history, and in world history, for a reason more profound than the Harrison Centennial. This was the year of the Japanese attack on Pearl Harbor. So it happened that a short time after graduation, Huey Coward, along with most of his Taylor High classmates, went off to war. Huey eventually became Lieutenant Coward, fighter pilot, and made an honorable record for himself before being shot down over Germany. Like General Harrison of old, whom he had venerated, Huey Coward also served his country well.

The road winding round the Harrison Memorial Park passes Congress Green Cemetery and leads to Cliff Road, high above the Ohio, where many years earlier the Guard brothers rolled their logs down a chute to the waiting steamers. Here, today--as then, is afforded one of the most lovely and wide-sweeping views to be seen anywhere. From this vista can be seen the Boone County, Kentucky, hills, and the stately old Cave Johnson home, built about 1796, near where Col. "Dick" Johnson rendezvoused his regiment of cavalry when it was recruited and drilled in preparation for the campaign in the War of 1812, which ended in the British defeat at the Thames and the death of the Indian chief, Tecumseh. Benjamin Stites and John Cleves Symmes, who first viewed the scene in 1786 and 1787, certainly knew beautiful country when they saw it.

This view recently inspired musician Edward F. Howard, a native of Cleves, to compose, while studying at Miami University, a brilliant symphonic band arrangement which he entitled "North Bend Suite." The modern composition, in four movements, is based upon scenes and events along the historic Ohio River and Harrison Memorial Park. It is Ed Howard's song of homage to North Bend's past. In sounding his notes of praise, the young musician joined the throng of men before him who had paid tribute, in countless ways, to General Harrison.

Innumerable persons, through the ages, have paid tribute to William Henry Harrison in yet another way, and that has been with their pens. Among these countless writers have been James Albert Green, Cincinnatian, who in 1941 contributed an excellent biography entitled William Henry Harrison: His Life and Times, and Alta Harvey Heiser, who, in her book West to Ohio, presented an equally fine historical account of the Harrison family.

For many years history classes of Taylor High School, in a step initiated by Mrs. Maye (DeLay) Wright, annually assembled at the tomb on the occasion of President Harrison's birthday. This act helped to instill in the students a spirit of patriotism and respect for their country. Today, on a wider scale, a national program honoring the memory of American Presidents has recently been inaugurated and annual ceremonies are presently being conducted at the memorial site. The grounds of the Harrison Memorial Park are beautifully maintained, and the old cedar trees, dating from 1841, and straggly with age, yet grace the path to the tomb of North Bend's "favorite son."

Much has been recorded already of the Harrisons and Judge Symmes and the roles they played in the settlement of North Bend and Miami Township. But there are also many stories waiting to be told, or to be refreshed to mind, about other pioneers, their trials and occupations and their places in the history of this community. With the foregoing accounts of Judge Symmes and General Harrison as background, it is time now to recount something of those lesser known tales.

The Family of Wm. H. & Anna Symmes Harrison
(for the reader's reference)

Betsy-b. 1796, d. 1846, m. John Cleves Short (Son of Maria Symmes & Peyton Short, her first cousin)
John C. Symmes-b. 1798, d. 1830, m. Clarissa Pike (Daughter of Gen. Zebulon & Clara Brown Pike)
Lucy Singleton-b. 1800, d. 1826, m. David K. Este (He was a prominent Cincinnati judge)
Wm. Henry, Jr.-b. 1802, d. 1838, m. Jane Irwin (She acted as hostess at the White House in 1841)
John Scott-b. 1804, d. 1878, m. Lucretia Johnson, #2. Elizabeth Irwin (Elizabeth was mother of Pres. Benjamin Harrison)
Benjamin-b. 1806, d. 1840, m. Louise Bonner, #2. Mary Raney (He studied medicine)
Mary Symmes-b. 1809, d. 1842, m. John H. F. Thornton (He was a physician; resided on State Rd., Cleves)
Carter Bassett-b. 1811, d. 1839, m. Mary A. Sutherland (Only daughter, Anna Carter, wed D. W. McClung)
Anna Tuthill-b. 1814, d. 1865, m. W. H. H. Taylor (Her distant cousin; colonel in Civil War)
James Findlay-died in infancy; named for Gen. Findlay, early mayor of Cincinnati.

Congress Green Cemetery Readings
(Those able to be read in 1967; many unmarked stones)

Ackman, Margaret wife of Jacob Ackman; d. July 13, 1834-age 49
Alison, Daniel son of S. & E.
Allison, child of Elizabeth Allison; d. 1845, age 22 years.
Bailey, Daniel husband of Phebe Bailey d. 1824, 42 years.
Banks, Symmes son of M. & Clara Banks 1810
Buckingham, Mary b. 1821 d. 1883 age 62
Carr, Samuel W. b. Conn. 1817 d. 1874
Carr, Mary Louisa dau. of Samuel & Harriet Carr, d. 1840, 19 mo.
Coughlan, Wm. Thomas son of James L. & Janeva, d. 1845
Easter, Henry Oct. 30, 1812
Eaton, George C. MD 1820-1866
Eaton, Nannie dau. of Geo. & Bessie H. Eaton, d. 1857 age 14 mo.
Eaton, Mary 1851-1877 (also a stone "Little Mary")
Eaton, Scott Harrison 1848-1878
Eckman, Geo. W. d. age 55
Frese, Ida b. 1869 d. 1869 (?)
Ginter, Charles son of Henry & Louise Ginter b. 1844
Ginter, Henry d. 1851 age 54
Ginter, Louise wife of Henry d. 1849 age 55
Griffin, Samuel H. b. 1836 d. 1848, son of Wm. & Elizabeth Griffin
Harrison, Anna Symmes dau. of J. Scott & Elizabeth Harrison, d. Aug. 26, 1838 age 1 yr. 3 da.
Harrison, John Irwin son of J. Scott & Elizabeth Harrison, d. Oct. 25, 1839 age 4 mo.
Harrison, James Findlay son of J. Scott & Elizabeth Harrison, d. Jan. 3, 1848, 11 mo.
Harrison, Dr. Benjamin, son of W. H. Harrison, b. Vincennes, Ia., 1806, d. 1840, age 34 yrs.
Harrison, Carter B. d. at Hamilton, Ohio, Aug. 12, 1839, 28 yrs., b. Vincennes, Ia. Oct. 26, 1811.
Harrison, Wm. Henry, Jr. son of W. H. Harrison, b. Vincennes, Ia., Sept. 3, 1802, d. 1838 36th yr.
Harrison, William H., son of Doctor Benj., & Mary B. Harrison, b. 1839 d. 1850
Harrison, James Irwin son of J. Scott & Elizabeth Harrison, b. 1849 d. 1850
Harrison, Elizabeth wife of J. Scott Harrison, 1810-1850

Harrison, Wm. Henry, son of John Scott & Lucretia Harrison, b. North Bend, 1827 d. 1829
Klumpp, Karl D. b. 1831 Germany, d. 1875 in Clevetown, Ohio
Ladd,
Laird, Mary b. Ireland d. 1867 age 76
Laird, Samuel b. Ireland d. 1851 age 44
Lockhart, Dora dau. of G. Lockhart d. 1866, age 3
Love, Stephen H. son of M. S. & B. G. Love b. 1854, d. 1855
Malone, John d. 1868 22 yrs.
McClelland, Nancy wife of Benjamin H. d. 1874 age 24
Moore, Doc. & Mary (Mother & Father on the stone)
Pfeffer, John 1860-1861
Pfeffer, Carl 1862-1870
Popham, Willie son of Charles & Mahala
Rittenhouse, Wm. Keen b. 1802 d. 1875
Rittenhouse, Ann M. wife, b. 1804 d. 1872 *(Cora Rittenhouse says she was called "Amy"; also believed that other Rittenhouses were buried on this lot.)
Runyan, Mary mother of J. M. Runyan, d. 1832, 70th year.
Runyan, Abigale dau. of J. M. Runyan d. 1832, 3 yrs.
Runyan, Joseph son of J. M. Runyan 2 yrs.
Runyan, Polly W. wife of J. M. Runyan, d. 1833 age 32
Short, Betsy Bassett, wife of John Cleves Short, (Large Marker), b. Sept. 29, 1796; m. June 29, 1814; d. Sept. 29, 1846.)
Silver, James d. Oct. 6, 1822 56th yr.
Silver, D.S.S. on another small stone nearby James Silver.
Silver, John B. July 20, 1832 26 yrs.
Silver, Mary Eliza., dau. of James & Eliza Silver, age 1 yr., d. Mar. 24, 1842.
Symmes, John Cleves "Here rest the remains of John Cleves Symmes who, at the foot of these hills, made the first settlement between the Miami Rivers. Born on Long Island, in the state of New York, July 21, 1742, Died at Cincinnati, February 26, AD 1814."
Taylor, Anna Tuthill dau. of Gen. Harrison, wife of Wm. H. H. Taylor, d. July, 1865, age 50 years.
Taylor, Nellie (small stone nearby)
Thornton, Wm. H. H. b. 1830 at North Bend, d. 1903 at Ellettsville, Ind.
Thornton, Chas. MD b. North Bend, July 1832; d. June 22, 1868.
Thornton, J. H. F., MD b. 1798 d. 1871 at Newstead, Ohio (*Note: Wm. H. H. & Chas. Thornton were sons of J. H. F. & Mary Harrison Thornton)
Thornton, Lucy H., d. Dec. 16, 1840; dau. of J. H. F. & Mary Thornton
Thornton, Joseph C. son of J. H. F. & Eliza Thornton, died 1846.
Thornton, Persis C. dau. of J. H. F. & Eliza Thornton, b. Mar. 27, 1849, d. July 1850.
Towner, Homer d. 1823 age 55 yrs.
Towner, Abigal d. 1836 age 55, (*Note: Stones placed by sons, H. N. & H. W. Towner)
Welsh, Mary E. dau. of G. S. & E. S. Welsh d. 1862 age 1 yr.
Welsh, Geo. A. son of G. S. & E. S. Welsh d. 1862 4 yrs.
Zondler, Jakob b. 1829 d. 1873 43 years, (*Note: This was the grandfather of Mrs. Margaret Keller Frankenhauser)

There are some rough stones unable to be read; also many burials were no doubt made here without markers. Maple Grove Cemetery was opened in 1884. It is said that several Civil War soldiers were moved from Congress Green and reinterred at Maple Grove in the "Soldiers Ring."

These Congress Green Readings were made in 1967 by Marjorie Brynside Burress.

★★★★★★★★★★★

Judge John Matson, one of the earliest pioneers of Miami Township, was among the honorary pallbearers at the funeral of Wm. H. Harrison.

Harrison Pilgrimage North Bend, O. Oct. 5, 1887

TIPPECANOE.

PRICE, 5 CENTS.   Words and Music by MAXIMILIAN BRAAM.

1. 'Twas in the good old days of yore, When dear "Old Sammy" was a boy,

The Brits and Indians as before, Combined and sought him to destroy.

But Harrison came, "Old Tippecanoe," Who whipped the British and Indians too.

But Harrison came, "Old Tippecanoe," Who whipped the British and Indians too.

2 Brock and Tecumsee in accord
   Set out to conquer Michigan,
   When cowardly Hull put up his sword
   And so defeated Sammy's plan.
                But Harrison came, etc.

3 Then Proctor and his savage mate
   On Raisin river and Maumee,
   Intent on sealing Sammy's fate,
   Began to kill and sell the free.
                But Harrison came, etc.

4 But fearless of the treacherous foe,
   Our hero came in good array,
   At river Thames to strike the blow,
   And with his warriors won the day.
                Our Harrison came, etc.

5 Come then, ye people of the land,
   Revere our hero's sacred name,
   Join with us as a happy band
   To sing his praises and his fame.
                For Harrison came, etc.

Song composed by village schoolmaster, Max Braam, and sung by North Bend children at the Harrison Tomb Pilgrimage October 5, 1887.

★★★★★★★★★★★

Horace Bonser, chairman of the Wm. H. Harrison Memorial Commission, was largely responsible for seeing the improvements at the tomb, the magnificent entrance and monument, become a reality. He was a Representative from Cincinnati to the Ohio Legislature and from childhood had looked upon General Harrison as his hero. Bonser was intensely dedicated to his responsibility. Carved on a column at the entrance are the names of the commission: Bonser, chairman; Wm. Whipple Symmes (descendant of Timothy Symmes, brother of Judge Symmes); Harry Hake, architect; and Hallie S. Caine, who was appointed to fill the vacancy of Cong. A. G. Allen, an original member of the commission.

Chapter 3

PIONEERS: Their Trials And Occupations

"Those simple people--our ancestors--achieved little that is glory, did nothing to interest a historian. But their characters and labors were instrumental in laying the foundations, political, religious and social, of this great state, which we call Ohio. A few so called leaders have been accorded the honors for those early accomplishments, but the common people, like our people, carried the burden."
From "Ohio in Homespun and Calico" by I. T. Frary

The men who came to this Miami country with John Cleves Symmes were doers who, despite overwhelming hardships, lost no time putting talents and ingenuity to work for the betterment of the new community. Doctor, store keeper, saw mill operator, justice of the peace, treasurer and legislator were all positions that needed to be filled if the settlement were to survive. Unbelievable as it may seem, Judge Symmes brought with him a man who filled all of these positions himself. He was Dr. Stephen Wood (1773-1844), pioneer physician.

History records something of Dr. Wood's services to Miami Township and Hamilton County. He was appointed first Justice of the Peace of Miami Township, first treasurer of Hamilton County, about 1792, and Judge of the Court of Common Pleas, 1795. As justice of the peace, he united many couples in marriage, among them William Henry Harrison and Anna Symmes, November 1795. Along with Symmes and Harrison, Dr. Wood subscribed to the Mill Creek Bridge, April 10, 1798. He served many terms in the Ohio State Legislature. He was reappointed a justice of the peace, along with Garah Markland, in 1807, and served as associate judge of the Common Pleas Court from 1810 to 1816. Stephen Wood was elected 4th vice president of the Hamilton County Agricultural Society, organized in 1819, of which General Harrison was president. He was one of the first elders in the Cleves Presbyterian Church, organized in 1830, and a subscriber, along with his sons, to the Cleves Bridge Company in 1833. With such achievements to his credit, it is easy to see the caliber of this man, Stephen Wood.

On January 26, 1795, Dr. Stephen Wood, having built a house and resided the required 3 years in North Bend, was deeded a lot by John Cleves Symmes. He and Catherine Freeman were issued a marriage license, Feb. 24, 1796, by Gov. Arthur St. Clair. The Woods had a number of children, all of whom later acquired lands in Miami and Green Townships.

In those days when Dr. Wood was practicing medicine, it was common for physicians to collect about 25¢ per call, perhaps a little more for mileage. Any wonder that he operated a store and also a saw mill near the mouth of Muddy Creek.

Stephen Wood was the subject of a sketch written by the late Judge Stanley Struble, Cleves, for The Valley Journal. Both Stephen Wood and Stanley Struble, illustrious citizens of their respective days, served as Judge of the Court of Common Pleas of Hamilton County. The following account is as recorded by Judge Struble:

"Dr. Stpehen Wood, one of our first pioneers, is buried on the farm of Gus Frondorf on Bridgetown Road. The inscription on his tomb reads: 'Dr. Stephen Wood, born May 3rd, 1773, died May 11, 1844. Emigrated from Long Island to North Bend, Nov. 1790 with John Cleves Symmes. Lived to see the inhabitants of the state increase from 3,000 to 3,000,000. He chased elk, bear and wolf over grounds now occupied by canals and railroads.'

"Gus Frondorf's grandfather, Philip Frondorf, purchased this farm in 1864 from Frances Worthington, daughter of Dr. Wood, who married Amos Worthington.

"When Dr. Wood came to North Bend everything about was primeval forest, infested with wild beasts and marauding Indians. The scalping knife was an ever-present threat, so much so that when Fort Washington was built many of the residents of North Bend left. Dr. Wood stayed on although his rounds of calls on patients subjected him to greater danger than other settlers. It appears that Dr. Wood could not get enough from his medical practice to live on, for he operated a small store at North Bend and a saw mill on Muddy Creek. He was also justice of the peace of Miami Township.

"In this position as justice of the peace, Dr. Wood had the distinction of joining in marriage William Henry Harrison and Anna Symmes, Nov. 1795. Without a doubt, Dr. Wood was also present on Monday, January 25, 1841, when President-elect Harrison left North Bend for Washington."

Letters written by Daniel and Eunice Keen Howell reveal much of the trials and living conditions in the early North Bend settlement. These letters, copies of which are in the hands of Miss Cora Rittenhouse and in a publication of the Cincinnati Historical Society, also mention the Muddy Creek saw mill.

In the fall of 1789, Capt. James Keen and his family, accompanied by son-in-law Daniel Howell and his bride, Eunice Keen Howell, married Sept. 1, 1789, went from New Jersey to Ohio. A letter from the young Howells, dated at North Bend, April 2, 1790, and mailed to Gideon Howell and his wife, Sarah, at Morristown, N. J., informed them that blockhouses were being built, and that Job Gard (Guard) expected to come to North Bend in the fall.

On April 23, 1790, Daniel Howell again wrote to his parents:

"I shall try to inform you of our well fare which is sometimes melancholy on account of the Indians. They have killed one Stephen Carter in sight of our door. They shot him through the breast, cut his throat and scalped him."

To his brother, Ezekiel, Howell wrote:

"We are going to fortify and build a blockhouse. I can't invite you or any of my relatives to come here till there is better prospects of peace."

During the summer of 1790, a foe more deadly than Indians attacked the settlers. This was an epidemic of fever. Entire families were struck down.

A subsequent letter from Eunice Howell to the Senior Howells related that her husband had died July 6, 1790, and that her sisters, Elizabeth and Sibel Keen, had also died along with Daniel Gard. Her son, Daniel Gideon, had been born August, 1790, a month after his father's death.

(The block house at North Bend, where Howell was born, was described in 1876 by B. W. Chidlaw in his paper entitled Early Times: "The block house was located near the site of the entrance of the (canal) tunnel about midway between the foot of the hill and the river. It was built of heavy logs 18 feet long, had 6 corners and a height of 10 feet. From a projection of 2 feet were port holes. Around this place of security and defense the pioneers built their cabins and cultivated their patches of corn, beans and pumpkins. No plows were yet used, the hoe in the hands of the females did the work of cultivation while the men with their rifles supplied their families with meat. Tea and coffee were unknown. Sassafras and spice wood answered for China and Java. Life among the squatters around the North Bend block house was full of adventure, privations and dangers.")

(Concerning spice wood, John Matson, in his accounts found among Cist's writings, stated that spice wood bush grew so thick at North Bend in 1794 that he was unable even after cutting them to lift, unassisted, the clumps out of the ground.)

An autobiography by one Jacob Parkhurst (1772-1863), published by Eastern Indiana Publishing Co., Knightstown, Indiana, tells more about the hardships and epidemic at North Bend. In this account, the author stated that his uncle Gershum Guard, with his family, left their Pennsylvania home and went to North Bend in the spring of 1789, and that his (Parkhust's) sister and her husband, Stephen Carter, went along. Parkhust, then a young man, joined the Kentucky militia in August, 1790, and a month later found himself camping near Cincinnati. Wanting to check upon his widowed sister at North Bend, whose husband, Stephen Carter, had been killed by the Indians that spring, Parkhurst went with Captain Brice Virgin, who had also visited the camp, to see her. There he found that, as a result of a siege of fever, she had been left bald-headed and hard of hearing.

Parkhurst later returned to North Bend to spend the winter with his sister, to help her cut wood, grind corn on a hand mill and hunt buck, turkey and possum. He joined Capt. Virgin's volunteers, who acted as a defense to the garrison at North Bend.

On Christmas Day, 1790, Parkhurst recorded that Judge Symmes had invited the whole garrison of men to the raising of a fort, or blockhouse, over on the Miami bottom. It was a log cabin with 16 corners and was not completed that day. Hard weather set in, and the fort was not yet finished in February, 1791, when Jacob Parkhurst took leave of his friends and "fellow Rangers" at the Bend.

This account by Parkhurst sheds a great deal of light on conditions at North Bend. His dates coincide with those given in the Howell letters. Since the Howells knew both the Gards (Guards) and Stephen Carter, they undoubtedly were acquainted with young Jacob Parkhurst.

(What type of epidemic of fever it was that lay siege to the settlers at North Bend in 1790 is not known. However, legend tells that a third of Cincinnati's population of 900 perished in 1793 in a smallpox epidemic.)

Widow Eunice Keen Howell, in a letter dated Feb. 1793, stated that she had remarried in 1791, to William Rittenhouse, and that Captain Keen had moved to Muddy Creek to tend the saw mill. This was no doubt the mill of Dr. Wood.

Stephen Wood's mill must not be confused with another early mill on Muddy Creek, near Devil's Backbone Road, which was called "General Findlay's Mill" and "Muddy Creek Mill." This mill stood farther up the creek than Dr. Wood's mill, and has been the subject of much controversy as to when it was built. As late as 1887, this saw and flour mill was being operated by A. J. Kuehn of Delhi. It is also interesting to note that Muddy Creek, according to legend, was originally called "Motto Creek" by the Indians.

Of specific interest in North Bend history is the "Diary of Major William Stanley," 1790 to 1809. This diary, found at CHS Library, although difficult to read, indicates that Major Stanley, a merchant and trader, had business transactions with Stephen Wood, delivering goods by boat to North Bend for Dr. Wood's store. While staying at Major S. Howell's tavern in North Bend, William Stanley met and shortly after, on April 30, 1797, married Howell's daughter, Sally. The wedding was performed by "justice-judge, Dr. Wood." The diary also notes that Capt. Keen was master of the schooner BETSY, undoubtedly the boat used in the trade.

Capt. William Rittenhouse, who married widow Eunice Keen Howell, is known to have operated a tavern, as well as a ferry and grist mill, at North Bend. A relationship is not stated but it is likely that Major S. Howell was of the same family as Daniel Howell. Possibly they managed the same tavern. (See "The Story of Mt. Nebo From Ledger and Legend.")

In writing to a member of his family, Judge Symmes stated that he had loaned a mare to Capt. Howell. In another letter to a friend in Morristown, N. J., he stated that Capt. Howell's family were well. The Judge cheerfully noted, in that same letter, that the "whole Country is busy making sugar from the "Myrtle Tree."

History reveals that these early families, the Woods, Rittenhouses and Howells, were closely associated in personal and community affairs. Stephen Wood, D. G. Howell and Charles Albert Wood, grandson of Stephen Wood, each in his time served as elders of the Presbyterian Church. Eunice and William Rittenhouse named one of their sons Stephen Wood Rittenhouse (1805-1848). Furthermore, the daughter of Stephen Wood Rittenhouse, Susan, a niece of D. G. Howell, married Charles Albert Wood, Dr. Wood's grandson. She lived but a short time after marriage, unfortunately. (C. A. Wood built the large home on State Road just outside of Cleves where the Colemans now reside.)

Daniel G. Howell (1790-1866), who had the distinction of being the first white child born in the North Bend settlement, lived all his life in the region. He and his heirs occupied a great piece of land at the foot of Mt. Nebo, along the Great Miami on the west side of Cleves. The family farmed and operated a tanyard. D. G. Howell is buried in pioneer Berea Cemetery, Hooven, Ohio. David H. Rittenhouse, in his diaries, referred to this uncle as "Uncle Howell."

A humorous legend is told about Daniel G. Howell. In the year 1900, Martin Harrell--a former Hamilton County Commissioner--resided on land once occupied by D. G. Howell. At the Harrell residence stood two giant hickory trees. Legend told that these were planted by Howell in 1828, during General Andrew Jackson's first candidacy for President. Howell christened the hickory trees "Jefferson" and "Jackson", by which names they were yet known at the turn of the century. Because of his admiration for "Old Hickory," Daniel G. Howell had changed his politics.

The name of Daniel G. Howell, along with those of pioneers Stephen Wood and William Rittenhouse, holds a legendary place among the annals of Miami Township.

****

Medicine in 1825

Lawrenceburgh, Ind., Aug. 12, 1825, Indiana Palladium: Dr. Ezra Ferris has just received from New Orleans a general assortment of fresh medicines which he offers for sale at his old stand on High Street, on better terms than medicine has ever been sold in the state. Persons wishing to purchase are solicited to call with the assurance that they can be supplied as cheap for cash, as they can in Cincinnati. He intends to keep on hand a constant supply of Lee's, Dyott's, Hooper's, and Anderson's Pills; Bateman's Drops; Godfrey's Cordial; British Oil; Balsalm of Life; Harlem Oil; Essence of Peppermint etc.; also Pukes, Purges, Bitters and Worm Medicine done up in doses with printed directions for using for benefit of families who live at a distance from a physician.

Chapter 4

IT HAPPENED 'ROUND THE POINT

The region surrounding The Point, that area near the mouth of the Great Miami, is undoubtedly the richest site, historically speaking, in all of the Symmes Purchase.

Here stands Miami Fort, earlier called Fort Hill, constructed--historians believe--by mound builders for the chief purpose of defense in time of war, as a refuge for the tribes who lived on the lower farm lands.

Here, at the confluence of the rivers, in 1749, Captain Celeron de Bienville buried a lead plate, never found, as declaration of ownership of the land for King Louis XV of France.

The Point was also the site of historic Fort Finney, where in 1785, the first white men to inhabit the region had camped. Here, Jan. 31, 1786, (some historians give the date as Feb. 2, 1786) a treaty with the Indians was signed, the first surrender of lands to the United States by tribes west of the Alleghenies. This treaty cleared the way for Symmes, and others like him, to purchase land in the Northwest Territory.

Goose Pond, known as such from earliest times, was a settlement in the vicinity of The Point. It derived its name from the fact that the region had a remarkable attraction for wild birds, and it was here the pioneers duckhunted. Some years later, it also became known as an ice-skating pond.

An account concerning early settlement at Goose Pond, written by Dr. Ezra Ferris, pioneer of the Cincinnati settlement at Columbia, and later resident of Dearborn County, appeared in a Lawrenceburg, Indiana paper, Independent Press, Jan. 16, 1852:

"A number of families from Columbia in the spring of 1793, made a settlement on the east side of the Big Miami, a little above the junction with the Ohio, near a place called goose pond. During the season a Mr. Rittenhouse built a mill to grind corn on a small stream passing down from the hill to the Miami, through where the town of Cleves now stands. . . It was a great accommodation to the people. A Mr. Demoss and Micajah Dunn went from the goose pond settlement to Mr. Rittenhouse's mill, each with a bag of corn to have ground. . ." In his narrative Ferris related that Indians attacked the settlers on their return from the mill and killed Mr. Demoss.

It was not far from Goose Pond that Abraham and Lydia Garrison settled, as early as 1799--perhaps before. They had earlier spent a few years at Losantiville where Lydia Garrison had done "considerable doctoring among the people, and she, in a small way, introduced the manufacture of soap in Cincinnati. Abraham Garrison built and operated a horsemill on Third Street." Their son, Joseph, had been born some years prior to their arrival in Losantiville. Abraham Garrison moved his family to The Point region sometime before 1799. In time, his son acquired great tracts of land in the Miami River bottoms.

From Ford's History of Hamilton County:

"Joseph Garrison married Merab Conner, near Lawrenceburg, Ind., in 1805, and after some service in aid of the government surveyors, settled at the Goose Pond, where Joseph Dixon Garrison was born in 1816. The latter, in early life, tended Garrison's Ferry over the Great Miami where the Cleves bridge stands (along State Line Road), and made several trading trips with boats to New Orleans. He married in 1852, to Sarah Ann Leonard, and the same day they started for California with a company he had agreed to take through. He there engaged in gold mining until Feb. 1855, when they started on their return to the states. Joseph D. Garrison pursued farming for a time until he bought a hotel in North Bend."

Independent Press, Lawrenceburg, Ind., Feb. 25, 1852:

"Gold seekers from the Cleves area, a few of whom will go overland via St. Joseph, include: J. D. Garrison, Sam'l Wamsley, Leander Markland, Steve Cooper, Sam'l Laird, James Morgan, Truman L. Hursey, Richard Simpers, Sam'l Carr, Frank Rogers, Wm. C. Rittenhouse, two of old Father Bateman's sons, and a few others whose names I have not learned; also Wm. E. Rittenhouse, who left here a few days ago enroute for New York. Boys are now busily engaged fixing their out-fits; they intend going through with mules and light wagons. May success attend them and hasten back loaded with precious truck." Signed by J.W.M., Cleves, Feb. 24, 1852.

Descendants of the family tell that Joseph D. and Sarah Garrison traveled to California in a covered wagon and returned with a sizeable can of gold nuggets. They farmed for some years, raised a family and later bought a hotel in North Bend, probably the one known as the North Bend Hotel operated in 1871 by S. V. Hayes. This boarding house burned about 1889. (It stood on the site where Bernard Sheridan later built a home, now known as the Lawrence Fisher house.) After the fire destroyed their hotel, the Garrisons moved to a house just behind their former home, one facing Washington Street, (occupied in recent years by Willard Hayes, and now by Ray Gillum), where "Aunt Sarah," as she was familiarly known to everyone, ran the North Bend post office.

This account of the Garrison family and their undertakings points again to the fact that those pioneers who came to Judge Symmes' settlement were stalwart citizens and courageous doers.

Among other doers were the pioneer Hayes and Guard families, who came to own thousands of acres of land in the region of The Point and the Miami bottoms. A history of the Hayes family, edited by Royal S. Hayes, gives accounts of the settlement of the lands around the mouth of the Great Miami, along the Ohio and Indiana border, where the Hayes, Miller and Guard families were first to occupy the soil. Descendants of Capt. Joseph Hayes, who had first leased land at The Point from Judge Symmes in 1793, bought some of that very land their grandfather Hayes had earlier rented.

Western Statesman, Lawrenceburg, June 2, 1830:

"Land for Sale. I will sell 150 A. of my bottom land near the mouth of the Great Miami in the Horst Shoe Bend. I should prefer to sell the part of the bottom which lies in in Indiana. A liberal credit will be given for the greater part of the purchase price, say 1/3 in hand, one at the end of the 2, and the remaining third at the termination of 3 years. W. H. Harrison, North Bend, 18th May, 1830."

This foregoing notice of land for sale was without a doubt the land at The Point which General Harrison sold in 1830 for $21,000, in order to help pay off some of his sons' debts. (See West to Ohio, page 150, by Alta Harvey Heiser.)

David, Ezra and Bailey Guard, whose father Alexander Guard first brought his family to the blockhouse at North Bend in the spring of 1790, bought an island in the Big Miami River, near its mouth, which they called Guard's Island. There Bailey Guard moved, built a home, cleared the ground and cultivated the land in corn. The Guard brothers joined in extensive shipping operations, bought several old steamboats, loaded them with cattle, hogs, sheep, bacon, corn, flour and hay, and towed them to markets in New Orleans.

It was Bailey Guard's son, Chalon, who lived on Mount Nebo at Dugan's Gap. Chalon had bought his farm about 1841, from his Uncle Hardin Ferry, who had purchased it directly from Judge Symmes. (Hardin Ferry had wed Hannah Guard, daughter of Alexander, sister of Bailey.) There Chalon and his young family had lived in a log house until 1849, when he built a fine brick farmhouse. Bricks for the house were kilned right in the front yard. That home, yet standing today, was recently acquired, along with ground around it, by the Hamilton County Park Board to be used in development of Miami Fort-Shawnee Lookout Park.

It was at The Point, in the shadow of the prehistoric fort, not far from Guard's Island and Goose Pond, that General Harrison, about 1837, built for his son, John Scott, a handsome brick farmhouse, which became the boyhood home of Benjamin, future President.

J. Scott Harrison home; boyhood home of President Benjamin Harrison. Built Ca. 1837 by Wm. H. Harrison. The house stood along the Ohio River, near the mouth of the Great Miami. It was razed in 1959.

The name Fort Hill could have been called so because of its having been an Indian fortification, or because of its proximity to Fort Finney. General Harrison, himself, gave a great deal of study to this fortification. He believed that it was built as a last place of resistance by Aztec Indians before their retreat south into Mexico. Harrison noted that the fort showed the great military skill of its builders and wrote one of the earliest papers on the subject, entitled, "Discourse on the Aborigines of the Ohio Valley," 1838.

(Dec. 30, 1837. Cincinnati Chronicle. "General Harrison was prevented from attending the Ohio Historical Society meeting in Columbus. His discourse upon the Aborigines and ancient mounds of Ohio, which was forwarded by mail, did not reach Columbus until after the society's adjournment. The report will appear in the volume of transactions which the society has now in press."

Another site of prehistoric interest, not far from Fort Hill, which also captured the attention of General Harrison as well as that of earlier day settlers of the region, was Big Bone Lick, Kentucky, lying just a few miles downstream. Here in the early 1700's, a saline-sulphur spring was discovered by the French during their early explorations of the Ohio Valley. The spring bore evidence of having been frequented for thousands of years by Indians and vast herds of buffalo and deer. The first English explorers found scattered over the lick great bones and teeth of extinct mammoth and mastadon. Soldiers stationed at Fort Finney in 1785-1786, made exploratory trips to Big Bone, records of which are found in Lieutenant Ebenezer Denny's Journal. The ancient bones found at Big Bone came to be desired for scientific study as well as sought after by the curious. Legend tells that General Harrison, himself, shipped, in 1795, thirteen barrels (hogsheads) of the relics from Big Bone, which, however, were lost when the flatboat capsized below Fort Pitt. Accounts of early pioneers in the region of The Point also relate that men journeyed to Big Bone Lick to manufacture salt for the needs of their households. In view of the health-lending qualities of mineral baths, a fashionable hotel and mineral spa was established at Big Bone in the mid 1800's, which attracted persons from far and wide. After the decline of the resort, interest in Big Bone diminished for many years. That interest was revived when, around 1960, Big Bone became the site of an extensive geological survey conducted by teams of university students. Subsequently a beautiful park was developed here by the state of Kentucky.

In addition to the above geologically significant facts concerning Big Bone, the place boasts yet another claim to fame, a minor one, in river history. Around 1825, it was the location of a small shipyard. Most famous of the boats built there was the GENERAL PIKE, named for Zebulon Pike, founder of Pike's Peak, whose widow lies buried at Sugar Grove, Kentucky, downriver from North Bend, not far from the site of old Fort Finney.

It was at The Point in the midst of such a wealth of history for a background that the children of John Scott Harrison were reared. Even as late as 1866, remains of the old blockhouse at Fort Finney could yet be seen lying a short distance upstream from the Harrison home.

Members of the Symmes, Harrison and Short families controlled vast acres of the surrounding farm lands for many decades, renting or leasing the ground for shares of the crops. Some of the earliest known people who settled about The Point and farmed for, or leased ground from, the owners included the Demoss, Anthony, Garrison, Strong, Moak, Bump, Bevens, Bingle, Cady, Cooper and VanGorder families. These names appear in early records. Many of the families intermarried and remained in the location throughout several generations.

Barnabas Strong was an early settler at The Point who acted as an overseer of the lands for General Harrison. The following record is found at CHS Library:

"$100 Reward: Tenement log cabin on property of William H. Harrison in Miami Township, mouth of Great Miami, occupied by Pardon Monroe, set on fire with intent of murder, will pay for conviction." May 6, 1813. Barnabas Strong, agent for W. H. Harrison.

There are yet descendants of Barnabas Strong around Miami Township.

Another who settled in the township as early as 1820 was Aaron Bateman, a flatboatman on the Ohio River. Bateman and his son, Harris, operated a ferry at one time at the mouth of the Miami. He was buried in an old grave yard on the site of the present power plant and, as late as 1926, two of the Bateman head stones could yet be seen. Descendants of this family settled in Cleves and Lawrenceburg. Inscriptions on the stones read: (Nov. 25, 1926, Lawrenceburg Press)

"In memory of Elizabeth, consort of Aaron Bateman, who died Sept. 1824, in the 40th yr. of age."
"In memory of Aaron Bateman, who died Nov. 28, 1833, in the 57th yr. of age."

Mrs. Nellie VanGorder Blackford, daughter of Harriet Cady and Harry VanGorder, recalls something of her family's relationships at The Point. A number of Cadys and VanGorders intermarried. Her grandmother, Jane VanGorder, sewed for members of the J. Scott Harrison family, and made both wedding and baby clothes for Bettie Harrison Eaton. The latter was Harry VanGorder's Sabbath school teacher at Cleves

Presbyterian Church, and Mrs. Blackford cherishes a book given to her father by Bettie Eaton. "When Grandmother VanGorder went from The Point to Cleves," stated Mrs. Blackford, "she always called on Mrs. Eaton."

The VanGorder, Cady, Bingle, Bevens and Myers families lived in dwellings on the Harrison lands. That these families held high regard for the J. Scott Harrisons is evidenced in the great number of sons of these families who, for several generations, were named "Harrison" and "Scott."

Although J. Scott Harrison studied law and, for a time, practiced in the firm of Nicholas Longworth, he was a farmer at heart. (See Benjamin Harrison: Hoosier Warrior, p. 17, by Harry J. Sievers, S. J.) He gave up his professional career to manage the farm lands of his father. Scott Harrison served for many years as justice of the peace of Miami Township, as early as 1829. In this capacity he united many couples in marriage, among them Job C. Hayes and Mary McCance in 1836. Harrison represented Ohio in Congress for two terms, 1853-1857, but was most active in public affairs on the local level. He was dedicated to the Cleves Presbyterian Church, as were the members of his family. All of his children were baptized there.

The following item was found in the Lawrenceburg Press:
June 19, 1873. "I will rent for the season 130 acres of fine wood land pasture, plenty of water and good fences. I have other fine pastures on which I will receive horses and cattle by the month. Signed, J. Scott Harrison, Point Farm."

The character of John Scott Harrison was revealed in an article that appeared in the Cincinnati Times-Star, May 16, 1940, of an interview with his granddaughter, the late Elizabeth Harrison Buckner, daughter of Carter Harrison, one of the five sons of J. Scott Harrison.

Elizabeth Buckner reminisced about her early childhood days at The Point. She stated that she often sat upon her grandfather's knee and it was there, from his newspaper, that she learned her letters. A fire burned in the fireplace year round to ward off the dampness from the rivers. She recalled the fine orchards at The Point from which none of the yield was sold.

Elizabeth Buckner said, "The neighbors were at liberty to come and take what they wished. My mother (Sophie Ridgely Dashiell Harrison), while we lived there with grandfather, often 'put up' the big, yellow, bellflower apples for winter use. Grandfather was a gentleman of the old school. He was generosity itself. In fact it was his signing of notes for friends that in later years caused shrinkage of his holdings.

"Grandfather was a voracious reader, as were my parents. There were always uncles and cousins and kinfolk coming for visits or departing. Often in the evenings there would be pantomimes or charades enacted on the spur of the moment. Those were the days when conversation was a fine art and when time was devoted to letter writing. Grandfather took great care of his letters, and those of his which I have show real literary style.

"My grandfather and all the family loved to ride the fine horses. He rode his horse until the day of his death, always seated erect in his saddle."

Elizabeth Buckner recalled vividly her grandfather's death. "I had had a birthday party," she said. "He took some of the cake upstairs with him and put it beside his bed on a little table. In the night he was stricken with a heart attack from which he never rallied."

John Scott Harrison became better known after his death, than before, on two extremely different counts, both of interest on a national scope. The first of these, the tragedy of his grave robbery, is known by all.

As it happened, J. Scott Harrison died suddenly at his home on May 26, 1878. His funeral was conducted at Cleves Presbyterian on May 29th, with addresses by Rev. Horace Bushnell, Rev. B. W. Chidlaw and Rev. R. E. Hawley. Mr. Bushnell, old friend, blind and inform, preached the sermon from memory. Pallbearers were: Wm. S. Groesbeck, S. S. Smith, John B. Whitman, Robert Brown, James J. Farar, Robert Hodge, Ebenezer Argo and Philander Gillespie. Mr. Smith had been a pallbearer at the funeral of President Harrison, 37 years earlier. Other old acquaintances present included W. F. Irwin, James F. Torrance, Dr. John Warder, Richard Stone, John A. Gano, Thomas Yeatman and John Noble.

Following the service, J. Scott Harrison was interred in Congress Green Cemetery, where members of the Harrison families and other pioneer settlers around North Bend were buried. During the graveside proceedings, it was discovered that the nearby grave of Augustus Devin, a young family connection of the Harrisons, who had lived at Devin's Station above North Bend, and who had died a little over a week before, had been molested. Further investigation revealed that his body had been removed. (Ironically, J. Scott Harrison, himself, had ridden horseback about 10 days earlier to the Devin home to offer his sympathy to the family of the young man.)

It was a known fact that "resurrectionists" were active in the city, at that time, and that colleges, needing bodies for study and dissection, were buying from these grave robbers.
The day after J. Scott Harrison's burial, his son, John, and grandson, George Eaton, obtained a search warrant and went to Cincinnati to look around the medical colleges in hopes of finding young Augustus Devin's body.

At Ohio Medical College no trace of Devin's body was found. The two men were about to abandon their search when they noticed that a rope attached to a windlass was down the chute of a trap door in the floor. Upon giving the rope a hard tug, they--to their profound shock--brought up a naked corpse. One look at the face quickly revealed that it was John's own father, J. Scott Harrison, buried so securely at Congress Green just 24 hours before!

The college denied any knowledge as to how the body had arrived there. Benjamin Harrison returned to Cincinnati from Indianapolis the following day for the reburial, temporarily, in the Jacob Strader vault at Spring Grove Cemetery. (Cincinnati Commercial, June 1, 1875) (For additional details concerning the episode see Cincinnati Commercial, May 30, May 31, and June 1, 1878; Lawrenceburg Press, May 30, and June 6, 1878.)

Cleves lawyer Harry L. Cooper immediately drew up search warrants for all the medical colleges, and assisted in the prosecution of the notorious case. Peter Zinn, attorney and esteemed resident of Delhi, a friend of J. Scott Harrison, visited Cooper's office, encouraged him to pursue the case to the utmost extent, and thrust into the younger lawyer's hand a generous fee to aid in this task. Eventually, the "grave snatchers" were apprehended.

Cincinnati Daily Gazette, Nov. 10, 1879:
"Capt. Carter Harrison of Point Farm and his brother, General Benjamin Harrison, have repaired the tomb of their honored grandfather. The work has been done in a thorough manner. It is warranted to last for 50 years. The remains of their honored father (J. Scott Harrison) will be placed in the tomb shortly."

(Congress Green figured in the news again in 1962, in a case of much less notoriety than in 1878, when a group of students from the nearby communities voluntarily staged a clean-up day at the pioneer burial grounds. With pride and enthusiasm, weeds were cut, brush removed, branches trimmed, graves raked and tombstones righted. In a sincere act of good faith, but without adult guidance, some of the young people, thinking yet further improvement could be made to the long neglected cemetery, whitewashed several of the blackened, century-and-a-half old headstones.

This latter incident did not go unnoticed. Within a few days, the act was reported to civil authorities. The young people were identified, cited to juvenile court and grossly misrepresented as a bunch of tombstone-whitewashing delinquents. A member of the local school board and the students' history teacher, knowing full well of their sincerity and integrity, went to their defense. Needless to add, the patriotic spirits of the misunderstood youth were dampened by the Congress Green incident.)

The spotlight was once more turned on the name of J. Scott Harrison in 1888, just ten years after his death and burial at Congress Green, when his son was elected twenty-third President. Having been the son of a President and the father of a President placed him in an unparalleled position of honor, one which has never been matched.

Benjamin Harrison, named for his great-grandfather--a signer of the Declaration of Independence, was born in his grandfather's home at North Bend. His mother, Elizabeth Irwin Harrison, was J. Scott's second wife. The baby's birth occurred on August 20, 1833, following--so legend tells--an evening of musical entertainment.

Legend also tells that Harriet Beecher Stowe and her husband were present at the Harrison homestead that night.* While it is possible that Harriet Beecher was present, records show that she and Calvin Stowe did not marry until 1836. The Harrisons, being so closely associated with the Presbyterian Church, became well acquainted with the Beechers. Harriet's brother, Henry Ward Beecher, pastor of Lawrenceburg, Indiana, Presbyterian Church from 1837 to 1839, was befriended by Anna Harrison. (*Commercial Tribune, Sept. 19, 1897.)

When Ben was very young his father moved the family to the new home at The Point. There the boy spent his youth. Much of his early education was gained from private tutors within his home or at the little log school erected closeby. This old school collapsed in 1848. (See Benjamin Harrison: Hoosier Warrior, page 25, by H. J. Sievers.)

The reminiscences of Ezra G. Hayes (1827-1919), related in The Hayes Family, by Royal S. Hayes, reveal some of his boyhood experiences at The Point, where the Hayes family farmed and raised cattle. During the years when Ezra lived there, he was a friend and playmate of the Harrison boys and frequently accompanied them to their grandmother Harrison's house. He recalled attending President William H. Harrison's funeral service at North Bend in the company of his parents. As a youth, Ezra Hayes attended--for three years--a private school conducted in the J. Scott Harrison home. The tutor, Joseph Porter, later president of Yale, received a salary of $1500. Ezra's father paid one-third of this expense.

Thomas N. Lind (1813-1875) was also known to have been a tutor in the Harrison family. He later taught school at Mount Nebo where he lived and became a dedicated Sabbath school teacher in the Mount Nebo M. E. Church. Benjamin Harrison is said to have been one of Thomas Lind's scholars. (See Benjamin Harrison: Hoosier Warrior, p. 26, by H. J. Sievers, S. J.; concerning the early teachers of Ben Harrison, "it was the face of Thomas Lynn (sp.) that lingered longest in Ben's memory.")

Following his early years of schooling at home, Ben was sent to Farmer's College, originally Cary's Academy, (College Hill) and on to Miami University, Oxford, Ohio, where he graduated in 1852. The next year he married Caroline "Carrie" Scott, whose father, Dr. John W. Scott, was president of a woman's college in Oxford.

The young couple first settled in the Harrison home at The Point and Benjamin pursued his study of law in the office of Bellamy Storer, Cincinnati. Some months later, they moved to Indianapolis, and this was to become their lifetime home. (The Harrison home, preserved as a national shrine, may be seen today at 1230 N. Delaware St., Indianapolis, Indiana.)

As Benjamin began to move ahead in politics, his father wrote him that "none but knaves should ever enter the political arena." Nevertheless, he joined the new Republican party and achieved prominence as a lawyer. During the Civil War, Ben organized a regiment in Indianapolis and went off to the battlefields. Like his grandfather, he rose to the position of General. After the war, he returned to his law practice and, in time, went on to the United States Senate.

A Republican campaign song, "Grandfather's Hat Fits Ben," is credited with helping to elect him to the Presidency in 1888. Among Ben Harrison's first moves as President was that of contacting his boyhood friend Ezra G. Hayes--then of Lawrenceburg, Indiana, and requesting him to come to Washington to act as an advisor to the new Cabinet. Ezra Hayes had achieved success in the railroad business and had a good knowledge of finance. He complied with the President's request and remained in the Capitol for about a year.

As President, Benjamin Harrison did more than any other before him to promote a greater respect for the United States flag. By his order, the colors waved above the White House and other government buildings, and he urged that "Old Glory" be flown over every schoolhouse in the land. He also founded the National Park Service, manifesting his long interest in conservation.

Ben must have carried with him to the White House memories of gay but simple Christmases he had known as a lad at The Point, when the family prepared presents for each other and when holiday treats consisted of a bit of candy or a few shooting crackers. (See Benjamin Harrison: Hoosier Warrior, pp. 42-43) In 1889, he and Mrs. Harrison set up the nation's first White House Christmas tree, a custom that continues to this day.

Benjamin Harrison's humble background and farm-centered homelife, his everyday communion with nature in the magnificent setting at The Point, the Christian teachings and honorable examples planted by his respected father, and the family's illustrious heritage all worked together to produce this spirit of dedication and concern for his country. What better harvest might the soil at The Point have yielded?

After J. Scott Harrison's death in 1878, the old homestead continued to be occupied for a time by his son, Capt. Carter B. Harrison. In late 1879, the home and some farm land around it was sold by Charles W. Short (whose father, Judge John C. Short, had assumed ownership of the place many years earlier) to Dr. Sylvan B. Robbins, Lawrenceburg physician. Dr. Robbins had, for many years previous to 1879, leased farm land in this region.

From Cincinnati Daily Gazette, Mar. 10, 1880, comes this pertinent item:

"Dr. S. Robbins will move his family to the Scott Harrison farm just above the Miami River. Dr. Robbins goes to the country for his health with the well wishes of the community (Lawrenceburg)."

"The explosion was heard for miles around. So terrible was the force of the explosion that the engine was shattered into a thousand fragments, some of which were blown to the Kentucky side of the river."

Oct. 6, 1870. "A passenger train and freight train came into collision at the Gravel Pit on the O&M R.R. Serious damage was done to the machinery but no one was seriously injured."

That passengers on the trains objected to increases in fares, just the same as today, is noted in the following items:

Jan. 5, 1871. Lawrenceburg Press. "A fuss was kicked up among commuters on the IC&L Railroad on account of the receivers of the road raising the price of commutation travel to almost double. Several meetings were held in Cincinnati and Milton Sayler, attorney, appointed a committee to visit and consult with receivers. The result was that the price was put back to the old rate. Monthly, instead of quarterly, commutation tickets are now issued."

Several months later, however, the fares were again raised. As a result a Mr. Anderson of Lawrenceburg sold many tickets on his omnibus line to the city. The commuters showed their indignation. Fares were again reduced in July, 1871. Fare from Lawrenceburg to Cincinnati was 65¢ on the O&M.

John B. Matson (1831-1902), who lived along the Big Miami near Lost Bridge, wrote in February, 1874, that he went to Cincinnati on the "accommodation." He noted in his ledger that the fare from Elizabethtown to the city had been reduced to 80¢ a round trip.

Conditions of the Cleves depot were noted in the following item:

Feb. 22, 1872. "Our depot is no fit place for any respectable lady or gentleman to enter. No matter how many go on the accommodation they are compelled to stand in the cold until arrival of the train. Six to ten young fellows lounge here about the depot, use obscene language etc. We hope the matter will be looked into by authorities."

With the coming of trains, villages began to grow. Businessmen moved their families to the suburbs, but continued to engage in occupations in the city. Commuter trains, "the accommodation," became an integral part of the lives of the townspeople. So it was with residents of the downriver localities. Passengers on the railroad, at first, paid 5 cents a mile; later the fare was reduced and a special low rate set for commuters. The close, daily contact among regular riders on the "accomodation" brought about a unique camaraderie. One direct result of this was that many a romance was kindled on the commuters' special.

On June 28, 1890, the first issue of "The Commuter," a newssheet published at Home City for the benefit of the residents and passengers on the Big Four and O&M Railroads, appeared. Its format included news items, humor and gossip of particular interest to local commuters. The following news was printed in the first issue:

North Bend Notes: "Mr. A. E. B. Stephens has been employed as principal and Miss Jessie M. Hunt, assistant, of North Bend School."
Home City Notes: "The annual excursion to Coney Island was largely attended. Early in the morning, families were swarming toward the river with loaded baskets, which indicated a good time for all."

The life of "The Commuter" newssheet was of short duration, but it must have been enjoyed by the passengers while it lasted.

Additional problems of the railroad companies are seen in the following Delhi items:

Mar. 25, 1883. Commercial Gazette. "A large and substantial platform has been erected by the O&M Railroad to replace the one destroyed by the recent high water."
May 3, 1893. Cincinnati Enquirer. "The storm which passed over the city spent its force at Delhi and flooded the country for miles. A culvert spanning Rapid Run, a small stream, was washed out and with it 100 feet of the O&M track which passes over it . . ."

The two most serious train wrecks to take place in this locality were undoubtedly those at Cleves, on May 15, 1892, and at Griffith's Station, North Bend, on July 23, 1894. Reports of these accidents were told at length in the Cincinnati Commercial Gazette.

From the Cleves Review, a Cleves publication of around 1894 to 1896, comes these lines:

Jan. 10, 1896. "Last Saturday the electric alarm bell at the C C C & St L (Big Four) crossing near Hafner's Mill was out of order. It failed to operate in the passing of trains, from either way."

One hazard or misfortune directly related to early railroads was seen in the unbelievably high numbers of accidents and deaths attributed to passing trains. Since roads were, in general, so poor until after the Civil War era, travelers chose to walk the railroad tracks, often the only clear path for miles around. Every newspaper carried accounts of persons or workmen injured or killed while walking the tracks or working on the railroad lines or bridges. Warning bells and signal lights were to come at a later date.

Following are two poems written by early residents of Cleves on the subject of trains. The first was penned by William C. Cooper, Cleves physician, and appeared in his book Tethered Truants, 1897. The author noted that his poem was written in competition with a couple of "doggerel grinders" who had contributed "pomes" on the same subject to a village paper:

THE LOCOMOTIVE

The locomotive is a rapid thing
It flies along on a rapid wing.
Nothing its velocity can scarcely restrain-
It rushes along with might-likewise with main.

Nothing in the world is a prettier sight
Than to hear one thundering along in the night-
The sparks fly right-they also fly left,
And the locomotive never gets out of breath.

Woe unto the cows which on the track remain,
When the iron horse comes with its rattling train;
Ten chances to one they'll all get freighted
To another world by being eviscerated.

The locomotive was invented many years ago
By a man who was tired of riding slow;
We ought to all join in giving him praise
For inventing an article so useful in these days.

Within a few years after 1880, The Point farm, along with hundreds of acres of land formerly held by C. W. Short, was in the hands of Abram Brower. A long chapter in the history and legend of life at The Point, at Goose Pond, and at the site of old Fort Finney had come to a close. However, a new chapter was beginning. That account is told in "New Life at The Point."

(Author's note: The Point was known as such from earliest times. It was also called Miami Point. A news item from the Western Statesman, early Lawrenceburg paper, tells of this:

> June 3, 1830. "Andrew Lind, Esq., performed the marriage of Mr. Warren Farmer and Miss Mary Cheek on Miami Point, O."

Andrew R. Lind is named in the 1830 Miami Twp. Census as head of a household; in 1834, as a stockholder in the Cleves Bridge Company; in 1835, as a patron of Ogden's Store. He was a justice of the peace in 1839. Mrs. Matilda Lind of Cleves has a record book kept by Andrew R. Lind in 1839, and as justice of the peace he was an overseer of the poor and in charge of placing bound children and orphans in foster homes to be cared for and protected until they came of age. Thomas Silver and Jeremiah Goodrich were among those named, in this interesting record book, as ones who took bound children into their homes. Whether the above Andrew Lind, justice of the peace who performed the marriage in 1830 at Miami Point, was the same as A. Richard Lind (b. ca. 1810), longtime magistrate of Miami Township in later years, 1865-1880 era, has not been learned.)

****

Why Symmes First Chose "The Point" For Proposed City
(from "History of Cincinnati", 1888, by A. E. Jones)

The reasons Judge J. C. Symmes selected the site at "The Point" for erection of his proposed city were given in a letter to Col. Jonathan Dayton. Symmes stated that there would be a large number of towns located on the Ohio above and below the mouth of the Great Miami, from Pittsburgh to the falls, and trade would center from there. The extent of country along the Miami spreading for many miles on both sides had superior qualities in point of soil, water and timber to any tract of equal area to be found in U.S. From this "Egypt of the Miami", as Symmes styled it, the produce of the country would be poured down the stream for 200 miles above its mouth, which could be collected there if the city was built at that point; whereas, if built above, at North Bend, the settlers could not work their boats 8 or 9 miles up the Ohio above the mouth and the produce would pass down the Ohio to towns below. (Symmes was obliged to abandon his proposal when he learned how readily the Big Miami bottoms flooded. He made his settlement at North Bend, instead.)

Brief Archaeological History of Miami Fort
(taken from notes of lecture by Fred W. Fischer to Three Rivers Historical Society, July 9, 1967)

Earliest occupants of Miami Fort were determined to have been those of the Early Woodland Period, 1000 BC to 500 BC. Their pottery was thick. The Middle Woodland group was responsible for constructing the fort, ca. 270 AD (150 years more or less) as indicated by isotope tests on charcoal found at the fort.

10,000 BC, Paleo Period. Nomadic tribes.
5,000 BC, Archaic Period.
1000 BC to 1 AD, Early Woodland Period. Permanent villages, some animals, some domestic plants, squash.
1 AD to 600 AD, Middle Woodland Period. Large villages of permanent type, hunting, agriculture, cultivated plants.
600 AD to 1100 AD, Late Woodland Period. Small villages, dependent upon agriculture and corn (maize) economy.
1100 AD to 1600 AD, Mississippian Period. New peoples in the Ohio Valley, some from Spanish area (bringing a return of squash and beans), and others which included French traders.

A pioneer fort or military station once stood just north of Cleves along East Miami River Road, according to a map drawn by Hamilton County surveyor Alfred West Gilbert in 1848. This old landmark, then in 1848, lay on property of L. (probably Lewis) Morgan, just beyond the Wm. young farm.

Mr. Charles B. Winter recalls that John Myers, long a tenant on The Point Farm, once contributed a collection of Indian relics to the Smithsonian Institute. The collection was labeled as having come from land around the boyhood home of Pres. Benjamin Harrison.

The Buckeye of Ohio

> "They said the buckeye leaves expand
> Five-fingered as an open hand,
> Of love and brotherhood the sign
> Be welcome! What is mine is thine!"

Indians called the buckeye tree "hetuck" which meant eye of the buck, for the nut which grew on the tree looked like the eye of the buck both in color and shape. Early settlers adopted the English meaning, calling it buckeye. Buckeye trees grew more abundantly in Ohio than elsewhere and they were very useful to the pioneers. Many log cabins were built of them. A poem entitled "The Buckeye Tree" appeared in the Western Statesman, early Lawrenceburg paper, in 1834. The last line of each verse was: "Ohio is the dandy." It was not until 1840, however, when General Harrison was a candidate for President, that the name "Buckeye State" became firmly fixed in the minds of the people.

Chapter 5

THE STORY OF MOUNT NEBO, FROM LEDGER AND LEGEND

An interesting legend surrounds the history of the settling of Mount Nebo. For many years this hilltop was called Rittenhouse Hill, and rightly so. Among the first sturdy pioneers to set foot at North Bend in the late 1700's were the Guards, Howells, Hayeses and Rittenhouses. William Rittenhouse, who had arrived by flatboat from Pennsylvania, blazed the first trail to the heights of what is now Mount Nebo.

(The following account is compiled from numerous sources, the principal help coming from Miss Cora Rittenhouse. Notes, concerning the legend, were copied from a paper presented to the Mount Nebo Society, Sept. 12, 1926, by Fanny Galt Taylor Hendryx, (Mrs. Charles F. Hendryx), daughter of Anna T. Harrison and W.H.H. Taylor, and great-granddaughter of John Cleves Symmes.)

When Judge Symmes and his partners purchased these lands, so the story goes, the government--as was the custom--reserved the great knobs of ground, the high hills, that promised to be places of mineral deposit, until such a time when they could be explored and examined by government experts. If found to contain valuable mines, the price of this land would be set at a higher rate per acre than adjoining ground. However, a promise had been made whereby the first opportunity to purchase this reserved ground at North Bend (Mt. Nebo), whether minerals were found or not, would be given to the "Miami Enterprises," as the Symmes' land company was called.

Legend says that when announcement came that the mining engineers had found no great mineral deposits, Judge Symmes departed for the East. Instead of going directly to the seat of the government land office in Philadelphia, he went first, for several days, to confer with his business partners in New Jersey. When he later arrived at Philadelphia to make payment for the "big hill," he was informed that it had been sold a few days earlier to a man who had paid for it in gold. The explanation given to Judge Symmes was that since the land office had received no word from him, it had been assumed he no longer cared to purchase the knob.

As it turned out, the man who had made the purchase, William Rittenhouse, had been living as a squatter for a number of years near the foot of the big hill, where he kept a roadhouse. He had come to the region as a soldier in the Northwest Territory Militia and was commissioned a lieutenant on March 7, 1792. The document granting this commission, yet in the hands of his descendants, was signed by Winthrop Sargent, "Secretary of the Territory of the United States, North-West of the River Ohio," and also sworn before and signed by Judge John Cleves Symmes. Lieutenant Rittenhouse also operated a ferry across the Great Miami, the course of which followed a slightly different route than it does today. The government mining engineers who had inspected the hill for mineral wealth, so the story goes, just happened to have been lodgers at his roadhouse. From them William Rittenhouse had learned, firsthand, the facts concerning the knob. Being among the earliest to know that the land was for sale, he had a head start on the Judge.

Legend tells that for many years men of the Rittenhouse and Hayes families had taken turns standing guard near the foot of Rittenhouse Hill to ward off squatters who might try to encroach on their domain.

William Rittenhouse had married, about 1791, the widow of Daniel Gideon Howell, Eunice Keen Howell, whose son was Daniel G. Howell, first white child to be born in the blockhouse in the North Bend settlement. With their five sons and one daughter, William and Eunice Rittenhouse commenced settling and clearing the virgin land. Each of the six children were in time deeded a parcel of land on the hilltop which overlooked three river valleys. Those children, in addition to Daniel G. Howell, were: Hiram Harrison, Joseph Howell, William Keen, Stephen Wood, Lewis and Nancy R. Hutchinson. (Lewis either died or left the area around 1830. Nothing is known of him after that time.)

Legend also says that the hilltop section, when yet reserved by the government for mineral rights, was referred to as "Congress green." Whether or not this is fact has not been determined. It is known, however, that Judge Symmes had reserved a section of land in the village of North Bend which he called "Congress Green," and it was meant to be the public ground, the town park, of his proposed city. Perhaps that original reserved section extended on up the hill past the pioneer burial grounds and on to Mt. Nebo, and for this reason the hilltop was also called "Congress Green." Although Judge Symmes' city never came into being, the term "Congress Green" remained as the name of the pioneer cemetery.

Nevertheless, it was finally in 1812, after purchasing--for $1.25 an acre--a tract in Section 26 of Miami Township of the originally reserved hilltop, that William Rittenhouse received his deed, written on parchment and signed by President James Madison. This unusual document is still in the hands of the Rittenhouse descendants. Following a Hamilton County Court House fire, in 1884, in which many records were burned, the Rittenhouse deeds and family papers were used by the court as copies in making duplicate records and surveys.

How much fact there is to the legend that William Rittenhouse outwitted Judge Symmes in acquiring a parcel of land on the hilltop is unknown. There are, however, a number of deeds in early Hamilton County court records showing transfer of land from Symmes to Rittenhouse. One such record, dated May 10, 1795, shows that "certain out lots in the vicinity of the village of North Bend were sold to Rittenhouse for 10 pounds currency." This deed was signed by Symmes in the presence of Isaac Matson and N. Carr. (See Hamilton County, Ohio, Court and Other Records, Volumes I & II, compiled by Virginia Raymond Cummins.)

Another interesting record, dated Sept. 16, 1796, shows that *Symmes deeded to Rittenhouse, a volunteer settler, 106 acres.* The record states:

"Rittenhouse improved the land and voluntarily at all times represented the section for 7 years last past, and being settled thereon, is entitled to his deed."

Among the Rittenhouse papers are receipts showing that William paid for his ferry operator's license. In December 1813, his step-son, Daniel G. Howell, and John Applegate, of Green Township, entered into a partnership to run William Rittenhouse's Ferry.

Members of the Rittenhouse family yet live on Mount Nebo in a comfortable farm home on the exact site of their forefather William's first permanent home. Four generations have been born here. The dining room of the homestead, built of logs, is part of the original block house. Still in perfect condition are the old andirons and crane placed in use in the home in pioneer days. The road running past the place is now Rittenhouse Road. In earlier days it was called "Orphans Lane," no doubt from the fact that Stephen Wood Rittenhouse, son of William, passed away in 1848, leaving three very young children, the Rittenhouse orphans.

In the earliest settlements pioneers were subjected to many inconveniences, among these being remoteness from mills. That William Rittenhouse contributed to the progress of the North Bend community is evidenced in the following words, recorded in History of Dearborn and Ohio Counties:

"During the period 1792 to 1794, a Mr. Rittenhouse built a mill to grind corn, on a small stream passing down from the hill to the Miami, through where the town of Cleves now stands. The mill was a wet weather concern, the stream being so small, but it was a great accommodation to the people at that time."

Furthermore, John Cleves Symmes, in writing to a member of his family, August 3, 1807, stated:

"Captain Rittenhouse has been running a gristmill at the place where he raised his sawmill; we find it very convenient for the neighborhood."

Judge Symmes would most certainly have known of William Rittenhouse's pursuits because he had built his fine home just a few hundred steps beyond the foot of Rittenhouse Hill. This was the home which burned in 1811, and with it countless papers and land records.

That William Rittenhouse was active in the government of Miami Township is also a matter of record. Handed down among family papers is a document, dated February 1798, signed by John S. Gano, Clerk of Hamilton County, that states he was appointed for a term as Overseer of the Poor. He must have served many years in this capacity. A number of receipts signed by Jacob Burnet show that William Rittenhouse purchased numerous yards of cloth dressings, presumably used in attending to his duties as overseer of the poor of Miami Township.

In those days it was common for children, often orphans, from large or poor families to be placed in private homes as servants, to be trained in housekeeping and farming, sometimes in a trade, as well as educated, clothed and cared for by their master until they became of age. A young girl named Sarah Armstrong was indentured to William Rittenhouse in 1818. That document, a most interesting one, reads as follows:

"This indenture witnesseth that Sarah Armstrong, now aged seven years, five months and eight days, by and with the consent of her father, Stephen Armstrong, hath put herself and by these presents doth bind herself of her own free will and accord as an apprentice to William Rittenhouse, Senior, to learn the art and mystery of housewifery and after the manner of an apprentice to serve from the day of this date said Sarah shall serve to the age of eighteen during all which time the said apprentice her master faithfully shall serve, his secrets keep, his lawfull commands every where readily obey; she shall do no damage to her said master, nor see it done by others without letting or giving notice, thereof to her master. She shall not waste her said master's goods nor lend them unlawfully to any. She shall not contract matrimony within the said term without permission of her said master. She shall not absent herself day nor night from her said master's service without his leave, but in all things behave herself as a faithful apprentice ought to do. During the said term the said master is to school or cause the said apprentice to be taught reading and writing in a regular way so as to read plain and write a plain commonlike woman's hand. Further the said master is to use the best of his endeavors to teach or cause to be taught or instructed the said apprentice in the art and mystery of decent housewifery, in particular knitting, sewing, spinning and the like, and to furnish said apprentice with sufficient meat, drink, washing and lodging and wearing apparel during said term of time and at the end of the said term of time to give to the said apprentice one complete good new suit for the performance of all and singular the covenants and agreements aforesaid. The said parties bind themselves each unto the other firmly by these presents. In testimony whereof the said parties have here unto interchangeably set their hands and seals; dated the 29th day of June in the year of our Lord 1818."

                        Stephen Armstrong
                        William Rittenhouse

Signed, sealed and delivered
in the presence of
Daniel Bailey
John Ball, Jr.

(Note: Miami Township Census of 1820 shows one Ruth Armstrong as head of a household. Possibly she was the mother of the above Sarah, and, by then in 1820, the widow of Stephen Armstrong.)

William Rittenhouse, first settler of Mt. Nebo, died in 1831. He was buried in Congress Green cemetery.

Settlers on Rittenhouse Hill found it densely forested. Among early pioneers was Chalon Guard who acquired extensive property in the Dugan Gap section of the hill. William L. and John Guard owned a large farm, adjoining the Rittenhouse land, along Cliff Road facing out over the Ohio River. In clearing their fields of trees, the Guards easily disposed of the timber by building a log chute from the top of the cliffs down to the Ohio. There the wood was loaded on steamboats. Larger steamers of the mid 1800's burned from 50 to 75 cords of wood daily. This act of landing for fuel was called "wooding up."

As late as 1887, the hilltop was yet listed as Rittenhouse Hill in the Hamilton County Directory, although the region had gradually come to be called Mount Nebo, after the church of that name. Legend says that a circuit riding preacher, Reverend Caughman, thought the hill, high above the beautiful Ohio, the closest place to heaven one could ever reach, affirming, as Moses of old, that it was truly a "land of milk and honey." Credited with helping Rev. Caughman select the name "Mount Nebo" were Chalon Guard, Job Hayes and Thomas N. Lind.

Thomas N. Lind (1813-1875) was an early tutor in the Harrison families and a longtime teacher in the Mount Nebo and Cleves area. He married, about 1835, Jane A. Glass. They had a son, Whipple, named for their family physician, Dr. Abel Whipple, early doctor in the Miami Township locale. Thomas Lind's wife died shortly after the baby's birth and Whipple Lind was raised by his grandfather Glass. Thomas Lind was remarried, on Christmas Day of 1848, to Sarah Ewing Rittenhouse, widow of Joseph Rittenhouse (son of William). The Linds resided at the very top of Rittenhouse Hill in a home that had a view of the entire valley. In addition to Sarah Lind's five Rittenhouse sons, the couple had a daughter, Frances Lind, who became a school teacher at Mount Nebo and Cleves. Whipple Lind became a bridge contractor and is known to have built a bridge across the Big Miami at Miamitown that withstood the floods for many years.

It is known that Thomas Lind taught on Mount Nebo during 1847-1848, and perhaps much earlier, because a record of the list of parents to whom he sent "school bills" that term is found in the back of the Ogden Store Ledger, which is in the hands of Dennis W. Collins. Knowing the locations of the farms of some of these families, it can readily be seen that the students came many miles to school.

In addition to teaching school, Thomas Lind was also a dedicated Sabbath school teacher at Mount Nebo M. E. Church. For faithful service his Sunday school class presented him with an ebony cane, silver mounted and incribed. This prized possession he willed to his grandson--and namesake, Tom

Lind, son of Whipple, who too lived all his years in the house at the very top of Rittenhouse Hill.

Another legend, loved by those who are charmed with the history of the region, tells of a boatman's bell. This account is based upon several sources, chiefly the Rittenhouse family papers and "The Story of the Bell," as recorded by Mattie Irene Chidlaw and read to the Mount Nebo Society about 1932.

It happened, so the story goes, that during the early 1800's, Mount Nebo's scattered settlers realized the need for a special place of worship. Religious services conducted by circuit riding preachers, carrying their Bibles, shirts and green baize leggings in saddle bags, were held in various homes. After long months of self denial, a church was built in 1852. It stood along the roadway of what is now Mount Nebo Road, near the entrance to the present John Bonham farm.

Ground for the church building had been provided by Stephen Wood Rittenhouse, son of William. The families of the Mount Nebo congregation used the new church faithfully. A singing school and a Mite Society were organized, which drew out the young people. Oyster suppers, strawberry socials and exhibitions were featured. One important object, however, was needed to make the services complete and that was a church bell which might summon all to worship.

A committee was appointed to consider purchase of a bell. This group thoroughly investigated the matter at the bell foundries in Cincinnati and duly reported that none could be bought for less than $125, a princely sum to the small, rural congregation.

The matter of acquiring a bell seemed to be at a standstill until some months later when June Balsley of Boone County, Kentucky, a boatman who traveled up and down the Ohio selling produce, heard of their need. He contacted the committee, informing them that he owned a large bell which he would sell for $100. This he had secured some years earlier in exchange for a barrel of cider. The bell had hung on the plantation of a Mr. Bartholomew, who had sounded it to call his slaves from their work. June Balsley had placed the plantation bell on his boat. He rang it as he paddled up and down the river. Its tone was so clear it could signal prospective customers a fair distance inland, announcing to all that the peddler was approaching with his apples or potatoes, for sale or barter.

Mount Nebo's congregation readily agreed to purchase June Balsley's bell. Women solicited for contributions from among all the settlers in the area. Reported to have made most generous donations of five dollars each were J. Scott Harrison and the family of Judge John C. Short.

After the money was secured, the boat bell was brought across the river to Dugan's Gap, from where it was hauled up to Mount Nebo. On October 2, 1867, the church trustees met to consult as to how best to hang the bell. So it was that William Burdsall, a carpenter by trade and a Mount Nebo resident, erected a belfry and superintended its hanging, on Saturday, Nov. 16, 1867. Henry and David H. Rittenhouse, grandsons of William, were among those who helped to raise the bell. Soon its clear notes were ringing again, this time high up above the river, over the hills. Its melody was much admired. Through the years the bell served its people well.

During the 1870's, Mount Nebo's congregation began to scatter and Sabbath school attendance declined. The old burying ground nearby showed increased signs of neglect. Efforts were made to get the congregation to attach themselves to Cleves or Elizabethtown M. E. Churches, both served by the same circuit riding preachers as Mount Nebo Church. Some members began to unite with these neighboring groups. Finally, shortly after 1880, the old church was closed. Its bell, no longer needed, was eventually removed, Oct. 4, 1884, and carried down Rittenhouse Hill to the newly erected Cleves M. E. Church. The diary of a Cleves resident disclosed the following pertinent statement:

"October 5, 1884. Cleves went daft last night! The bell was yesterday brought down from Mount Nebo for the new church and a number of men and boys were pounding it half the night. It was the old plantation bell brought from the South by June Balsley, the Boone County boat peddler."

It is pleasant to note that the bell yet hangs today in the belfry of the Cleves United Methodist Church. It is likewise interesting to know that the Rittenhouse family has an old flat ironing board hewed from one of the crude, worn benches that was salvaged from the Mount Nebo Church when it was dismantled and sold for scrap in the mid 1880's.

The Mount Nebo Society, organized in 1905, was a reunion society. Its membership included early pioneers, teachers and scholars of the area. The group met annually for a basket picnic at the old school house or at farm homes around Mount Nebo. The calendar was turned back to earlier days on the hilltop, often there was music, and someone usually prepared a paper of particular interest to those gathered at the reunion. The society functioned until the beginning of World War II.

Ezra Guard (1849-1943), early Mount Nebo scholar and teacher, was one of the founders of the society. He was elected first historian and maintained a life long interest in the group. At the first assembly in 1905, Will Rittenhouse told of his experiences as a school boy, of how the earliest school was located in the pasture of Job Hayes, and how frightened the younger children were of the animals in the unfenced school yard.

On October 6, 1907, Alta McKinney Baker--then Mount Nebo's teacher--presented her account, "Former Days at Mount Nebo," which also told of school and how it was conducted.

The next year, on Sept. 13, 1908, Alta Baker again delivered a very interesting history of Mount Nebo. This history was read again at the society's meeting of Sept. 1931, and printed in the Lawrenceburg Press. (This 1908 report of Mrs. Baker has been an invaluable source of information for this writer.)

On Sept. 16, 1917, Judge Stanley Struble told the Mount Nebo assembly, in commenting favorably on the subject of women teachers, quote: "The factors bringing on the War (World War I) were due to the mismanagement of men, and the outcome will be that women will have a larger part in affairs of the government." The Judge's prediction proved true.

At another reunion, Hallie Stephens Caine read a collection of interesting facts pertaining to the general history of the region. She pointed out prominent persons who had lived, at one time, on or near Mount Nebo. These names included: John James Piatt, consul to Ireland and noted poet; Murat Halstead, journalist; John S. Conner, judge; William A. Davidson, attorney; John King, physician; and Charles W. Karr, attorney who had earned the title of general in the Civil War.

At the society's meeting in September, 1925, Archibald Shaw, editor of History of Dearborn County, Indiana (1915) and, himself, a descendant of the Hayes and Guard families, presented the story of the founding of Fort Finney.

On another occasion, Joseph H. Heimbrock, then chief

engineer at Columbia Power Plant, now Miami Fort Station, spoke to the society of his particular interest, that of Fort Hill and its prehistoric inhabitants.

On Sept. 9, 1934, Miss Cora Rittenhouse read her account of the Symmes settlement at North Bend. Hardships of the pioneers were described with excerpts of letters of the Keen, Howell and Rittenhouse families.

Throughout its years of existence, the programs of the Mount Nebo Society were outstanding. As the old teachers and scholars passed away, interest declined and the organization was disbanded. Miss Katherine Hayes, who was the last historian, placed the records at the Cleves Library. When the Library was closed, the papers were turned over for safe keeping to the administrators at Taylor High School.

A short but interesting history of Mount Nebo was written by Waldo Jackson when he was an 8th grade pupil at Mount Nebo School. His teacher then was Sewell G. Chance. The article was printed in Lawrenceburg Press, Feb. 17, 1921.

"Alexander Guard, an early settler, had a trail from North Bend over Mount Nebo hill to Double Lick, a creek at the Indiana and Ohio state line.

"At the dedication of the Mount Nebo Church which was located 1/2 mile east of the present (1921) schoolhouse, the main speaker said, 'This certainly is my Mount Nebo.' Hence the name.

"The first schoolhouse was a log one built in 1832 by John Wright* on Mount Nebo Road, just south of the stone house which was then occupied by Job Hayes. The first church was built on a site donated by Stephen Wood Rittenhouse. To this church came 2 itinerant preachers, a senior and a junior, who held services alternately and at regular intervals.

"Some of the early amusements were singing schools, corn huskings, quilting parties and apple peelings. This added to a general feeling of good will. When Abraham Lincoln made a call for volunteers in 1860, no section made a more liberal response for its size than Mount Nebo, which sent 30 soldiers."

*(Miami Township Census of 1830 shows one John Wright.)

Note: For more about Mount Nebo see "History of Mount Nebo Schools."

★★★★★★★★★★★★

Food and Labor Prices of the Region in 1818

Examples: Good wagon horse, $70 to $100; Milch cow, $16 to $24; Beef, $4 to $5 a hundred pounds; pork about the same; Rye and Indian corn, half dollar a bushel; Flax, 1/8 dollar per pound; Potatoes, 3 bu. for one dollar; Wheat, 3 quarter dollars a bushel. The dollar was equal to 4S 6d (shillings and pennies) of Welsh or English money. For instance, wheat was 3S 4 1/2d per bushel. A days labor was half a dollar per day and found (board and lodging), or a bushel of wheat and "find themselfs". Blacksmiths, carpenters and masons got about a dollar and fifty cents, per day. (From The Saga of the Paddy's Run by S.R. Williams)

Pioneer Religious Services at North Bend

Rev. James Kemper, pioneer in the cause of religion in Cincinnati, was ordered by the Cincinnati Presbytery, Apr. 2, 1792, to give a Sabbath at North Bend of the Miami (settlement) and Rev. Mr. Rice to give 2 Sabbaths. (Greve's Centennial History of Cincinnati.)

Henrie-Jackson home on Brower Road, near Dugan's Gap. Built during the 1840's by James Hayes, Jr.

Oldest Living Pioneers of Miami Township, Nov. 2, 1871 from Lawrenceburg Press

Jacob Eckman, 81; Jonathan Markland, 83; Wm. McConnell, 84; Samuel Price, 84; all four of these men were soldiers in the War of 1812; McConnell served as justice of the peace for 24 years; other pioneers, Michael Shotts, 81; Mrs. Skidmore, 85; Joseph M. Runyan, 84; Mrs. Wm. Bateman, 81; and Mrs. Carpenter, 88; John D. Matson, 76, lives in same house in which he was born; Mrs. Morgan, 72; Dr. J. H. Thornton, 75; Hon. J. Scott Harrison, 70; Mrs. D. G. Howell, 75; Thomas Miller, 76, of Whitewater Township, was born at North Bend.

Old County Histories

County histories were popular books of the late 19th century. These volumes were sold in advance of publication by salesmen who canvassed the neighborhoods. Families ordering books usually supplied biographical sketches to the publishing firm. These histories sold for around $12.50, a great sum in that day. If an account of one's ancestor does not appear in the county history, he either may not have been contacted to order a book or he may have felt the cost too great. The biographical sketches were not always factual, every family wanting to show itself in the best light and to leave a faultless record; however, the books still offer useful leads to family historians and genealogists.

The histories of the Fords, History of Hamilton County, and History of Cincinnati, 1881, and the History of Dearborn and Ohio Counties, Indiana, published in Chicago, 1885, by F. E. Weakley, are yet the best sources of early accounts of this region. (The latter book is presently being reprinted and will be sold by the Hillforest Historical Foundation, Aurora, Indiana.)

Henry Howe published his Historical Collections of Ohio in 1847 and again in 1888. These volumes include chapters on every county. One outstanding feature of Howe's books were his drawings of historic landmarks then standing, or as described by older residents of the locale.

Chapter 6
GRIST AND SAWMILLS

Grist and saw mills, so vital to our forefathers, were operated in a number of places around Miami and Whitewater Townships, but those of Capt. Wm. Rittenhouse, Dr. Stephen Wood, Judge Symmes, General Harrison, John Matson, Samuel Bond, Col. Benjamin Cilley, Jacob Herrider, Joseph Hafner, Daniel Keller and W. W. and Moses Whitney were probably the best known of them all.

Earliest references to mills in the North Bend settlement are found in the historical recollections of Dr. Ezra Ferris and John Scott Harrison, and in the letters of Judge Symmes. These records all refer to the same mill, that of Capt. Rittenhouse, in operation as early as 1793, located on Mount Nebo hill. (See chapter "Mount Nebo, From Ledger and Legend"). Ferris related that settlers, including one Mr. Demoss, went from the Goose Pond region at The Point to the Rittenhouse mill to have corn ground. Demoss was killed by Indians on his return. Harrison tells of this same incident, as told to him by his mother, Anna Symmes Harrison, of the murder of Demoss, along with additional details, although he does not specifically name the operator of the mill. Judge Symmes also wrote of the Rittenhouse mill in his letters.

From all records it is apparent that pioneers journeyed great distances to mills and they were most grateful to the men who operated them. When mills were not available, corn had to be ground on a hand mill, a tedious process. Getting the grain to the mill was often the most difficult task for settlers in some localities. Wagon trips over rough trails required much time. Operators of the early mills were invariably men of integrity, who had the interest of their communities at heart. And, as a result, early millers often asserted great influence in their settlements.

Saw mills were as necessary as grist mills to the early pioneers. After the coming of steamboats, floating saw mills were often erected on crude barges and moved from town to town. Later, floating mills were also employed along the canals. Probably the earliest saw mill in the North Bend settlement was that of Dr. Stephen Wood. In operation as early as 1793, it lay at the mouth of Muddy Creek. (See "Pioneers: Their Trials and Occupations.")

Judge Symmes is said to have erected two stone mills on Indian Creek, a sizeable stream which emptied into the Ohio close to the site of General Harrison's home. (See "Indian Creek".) In a letter dated at North Bend, July 29, 1796, to Capt. John Matson, Symmes requested Matson to purchase for him in the Redstone country "a number of articles for the purpose of erecting grist mills to run with one waterwheel and two pair of millstones."

On August 10, 1796, the Judge wrote: "I am building a house and grist mill on pretty extensive plans."

In a subsequent letter, written to members of his family, Dec. 26, 1799, Symmes noted that "Capt. Howel (Howell) has a good yoak (sic) of oxen & we have cut a waggon (sic) road to his house; he can therefore come to mill with a sled . . ."

Hutchinson's Mill, named in Harrison papers at CHS Library, was in operation in 1814, somewhere along the Big Miami.

Matson's Mill is another frequently mentioned mill, and ranks near the top of all in years of continuous service. Capt. John Matson, Sr., and his family, including four sons, came to North Bend with Judge Symmes around 1789. Hamilton County Court records show:

"Symmes deeded to John Matson, Jr., Jan. 10, 1796, in consideration of currency paid by John Matson, Jr., or by Capt. Matson on behalf of his son, a tract at a place called the Judge's bottom on the east bank of the Great Miami."

It appears that John Matson, Jr., (ca. 1770-1847) and some of his brothers built a saw and grist mill in this area along the river north of Cleves along the road now known as East Miami River Road, in earlier days called Matson Mill Road. An incident of early settlers going to Matson's Mill to have corn ground is cited in Pioneer Annals of Green Township. David Rittenhouse, in his diary, mentioned going to Matson's Mill, May, 1865. That mill was a thriving concern for many years, last operated by the sons and sons-in-law of John D. Matson (1796-1876). John D. Matson was the son of James Matson. In his obituary it was stated that he died near Matson's Mill and was buried on the same farm where he was born. Matson's Mill was yet in operation in the 1880's but when it was closed has not been learned. It likely was destroyed in the flood of 1884. The mill was definitely gone by 1894. An article pertaining to places around Cleves appeared in the Cincinnati Commercial Gazette, July 29, 1894, which noted that "the blacksmith shop has defied the troops of time, but Matson's Mill, the millstone and water wheel, has passed away." A verse of poetry, author unknown, described the old mill:

"Hushed is the sound of the water-mill wheel
Sleeping the echoes that waked at its call;
Musing, the mill-race flows murmuring softly,
Dirges in cadence with rain and fall."

In the Matson family burial ground, located near the gravel pit, just south of the residence of Al Minges on East Miami River Road, this writer saw a broken marker inscribed with the name of James Matson, who died in 1831 in his 65th year of age. He was the father of John D. Matson, and, without a doubt, he, too, had a hand in running the pioneer mill on the Big Miami.

Mills best known in Whitewater Township included the Samuel Bond Mill, in operation as early as 1831, probably much sooner, along the Whitewater River near Elizabethtown. In 1872, Thomas H. Hunt and W. P. Rees took over the old Bond Mill, for some time idle, repaired it and put in into running condition. Renamed "Whitewater Mill," Hunt & Rees advertised: "Choice flour, bolted meal, corn flour and feed."

In 1872, a hominy mill was built at Valley Junction. Temperance minded farmers in the Great Miami corn bottoms of that era prided themselves on the fact that they shipped the product of their labor to the wholesome grist or hominy mills, rather than to the distilleries located at nearby Lawrenceburg or Riverside, where the Fleischmann distillery was situated. (Fleischmanns were to become known for their compressed yeast which revolutionized the baking methods of the country.)

Other well known mills along the Miami, north of Cleves, were those of Col. Benjamin Cilley, along the west bank of the river in the Berea community (now Hooven), and Jacob Herrider, at Miamitown, destroyed in the 1913 flood.

Mills often experienced mechanical troubles and low water lines, but located as they necessarily were, along rivers and streams, they were subject most frequently to damage caused by floods, ice and severe winters, as seen in the following Lawrenceburg Press items:

Feb. 20, 1873. "Great Miami mills having heavy ice damage include Herrider's at Miamitown, Matson's above Cleves, and Keller's. None can grind."

Jan. 23, 1873. "The break in the Hunt & Rees mill dam caused by the heavy run of ice is a small break. No delay in business."

Along the Great Miami, west of Cleves, (Miamiview Road this side of Lost Bridge) where the Whitewater River enters the Miami, was the site of a saw and grist mill that dated from pioneer times. It may have been the site of the Hutchinson Mill, already mentioned. Members of the Noble family ran a mill here in early days, how early is unknown, but the mill was in operation in 1847, as indicated on a map of that year. Mahlon B. Creemer, listed in the 1880 Cleves census as a miller, resided in the general location of the mill around 1850. Possibly he worked at the Noble mill. Near the site of this mill (now the present Saur farm), in the days before Lost Bridge existed, was a ford where Mt. Nebo settlers crossed the river to Berea or Elizabethtown.

The old Noble mill was being operated in the 1860's by Joseph Hafner, Sr. Prior to owning the mill in the Miami, Hafner had been principal miller for many years at the old Lewis & Eichelberger Flour Mills along the Whitewater Canal in Lawrenceburg. He died in February, 1867, as a result of being hit by a train at North Bend. His son, Joseph (II), also operated the mill for a time at this site. In January, 1872, Daniel Keller took over the management of the former Hafner mill. This mill was a convenience for both the residents of Cleves and Mt. Nebo. In those days a road ran off from Mt. Nebo Road, near the old M. E. Church, through the Stephen B. Hayes farm--later the Peter McIntyre farm, down to the Big Miami not far from where the mill was situated. (Hamilton County Atlas of 1869, by Titus, shows that Peter McIntyre, himself, was proprietor of a saw mill and a dealer in lumber, although his grandson, Arthur "Bud" McIntyre, knows nothing of this.) Motto of Daniel Keller's Mill was: "First to the mill, first served with the best family flour." (from Lawrenceburg Press, Jan. 11, 1872.) This mill was yet in operation in 1883, Keller's sons, Edward and Peter, then working with him. It's location is best described as having stood near the site of the old Jacob Pittner dining place, "Riverdale."

The diasatrous flood of 1884 changed the course of the Great Miami River, and the old Noble-Hafner-Keller grist mill was put out of business due to the loss of its water supply.

Sometime therafter, Joseph Hafner (II) built a mill in Cleves just beyond the railroad tracks on Mt. Nebo Road. Here he erected a three-storied building and operated his mill by steam power. This was a lumber mill as well as a flour mill. Small furniture parts, such as chair and table legs, were also turned out. Hafner and several of his sons worked for a time at the trade. The "Miami Flour Mill," as it was called, stood where Jack Moreland's garage now stands, along the alley commonly known as Hafner's Alley. (Hamilton County Directory of 1887, lists Joseph Hafner, proprietor of Miami Flour Mill, Miami River Road, with sons, Joseph, Jr., and John as millers.) This mill was in operation until shortly after 1900.

Several interesting legends have been passed down in the Hafner family concerning happenings at the old mill along the Miami. One account tells that Joseph Hafner was once cited to court on the grounds that he was running a fish trap at his mill. Before the judge, Hafner explained how fish--quite naturally--became caught in the race under the slats used to keep debris from the water wheel. Fish trapped in this manner were handed out daily to whoever happened by the mill. The understanding judge, upon hearing the testimony, could find no guilt on the miller's part, and he appeared, himself, next day at the Hafner mill to "catch some fish." (See also "The Legend of the Wamsley Madstone.")

North Bend is known to have had a saw mill, and later a veneer mill, near the river just below Harrison's Tomb. This mill, operated over the years by several families including those of W. W. and Moses Whitney, and later Henry Graham, stood for at least fifty years. David Rittenhouse, in his diary, noted several times between 1866-1868 that he took a log to the mill or went to the Bend for lumber. Before the existence of the town hall and school house at North Bend in 1877, lectures and meetings were held at Whitney's saw mill, with logs serving as benches. From the Lawrenceburg Press comes this item:

Aug. 6, 1874. "Robert Warder addressed the people of North Bend at Whitney's Mill on the subject 'Prodigal Son'."

Arthur "Bud" McIntyre, life long resident of Mt. Nebo, North Bend and Cleves, and former chief of Cleves waterworks, recalls that as a young lad of about 10 or 12, he had his first paying job at the veneer mill below Harrison's Tomb.

This foregoing account concerning grist and saw mills built and used by pioneers of the region in and bordering Miami Township, although by no means complete, gives some picture as to how hard our forefathers worked to accomplish and acquire the needs of their day.

Ruins Of Harrison Mill At North Bend, Ca 1890. Victor Truitt On Log.

★★★★★★★★★★

Perrines' Mill on the Whitewater

John and Peter Perrine were among the earliest landowners west of the Great Miami. The Perrines are said to have built the first mill on the Whitewater River, for which they received a bonus of a quarter section of land. A number of this pioneer family are buried in the old Whitewater Township Cemetery near the place once called Hunt's Grove and Whitewater Park.

Another Mill on the Great Miami

The 1856 map of Hamilton County Surveyor A. W. Gilbert indicates that S. C. Andrews operated a mill along the west side of the Great Miami just opposite the Matson Mill.

Chapter 7

THE MIAMI AND WHITEWATER VALLEY PIONEER ASSOCIATION: "THE PIONEER SOCIETY"

"The Miami and Whitewater Valley Pioneer Association was organized June 20, 1866, by a group of gentlemen of Elizabethtown, Ohio, to whom the reminiscences of pioneer life and the settlement of these valleys possessed an interest and in which their parents and grand-parents had acted a part.

"The organization became no insignificant feature in the west end of Hamilton County and a part of Dearborn County, Indiana. Its annual reunion became, so as to speak, 'the Derby Day' of this section.

"With its growth in popularity it lost some of its simplicity but preserved its original intent of collecting and preserving the facts of early pioneer life and the memory of the early settlers." (Copied from the organization's by-laws and membership roster of 1883.)

The move to organize such a society in 1866, was no doubt influenced by the existence of the Cincinnati Pioneer Association, in which many local pioneers participated. That group had enjoyed a picnic at Hunt's Grove, near Valley Junction, just two years before, on July 17, 1864. Rev. B. W. Chidlaw of Whitewater Township had given the pioneer address and Jose Tosso, Cincinnati violinist, best known for his composition "The Arkansas Traveler," had entertained with music.

On September 8, 1866, the Honorable J. Scott Harrison delivered the first paper to the newly formed Miami and Whitewater Society entitled "Pioneer Life at North Bend." From his paper the following narrative concerning an experience at the early North Bend settlement is taken:

"A party of men, residing at the Point (mouth of the Big Miami), were returning from a small mill near North Bend and, with one exception, stopped at the old log house, lately occupied by Andrew McDonald, where a tavern was then kept. One man, Demoss, more temperate, perhaps, than his fellows, continued on his way up the hill--the trace to the Point then running over the hill, near the old graveyard, and on the bluff of the ridge. The revelers had hardly time to accomplish the object of their stop before the report of a rifle was heard on the hill. The party at the tavern, supposing it was only an intimation from their more sober companion to cease their revels and continue their way home, rushed out of the house with a wild whoop, mounted their horses and rode up the hill. But what must have been the horror of the party, on arriving at the crown of the hill, to find their companion dead and weltering in his own blood! The undischarged rifle of Demoss, and the missing mealbag, too plainly explained the manner and the cause of his death. Pursuit was immediately given, in a northwesterly direction, and the meal, but not the Indian, found. The Indian, in order to save his own life, had dropped that which had evidently incited him to commit murder.

The tale of Indian murder has always had a peculiar personal interest to me. My mother, (Anna Symmes Harrison), then unmarried and living with her father, Judge Symmes, at North Bend, had been on a riding excursion, (horseback, of course), to the Point, the very afternoon of this murder, and has often told me that the horses of their party were still at the door after their return, when the fatal shot that killed Demoss was plainly heard. My mother was always under the impression that the Indian saw her party pass, but the bread, rather than blood, was the object of the murderer." (Page 322, Ford's History of Hamilton County).

At the Pioneer Society's meeting of July 3, 1869, Rev. Benjamin W. Chidlaw presented his paper entitled "Sketch of the Early Life and Times of Bailey Guard, Esq." (See also another chapter "It Happened 'Round the Point.") Rev. Chidlaw's account portrayed an excellent picture of pioneer life. Briefly condensed, herewith, his report was given something like this:

The necessities of time chartered the course for those who first settled at North Bend and ports round about.

During the spring of 1790, several families named Guard came by flatboat to Judge Symmes' colony at North Bend. The entire settlement existed as best they could on their scanty means, hunting and farming, while at the same time keeping a sharp lookout for Indians. Some of their number boated downriver to Big Bone Licks near the Kentucky shore to manufacture salt.

Captain Joseph Hayes, in 1793, leased a vast tract of fertile land belonging to John Cleves Symmes at the mouth of the Great Miami, four miles below the Bend. In that same year, Alexander Guard, his wife, Mary, (sometimes given as Hannah), and their four sons, Timothy, David, Ezra and Bailey, decided to leave the blockhouse at North Bend and join the Hayes family downstream. On moving day they packed their belongings into a hollowed-out log boat, called a pirogue, and bid farewell to their friends at the Bend.

Alexander Guard poled the pirogue downstream. His wife and young sons followed on foot. The Great Miami was swollen and running with a strong current where it emptied into the Ohio. Here, the boat upset. All the family's worldly goods was lost, even their money--which was in silver. Alexander Guard, fortunately, reached safety.

Mary Guard, who was familiar with the cultivation of flax and cotton and the weaving of cloth, had noticed, as she made the journey, that wild nettles, having tough fiber, grew in great profusion about the river bottoms. She and her children later gathered enough of these nettles, in one season, to make 200 yards of strong cloth. This was but one instance of ingenuity that grew out of the necessities of the time.

At a later pioneer gathering at Berea Chapel, July 16, 1876, in a special Centennial Service (1776-1876), Rev. Chidlaw read a paper called "Early Times." In this he explained in detail the process of cloth making from nettles and flax as related to him by Sarah Guard Bonham, daughter of Alexander Guard. On this occasion, Dr. Walter Clark displayed a well preserved specimen of nettle cloth. In his account, Rev. Chidlaw stated--in the words of Sarah Bonham:

"Our men folk went in the canoe to the mouth of the Whitewater and gathered nettles that had rotted during the winter. They were from 12 to 16 feet long. They broke and scutched these reeds and the women heckled, spun and wove the sloth. We made over 200 yards and used most of it in the family, but sold some to neighbors. Some families sowed flax and planted cotton. They all grew some indigo and manufactured linen and cotton goods fit to make garments for kings--or presidents. Woolen goods, genuine linsey-woolsey, and Kentucky jeans were produced at a later day and added greatly to the wardrobes of the families of our grandparents."

The place where the principal business of the Miami and Whitewater Valley Pioneer Association was transacted was Hunt's Grove, later called Whitewater Park. In earlier days, as early as 1850, Hunt's Grove, then situated near the Whitewater Canal, was the site of regional Sunday School rallies and mass meetings, promoted largely by Rev. B. W. Chidlaw. Rev. Chidlaw was active in the work of the American Sunday School Union and was founder of the Hamilton County Sunday School Union, organized in 1862, to promote interest in Sunday School work. First officers of the Hamilton County Union included: Dr. J. M. McKenzie, president of Delhi Township S. S. Union; Walter Howell, Miami Township president; and Rev. Chidlaw, Whitewater Township president. The following news item appeared in the Independent Press, Lawrenceburg, August 10, 1853:

"The Basket Mass Meeting of the Sunday Schools at a grove near Cleves came off in fine style. An address was given by Rev. B. W. Chidlaw and Dr. W. Clark of Elizabethtown spoke. A canal boat load of persons came from Harrison. The grove is a delightful place."

The grove was leased from the Hunt family by the I&C Railroad about 1870, the grounds were improved and in time the park became known as a meeting spot for miles around. Situated on the Whitewater Valley Branch of the I&C Railway, about 2 miles north of Valley Junction, Whitewater Park came to be the favorite amusement grounds of the region. The railroad company sponsored excursions to the park, where large business concerns entertained their employees with outings. Special coaches carried picnickers from Cincinnati to the well-kept grove. Amusement features came to include a bowling alley, a "flying Dutchman," dance pavilion and bands. Ice cream, all-time favorite, was the specialty of the park. Among those who served as superintendents of the park grounds were James Kendrick and Erastus Hayes, both members of the Miami and Whitewater Pioneer Society. A more pleasant spot to hold reunions could not have been found. For those attending the pioneer meetings, half-fare arrangements were made by the railroad company.

Officers elected at the society's meeting in August, 1871 were: President, Gen. John McMakin; Secretary, William P. Reece; Treasurer, S. Van Hayes; Historian, John Crookshank. Eight vice-presidents were also elected. Persons who had lived in the region since 1840 were invited to become members by paying one-dollar. At this 1871 gathering, Rev. Samuel Browne spoke. His father was credited with preaching one of the earliest sermons west of the Miami River, in Whitewater Township.

The 8th annual reunion of the Pioneer Society was held at Hunt's Grove, August, 1873. Dr. Edward Crookshank of Cheviot presided and Hon. D. K. Este of Cincinnati delivered the address. The oldest member present was 93 years old.

At the 1874 meeting, a pioneer foot race was featured, the competitors being Mr. Toph of Miamitown, Mr. Hartpence of Harrison, and Noah Markland of Cleves, all nearly 72 years of age. Mr. Markland won the prize, a pair of gold spectacles.

The yearly reunion at Hunt's Grove, August 7, 1875, was not well attended due to floods and high water. Hon. Will Crumbach was the speaker.

In 1882, the Miami and Whitewater Pioneer Society was incorporated under the laws of Ohio for Harvest Home Associations, subscribed to by James Kendrick, M. B. Wamsley, Warren West, B. W. Chidlaw, S. V. Hayes and Joseph Cilley. Officially it became "The Miami and Whitewater Valley Pioneer and Harvest Home Association," but it was best known to everyone as "The Pioneer (Pia-neer) Society."

Presidents of the organization from 1866 to 1883 were: Dr. J. H. F. Thornton, 1866-67; Edward Hunt, 1868-71; John McMakin, 1872; Dr. E. D. Cruikshank, 1873; A. B. Lind, 1874; William Jessup, 1875; Dr. J. C. McGuire, 1876; S. V. Hayes, 1877; G. W. Haire, 1878; Thos. E. Sater, 1879; Dr. Myron H. Harding, 1880; George Bowlby, 1881; G. W. Lane, 1882; and William Cone, 1883.

Brief notes concerning the reunion of August 4, 1883, were copied from the Commercial Gazette:

The picnic was held at Hunt's Grove on the Harrison Branch of the Big Four. It was estimated that 5,000 attended. The program was opened with music from Ruff's Band of Harrison, Ohio, a new organization with handsome uniforms, bright instruments and a dizzy band wagon, decorated with portraits of Haydn, Handel, Weber, Beethoven and others of the great musical masters.

Prayer was given by Robert Gwaltney, chaplain. General Ward was the guest speaker. Judge A. G. W. Carter reported on the background of Cincinnati's settlement in 1788.

Elected as president for the coming year was Warren Tebbs of Lawrenceburg.

Obituaries of three departed members, Dr. J. C. McGuire, Major John Anderegg, and Dr. John A. Warder, were read. A resolution was given in regard to the life and service of Dr. Warder, who had been a most worthy and honorable helper in promoting the objects of the pioneer association.

At the gathering August 6, 1892, a poem "The Old Log Cabin," written by W. R. Hartpence of Harrison, was read and dedicated to the Association.

The 26th annual meeting was held at Whitewater Park, August 5, 1894. Officers elected were: President, Hon. R. E. Slater; Secretary, Geo. W. Haire; Treasurer, Daniel Jessup; Vice-presidents, Ambose E. Nowlin, Moses B. Wamsley, Walter Hartpence, J. E. Slater, David Lowstutter; and Historian, Harry Bowles.

Highlight of the Pioneer Picnic at Whitewater Park, in August of 1901, was the awarding of gold spectacles to the oldest woman present, and a gold-headed cane to the oldest man present. Winners were Mrs. Eliza Hayes and Mr. George Roberts.

Among the premiums offered at the Pioneer Reunion, September 10, 1904, were the following:

F. A. Grossman, Druggist, Cleves, Ohio: 1 silver mounted toilet set for the best piece of needlework.

Ideal Clothing Co., Harrison, Ohio: $1 neck tie to the best looking man present.

Cincinnati Times-Star: 1 year's subscription to each for the oldest U.S. coin; for the best display of needlework; for the best farm products display.

George E. Caine, Leading Grocer, Cleves, Ohio: 1# best coffee for the best loaf of salt rising bread.

Hamilton County National Bank, Cleves, Ohio: 50¢ each for best 5 nutmegs; best half peck of oats; best plate of tomatoes; best 12 ears of corn.

At the picnic September 9, 1905, Henry H. Rittenhouse received a premium of 1 quart of wine together with a certificate stating that he was judged the "best looking young man present." (He was around 60 at that time.)

W. C. Cooper, Cleves physician and writer, read his humorous poem "A Brief Courtship" to the society, September 7, 1907, which told how a young couple met at the Pioneer Reunion. At their marriage they vowed to "allus tend the blessed Pioneer."

A BRIEF COURTSHIP
by W. C. Cooper, Cleves, Ohio

Prehaps you've never heered before of Jeremiar Higgins,
An' mebbe you have never met one Miss Jerusha Spriggins.
Well, Jerry he was tall and lank, an' awk'ard in his manner,
An' lived jes' on the eastern aidge of southern Indianner.
Now Jerry had acquired some wealth (three dollars), an' last year

He tuck it in his head, he did, he'd 'tend the Pianeer.
An' when the time came fer to go, he humped him with a will;
He shaved hisself, an' breshed his hair, an' spruced up fit to kill.
He didn't want to kill no one, but he was bound to resk it,
An' so he wore his striped pants; also his speckled weskit,
An' wore his allypacky coat that allus ketched the eye,
But the stunniest of all he wore was that there red neck-tie.
He found more people there than all he'd ever saw before;
He vowed they was ten thousand, an' prehaps a whole lot more;
An gyrls--they wan't no eend of them as fer as he could see--
"Just whirls and swirls of pretty girls in dainty dimity."
(Which that was what a feller that stood closte to Jerry said,
An' Jerry ketched it, so he did, an' crammed it in his head).
At last he come acrost a gyrl that wasn't dressed so proud
As nearly all the rest was in that vasty, vasty crowd,
An' somethin' 'bout her drawed him in the fetchinest of styles,
An' somethin' 'bout him drawed her--prehaps it was his smiles;
So he went to her an' bravely said: "I'm Jeremiar Higgins,"
An' then she 'jes as bravely said: "I'm Miss Jerusha Spriggins,"
He tucked her tremblin' hand in hisn an' squeezed it sev'ral times,
Then said: "I hope you notus Miss, how nice our two names rymes.
They naicherly--your name an' mine--jes' seems to hug each other
So tarnal close it would be hard to tell the which from tother.
Now don't you think that you an' me would make a purty verse?"
Said she: "I really must own up, I think they could be worse."
Then follered leminade an' sech, as round the stands they hovered,
Till Jerry's funds was runnin' low, he painfully discovered;
An' so he said to Rushy in a whisper half aloud,
"Les meander to the sooburbs of this everlastin' crowd."
She tuck his arm an' they walked out behind an underbresh,
Where they could talk an' not be herred, an' no one see her blesh.
They sot down on a mossy log, an' losin' self-control,
Poor Jerry, fearin' he'd explode, jes' emptied out his soul!
He vowed he loved her fiercer than blue lightnin' strikes a tree;
In fact he loved her way beyend the uttermost degree;
"Toad of the world!" he sighed to her, will you, will you be mine?
"It's suddint-like," said she, "but then, dear Jerry, I'll be thine!
She fell into his waitin' arms, fer nothin' then seemed missin',
An' all their bosom-loads of bliss then busted out in kissin'!

* * * *

They're morried now, this happy pair, an' both of them is here,
Fer they are bound to allus tend the blessed Pianeer.

At the 45th annual reunion of the Pioneer Society, 5,000 persons attended. Prizes for the oldest woman and man present went to Mrs. A. S. Bennett, 89, and E. W. Crow, 87, both of Harrison, Ohio. Officers elected at that gathering of August 20, 1910, were: President, Martin Hartpence; Trustees, D. W. Gwaltney, Peter Menges, John Wentzel; Vice-president, Martin Weber; Secretary, Harry L. Cooper; Treasurer, Dr. Fred Grossman; and Historian, Dr. W. C. Cooper.

The meeting of 1912 was cancelled for the first time since the association's inception in 1866, because of numerous other events scheduled on the regular reunion date.

By this time, interest in the pioneer organization had waned and the original purpose of the society had dimmed. The reunion had come to be no more than a carnival replete with all the usual money-making attractions. Several more Pioneer Picnics were held after 1912, but in the year 1916, the Miami and Whitewater Valley Pioneer Association was disbanded. D. W. Gwaltney served as the society's last president.

Sometime shortly after, Whitewater Park itself was abandoned. Several years later, the Pope family opened a similar type picnic grove and amusement park, very close by, at the site of the suspension bridge spanning the Whitewater. At that point in the river is an island--so the park became "Long Island Park." It quickly took the place of Whitewater Park and continued as a popular beach resort for many years.

It is interesting to note that on this island, shortly before 1930, Boy Scout Troop #26 of Sayler Park, under Scoutmasters A. G. Colburn, Sr., and Christie Burger, built a lodge. Other leaders who assisted in the erection of the cabin included E. W. Volz. Entire families of the Scouts packed their lunches, boarded traction cars to Long Island Park and spent their meeting days in the work of building the lodge. The Scout cabin was reached by walking over a narrow swinging bridge, suspended by cables across the Whitewater River. Troop #26 was most generous with their lodge and camp ground; many local Scouts, girls as well as boys, enjoyed memorable weekends camping on Long Island.

Frequent floods caused the downfall of Long Island Park. It became a thing of the past along with Whitewater Park, Hunt's Grove and the old Pioneer Society.

The very first meeting of the old Miami and Whitewater Valley Pioneer Association had been held at the new town hall in Cleves, Sept. 8, 1866, with J. Scott Harrison delivering the pioneer address. Judge Bellamy Storer also spoke. Following the program a public dinner was held in the dining room of the hall. This town building had only recently been completed by veterans of the Civil War and citizens of the community. It became the meeting place and official headquarters of the Charles S. Hayes G.A.R. Post No. 224. Major Hayes, of the 5th Ohio Cavalry, a native of Elizabethtown, had been killed in action in the south. The town hall was turned over, several years after its construction, to Miami Township. Since that time it has seen continual use as a court room, a church, an entertainment hall and a meeting place for many organizations.

Among the builders of the old Cleves Town Hall was Jacob Zondler (1829-1873) a native of Wurttemberg, Germany, who settled in Cleves about 1858. He was a bricklayer and stone mason by trade. When the venerable town building was being remodeled in 1929 and 1930, an old brick* was found among the rubble which bore the signature Jacob Zondler of Wurttemberg. His son, Philip Zondler, and daughter, Emma Z. Keller, immediately recognized it as that of their father, long before buried at pioneer Congress Green, who had helped lay the bricks of the old hall.

The newly designed Miami Township Hall was dedicated in April, 1930, with an appropriate ceremony. Speakers included: Hon. James Albert Green, "Historic Address;" Prof. Charles T. Young, "Educational Advantages of Miami Township;" and Judge Stanley Struble, "Civic and Industrial Life of Miami Township." William A. Smith, Cleves contractor, presented the keys of the new hall. Then, in 1930, Perry Stoneking was president of the Miami Township board of trustees, and John Balser, clerk. New features of the enlarged building were a spacious auditorium, dining room and kitchen, and a room for a public library. Stephen J. Alling of Fernbank was one of the architects who assisted in designing the plans for rebuilding the hall.

A counterpart, today, of the old Miami and Whitewater Valley Pioneer Association, organized in 1866, is the new Three Rivers Historical Society, chartered in 1967. Appropriately, the meetings of the new society are conducted in Miami Township Hall, Cleves, where the first meeting and program of the old pioneer association was held. The purposes of the new historical society closely parallel those of the old. First to serve as president of the new organization was Stephen J. Alling.

It is interesting to note in his closing remarks to the newly formed Miami and Whitewater Valley Pioneer Association-- over 100 years ago--that the speaker, J. Scott Harrison, implored the society:

". . .not to forget the services of those brave men who macadamized with their blood the highway to this land of 'milk and honey.'. . .It is your duty to preserve the good name and fame of these worthy ancestors... You gentlemen in your researches after the buried gems of Western history will find much that is worthless, but persevere--the gold will be found at last."

~~~~~~~~~~~~~~~~

The narrative and closing remarks of J. Scott Harrison were taken from his paper "Pioneer Life at North Bend," delivered before the Miami and Whitewater Valley Pioneer Association, at Cleves, Ohio, Sept. 8, 1866. Published by Robert Clarke & Co., Cincinnati, 1867.

*The brick from the old town hall is in the hands of Mrs. Margaret Keller Frankenhauser of Cleves. 1968

What ever happened to the records of the Miami and Whitewater Valley Pioneer Association is unknown. Much of the information included in this account was taken from old Lawrenceburg and Cincinnati newspapers, and from an 1883 association roster, with by-laws, loaned by Miss Cora Rittenhouse.

A complete copy of Rev. B. W. Chidlaw's address of July 3, 1869, entitled "Sketch of the Early Life and Times of Bailey Guard, Esq.", appeared in the Lawrenceburg Press, July 15, 1869. A copy was made by this writer, 1968.

Rev. Chidlaw's paper, delivered at Berea Chapel, July 16, 1876, in a special Centennial Service (1776-1876), entitled "Early Times," was copied by D. W. Collins from the original manuscript through the courtesy of the Chidlaw family.

A copy of the Premium List for the Pioneer Reunion Picnic at Whitewater Park, Sept. 10, 1904, may be found at CHS Library.

★★★★★★★★★★★

Miami Township

Miami Township, created in 1791, situated in the southwesternmost corner of Hamilton County, originally encompassed not only the present Miami Township tract but also parts of what now lie in Delhi, Green and Colerain Townships.

First officers of the township were Lynde Elliott, clerk; Darius C. Orcutt, overseer of roads; Henry Brazier, overseer of the poor. Early justices of the peace were Stephen Wood and Garah Markland. Township constables were Andrew Hill, 1797-98; John Wilkinson, 1799. The cattle brand for the township was fixed by the court as the letter D.

Travel Improvements Witnessed by Job Miller, Sr.

Job Miller, Sr., came to North Bend with his father, Thomas Miller, Sr., in 1791. He lived all of his life in this general area. Upon Job Miller's death in 1865, a pioneer friend wrote a short sketch of his life and included in it brief mentions of events and improvements that the subject had witnessed during the course of his lifetime. The following paragraph concerns travel. Quote:

"Then the improvement in navigation of the beautiful Ohio River, from the bark and other canoes, perogues, and batteaus, which gave place to the keelboat and barges, these gave place to the majestic steamboat. Job Miller came home from New Orleans on the 'ROBERT FULTON', one among the first steamboats that ran the western rivers. (During the early period of his life he engaged in agricultural pursuits and of shipping his products to New Orleans markets and walking back over land to his home.) The primitive ferries, of swimming the horse beside the canoe, have given place to magnificent bridges and steam ferries. The U.S. mails from the postboy and trumpets on horseback to stage-coaches, canal packets and steamboats. Now (1865) the rail car drawn by the locomotive, whose shrill whistle startles the inhabitants by day and night as it darts through town and country. Then the majestic telegraph spans the continent from the Atlantic to the Pacific Oceans and with the twinkling of an eye dispatches are transmitted from San Francisco to New York and every flash brings tidings from all parts of the country. All these and many more of the most valuable and wonderful improvements in the world have been produced in the lifetime of Job Miller." (copied from The Union Press, Lawrenceburg, Ind., Feb. 2, 1865)

Miami Township Justices of the Peace

1819, John Palmer, Daniel Bailey; 1825, Wm. Harrell, James Martin; 1829, John Scott Harrison, J. L. Watson, Isaac Morgan; Wm. McConnell served during this period for 24 years; 1865, John D. Matson, A. R. Lind; 1866, A. R. Lind, James Carlin; 1867-69, Carlin and James Herron; 1870-72, Carlin and Wm. B. Welsh; 1873-74, Carlin, James Herron, Wm. Ayr; 1875, Carlin and Ayr; 1876-78, Wm. Jessup, A. R. Lind; 1879-80, Carlin and Lind; 1882, Carlin and James B. Matson.

Miami Township Festival

Sept. 1, 1869. Cincinnati Commercial. "In a lovely grove on the bank of the Ohio in sight of the tomb of President Harrison at North Bend the "Feast of Harvest" was celebrated yesterday. On the motion of Capt. G. W. Boyer, Judge Spooner was called to preside. Before dinner "How to Elevate the Laborer" was the subject of an address by Rev. B. W. Chidlaw, followed by C. W. Spooner, Esq., of Cincinnati, on the History of Agriculture." After dinner Hon. Judge Woodruff and others entertained the audience. Young people enjoyed recreation and rural sports. Miami Township made a fine show of youth and beauty, the scores of country girls gracing the assembled crowd, as well as the sturdy, intelligent yeomanry -- the boys -- that hold the plow and gather the abundant harvest."

Whitewater Township

Whitewater Township was originally set off to include all that part of Hamilton County west of the Great Miami. It comprised the large tract now occupied by Whitewater, Crosby and Harrison Townships. In 1804 this large township was subdivided and Crosby Township was formed of the five northernmost tiers of sections. In 1853 Harrison Township was formed from Whitewater and Crosby Townships.

Chapter 8

SKETCH OF THE EARLY LIFE AND TIMES OF BAILEY GUARD, ESQ.

Delivered by Rev. B. W. Chidlaw at the Pioneer's celebration at Hunt's Grove, July 3, 1869.
Copied from The Lawrenceburg Press, July 15, 1869.

In 1787, the Congress of United States, by a memorable ordinance, secured to freedom and free labor the territory northwest of the Ohio River. This guarantee, that the broad acres of the garden of this continent should be forever the inheritance of freemen, inspired the liberty loving hearts of the enterprising yeomanry of the new-born Republic to go up and possess the land.

New England sent her sons and daughters under adventurous leaders to plant the standard of Christian civilization and religion at the mouth of the Muskingum River. New Jersey sent her children on the same exalted errand to a point lower down the Ohio Valley between the Little and Great Miami Rivers in the spring of 1790. Several families left Elizabethtown (N.J.) to seek a home in the fertile valleys of the west. Among these was Alexander Guard, his wife and three small children.

The youngest was Bailey, who died last June 6th at his residence near Elizabethtown (Ohio), at the advanced age of 82 years. Having spent 79 years of his life within 10 miles of this pleasant grove. Mr. Guard's family, with four others, formed a mess and journeyed in two wagons to Red Stone, an old fort on the Monongahela River, 40 miles above Fort Pitt. This point of embarkation was the gate opening to the boundless and unexplored regions toward the setting of the sun. Here was the grand entrance to the Northwest Territory, and here the adventurous emigrants made arrangements to prosecute their journey westward.

Mr. (Alexander) Guard and his companions in travel built a flatboat and embarked with his earthly goods on the gentle Monongahela, then at flood height, and voyaged amid perils and privation on the majestic Ohio, arriving at North Bend April 4, 1790. Two years previous the site of Cincinnati, now (1869) a city of 250,000 inhabitants, was covered by a dense forest and the first cabins in Losantiville were built.

The same year, 1788, Judge Symmes with several boats and families landed at North Bend and commenced the settlement of his new purchase. In the military journal of Maj. Ebenezer Denny, published by the Pennsylvania Historical Society, page 327, we find the following record:

"The major was then stationed at Fort Harmar, at the mouth of the Muskingum, August 27th. Judge Symmes arrived on his way to his new purchase at the Miami. He had his daughter Polly along.

"They lodge with the General and Mrs. Harmar, and will stay three days and then depart.

"If I am not greatly mistaken Miss Symmes will make a fine woman, has an amiable disposition and highly cultivated mind.

"In December, 1789, Gen. Harmar located a garrison on the banks of the Ohio, opposite the mouth of the Licking, and east of the log-cabin village of Losantiville. Writing to General Knox, Secretary of War, at New York, he thus described the fort: This will be one of the most solid and substantial fortresses in the western territory; it is built of hewed timber, and is a perfect square, two stories high, with four block houses at the angles.

"On account of its supreme excellence, I have thought to honor it with the name Fort Washington. Appendix, Denny's journal, page 448, he also adds; the difficulty of forwarding my dispatches from this post to the war office is very great up the River to Fort Pitt. It is about 500 miles. It is too fatiguing to be monthly sending a boat against the stream for that purpose unless an extraordinary occasion shall require it.

"I am therefore making arrangements to send my letters to Danville, Ky., from whence to be forwarded through the wilderness and deposited in the post office at Richmond, Va., which I believe to be the most expeditious conveyance.

On page 439, General Harmar writes to Major Willis: "It is not improbable but that two companies will be ordered to be stationed at the mouth of the Great Miami, not only as a better cover for Kentucky, but also afford protection to Judge Symmes in his intended settlement there."

In another dispatch he writes near the Little Miami: This is a settlement called Columbia. here: seven miles distant from Columbia there is another named Losantiville, but lately changed to Cincinnati, and Judge Symmes himself resides at the other called Miami City at the north bend of the Ohio river. They are in general but small cabins, and the inhabitants are of the poorest class of people."

Three months after, the General, however, thus dispatched to the war office: "Mr. Guard and family cast their lots with the Webb families, then living at the north bend, and protected from hostile savages by a garrison of United States troops."

Mr. Guard remained a squatter at the bend for (several) years, enduring many privations, and earning a scanty living. In 1793, he leased some land from Judge Symmes at the point four or five miles below the bend.

His wife and children walked over the hills to their new home, while he took his movables in a barge down the Ohio. Entering the Miami he met with a disaster, his boat was upset, and much of his property was lost, and by clinging to a snag for several hours until a canoe could be obtained for his rescue, he narrowly escaped a watery grave.

Near this new home was once located Fort Finney. On page 268 of the journal already referred to, we have an account of the location of this post, October 22, 1785.

"The fleet arrived at the Great Miami the best ground for our station about a mile above the mouth, where the boats were brought, and everything unloaded.

All hands set to work preparing lumber for block houses and for the pickets, and on the 8th of November had ourselves inclosed, and hoisted the U.S. flag, and christened the place Fort Finney, in compliment to Capt. Finney, the commanding officer.

Our work is a square stockade fort, 24x18 feet in each angle. It contains 100 feet of stout pickets, 4 feet in the ground and 9 feet above, situated 150 feet from the river, on a rising second bank.

Here the Indian chiefs assembled and councils were held here. Generals Clark, Butler, and Parson treated with the Wyandots and Delawares, the Ottawas and the Shawnees.

Captain Johnny, Halfpole, White Eyes, Half King, Crane Pipe and Wingmen--all were glad to see us brothers; some grog and a smoke. This post was abandoned.

When Fort Washington was garrisoned, some of the ruins of this important post of the early military occupancy of the West still remained. At the point, Bailey Guard spent several years of his early life, and his child memories of that period he retained vividly and related with much pleasure. The home of the pioneer was generally erected in a day. In the morning the trees out of which it was built were growing and at sunset the axe and handspike and the willing hands of friendly neighbors had finished the cabin, and it was ready to domicil the new comer.

The habitations of the first settlers were not equal in architectural style and finish to the shanty now built in an hour with the help of the saw mill and the nail keg. In its construction entered neither iron or glass. Slit clapboards answered for the roof and ceiling, hewed slabs for flooring, and greased paper for window glass. The furniture was in perfect keeping with the house. Chairs, bedsteads and tables were made with an axe, a drawing knife and an auger.

The larder was supplied from the truck patch, the forest and the river with occasional additions in the way of luxuries obtained in barter for venison or peltries at the trader's counter or the store at the block house.

Mr. Guard, in referring to the style of living in early times, would relate with great pleasantry that one of the dishes held in high esteem and considered a perfect luxury, the very delicacy of the season was prepared with wild onions and wild turkey eggs fried in oppossum fat.

In the autumn, when the oppossum were plenty and in good condition, the thoughtful wife was careful to render and preserve the fat to be used on extra occasions as a substitute for lard and butter. Manufacturers in those pioneer days, before Onandago and Pornesey were known, of salt, so indispensable in the culinary art, were scarce and high.

At the lick, west of Elizabethtown, almost in sight of where we are now assembled, in 1796, salt was manufactured and sold at $4 a bushel, hot from kettles. The well was sixteen feet deep, and the kettles used were brought from the ironworks in western Pennsylvania. Salt was also made at Big Bone (B.W.C. wrote Big Bend, or the paper miscopied) Lick, Ky., greatly to the comfort and advantage of the early settlement.

"Necessity being the mother of invention," when the stock of clothing brought from the old State was exhausted, their necessities compelled the pioneers to depend upon their own labor in producing the raw material and upon their skill in manufacturing fabrics from which their bed clothes and wearing apparel could be made.

The skins and furs of wild animals especially the deer and the raccoon, properly prepared at these house shops, supplied the men with caps, pants and fringed hunting shirts, and both sexes, old and young, with moccasin for the feet. Around the cabin grew the corn, the vegetables, and a small patch of cotton. The seed of the cotton was brought from Kentucky, and its culture decided the enterprise and progress of the family.

But the quantity produced was inadequate to meet the wants of the growing population, and something else must be found that the naked might be clothed and the bed-chamber supplied. In these alluvial bottoms the wild nettle grew luxuriantly and abundantly. In the spring of the year, on this crop of nettles, which had been rotted during the winter, was found a fiber out of which, with labor and skills, linen could be manufactured.

The venerable mother of Bailey Guard, in view of the necessities of her household, determined to test the capacity of the nettle for manufacturing purposes. At the mouth of the Whitewater a large supply of rotted nettle could be found, and thither in a canoe up the Miami, from their dwelling at the Point, the family proceeded for a cargo.

A load was soon obtained and stowed safely on board their gallant craft. The reeds were from 8 to 10 feet long and well covered with the desired fiber and well dried in the sun. The process of cleaning commenced by breaking the reeds and separating the stock from the fiber by scutching. This work was performed by father and the boys. The hackling, the spinning, the weaving and making of the garments belonged to mother and the girls. Rude cords were used in preparing the cotton for the distaff and home-made looms for the weaving. The cotton goods thus manufactured were used in making fenines for the ladies and Sunday shirts and white stockings for the gentlemen, while the nettle cloth, coarse and strong, was made up for every day use and hard service.

During one season Mrs. Guard manufactured over 200 yards of nettle cloth, which was found useful and serviceable in her own household and among the neighbors. In a few years the growth of flax and the introduction of goods superceeded the use of the indigenous nettle in manufacturing, and the primitive way of helping themselves disappeared from the Miami and Whitewater settlements; but in those early days, when parent and child were clad in homespun, when true social cheer was the universal and never varying custom, every heart, every cabin, when the strong arms and willing hearts leveled the forests, cultivated the virgin soil and laid the foundations of future prosperity; were days of family happiness and progress never to be forgotten. The child life of Bailey Guard was spent amid the scattered cabins surrounding the blockhouse at North Bend, when painted Indians, uniformed soldiers and adventurous hunters filled his mind with horror, amazement and delight. When his young feet first trod the soil of Ohio, in 1790, the white population living in our great commonwealth, now the home of 3,000,000, was made up of the Moravian missionary households. On the Tuscarawas were a few families around 3 military posts along the Ohio river, with occasional trappers and hunters in the interior. When he was 15 years of age, having lived 12 of those years in Ohio, Cincinnati was a village of less than 500 inhabitants going to mill with a few bushels of corn in a canoe up the Ohio and Mill Creek, near where the Brighton House now stands, gave him an opportunity of visiting the town and seeing the sights.

His school days, which were few and irregular, were spent in a long schoolhouse, on the west side of the stream whither his parents had moved after residing at the point of their lease hold for several years, on split log benches, with Delworth's spelling book for his guide.

He pursued his education attending school for a few weeks in the winter. His great ambition was to learn to read and write. In youth he enjoyed but few religious privileges, yet he attained manhood free from the prevailing vices of the times. He was a sober, honest and industrious young man. At the age of 40, his mind was interested in the claims and duties of personal piety.

Under the labors of Rev. Ellinger, a Methodist minister, whose name and labors are still fragrant in the Church of Christ in these two valleys, Bailey Guard decided to be a Christian, and entered with soul on Christian life; he was always ready to do his duty, and never sought the retired list in the church. His piety was intelligent, humble and genial.

Brother Guard, in his vigorous manhood and declining age, successfully battled against the inordinate love of the world, and its useless pursuits, allied with temptation, to be richly furnished by the broad acres of the Miami bottoms; he lived above the world, and at the same time enjoyed a full measure of real comfort and solid happiness; his divine philosophy made him happy, useful and universally honored and respected. Few men have gone down to the grave leaving a better record of a well spent and happy life as Bailey Guard. He loved and cherished the M. E. Church; all her doctrines and adages were precious to his soul yet he was free from all bigotry. He was a kind and faithful friend, a good neighbor, ready to accommodate, a pattern of good works and all that knew him arise and call him blessed.

Thus lived and died our venerated friend, leaving to his numerous posterity a good name, an inheritance more precious than glittering gold, and to us all an example worthy of sincere admiration and earnest imitation.

*Note. Chalon Guard, the son of Bailey Guard, built a brick farm house on Dugan Gap Road, Mt. Nebo, in 1849. This is the old home recently acquired by the Hamilton County Park Board and it lies within the boundaries of Shawnee Lookout Park.

★★★★★★★★★★★

Alfred J. Cotton: Extracts from "Cotton's Keepsakes"

Alfred J. Cotton, a descendant of Rev. John Cotton of Plymouth Colony, was born in 1800 at Pownal, Maine. He came to Lawrenceburg in 1818, started out as a preacher--which he continued to do all of his life, and subsequently became a teacher, poet, author, judge on the Dearborn County bench for 12 years, and elder and deacon in the M.E. Church. Rev. Cotton returned to Maine in late life and died there in 1875. (Obituary, Lawrenceburg Press, July 15, 1875)

In 1858, Cotton published a book entitled "Cotton's Keepsakes," which was made up of his poems, personal experiences and recollections--many tragic--of people whom he had known and of places where he had lived and worked in the general vicinity of Dearborn County and Elizabethtown. Names and references to many pioneer families of the region may be found herein.

Cotton stated that Dr. Jeremiah Brower befriended him, got him a school at Elizabethtown, aided him in passing the school examination, and "in some sense was the maker of me." He noted that Brower was one of the most justly celebrated physicians and surgeons in our midst. At Elizabethtown, Cotton had among his pupils Dr. Brower's son Abram. Cotton stated that Abram later served as a clerk in his (Judge Cotton's) court and became a skilled lawyer; he was "proud of his former pupil."

Cotton described that first school where he taught thusly: "My first school, a poor log cabin with a 'cat and mud' chimney, puncheon floor and oiled-paper for glass, was the best the county could afford. Still we were happy and got along well." Cotton advised: "Children (now, 1858), think and be thankful that you have a better inheritance."

Judge Cotton had a son, Alfred B. Cotton, who went to California in the gold rush in 1852 with others from around Lawrenceburg, E-town and Cleves. In a poem to the memory of those who drowned in California during that period, Cotton named James Lozier, Clinton P. Craig, Capt. Geo. Dunn and Gilbert Angevine as "those who sleep there."

In his book the author recalled one Capt. John Montgomery, early steamboat captain, who when a young man was bitten by a copperhead. Rock fern boiled in sweet milk was fed to the victim and the plant applied to the bite. This treatment gave immediate relief, so stated Cotton. He noted that rock fern "grows in richest places in the woods and has a white blossom and scalloped leaf."

The Flatboat, Early Method Of Navigation On The Ohio River. (Sketch from Leslie's Monthly Magazine, 1888.)

Chapter 9

THE ROLE OF THE RIVER IN EARLY LIFE AND SETTLEMENT: ITS PLACE IN TRAVEL AND TRADE

The river for many years was the best highway our forefathers knew. Travel in any manner was full of hardships but a journey downstream by flatboat was preferred to one by wagon or horseback through uncharted wilderness country. A good description of a flatboat is found, as follows, in History of Dearborn and Ohio Counties, Indiana:

> These flat bottomed crafts, sometimes called arks or Kentucky boats, in which the early emigrants descended the Ohio were often immense structures. They were built of stout oak plank, fastened by wooden pins to frames of timber. The cabin was well protected and placed in the stern; from it smoke curled up gracefully. The fire within gave warmth and comfort for women and children. Cattle, provisions and furniture was placed in the bow. Had it not been for savages lurking about, it was a pleasant enough mode of travel. The boats were propelled by oars and setting poles. Frequently, several of these rafts would be joined together, forming a floating village. .

Often the crude flatboats served as homes and shelters for families long after destinations had been reached. Planks from dismantled crafts usually went into the building of the pioneers' first cabins. Legend tells that the first school in Cincinnati was conducted, in 1790, aboard a flatboat. As a symbol of the unique role it played in the settlement of the Ohio Valley, the flatboat was depicted on the seal of the Cincinnati Historical Society.

A voyage by flatboat to New Orleans, in 1799, took roughly 100 days. Although profits on home produce were low, pioneer Miami Valley farmers found a ready market for their surplus products downstream. They pooled their crops and floated them downriver at little expense, although such undertakings--as legend tells--often proved hazardous. In that era, corn and oats sold for 8 to 12¢ a bushel; wheat, 30 to 40¢ a bushel; beef, $1.50 to $2, and pork, $1 to $2 per 100 pounds. These prices were low but cash was needed for trade. Pioneers in Cincinnati in that day had to pay high prices for foreign articles. This merchandise, carried overland from eastern markets and down the Ohio or brought upstream from New Orleans, included such commodities as:

> Coffee, 50¢ per pound; tea, 80¢ per pound; pins, 25¢ a paper; gingham, 50¢ a yard; fine linen, $1 per yard; cotton stockings, 6 to 15 shillings; bonnet ribbon, $1 per yard; thin linen for flour sifters, 10 shillings per yard.

Cash for their surplus home produce enabled the pioneers to purchase these needed foreign goods. Even after the coming of the steamboat, flatboats continued to serve for many years as chief means of transportation and trade. The cost of operating steamboats was prohibitive for most pioneer shippers.

Having the river at their doorstep was a distinct advantage in other ways for settlers in the little towns. News of events of importance taking place elsewhere in the country reached them first. Although newspapers were published in the larger towns, news--for the most part--was carried slowly from place to place by word of mouth. Post riders bearing mail and newspapers in saddle bags through the wilderness brought news gathered along the route. Peter Williams of Delhi Township was the pioneer mail route agent for the government from 1807 to 1820, carrying the mail to this region on packhorses. Flatboat traders and river peddlers also relayed the latest gossip from settlements up and downstream. In 1794, mail was first carried between Pittsburgh and Cincinnati in canoes. During that period, William Maxwell, publisher of Cincinnati's first newspaper, Centinel of the Northwest, was postmaster in the city. He kept the post office in his printing shop. These forms of communication, the mail and the paper, were then greatly dependent on each other. Early papers frequently published lists of names for whom the post office was holding letters. Pioneers walked, or rode horseback, many miles to the city to get their mail. Communications in early settlements, in general, were slow and undependable, but the river played an important role in supplying this need. It was in 1819 that Congress passed an act permitting mail to be carried in a new way--aboard steamboats.

Back in the fall of 1811, North Bend's settlers had the privilege of witnessing, before their very eyes, an event of national importance in river chronicles. This was the passage downstream of the first steamboat, the NEW ORLEANS. Legend tells that the scene was viewed in fright and with mixed emotions. The following account, written by P. S. Bush and found in Cist's writings, tells of that historical event, as viewed across from North Bend:

> "In the fall of 1811, before the earthquakes of December, 1811, my father was residing in Boone County opposite General Harrison's farm at North Bend. The family was one day much surprised at seeing the young Mr. Weldon running down the river much alarmed and shouting, 'The British are coming down the river!' There had been a current rumor of a war with that power. All of the family immediately ran to the bank. We saw something, I knew not what, but supposed it was a saw mill from the working of the lever beam, making its slow but solemn progress with the current. We were shortly afterward informed it was a steamboat."

That frightening impression created by the sight of the first steamboat upon the Bush family was no doubt typical of the reactions of other North Bend inhabitants who chanced to see the NEW ORLEANS as she passed by, for not even the rumor of such an invention had yet reached there.

There were no known boat-building docks at North Bend, but Aurora and Rising Sun, Indiana, and Big Bone, Kentucky, nearby, are on record as having had very early ship-building yards. (During the era of the operation of the Whitewater Canal, canal boats were designed and built at a dry dock in Cleves, and, in later years, steamboats were built at Delhi.) The life span of a steamboat was extremely short. They were subject to fires, explosions and snags in the river. Early-day steamers were nothing more than clumsy barges fitted with crude engines.

Steamboat travel was slow, especially upstream. Evidence of just how slow it was was reported in the following account from History of Dearborn and Ohio Counties:

> "The Steamer INDEPENDENCE, after having been pressed into service at New Orleans by General Andy Jackson, began her upward journey to Cincinnati in 1815. After a voyage of nearly four months, she arrived at Rising Sun, where she stopped for wood, but none could be obtained. John James, however, furnished her with fence-rails for fuel and agreed to take his pay in a passage to Cincinnati. He embarked, but such was the slow speed of the INDEPENDENCE that when she got to North Bend, James left the boat and walked to Cincinnati, arriving some twelve hours before the steamer."

(Although there are historical inaccuracies in this foregoing account, see James Hall's Statistics of the West, 1836, it is certain that earliest steamers moved very slowly.)

Near Anderson's Ferry in early times was a place known as Cullom's Ripple (probably called riffle by old-time boatmen). Here, in pioneer days of steamboating, so legend tells, Mr. Cullom, who had a farm there, kept a large and powerful ox, which he used to hire, hitched to a strong cable to early steamboats struggling up the swift current on the Ohio side, and thus made up-the-river navigation speedier for some vessels.

By 1830, travel and shipping conditions had improved greatly due to the progress in steamboat building and trade. Merchandise was becoming more easily obtainable. Customers at James L. Ogden's General Store in North Bend were buying, in 1835, the following items:

"1 1/2 yards yellow linen, 56¢; 1 palm hat, 31 1/2¢; 1 hoe, 50¢; 1 set teaspoons, 25¢; spelling book, 12 1/2¢; 1 # sugar, 16¢; 1# coffee, 25¢; 1# butter, 15¢; 1 dozen eggs, 6 1/2¢."

Ogden's Store was well stocked with goods from abroad, for the account ledger, in the hands of D. W. Collins, North Bend, shows sales of Imperial tea, Cavendish tobacco, Barcelona handkerchiefs, Holland circassian, jaconet, bombazetti, necklaces and fur caps. In addition to food items, customers purchased such home remedies as camphor, castor oil, turpentine, paragoric, Godfrey's cordial and antimonial wine, opodeldoc (which was camphorated soap liniment), Bateman's drops, vials of hemlock, laudanum (which was tincture of opium), brandy, Scotch snuff and epsom salts. Sales of all types of notions in the sewing and hardware lines are recorded in the Ogden ledger.

Food prices as published in the Western Statesman, Lawrenceburg, Ind., Oct. 9, 1833, included:

Apples, bu. 25¢	Hams lb. 7¢
Beef, choice pieces, lb. 5¢	Hay ton $8-$9.00
Beans bu. 45-50¢	Lard lb. 7¢
Butter lb. 12 1/2-18 3/4¢	Mutton lb. 3-3 1/2¢
Cheese lb. 7-9¢	Onions bu. 50¢
Corn bu. 37 1/2¢	Oats, demand, 15-18 3/4¢
Corn meal bu. 37 1/2-50¢	Pork, small quantities, lb. 3¢
Chickens doz. $1.00	Potatoes, sweet, bu. 75¢
Ducks doz. $1.-$1.25	Potatoes, Irish, bu. 25¢
Eggs doz. 6-8¢	Peaches, dried, bu. 75¢
Flour cwt. $1.50-$2.00	Quinces, bu. $1.00
Flour bbl. $3.50-$4.00	Veal, choice pieces, lb. 3-3 1/2¢
Hops lb. 16-18 3/4¢	Wheat bu. 50¢

Miscellaneous prices of articles in the Cincinnati market, Oct. 9, 1833, listed in the Western Statesman.

Coal, at river, bu. 10-14¢	Ginseng, lb. 17-18¢
Coffee, Havana, lb. 15-15 1/2¢	Glass (12x18) box $9.
Cotton, Ala. & Tenn. lb. 12-14¢	" (8x10) box $4.-$4.25
Cotton, yarn, lb. 26 3/4-30¢	Gunpowder, keg, $7.-$7.25
Wool, clean washed, lb. 25¢	Honey, gal. 62 1/2-75¢
Feathers, lb. 30-31¢	Hay, ton, $8.00
Hides, dried, lb. 12 1/2-14 1/2¢	Logwood, ton, 40¢
Hides, salted, lb. 12-12 1/2¢	Nails, ass't, lb. 6 3/4-7¢
Leather, sole (Cin'ti) lb. 22-25¢	Nutmegs, lb. $1.87-$2.00
Leather, upper, lb. $2.25-$2.50	Oil, olive, doz. $6.00
Leather, calfskin, doz. $27.-$30.	Oil, tanners, bbl. $12.00
Linen, brown tow, yd. 12-14%	Pepper, lb. 18-20¢
Linen, flax, yd. 20-22 1/2¢	Pork mess, bbl. $12.00
Madder, best Dutch, lb. 22-25¢	Potatoes, bu. 25-31 1/4¢
Molasses, sugar house, gal. 50¢	Rags, lb. 3-4¢
Molasses, plantation, gal. 40¢	Raisins, box, $4.-$5.00
Mustard, common, lb. 25-30¢	Sugar, N. O. lb. 10 1/2-11¢
Cogniac, Brandy, gal. $1.50-$2.25	Sugar, loaf, lb. 15-17¢
American brandy, gal. 40-62¢	Sugar, lump, lb. 12 1/2-16¢
Holland gin, gal. $1.25-$1.75	Salt, Kanawha, bu. 37 1/2¢
Country gin, gal. 30-37¢	Soap, yellow, lb. 5¢
New Orleans rum, gal. 62¢	Soap, common, lb. 4¢
Tobacco leaf, cwt. $3.-$5.	Twine, lb. 18¢
Tobacco, Va. man, lb. 37 1/2-50¢	Vinegar, bbl. $4.00
Tobacco, Ky. man, 7-8¢	Tar, lb. $2.50-$3.00
" Cincinnati man, lb. 8-10¢	Tea, Imperial, lb. $1.00
Whiskey, from wagon, gal. 25¢	Tin Plate, box, $12.00
Steel, cast No. 1, lb. 22 1/2¢	
Steel, No. 2 cast, lb. 20¢	

The above price lists will give the reader an idea what the settlers of the Miami Township locale were paying in 1833.

Packet lines ran scheduled trips from Cincinnati to towns along the river, carrying passengers and delivering goods to small shopkeepers. In early days, before steam whistles came into use, guns or rifles were discharged to announce that a craft was about to land. If a townsman wished to take passage on an approaching steamer, a shot was fired from shore, signaling the captain to dock. Freight and passenger fares were dear. The cost of a trip by steamer from Cincinnati upriver to the mouth of the Great Kanawha in 1835 was about $7. Even so, this was the most comfortable mode of travel yet available—and worth the price, first class.

In June, 1851, a splendid new steamer, the FOREST QUEEN, made her first trip in trade. Built by Capt. Isaac Pratzman of Lawrenceburg, and James Gaff of Aurora, the FOREST QUEEN plied between Cincinnati and Aurora, stopping at many landings along the route. Passenger fare from Lawrenceburg to the city was 50¢. The FOREST QUEEN and her competitor in trade, the REDSTONE, became familiar sights to early citizens of this Ohio River locale. According to Rev. B. W. Chidlaw, the FOREST QUEEN made frequent landings at North Bend in that day.

This same steamer, FOREST QUEEN, along with another called DIANA, both owned by the Gaffs, early Aurora industrialists whose interests included distilleries, turnpike construction and river shipping, later won claims to fame when they successfully ran the blockade at Vicksburg during the Civil War. (More of the Gaffs and their river interests may be seen in the restored mansion, "Hillforest," at Aurora.)

The side-wheelers UNITED STATES and AMERICA, sister boats of the U.S. Mail Line, Cincinnati to Louisville run, which figured in that historic river collision, Dec. 4, 1868, on the Ohio River just below Patriot, Indiana, both had, at earlier dates, figured to a lesser degree in North Bend river history. The UNITED STATES, on Christmas night, 1866, while downbound had collided with the Steamer SILVER SPRAY at North Bend. Luckily the SILVER SPRAY had aboard a cargo of cotton bales which served to buffer the impact. The AMERICA had made her trial run, April 27, 1867, from Cincinnati down to North Bend with several hundred guests aboard. On her return trip upstream, the AMERICA's speed was timed. In one hour flat she was at Sedamsville, doing 13 miles per hour, in that day quite a record! Both of these elaborately furnished steamers, with two decks of staterooms and accommodations for the most discriminating passengers, most surely were known to every resident along the old River Road, and to those who traveled between Cincinnati and Louisville. These boats also carried mail—as well as passengers—up and down the river.

Riverside towns frequently had an attraction not to be found in prairie or mountainous villages. This was the showboat. These colorful floating theaters with their steam calliopes whistling summonses to the townspeople, enticing them down to the riverbank to see the show, were familiar sights. Showboats did not move along the river under their own steam; they were shoved by companion towboats to the sites of their engagements. Performances were heralded, in advance, up and down the river towns with hand bills and banners. These announcements created an air of watchful anticipation, especially among the young people.

Mr. Arthur G. Colburn recalls that showboats always docked at Home City at the point along the river where the ice house is located today. A bit farther downstream was the site known as Lee's Landing (later Lee Park was established here) where Mr. Colburn recalls boarding, for his very first time, the old ISLAND QUEEN (ca. 1896) for an all-day picnic excursion to Coney Island.

Residents of the communities situated along the Ohio knew firsthand the advantages of the river at their doorsteps, but they also knew, full well, of its disadvantages--those caused by flood and ice. From local papers these items concerning hazards of the river were copied:

Jan. 18, 1877. Lawrenceburg Press. "Citizens from all around Miami Township visited the Bend to witness the break up of ice in the river. Boats and barges were scattered everywhere along the Ohio."

Feb. 24, 1883. Commercial Gazette. "Capt. Robert W. Wise of Delhi is home from a highwater trip on his steamer, J. W. GAFF, and says the destruction has been terrible all the way down the Ohio."

Capt. Wise became superintendent of the Cincinnati & Memphis Packet Co., which operated a number of sternwheelers including the OHIO, DeSOTO, BUCKEYE STATE and GRANITE STATE. He was a close associate of the Gaffs. Capt. James D. Parker of Home City was likewise associated with this steamboat line and was a bookkeeper and manager of the J. W. Gaff estate for many years. Capt. Parker had a fine voice, was in demand as a soloist, and, in 1883, was President of the Cincinnati Chamber of Commerce and a trustee of both Delhi Presbyterian Church and Home City School. (The description of this riverman, the reader must agree, is quite the opposite of those riverboat characters portrayed in the legends of Mike Fink.) Sarah Wise, wife of Capt. Wise, an early worker in the Delhi Methodist Church, must have had great faith in the travelers on the packets of her husband's line. Once around 1890, she placed mite boxes for her missionary society on the steamers. Her faith was justified when the boxes were opened and found to contain the great sum of $45.

(Further accounts concerning local floods may be found in the chapters on "Railroads" and "Bridges and Floods.")

Storeboat peddlers, hawking everything from tin ware to ribbons and laces, reached the height of their business activity during the middle 1800's era. One such peddler was June Balsley who lived opposite North Bend in Boone County. He traveled up and down the river selling and trading produce. The bell from his boat he later sold, in 1867, to the Mount Nebo Methodist Church. When that congregation finally disbanded, the boat peddler's bell was moved, in 1884, to the Cleves Methodist Church, where it yet hangs today.

Another peddler who used the river as his highway was Jonathan Newman Hamilton. He frequently landed at North Bend with his wares. The following notes, applicable to this account, have been taken from his 1839 journal, entitled "A Storeboat on the Ohio River," found at Cincinnati Public Library.

Peddler Hamilton recorded that he left home in Cincinnati in early August, 1839, on his boat HELEN, named for his little daughter. His trading stock included clothing, books and kitchenware. Accompanying him were his son, Ichabod, a Negro servant, a dog and "quite too many rats and mice."

Entries of August 13, 1839, reported that he ran down to General Harrison's "where they are constructing a culvert and tunnel. They have quite an extensive brick manufactory. . ." At this point the peddler described at length how bricks were being molded of clay for use in the canal tunnel. He continued in his diary: "Called on General Harrison; he was absent to Hamilton, his son having died last night. Another son of the General, Dr. Benjamin Harrison (uncle of the later President) called at the storeboat, looking not at all prepossessing. He bought two books for $4.30. . .could not pay for them down, but would in a month, would send it to Cincinnati. Don't sell on credit, but being General Harrison's son, can't refuse. Inquired, however, after he left and was told it was a dead sale, could not pay his debts--was intemperate. The General would pay sometime for him. . ."

"General Harrison returned and brought the corpse of his son (Carter Bassett Harrison), intending to bury him at home to-morrow. . ."

The next morning, Wednesday, August 14, 1839, the peddler recorded that he left General Harrison's landing at North Bend and moved his storeboat a short distance downstream to a spot in Boone County, Kentucky, then known as Sugar Grove--which got its name from the sugar maples growing there, situated nearly opposite the foot of Dugan's Gap Hill. There he put in at the landing of the "Widow" Pike, known as Pike's Landing.

Clara Pike, widow of the explorer, General Zebulon M. Pike, credited with the discovery of Pike's Peak, resided here. She was the daughter of Capt. John Brown, Revolutionary soldier, who had settled at this site along the river shortly after the arrival of Judge Symmes to North Bend. It was here that young Zebulon Pike, enroute to visit his father, Col. Zebulon Pike, in Dearborn County, met Clara Brown and shortly after married her. Their only daughter, Clarissa Pike (1803-1837), married John Cleves Symmes Harrison, known as Symmes, the General's oldest son. The young couple occupied Grouseland at Vincennes, for a time, where Symmes was Receiver of Land Affairs. (Grouseland, built in 1803-1804 by General Harrison, was the capital of the Indiana Territory. The mansion is now a public museum.) After Symmes died in 1830, and Clarissa died in 1837, General and Mrs. Harrison and Clara Brown Pike assumed responsibility for the five orphaned grandchildren. Records state that there was much coming and going by rowboat across the Ohio between North Bend and Sugar Grove in those days.

The storeboat peddler in his log book noted that Miss Zebela Harrison (Zebuline seems to have been her correct name) and her sisters, accompanied by their Grandmother Pike, came aboard to look at his wares, at the ribbons and bonnets. Since the family lived in such remote surroundings, it would be safe to say that the arrival of the riverboat vendor afforded untold pleasure for the young girls, judging from the popularity of "window shopping" today. Looking at the subject in this light, is it not easy to see why the traveling salesman became so admired by the farmer's daughter? Peddler Hamilton recorded several return stops at both Pike Landing and North Bend during 1839.

Today, several miles below Harrison Memorial Park, on a slight rise above the Ohio along the Kentucky shore, may be seen the monuments of those early inhabitants of Sugar Grove, who were known to the storeboat peddler. There sleep Capt. John Brown, his daughter, Clara Brown Pike, her daughter and son-in-law, Clarissa and John Cleves Symmes Harrison, and their daughter, Zebuline. For over a century the silence of the surroundings remained unbroken, except for the flight of bird and drone of bee. An occasional steamer puffed by the site, plowing up the quiet waters below. By rude contrast today, the air vibrates with the flight of planes and the drone of diesel boats. Nevertheless, the isolated locale is nearly as remote as it must have been back in 1839.

History reveals much of North Bend's legendary past, yet there are omissions. One little known story concerns a newcomer of 1839, who was carried here by the river.

As it happened, one day back in August of 1839, two orphan lads, Charles and John Myers, signed on as hands aboard a barge that was being floated down the Ohio from Pennsylvania. The boys took their places among eight or ten others of the crew, poling and steering the crude vessel through the deepest parts of the channel.

It was during this era of the middle 1800's that coal was carried southward in great, clumsy, frail boxes having flat bottoms and square ends, called "coal boats." These boxes were lashed together in pairs and floated downstream with the current, guided with oars by a dozen or more crew members. At their destination, the coal boats were broken up and sold along with the cargo.

When the barge carrying the Pennsylvania orphan lads put in at North Bend for supplies, on Wednesday, August 14, 1839, the crew eagerly climbed ashore. They found the little village bustling. Work on the Whitewater Canal was in full swing. A tunnel was being excavated through the hill that lay between the towns of North Bend and Cleves. Everywhere men were digging and shoveling. Horses were dragging sleds and pulling carts heaped high with clay and earth. Nearby, bricks were being molded in a press operated by horse power. The air resounded with shouts and laughter.

Amidst the hub-bub, a solemn funeral procession was winding its way along Front Street, heading toward the little cemetery rising on a knoll at the edge of the village.

The crew of the flatboat quickly scattered and were soon lost in the confusion of the town's activity. Cares of the barge were momentarily cast aside as they watched and listened to the canal workmen.

The burial rites captured the attention of thirteen-year-old John Myers, younger of the orphan lads. Carter Bassett Harrison, son of General Harrison--prominent man of the village, John learned--was the deceased. As the boy watched he became fully engrossed in the funeral proceedings. Time passed swiftly. When John suddenly realized that he was standing among complete strangers, with none of the barge crew anywhere in sight, he turned and ran at breakneck speed down to the riverbank. How horrified he was to find the coal boat gone, and his brother, Charlie, upon whom he so strongly relied, gone, too. Waves of panic and fright swept over him. Nevertheless, John, who had learned early in life the necessity of self-reliance, quickly recovered his composure. He turned back to the village in search of work. Overseers of the canal construction lent sympathetic ears to his tale. They hired him as water boy.

Several days later, John Scott Harrison--another of the General's sons--who resided below North Bend near the mouth of the Big Miami, happened by to see the canal's progress. It was upon the property of his father, who lived in the "Big House" on Front Street, that work on the Cincinnati branch of the Whitewater Canal had been started. J. Scott Harrison noticed the lad carrying the large, wooden, water buckets back and forth among the crude, rough-spoken workmen. On hearing of the boy's misfortune, he approached him and inquired if he would like to live and work on his farm at The Point.

So it was that at The Point, in the shadow of old Fort Hill, John Myers not only found work but he also found a home and happiness. As the years passed by, he married Ann (Hannah) Bevens, a nurse maid to the Harrison children. John and Ann Myers lived in a cottage on the Harrison estate, where they remained for nearly half a century, raising a large family. But, John never ever heard from his brother, Charlie, or learned what his fate had been.

An interesting reference to John Myers is found in the book Benjamin Harrison: Hoosier Warrior by Harry J. Sievers. A letter, listing Christmas requests, written Nov. 24, 1849, by Sallie Harrison, daughter of J. Scott Harrison, to her brother Ben at Farmer's College, stated that "Anna (her sister) wants some candy for John Myers' children..."

The 1850 Census of Miami Township showed that John and Ann Myers then had two children, Mary and Harrison. Their last child, born a number of years later, was Rhoda Myers, who married Lon Hay. The Hay's daughters, Mrs. Edith Bonham and Mrs. Emma Carlin, have been lifelong residents of North Bend and Cleves.

The necessities of the time had determined a strange course, almost fairy-tale-like in plot, for this 1839 newcomer to North Bend's shore. Isn't it likely that some great-great-great grandchild of John Myers may one day thrill at hearing of his storybook adventure down the Ohio by coal boat?

Strange as it may seem, General Harrison lost three of his sons, in addition to oldest son John Cleves Symmes, by death in the three successive years prior to his own death in 1841. The year 1838 took son and namesake, William Henry; August of 1839 saw the death of Carter Bassett, whose funeral thirteen-year-old John Myers happened upon the day his coal boat landed; and the following June, 1840 claimed the same Dr. Benjamin Harrison who had patronized the Ohio River storeboat peddler. Three identical stones mark their burial plots at Congress Green. Only surviving son J. Scott Harrison lived to see his father become President. Montgomery Pike Harrison, raised by his grandmother Pike at downriver Sugar Grove, was one of the very few family members who actually witnessed the Presidential Inauguration of his grandfather Harrison.

All evidence of the role that was played by the river in North Bend's past has long washed away in the channels of time. "Time," as Marcus Aurelius aptly described it, "is a sort of river of passing events, and strong is its current; no *sooner is a thing brought to sight than it is swept by and another* takes its place, and this too will be swept away." Nevertheless, history's pages are filled to overflowing with accounts that reveal with crystal clarity the depth of the river's course in shaping the events and destiny of this region.

★★★★★★★★★★
Steamboats

James Hall in his book "The West", 1848, wrote: "The introduction of steamboats upon western waters contributed more than any other single cause to advance the prosperity of the West." He also stated: "There is nothing in the topography of any other country to compare with the western rivers."

Steamboat Names

The steamboat J. M. GRUBBS (1898-1930) bore the name of a lady who lived along the Ohio just opposite Delhi. Since those days several towboats have carried names of local citizenry, including the Str. SAM P. SUIT, M/V A.L. LONG, and M/V BOB BENTER.

Chapter 10

EARLY ROADS
WITH EMPHASIS ON THE RIVER ROAD

Rev. Horace Bushnell (1802-1876), New England clergyman and writer, had this to say about roads:

> The road is that physical sign by which you will best understand any age or people... If there is any kind of advancement going on, if new ideas are abroad and new hopes arising, then you will see it by the roads that are building. Nothing makes an inroad without making a road...
> Rev. Horace Bushnell, D. D.

Although the founders of this community used the rivers as their first means of transportation and located as near to them as possible, pathways and roads became one of the prime concerns upon settlement. Therefore, it is interesting to know something of the early roads of this region.

In 1790, a road was laid from Cincinnati west along Ludlow's Trace, to Mill Creek, thence toward the Ohio and along the river bank to "the city of Miami," or "Symmes' City," as the Judge's settlement at North Bend was briefly known.

In that same year, a road from North Bend to South Bend was completed. South Bend, a short-lived establishment promoted by Judge Symmes and his brother, Timothy Symmes, embraced that region along the Ohio above the present Delhi and below Anderson's Ferry.

In 1793, the road from the mouth of Mill Creek to North Bend was improved. Aaron Caldwell (sometimes spelled Cadwell) surveyed this road running from Cincinnati to the mouth of the Big Miami. Described in the survey of 1806 as "River Road," it "ran from a hackberry tree 150 rods from the mouth of the Big Miami River to near the Meeting House in Cincinnati." The Meeting House is said to have stood at the corner of 4th and Main Streets. The early River Road followed the river more closely than it does today.

From North Bend to the confluence of the Ohio and Big Miami, this road for over a hundred years was never much more than a wagon trail. At the mouth of the Miami, in early days, was a ferry which carried travelers across to Indiana where they continued on the river route to Lawrenceburg and Aurora.

It is interesting to note that the name of the present North Bend Road came about because it was the early route to Judge Symmes's and General Harrison's at North Bend. This road began as a military trail starting at Ludlow, to Carthage, through Cary's (now North College Hill), Mt. Airy, Cheviot, past Seven-Mile House--which stood at the corner of the present Bridgetown Road and Harrison Avenue intersection, and on to North Bend. The main road through Cleves, even as late as 1870, was also called North Bend Road.

The famous Seven-Mile House, built in 1815 by Roswell Fenton, Sr., remained in operation as a tavern and inn, and lastly as a cafe, until 1924, when it was torn down to make ready for the building of Cheviot School.

The road from Cheviot to Cleves was early known as State Line Road. This came about because a bridle path led from Fort Washington, through Cheviot, to Cleves and on to the Indiana line. The Ohio and Indiana boundary line was first surveyed Oct. 11, 1798, by Israel Ludlow, surveyor of the Northwest Territory, who established a base line from the mouth of the Great Miami due north. This line was resurveyed in 1837, and a stone marker set in 1838, which may be seen today at the state border. State Line Road, later State Road, was so called for many years. It is now Bridgetown Road, with the exception of the stretch which passes through Cleves and this is yet State Road. At Cleves (at the intersection now marked by a traffic light at the new highway) this old State Line Route followed straight ahead, crossing over where later the canal and railroad ran, and on across the Great Miami, which flowed closer to the village in those days. The road continued on through the bottoms with branches going off to Miamitown, Harrison and Elizabethtown. Before the existence of the Cleves Bridge, built about 1834, Joseph D. Garrison operated a ferry over the Great Miami along this thoroughfare.

Several inns stood in Cleves, at one time, along the State Line route. One of the earliest was the tavern of J. L. Watkins, thought to have stood on the site of the present Central Trust Bank, near the old Howell homestead. Watkins must have been a "jack-of-all-trades," as were most innkeepers of that day. He was a justice of the peace of Miami Township in 1829. Evidence of another of his pursuits is seen in the following news item from the Indiana Palladium:

> Sept. 26, 1825. "Removal notice. The subscriber who is possession of the medicine for the cure of schirrous tumors and cancerous affections has left Lawrenceburgh and moved to Cleves, near North Bend, where he may be found at any time by those who wish to experience the good effects of his medicine for destroying the above disorders. John L. Watkins."

(Watkins is said to have been a kin of the family which founded, in 1868, the Watkins Company, whose first product was liniment.)

Watkins was appointed postmaster at Cleves, July 17, 1826. No doubt, he dispensed his cure-all, along with the mail, at his tavern. Legend tells that it was at this tavern, on the site of the bank, that General Harrison first heard the news of his election to the Presidency in 1840. (A map of 1847 shows a tavern at this place.) During the 1860's, this inn, then known as Cleves Hotel, was operated by John M. Flinchpaugh. Across the road, on the State Line route, stood the Gibson House, its proprietor being William Gibson, and beyond the railroad crossing was John Pfeffer's Hotel.

Notices of travel schedules of stage lines and post coaches on the State Line route, from Lawrenceburg (earlier spelled Lawrenceburgh) to Cincinnati via Elizabethtown, Cleves and Cheviot, appeared in the Western Statesman, early Lawrenceburg newspaper:

> August 11, 1830. "Stage line now in operation; every facility will be offered to passengers on this route. For passage call on Lawrenceburgh postmaster, James W. Hunter."

> April 29, 1831. "Post coach via Elizabethtown and Cleves leaves Lawrenceburgh at 6 AM and arrives at Cincinnati at 12 noon."

> Mar. 4, 1832. "The new and spacious U.S. Mail Coach 'Sam Patch'--the most splendid vehicle of the kind in the west--will commence running on the (State Line) route."

These big mail-coaches, drawn by four or six horses, and capable of carrying about twelve passengers, were long the only means of public conveyance available in some parts of the country.

Lawrenceburg, Elizabethtown and Cheviot, all important crossroads in their day, were known to have had early inns and taverns. Very important was the tavern, tavern-keeper, stage coach agent and stage driver to the pioneer traveler. Taverns served as coach stops--the mail bag was often thrown off here--and, as such, became news centers in those days when communications were poor and newspapers few. Distances were often given, not from town to town, but from tavern to tavern. Dr. Walter Clark ran a hotel and tavern at Elizabethtown. Rates of boarding at his place were posted on July 7, 1852, as "from $2 to $3 per week."

Early roads were extremely hard to travel. Charles Cist, Cincinnati historian, described them as follows:

"Until about 1835, the roads around Cincinnati were of that primitive character which is peculiar to all new countries. Many of them led over the top of the highest hills without reference to grading, while all were what are now called mud roads."

Back in the year 1806, under Judge Symmes' direction, early roads in the Miami Purchase were surveyed and laid out. Among these was Harrison Pike, laid out as a route from Cincinnati to Indiana Territory, the village of Harrison being at the western border. It was along this Harrison Pike that several famous inns, Seven-Mile House, Nine-Mile House and Eleven-Mile House, sprang up. These names designated the number of miles from the center of the city to the location of the inns. Both Seven-Mile House and Nine-Mile House are said to have been in existence by 1815. As early as 1836, a macadamized turnpike ran from Cincinnati to the state line at Harrison. Miamitown, along this route, boasted a fine toll bridge over the Big Miami. Situated along the well traveled Harrison Pike, the town also boasted several inns. From a notice in the Western Press:

April, 1831. "Miamitown Hotel, operated by T. G. Noble, opposite Charles Atherton's Columbian Inn. Bar, table and stable; well furnished yards for stock; charges low."

Construction of roads and bridges was frequently financed by private groups of citizens, organized as toll road and toll bridge companies, or stock companies. These companies elected officers and were given authority to collect tolls from all persons using the roads, the amount computed by distance or by weight of their animals or vehicles. In this way those citizens who had subscribed money to these stock companies received a return from their investments. They also used the roads or bridges toll-free, themselves, while non-subscribers paid a fare with each passage. The early toll roads were mere pathways or wagon trails but they showed improvements with each passing year and eventually became the turnpikes of that century. The story of the turnpike is as interesting as the story of the Indian trail.

("Turnpike," according to Webster, "turn pike, a sharp point; or pike, a weapon, is from the historical turnstile; a toll bar or tollgate; also a road having, or formerly having, a tollgate." At the turnstile, or turnpike, along the road a toll was charged; thus the words "tollgate" and "pike," short for turnpike, have derived. Tolls were collected on military roads of Babylon and Syria as early as 2000 B.C.)

Turnpike rates as they appeared on an old New England signboard, copied below, give a general idea of how fares were levied:

TURNPIKE FARE

Each person and horse.................4.
Each chair, chaise or sulkey............12.5
Each 4 wheeled pleasure carriage........25.
Each stage...........................25.
Each 2 horse pleasure sleigh...........12.5
Each 1 horse pleasure sleigh...........5.
Each loaded cart, sled or wagon........12.5
Each empty cart, sled or wagon........6.
Each 1 horse cart loaded..............6.
Each 1 horse cart empty...............4.
Each horse, cattle and mule............1.
Each sheep and swine..................3

June 15, 1839, Cincinnati Chronicle: "Turnpikes. The Harrison Road is about finished to the Indiana line. The law making the state a stockholder in public works has had a beneficial effect on our turnpike roads. They are rapidly progressing in every direction."

Although a few early turnpikes were macadamized, it was not until around 1865, during the Civil War era, that crushed stone and gravel came into general use for road building. News items from Lawrenceburg papers, 1865 to 1869, tell of local road conditions, as follows:

"The roads that are nor piked out are in a horrible condition all over the country. Wagoning has 'played out,' in fact, pikes in many places are fast losing their identity."

"Our friends in Elizabethtown have got out of the draft (Civil War) and are now striving to get out of the mud. They are graveling their streets and sidewalks."

"Supervisors of roads around Valley Junction are John Chidlaw and James Kendrick. Their new gravel roads are much appreciated."

"Chalon Guard, Mt. Nebo, has been for the past four weeks macadamizing the road from his farm, northwest for some distance, and says he isn't going to stick in the mud any longer." (Nov. 4, 1869)

Numerous entries in the diaries of David Rittenhouse, during the perod 1864 to 1870, tell of his working on the road, hauling gravel and "making money working on the road." Frequent mention is also made of George Haire stopping by the Rittenhouse home on Mt. Nebo while he was "engineering the road." In that era, George Haire of Elizabethtown was supervisor of the county roads. He later served as Hamilton County Surveyor, from 1876 to 1879.

Once a year, according to law, property holders were summoned by the supervisor to work out their road-tax, by plowing and scooping the thoroughfares into better shape, and perhaps hauling a few loads of creek-gravel to dump into the ruts.

Ethel V. Perkins of North Bend, who lived in the region of Columbus, Ohio, as a child, tells that her family kept their county road-taxes paid (ca. 1890) by regularly hauling gravel to a stretch of roadway in their neighborhood. One of her cherished recollections as a child was riding in the gravel wagon when her father or brother hauled gravel.

Officials of early towns or townships needing roads or bridges built or repaired often ordered them to be constructed and assessed the inhabitants for the costs, frequently setting up toll gates in order to collect.

Bridges became as important to early settlers as the roads over which they traveled. A common feature of road building during the 1805-1875 era was the covered bridge. Bridges of that day, built exclusively of wood and generally resting on stone piers, were covered with sheeting to keep the supporting timbers--the main beams and arches--dry and to prevent rot from exposure to rain, snow and sun. These were often called "kissing bridges." After the Civil War, when the iron age came to this country, construction of timber bridges declined.

A sign that appeared over an old Ohio covered bridge read as follows:
> Five dollars fine for driving more than
> 12 horses, mules or cattle, at any one
> time, or for leading any beast faster
> than a walk on--or across--this bridge.

Today there are three covered bridges yet standing in this general locality. One may be seen in the North College Hill area of Hamilton County, on Covered Bridge Road; another just outside the village of Oxford, Ohio; and the third--Bushing Covered Bridge--near the entrance to Versailles State Park, Versailles, Indiana.

(It is difficult to separate the subject of bridges from roads, one was so necessary to the other. However, for clarity, material on local bridges will be found in the account "Bridges and Floods," following the chapter on "Railroads.")

In many localities the construction of bridges took precedence over the improvement of roads. This condition was particularly true in the Miami and Whitewater Township region where there were so many streams to cross. Citizens of this locale organized, in 1833, the Cleves Bridge Company. Shares were sold for $50 each and a bridge was built over the Great Miami along the State Line route. This bridge, operated by its shareholders until 1870, when it was given over to the management of Hamilton County Commissioners, stood until the flood of 1883 washed it away. Standing along such a well-traveled thoroughfare as State Line Road, the early Cleves Bridge must surely have been a sturdy one to have withstood the tests of time for 50 years.

In 1878, the State Road or Cleves Road Turnpike Company was organized, and, as late as 1880, there existed yet 13 toll roads in Hamilton County, with a total length of 132 miles.

The last toll gate in Hamilton County stood along River Road at Anderson Ferry. Here, near the railroad tracks, stood the little toll gate house where the keepers lived, and from this point down along River Road ran a gravel road. The toll collector had the responsibility of keeping the road in good repair, and he could be seen each day with his horse and cart, raking and spreading gravel, grading and filling ruts along the toll road. Arthur G. Colburn, Sr., born in 1880 at Home City, recalls well this old toll gate. At the gate a long pole, often no more than a limb from a tree, extended across the road. When travelers approached the gate-house and paid their toll, the bar was raised. Fares were used for the upkeep of the road. Toll stations were placed at various intervals along the route, another well known one having stood at the intersection of River Road and the road leading up Mount St. Joseph Hill.

From The Cincinnati Enquirer, June 25, 1910:

"The last of the tollgates that made Cincinnati one of the few cities in the country where toll was charged from travelers over roads within the corporate limits was demolished by a crew of workmen. The road was assessed until this date by the Cincinnati, Lawrenceburg & Aurora Traction Company and lay between Anderson's Ferry and Delhi, which territory recently has been made a part of Cincinnati by annexation. The toll road was one of the primary causes of the organization of the Lower River Road Improvement Association and it was the work of this association that stimulated the purchase of the outstanding bonds by the county commissioners and made the toll road free."

An interesting copper, toll gate ticket was found by Mr. A. Sheckler of Cleves, in 1945. Imprinted on the tag was the following inscription:

2 Horse
Delhi to Hatch's
Round Trip
Ex. L. R. R. Co.

L. R. R. Co. probably stood for Lower River Road Company. William J. Hatch, early pioneer, resided along River Road in the Riverside-Sedamsville region. The Hatch residence was long a noted landmark in this locality. Perhaps this old tollgate tag was once used as fare on the River Road route. Superintendent of the River Road turnpike in 1880 was Andrew Rilea of Delhi.

The Cincinnati and Whitewater Canal, which followed along side River Road from the city to North Bend, was completed in 1843, and remained in operation for about 20 years. From North Bend the canal ran over through Cleves and on to Harrison. Although primarily constructed for the shipment of freight, canal boats were often the only means of transportation available to travelers in some regions.

In 1854, the O & M Railroad (now the B & O), laid along the river route from Cincinnati to the mouth of the Miami, commenced operations. A second railroad, the I & C (now the NY Central), opened its new line, Dec. 1863, directly through the channel and along the towpath of the old canal. This company also opened a branch railroad from Valley Junction to Harrison, January 1, 1864. So eager were the citizens of Harrison to have railroad service, they contributed $20,000 toward the total cost of $100,000 for building the 7 1/2 mile branch. Until this time, 1864, the people of Harrison had to rely on stage coaches, the canal or omnibus lines for public transportation. Two omnibus lines ran from Harrison to the city over the Harrison Turnpike, and one line ran from there to North Bend, where travelers boarded steamboats or trains and continued their journies on to Cincinnati.

Since River Road was the most direct way to the city, early settlers of the Miami and Delhi Township locale could not help but be aware and interested in all that transpired along this route. Stage coach lines, canal boats, toll gates, ferries, railroads and omnibuses were common to all who traveled this thoroughfare. Any measure of transportation betterment or road improvement was a direct assist to the welfare of each and every resident of the region.

The route along River Road was once exceptionally beautiful. The poplar-lined drive down through Riverside to Anderson Ferry was marked with lovely homes built by prominent families, including those of presidents of both railways along this route. It became a favorite pastime of the wealthy to take carriage drives out along River Road, to there view the scenery and dine at the Buckeye House, a tavern near the ferry, famous for its chicken dinners. Captain Joe Harrison, a native of New York, was proprietor of the Buckeye House around the 1840's; Ollie Pettit kept the inn during the Civil War era. This section of River Road, being so level, was once referred to as "The Stretch."

Major Peter Zinn, who was responsible for laying out Delhi, interested himself for many years with improvements along the River turnpike. He was president of the Lower River Extension Turnpike Company. Just the season before his death in 1880, Zinn set out 1000 trees along this route. Fernbank, Sayler Park and Delhi have long been admired for having beautiful trees. The credit for this should be given, in part, to Peter Zinn. Unfortunately, many of the old trees, some of unusual species, were cut when the new River Road was constructed in the 1950's.

Horse racing became a popular sport in the earliest days of Cincinnati, the soldiers at Fort Washington doing so for pastime. From this sport Race Street was named. Because of the desirable location of River Road, a race track was built close to the river, near the ferry, around 1843, one of the early Queen City tracks. The venture, however, was of short duration.

The Home City (later Sayler Park) and Fernbank communities did not actually begin to become settled until after the coming of the railroad in 1854. Prior to that time the land had passed through the hands of several owners. One of the first of these was said to have been Judge John Matson, son of Capt. John Matson--early settler with Judge Symmes. Some of the Matson land fell to Rees E. Price who had wed Sarah Matson (1802-1897). Legend says that Judge Matson gave to each of his children, several sons and a daughter, a homesite consisting of 82 1/2 acres along the Ohio in what is now Fernbank and Sayler Park. (General Rees E. Price was of the family which founded Price Hill, and Matson Place there was named for his wife, Sarah Matson Price. Their son, Rees B. Price, and his descendants lived many years in Fernbank.) Judge John C. Short and David Kirgan were also early owners of land in what became Fernbank. Major Daniel Gano, early clerk of Hamilton County, one-time proprietor of the land around the Indian mound, now Sayler Park, is said to have laid out a mile race track around the ancient mound, where he exercised his fine horses. Spectators, so legend tells, seated themselves atop the mound and watched with delight the horse races. (The Indian mound was excavated in 1955 and 1956. For information concerning the mound see The Archaeology of Hamilton County, Ohio, by S. F. Starr.) One of the next known proprietors of the land in the area of the Indian mound, before 1834, was a Mr. Mackey who called his place "The Home Farm." In 1834, he sold 140 acres of "The Home Farm" to George T. McIntyre. When the village here was laid out in 1849, it appropriately was named Home City. Home City, however, did not experience much growth until after the opening of the railroads, transportation being so vital to the development of the community. Prior to that time, residents of the area depended upon stage coaches, canal boats, steamers--which stopped at Lee's Landing, or omnibuses for travel and for receiving and shipping freight.

Omnibuses, operated by Peter Sindlinger in the 1860 era, carried passengers out River Road until the coming of mule drawn street cars. Union Omnibus Company on Bank Street in Cincinnati was known for the manufacture of fine omnibuses and carriages. These big buses, pulled by horses or mules, frequently had two decks, and it was on the top deck that young lads usually chose to ride. Cincinnati newspaperman Edwin Henderson wrote of his thrilling experiences as a young boy riding with friends atop an omnibus to Anderson Ferry, where they crossed the horse-driven ferry to Boone County, and from there climbed the hill to visit "Mother Apple" who had a dairy farm on top of the bluff. (Henderson wrote under the name of "Conteur" for The Cincinnati Enquirer.)

Operating an omnibus could be a dangerous occupation, as related in the following news item:

April 26, 1866. (Union Press, Lawrenceburg) "A driver on the Harrison Pike to Cincinnati Omnibus line fell from the bus while coming down the hill near the Five-Mile House, in consequence of the breaking of the footbar attached to the lock. He died instantly."

An outgrowth of the improved roadways was the extensive use of bicycles. Through the years they appeared in all shapes and sizes. The late 1800's saw the introduction of bicycling clubs. Groups of cyclists belonging to "Century Clubs" and aiming to travel 100 miles over the weekends passed along River Road or over Harrison Turnpike into Indiana. The Cincinnati Bicycle Club was organized in 1882. This group was affiliated with the League of American Wheelmen, forerunner of the present American Automobile Association. Country roads were poor and dusty but the wheelmen made their "century" runs every Sunday. Each club had its bugler and the cyclists maneuvered to his calls. It was real work to pump those high wheeled bikes. Delhi had its bicycle club, also, and each evening members raced on Western Avenue, now Home City Avenue, or around the Indian mound. At Harrison, Ohio, the fair association held annual bicycle races, which became a popular event all over the western part of the county. Members of the Cleves Bicycle Club in 1894 were: John and Frank Ingram, Charles and Walt Caine, Will Riehle, Virgil M. Henderson and Will Chidlaw. The latter two cyclists, residents of Cleves, became lifelong teachers in the community.

In addition to mud, gravel and macadamized roads, plank roads were common. The term "plank" was actually another name for a log or corduroy road. The road that we know today as Cleves-Warsaw Pike, leading into Addyston and River Road, was for many years identified as Plank Road. A Cincinnati map of 1855 clearly shows "Plank Road to Warsaw."

In the late 1860's, a saloon called Ten Mile House stood along Plank Road near Muddy Creek. Here in November, 1872, a shocking murder took place. William "Boone" Markland of Cleves was killed at the saloon on the old Plank Road near Muddy Creek. An account is given in the Cincinnati Daily Gazette, Nov. 5, 1872.

This saloon was being operated in 1887 by Peter Scheffel, who also made baskets in the building. Scheffel was among the early settlers of Delhi, having arrived in 1862.

Across the road from the tavern a farmhouse of stone was built by Benedict Yunker in 1873. This old home, at the foot of VanBlaricum Road, is yet occupied by the third generation of Yunkers, who operate a truck farm. It is interesting to note that a settlement called Ervina once existed during the 1840-1860 era in this general region around Plank and VanBlaricum Roads.

Plank Road was called by that name until about 1905. There are yet a few old-timers who recall walking along Plank Road on their way to Addyston or Fernbank Schools.

In attempting to record any kind of history a writer continually finds his material dated. Changes are always being made and new roads being built, just as Rev. Bushnell stated in the quote used at the introduction of this chapter:

The road is that physical sign by which you will best understand any age or people . . . If there is any kind of advancement going on, if new ideas are abroad and new hopes arising, then you will see it by the roads that are building. Nothing makes an inroad without making a road . . .

Something of the progress and growth of Miami Township and its borders can certainly be seen in the history of its roads. River Road, the oldest of them all, first laid out by John Cleves Symmes, has literally felt the feet of history tread over it.

(Superintendent of Miami Township roads now, in 1969, is Eugene Hoffman of Cleves, who is also superintendent of the township-maintained Maple Grove Cemetery, established in 1884.)

★★★★★★★★★★

Legend tells that there was once a stage coach robbery somewhere in the region of the Ohio and Indiana border. Gold taken during the robbery was said to have been hidden in the "Whitewater hills" and never found. The story was passed down by Albert Spraul to his descendants, including his niece, Miss Frances Robison of Bond Road.

A dearborn, named for its inventor, according to Webster, was a four-wheeled carriage with curtained sides. Frances Trollope mentioned riding in a dearborn in her book, Domestic Manners of the Americans, 1832.

38

Chapter 11
FERRIES

Regardless of how many roads were built, they would have been useless without ferries, for most roadways--sooner or later--ran into rivers. Small scale ferry operations are known to have existed, off and on, in earlier years at North Bend, around The Point from Ohio to Indiana across the Big Miami, at Cleves, along the route of the old State Line Road, and at Delhi, along the Ohio over to Kentucky. Yet none of these ferries has ever rivaled Anderson's Ferry. This ferry has the distinction of being one of the oldest in length of service in all of the United States, having operated continually for at least 150 years between Anderson's Ferry, Ohio and Constance, Kentucky.

Records indicate that a ferry existed in this place as early as 1817, and it is possible that the crossing was used by Indians before that time. It was in this region, in 1789, that Judge Symmes and his brother, Timothy Symmes, laid out the short-lived settlement called South Bend. It was between here and North Bend that that first stretch of the river road was laid.

On August 30, 1817, Raleigh Colston conveyed by deed to George Anderson "one ferry with sweeps and 103 3/4 acres of land for the sum of $351.87." On the Kentucky bank Anderson's brother, Montgomery Anderson, built one of the first stone houses erected in Boone County. This structure, although in dilapidated condition, yet stands. Between 1817 and 1865, the ferry changed hands 15 times. It was owned by George Anderson, who gave it its name, until June 21, 1836. Legend says that he lost the ferry in a poker game. Other members of the Anderson family operated it until 1841. From 1841 until 1865, the ferry was sold as often as 4 times in one year, and at prices ranging from $200 to $4,000.

According to another legend, a site near Anderson's Ferry, known as Cullom's Ripple, was once noted as a good place for fishing parties. Anglers used to camp along the shore, fish, drink and visit old Joe Harrison who had a bowling alley near the ferry. Harrison, early day steamboat captain, was known to have operated the Buckeye House, a hostelry along River Road, during the era of the 1840 Whig Campaign. This was a popular dining spot for those who took the fashionable drives out of the city, down along the river and out to North Bend to the tomb of Judge Symmes and still later of General Harrison.

Confederate General John Morgan is said, according to Constance tradition, to have crossed the Ohio at Anderson's Ferry in 1863, prior to his later crossing at Brandenburg. With this tradition in mind, Joseph Longworth, father of Nicholas Longworth, wrote a short novel, Silas Jackson's Wrongs: Or a Romance of Anderson's Ferry (1898), in which the snorting of the horses in the ferry treadmill betrayed a Confederate soldier wooing a Yankee girl. Although the story is fictitious, it has special appeal for those interested in the history of rural North Bend and Elizabethtown. Silas Jackson, subject of the novel, farmed in the Big Miami bottoms. Author Longworth adapted the story of General Morgan's crossing at Anderson's Ferry, whether fact or fantasy, to his short novel.

(There was naturally much pro-Southern sympathy in the region bordering the Ohio during the Civil War. John Morgan is also said to have been entertained in the old whitewashed Piatt house near Petersburg, Ky., according to an account by the late Charles H. Wesler, a native of Lawrenceburg. See Times-Star, June 3, 1949.)

The old horse ferry at Anderson's Ferry was sold, along with 2 acres and 4 poles of land, by John Wilson on March 6, 1865, to Charles Kottmyer for $2,800. Charles Kottmyer had earlier run an omnibus line from Fifth and Main down to Elkwood Park, located at Anderson's Ferry, and later operated the tavern there. When he bought Wilson's ferry, Kottmyer first had to retrieve his ferryboat which had broken away from its moorings several months earlier and was laying downstream at Stringtown, a mile away, before he could begin operations.

The new owner lived, at first, in the old ferryhouse at Constance until the river took it away. Next he lived in an old canal boat, but the river got that, too. Then he bought a Constance farmhouse into which the river still frequently flows, despite the fact that it was moved, some years ago, to higher ground. For a time, members of the Kottmyer family resided in the old stone Anderson house.

Until 1867, the ferryboat was run by horses walking on a treadmill. In that year Charles Kottmyer built a steamboat, Boone No. 1, the first of a long line of Boones. After that he built four more ferries. Henry Kottmyer, his son, constructed Boone No. 6 and Boone No. 7. Over his father's protests, Henry built Boone No. 6 right side up, instead of keel up, so that she did not require a steamer to turn her over after she was in the water. Boone No. 7, the boat now in operation, is 64 by 22 feet, divided lengthwise by a driveway; the engine room and smoke stack are on one side, with a small passenger cabin and pilot house opposite. In 1965, with increasing numbers of passengers using the ferry as a route to Greater Cincinnati Airport in Boone County, the Kottmyers added a second ferry, naming it "Little Boone."

Kottmeyer's Ferry, known as Anderson's Ferry, Ca. 1900. This was Boone No. 4. A ferry has been operated at this site since 1817. (Picture courtesy of Cora Rittenhouse.)

The Kottmyers claim that their ferry was the first double-ended ferry on Western waters, when it appeared in 1867. Double-ended meant that wagons and vehicles could drive onto the boat from one end and drive off at the other end upon landing.

Throughout many years small ferries, operated by several families, ran from Delhi over to Taylorsport or up to Parlor Grove on the Kentucky shore. The latter was an amusement park located along River Road between Taylorsport and Anderson's Ferry. Established in the late 1860's, perhaps a bit earlier, Parlor Grove featured wrestling, boxing, rooster and dog fights, flying Dutchman, dancing and band music. Picnickers boarded chartered steamers at the foot of Walnut Street in Cincinnati and rode down to Parlor Grove to spend the day. Some persons reached the park by way of ferries at Anderson's Ferry or Delhi. This 250 acre amusement ground was sold, around the turn of the century, to the Hempfling family. The Hempflings established a large fruit farm here, retaining the name Parlor Grove for their orchard. The third generation of this family yet operates the farm.

As early as 1869, Parlor Grove sponsored a baseball club. A newspaper clipping of July, 1869, tells that the team played a game against the Cleves "Blue Stockings," with Dr. Grubbs of Taylorsport acting as umpire. Undoubtedly the team crossed the river on one of the ferries, sometimes only a skiff at Delhi.

The community along River Road below Anderson's Ferry, earlier laid out as the town of South Bend, was never an incorporated village, as were Riverside and Sedamsville. The area became known for its dining spots and toll gate, and as a stopping point for horse drawn cars, trains, trolleys and busses, but best known for the ferry crossing. Legend tells that in the days before the Civil War the "underground railroad" ran slaves across the river on the ferry to Ohio and from there up Anderson Ferry Road--in earlier times called Cedar Grove Road, to Delhi and Green Township families who helped them on to freedom. The railroad stop just west of the ferry was widely known as "Trautman," named for a German gardener who settled there in 1846. It was between Trautman and Delhi that Henry Darby settled in 1818. He operated an inn for many years on old River Road, which then lay close to the river. This territory along the river, from the ferry down to Delhi, was annexed to Cincinnati in 1909.

Few ferries exist along the rivers today. Bridges at frequent intervals have replaced them. What a pity that today's children will never know the joy of walking, on a quiet summer's day, down a river bank to a ferryboat landing and there pulling a rope to ring the bell which would clearly summon the ferryman to steam across to his waiting passengers. What a pleasant memory for those fortunate enough to have had such an experience.

★★★★★★★★★★★★

Daniel Gano: His Farm at Home City

Major Daniel Gano, son of one of Cincinnati's first settlers, once owned several farms in the area, one at Carthage and another at Home City. On the farms he kept fine horses--imported Arabs and Conquerors, bred sheep and experimented with silk worms. He is known to have entertained Lafayette and other famous personages. One of the Gano country homes was a favorite visiting place of the Blackwell sisters during the 1839 era. (See the book Lone Woman, the story of Elizabeth Blackwell, by D. C. Wilson.) Elizabeth Blackwell was to become the first woman physician in United States. (Could it have been the Home City farm of Daniel Gano where she visited?)

The end of the Cincinnati And Whitewater Canal tunnel as seen from North Bend end. Ca. 1900. It was then blocked off with stone.

Peter Zinn (1819-1880)

Peter Zinn was a prominent citizen of Delhi Township. It was he who laid out the subdivision of Delhi and gave the land for the erection of both the Delhi Methodist and Delhi Presbyterian Churches. He was first educated as a printer but soon entered the practice of law. Zinn served as Representative from Hamilton County to the Ohio Legislature in 1849, and again in 1861 along with Milton Sayler. He was assigned the position of major of the 85th Reg't OVI in 1863. Lutheran by birth, Quaker by habit, Peter Zinn disliked pretense and show, was modest and sought no honors. Anxious for the betterment of every community in which he lived, he interested himself in improvements along the Ohio River turnpike and acted as president of the Lower River Extension Turnpike Company. He built a home at the corner of the present Gracely and Zinn, which for many years was occupied by the Butterfields.

Sedamsville was named for Col. Cornelius Sedam, prominent in public and military affairs in the early days. He came to the region as an officer in the Continental Army in 1789, and helped built Fort Washington. Later he invested in a large tract of land at the mouth of Bold Face Creek. Col. Sedam was a top military strategist and close friend of W. H. Harrison. He is credited with helping Gen. Harrison map the campaign of the War of 1812. He was justice of the peace from 1795 until his death in 1824.

CL&A line along the Whitewater Pike. The stone wall, beyond the car, is the ruins of a lock on the old Whitewater Canal. The tracks beyond are those of the Big Four Railroad.

Chapter 12

THE CINCINNATI AND WHITEWATER CANAL

In looking at the history of travel and transportation in Miami Township and its borders, the story of the Whitewater Canal and the part it played in the life of the community must next be told.

During General Harrison's years of absence from his North Bend farm, in the service of his country, J. Scott Harrison cared for the homestead and farm lands of his father. Here to his father's place, "The Cabin" or "Big House," he brought his bride, Lucretia Johnson, in 1824. Following her death in 1830, Scott married a second time to Elizabeth Irwin, and continued to live at "The Cabin" until about 1837. It was at this place, the home of his grandfather, that Benjamin--future President--was born.

General Harrison had done much for his other children and he wanted to do well for the son who had served him so faithfully. J. Scott had been educated, had practiced law for a short time, but he preferred farming. Now he needed a home of his own.

During this period negotiations were under way to build a Cincinnati branch of the Whitewater Canal. General Harrison contracted to sell bricks, wood and stone from his lands for the canal construction, the tunnel of which would be routed through his farm. So it was that from the sale of these materials for the canal he was enabled to build, about 1837, a fine brick home for his son at The Point, just below the site of old Fort Hill. This home became known as "Longview" and still later as "The Point Farm."

It was in the year 1838 that construction of the Cincinnati to Harrison section of the Whitewater Canal was begun. Since the canal was to be located for a lengthy stretch on the property of General Harrison, it was concluded appropriate to begin initial excavations on his farm. The specified day, March 31, 1838, was marked with a grand celebration at North Bend. Illustrious speakers and visitors were present. Harrison hospitality was much in evidence. An elegant new steamer, the MOSELLE, chartered by the canal directors, carried a great throng of spectators on an excursion from Cincinnati to the Bend.

(Incidentally, it was this same Steamer MOSELLE which blew up, less than a month later, near the Cincinnati wharf. Bound for New Orleans, the MOSELLE held a record number of passengers. More than 150 persons were killed, the greatest steamboat disaster in Ohio River history. This disaster was responsible for the Steamboat Act of 1838, which was the first governmental attempt at steamboat regulation.)

From Harrison, Ohio there were two branches of the canal, the east and west. The Harrison to Lawrenceburg branch, which followed the west bank of the Whitewater River, was begun in 1836 and completed in 1839. This section, with a feeder dam located at the site of the old Lawrenceburg Fair Grounds, emptied into the Ohio. The first boat to pass from Lawrenceburg to Brookville was the BEN FRANKLIN.

The Cincinnati-Whitewater Canal, the east branch, eighty miles in length, was completed in 1843. From Cincinnati (terminus between 2nd and 3rd Streets, near Western Row) it followed the Ohio to North Bend, on to Valley Junction, along the east side of the Whitewater to Harrison and on to Cambridge City, Indiana. At Harrison there was a lock and dam where boats from Lawrenceburg and Cincinnati joined into the Indiana branch.

Construction of the canal followed a strict code of regulations. Width at the bottom of the canal was to be 26 feet, with uniform width of 40 feet at the top of the water. Depth was to be not less than 4 feet. The towpath was to be 10 feet wide and the bank on the opposite side, 6 feet wide.

Builders of the canal received about 60¢ per day, $18 per month. The canal company paid $15 to $25 per acre for rights of way.

Canal boat crews consisted of captain, 2 steersmen, a cook and a driver of the horses, oxen or mules. The horses, two to six in number depending upon weight and size of load, were driven along the towpath. Workers on the Whitewater Canal in 1836, received 30 3/4¢ per day, 26 days per month. Their total average pay was less than $8 per month.

Canal boats were used chiefly for freight, a buggy ride to the city being much faster. Nevertheless, pioneers in some areas found the canal their best mode of travel. Passenger rates on canals in the west, $3.25 for 100 miles, were cheaper than steamboat fares. Eastern canals with more widely developed systems appear to have had even cheaper rates. Fares included room and board. Stove wood heated boat interiors.

The following record, copied from Old Towpaths by Alvin F. Harlow, is of particular interest to historians of this community. It concerns notes written by Rev. B. W. Chidlaw in 1839, when he made a trip from this valley to Wales. Rev. Chidlaw listed his various stages of travel, mostly by canal boat, and the costs over each stretch from New York to Cincinnati.

```
New York to Albany, 160 miles (steamboat ....... 2.00
Albany to Utica, 110 miles (stage & canal) ....... 1.50
Utica to Buffalo, 254 miles (canal) ............. 3.75
Buffalo to Cleveland, 193 miles (steamboat) ...... 2.50
Cleveland to Newark, 171 miles (canal) ......... 2.00
Newark to Columbus, 40 miles (canal) ........... .75
Newark to Columbus, 40 miles (canal) ........... .75
Columbus to Portsmouth, 82 miles (canal) ........1.25
Portsmouth to Cincinnati, 100 miles (steamboat) ... 1.00
   *Entire journey, 1,110 miles ............. $14.75
```

Although Rev. Chidlaw did not state how long the journey required, it is safe to guess it took nearly a month. It would also be safe to guess that he made many future trips on the Cincinnati-Whitewater Canal in his church and Sunday school work. The canal passed by Hunt's Grove, a picnic ground in Whitewater Township, the site of early Sunday school rallies. An item from the Independent Press, Lawrenceburg, tells of the place:

August 10, 1853. "The Basket Mass Meeting of the Sunday Schools at a grove near Cleves came off in fine style. An address was given by Rev. B. W. Chidlaw and Dr. W. Clark of Elizabethtown spoke. A canal boat load of persons came from Harrison. The grove is a delightful place."

Operators of canal boats often tried to pass each other on the water and this led to fights. Two boat crews at Cleves, Ohio, once fought to such a degree that one man was killed, so recalled old-time canal boatman Joseph McCafferty of Brookville.

One of the engineering feats in building this waterway was tunneling through the hill between North Bend and Cleves. Bricks for the construction of the tunnel were moulded right at the site of clay dug nearby. The art of tunnel building was new. Darius Lapham, resident engineer of the Miami Canal, engineered its construction. An account of this project is given in a recent edition of "Towpaths," the publication of the Canal Society of Ohio.

Upon reaching this 1900 foot long tunnel at North Bend, the horses were unhitched and led around to the other side of the hill. The canal boats were pulled through the underground passage by hand to hand pull on a rope fastened at each end of the tunnel. Once through, the animals were re-hitched to the tow-lines.

A lengthy discussion of the usefulness of the Whitewater Canal, along with an account of the source of its water power, is found in Cist's Cincinnati in 1841.

The Whitewater Canal was for two decades the important avenue from Cincinnati to the agricultural wealth of Indiana. Every farmer along its path had an abundance of water at his door and ready shipping accommodations at hand. Hogs and cattle, together with the harvest of big cornfields, became staple crops. Potatoes sold for 40¢ a bushel and wheat rose from 25¢ to $1 a bushel in 1836. The canal was a boon to agriculture.

The Ohio Gazeteer of 1841 reported that the Whitewater Canal passed through Elizabethtown. (This was the Lawrenceburg branch) It was the canal that gave impetus to many a little town's business activity and Elizabethtown was just such an example. Being located along the State Line Road, the town became known as a stopping-off point for weary travelers. Many businesses were established, a private school for young ladies was started and several large inns--with adjoining pens and corrals for holding pigs and stock enroute to Cincinnati markets--were built at Elizabethtown during this era.

With the canal as a source of water power, grist mills were established along its route. Floating saw mills were seen on some sections of the canal. These mills, erected on boats operated by steam power, traveled up and down the canal and cut logs into building timber.

Evidence that operation of the canal was not always smooth is shown in the following item:

"The first boats passed to the city on the Whitewater Canal in November, 1843. The great flood in the Whitewater River in December, 1846, swept away the feeder dam and about a mile of the canal at Harrison. The company repaired the damage during the summer and fall of 1847. In the fall of the same year, another flood swept away the entire canal at Harrison, which determined the company to re-locate on higher ground, which was done in 1848." (Cist In 1851)

The following poem presents a good picture of canal-boat days. Its author is unknown.

Old Canal-boat Song

Full free o'er the waters our bonny boat glides,
Nor wait we for fair winds nor stay we for tides;
Through fair fields and meadows--through country and town,
All gaily and gladly our course we hold on.

From the lake to the river, from river to lake,
Full freighted or light, we still leave a wake;
From the West bearing all that a rich country yields,
To the labor which makes the morn glad in the fields.

Returning again from the river's bright breast,
Bear the products of climes far off to the West,
And add to the backwoodsman's comfort and ease
All that commerce can give by its spoils of the seas.

In 1851, the Whitewater Canal Company was advertised as the "Rapid Transit" canal, noted for economy, comfort and speed. Two new boats, BUCKEYE STATE and HOOSIER BOY, were put into service. The fare from the city to North Bend was 45 cents.

Claus Drucker, one of Home City's first settlers, opened a grocery store (later Barman's) in 1855. Merchandise to stock his shelves reached Home City by canal boat.

The following item is from the Commercial Tribune:

Old Canal Boat 'JENNY LIND' Is Unearthed
Cleves, Ohio. Nov. 15, 1920. "Workmen digging for a sewer in Cleves struck a craft used on the Whitewater before the Civil War. A reminder of by-gone days was the discovery of the old Whitewater Canal boat JENNY LIND by workmen digging for a sewer beneath the Big Four Railroad here.

"Ezra Bussell had told the workmen they would strike the canal boat when they got down a little farther. They laughed at him. On Friday they struck the boat at a depth of ten feet. Part of the hull was still in first-class condition.

"Mr. Bussell obtained a portion of the bow piece. On his showing it to a pioneer resident, William R. Myers, who is 83 years old, Mr. Myers related some of the facts concerning this ancient craft.

"In the late fifties and early sixties, this boat, one of the handsomest of its day, plied between Harrison and Cincinnati, making a trip everyday, carrying freight and passengers. When the Ohio & Mississippi Railroad took over the old towpath and ran trains to North Bend, the boat was converted to a packet. It ran between North Bend and Harrison until the Whitewater Canal was abandoned. The boat was sunk where it was tied up at Cleves, at the Howell tanyards.

"Mr. Myers says that this was one of the most noted canal boats of the day. It was somewhat larger than the average boat, both longer and higher, and was fitted with all of the conveniences of the day. It was considered an honor to work on such a boat, and Mr. Myers is proud of the fact that he was a driver, steersman and pilot of the JENNY LIND in 1858 and 1859.

"Many stirring times were recalled by him. Crossing the Whitewater River at Harrison, above the dam, was a ticklish job. His boat was worked through the tunnel between North Bend and Cleves by means of ropes hung on rings in the roof of the tunnel. This was especially difficult when pulling against the current enroute to Harrison, as the canal flowed toward Cincinnati. He spoke of the big dry dock at Cleves, where canal boats of all designs were built for the trade, which was good from the opening of the canal until it was abandoned."

Erastus Bussell Hayes (1842-1911) was another who knew firsthand the workings of the old canal. "Rast" Hayes, father of Miss Katherine Hayes of Cleves, lived some of his early life on Mount Nebo. As a young man of about eighteen he worked as a driver along the Whitewater Canal. He guided his team of oxen, Jill and Jerry, as they pulled the boats through the water. One day the towpath was treacherously slippery and one of "Rast's" oxen, which he prized very highly, fell into the stream and drowned. The unfortunate experience put an end to the young man's work on the canal. He occupied himself for many years at farming and later was superintendent of the grounds of old Whitewater Park. However, in 1902, Erastus Hayes launched into a new type of service which proved to be every bit as important as his early work on the canal. In that year he organized the first Rural Free Delivery Service in Hamilton County. Starting from Cleves he went to Miamitown, thence over Harrison Pike to connect with Lawrenceburg Road and back to Cleves, driving his horse and buggy, carrying the mail around the countryside.

Incidentally, while Erastus Hayes was operating the rural mail route his horse was stolen at Hunt's Grove, near where the family lived. However, this time he was more fortunate than when he lost his prized oxen in the canal. The horse was traced to Cincinnati where it was found aboard a wharfboat ready to be shipped south. The animal was located by James Adams, a trader. Its discovery led to the formation of the Whitewater Detective Association, an organization which later numbered 150 members. This type of community service, along with Erastus Hayes' rural mail service, proved as vital to the progress of the region as did the operation of the Whitewater Canal.

Several denominations of notes used as tender on the Cincinnati and Whitewater Canal were issued. Pictures on the notes included the Harrison home, the tunnel and canal boat at North Bend. One scene of a driver with his team walking the towpath brings into vivid recall the story of young "Rast" Hayes. These notes were called scrip.

The canal was drawn into service on the home front during the Civil War. In September, 1862, there was a threat of Confederate attack on Cincinnati. North Bend, situated at a strategic point along the river, became a center of military movement between the mouth of the Great Miami and Cincinnati. Hundreds of patriotic men and boys from around the countryside, "Squirrel Hunters," heeded the call. The alert continued for about ten or twelve days. The home guard from Harrison came down to North Bend on a canal boat, bringing with them the "Jessie Fremont," a brass cannon. This was one of the last trips to be made on the canal. Its days were numbered.

The Cincinnati and Whitewater Canal was killed by the destruction of its Indiana connection--the Whitewater Canal--and by a railroad built alongside it in the 1850's. Some of the problems of the canal company may be detected in the following news items from the Independent Press, Lawrenceburg:

August 22, 1851: The Whitewater Canal from Lawrenceburg to Harrison is in bad condition. Canal boat companies are giving the canal company a few for their neglect!

Sept. 19, 1851: The Cincinnati branch of the Whitewater Canal now draws so largely on the Harrison dam that boats cannot have water enough to float them to Lawrenceburg branch. So our canal ceases business until we have a rise.

May 5, 1852: The water in the Cincinnati branch of the Whitewater canal will be let out for 4 months shortly, to enable the railroad company to build their track along the bank. (This was the O&M Railroad.)

In 1863, the canal company deeply in debt, the channel was sold to the I&C Railroad (later the Big Four) for its right of way. The railway company routed its train right through the old canal tunnel between North Bend and Cleves.

Like most vestiges of the past, little evidence remains today of the Whitewater Canal. However, parts of it have been restored at Metamora, Indiana, near Brookville. There on weekends in the summertime a boat takes passengers on short rides along the old canal. Also, alongside the new highway 50 at Cleves, a bit of the west entrance of the old tunnel may yet be seen. (Something more on this tunnel may be found in the account on "Railroads.")

(For the reader who may be interested, some information for this record was taken from a very complete manuscript, "The Old Whitewater Canal," written by C. H. Wesler and edited by Minnie Wycoff, President of Ripley County, Indiana, Historical Society, Batesville, Indiana. (1937) This manuscript may be read at CHS Library.

Charles Cist, Cincinnati historian, in his book Cincinnati In 1841, discussed water power on the Whitewater Canal and the usefulness of the Whitewater Canal.

(For the information of the reader who may want to know more of Ohio's canals, a map and history of the state's canal systems may be purchased from The Ohio Historical Society, Columbus, Ohio.)

BRICK MAKING AT NORTH BEND

The diary of an Ohio River storeboat peddler, Jonathan Newman Hamilton, found at Cincinnati Public Library, tells how bricks were being made for the building of the canal and tunnel at North Bend in August, 1839.

"August 13, 1839. Ran down to General Harrison's where they are constructing a culvert and tunnel. There are about 100 persons at work there. They have quite an extensive brick manufactory--on a new plan to me, at least; they have erected a circular building, about 60 feet in diameter. The area, with the exception of about 4 feet around the circumference which is left to shelter the moulders, is raised 2 1/2 or 3 feet above the level of the ground. A large post stands in the center to which is attached a beam and at the outer end of the beam is affixed a large roller, near 8 feet in diameter and 18 inches thick. This roller runs on the outside or outer edge of the elevated area. The track upon which the roller runs is depressed about 4 inches; in this track are placed the moulds for the brick. There are four moulds together and then a space of 1 foot and four moulds again. The moulds are lined with iron or steel, and bound on the upper edge, also. The bottom is fitted so as by means of a lever (upon which the moulder presses with his feet) to raise to the top of the mould and throw the brick out after the large roller has pressed it into the mould. The clay for the brick is dug out of the ground and while moist, hauled and thrown into small holes into the ground without being wet or tempered. The moulders thrust it into a box just the length and width of the four moulds and turn the box bottom upward on the mould and press it into the mould exceedingly hard. As soon as the roller passes off, the moulder with his shovel, which is much concave, throws the crust off the top of each brick, making it smooth. Then having a board at hand, places his foot on the handle of the lever and throws out the brick which is quite smooth and hard, and places it on the board. The offbarer puts the boards on a barrow and conveys them to the yard to dry. One man will attend 3 sets, viz. twelve moulds. The wheel or roller turned by horse power makes one revolution in 1 1/2 minutes."

In his diary the peddler also noted that workmen were cutting stone for lock walls in the Cincinnati and Whitewater Canal and that some German laborers had bought $9.20 worth of clothing. When business was slow the storekeeper went ashore to seek customers. He added that he was "all down in spirits owing to stoppage of the Whitewater Canal." (He was referring to an Indiana section already in use.)

(Note: The following material is condensed from an article that appeared in "Towpaths," publication of the Canal Society of Ohio, October, 1966. It is copied by permission of the author, Mr. F. W. Trevorrow, Oberlin.)

The Cincinnati and Whitewater Canal was one of the several canal projects being considered by the Legislature during

1836-1837. Although undertaken by a private company, the state was to subscribe to $150,000 of the stock.

A survey of the proposed canal was made in Dec. 1836, by Darius Lapham for the officers of the board of internal improvements of Cincinnati. Lapham was then Resident Engineer of the Miami Canal, but the expense of the survey was borne by Cincinnatians.

Lapham's report, dated Jan. 23, 1837, described the proposed route of the canal, the principal works required, the levels and estimate of cost. The unusual feature of his report was his recommendation of a tunnel through the ridge between the Great Miami and the Ohio Rivers.

Lapham's survey proposed that the Cincinnati and Whitewater Canal join the Whitewater Canal of Indiana in the pool of the dam three-fourths of a mile south of Harrison, or by continuing for a short distance into Indiana; if such provision could be made, a safer connection could be built. The construction of the Whitewater Canal in Indiana had only begun in 1836 and its route below Harrison was not settled, so the point of connection could not be fixed.

Lapham proposed an excavation through irregular terrain below Harrison for about two miles, where he would place the guard-lock, with four feet of lift. He recommended this position as affording protection against floods in the Whitewater. From the guard-lock, the canal was to continue on that level across the Dry Fork on an aqueduct, beyond which another lock would be necessary.

After crossing Dry Fork, the method of crossing the ridge between the Great Miami and Ohio would determine the amount of lockage required. Here, Lapham proposed a tunnel through the ridge in preference to an open cut. By means of the tunnel, the level of the canal would be brought down to the required level in the Ohio River valley by one lock and the expense of crossing the Great Miami would be reduced.

Lapham proposed to cut through the ridge by means of a tunnel 15 chains (990 feet) long, with the arch extended another 12 chains (792 feet) in the open cut, to protect the cut from filling by the wash from the banks. According to the proposal, the masonry arch would extend for a total distance of 1792 feet. He estimated the cost of the excavation and the tunnel thus:

Excavation in open cut, 55,390 yds. @ 25¢	$13,848
Excavation in tunnel, 12,450 yds. @ $1.50	$18,675
Masonry of arch in tunnel, 6,600 perches @ $3.00	$19,800
Masonry of arch in open cut, 5,280 perches @ $2.50	$13,200
Total	$65,523

Against the estimated cost of the tunnel, Lapham estimated the cost of an open cut at $91,434.50, involving 246,938 cubic yards of excavation and 11,880 perches of masonry arch. In either case, the arch was considered necessary.

The proposed tunnel was a daring engineering innovation at the time it was made. Only four canal tunnels had been dug in the U.S. up to that time. The Schuylkill and Union Canals each had one and the Pennsylvania Main Line had two tunnels. James Brindley's Harecastle tunnel on the Trent-Mersey Canal in England had set the example for the use of tunnels in canal construction. The art of tunnel building was new to Ohio, but Lapham was of the opinion that the conditions were favorable and had no hesitation in recommending the tunnel plan over the open cut. The tunnel was built and proved the most lasting work on this canal.

From the southern end of the tunnel, the survey ran the canal along the north bank of the Ohio, crossing Mill Creek on a masonry culvert, with the termination near the foot of Fifth Street in Cincinnati. The survey pointed out that the canal could be carried through the lower part of the city to connect with the Miami Canal. The level of the Cincinnati and Whitewater Canal, as proposed, corresponded with the level between the 5th and 6th locks on the Miami Canal.

An original drawing showing a cross section of the canal tunnel and method of construction is found in the Erasmus Gest Papers, Ohio Historical Society Library.

The upper center and two side sections of the tunnel were excavated first, leaving the lower center and two upper side sections as roof supports. These latter were removed just ahead of the masons and the lower center last of all.

The tunnel, over 1600 feet in length, was 24 feet wide at the water line and the center of the arch was 15 1/2 feet above the water, 20 1/2 feet above the bottom of the canal. A smaller drawing indicates a towpath about 4 feet wide on one side. It is not clear whether this was of masonry or timber.

The tunnel still exists under the hill, although not in condition for casual exploration.

The Cincinnati and Whitewater Canal is Completed (From Erasmus Gest Papers, OHS Library; undated manuscript, probably written in 1843-1844.)

Cincinnati and Whitewater Canal: Darius Lapham, Resident Engineer; Clement Dare, Senior Assistant; Charles Taylor, Erasmus Gest and Thomas Fallus, Assistant Engineers; Taylor and Morgan Ruffner, Rodmen.

$542,928 total cost at contract price, or $21,890 per mile. Original estimate made in Dec. 1837, $454,326, or $18,173 per mile.

The Indiana Canal is tapped on the farm of John Godley, Esq., on the level which receives its water supply from the foot of the dam.

After crossing into the State of Ohio it follows along the dividing ridge between the Whitewater and Miami until the termination of the same where it crosses the Miami over an aqueduct of 8 spans of 60 feet each to the town of Cleves. From Cleves it passes the hills dividing the Miami and Ohio Rivers through a tunnel of over 1600 feet in length to the left bank of the Ohio River which it follows to the city of Cincinnati.

The tunnel passes through clay mixed with small water worn pebbles and has pieces of limbs of trees also mixed with it. The arch is made of the best quality of brick made by a machine and burnt in kilns. It is 24 feet span and rises 12 feet above the abutments which are 5 1/2 feet high and 3 feet thick.

Near the State line is a guard and lift lock of 4 feet lift. Just below the Dry Fork Aqueduct is a lift lock, 8 feet, and at the end of the Miami Aqueduct is another of 5 feet lift. They are built of common limestone laid in mortar and grouted and lined with timber and plank similar to those on the Whitewater.

There are two aqueducts, one over the Dry Fork of 4 spans of 50 feet each, one over the Miami of 8 spans of 60 feet each. They are constructed of wooden trusses supported by wooden arches and rest on substantial stone abutments and piers founded upon two courses of timber.

There are several large culverts, one at Indian Creek of 18 feet span, at Muddy Creek, Rapid Run and Bold Face of 30 feet each and one at Mill Creek at the lower end of the canal of 50 feet span and 20 feet rise. It is an eliptical arch and stands upon stone abutments 10 feet high and 6 feet thick. The abutments are built of common limestone and the arch of sandstone brought from Rockport near Portsmouth.

From the foot of the lock at the Miami River to the city there is a descent in the canal of 7/100 to the mile.

****

On July 17, 1869, a Cincinnati paper recorded that Abram Brower had acquired Lot No. 31, containing 11.15 acres, from the subdivision of the W. H. and Anna Harrison estate for

$2,500. On this property, interesting to note, stood about one-half of the canal (then IC&L Railroad) tunnel on the Cleves end. (Brower also owned another large section of land in that area, acquired before that time.)

Coincidentally, on that same date as above, Henry C. Lord (president of IC&L R.R.) transferred 2 acres of land in Delhi Township to Brower. (Lord and Brower were then neighbors in Riverside.

(Note: Three Rivers Historical Society would like to acquire the property whereon the Cleves end of the old canal tunnel stands and restore a small plot of ground around it for the benefit of posterity.)

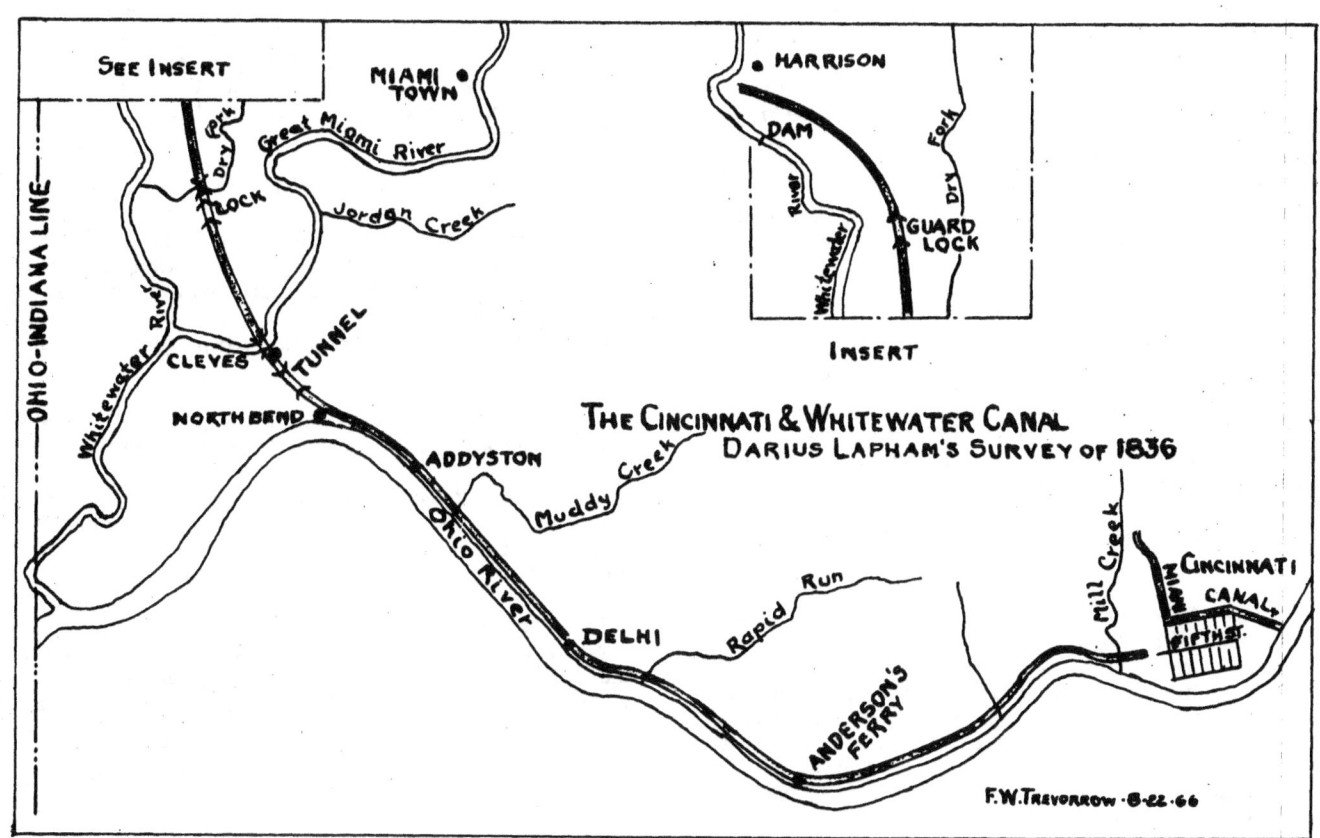

Sketch of the Ohio route of the Cincinnati And Whitewater Canal.

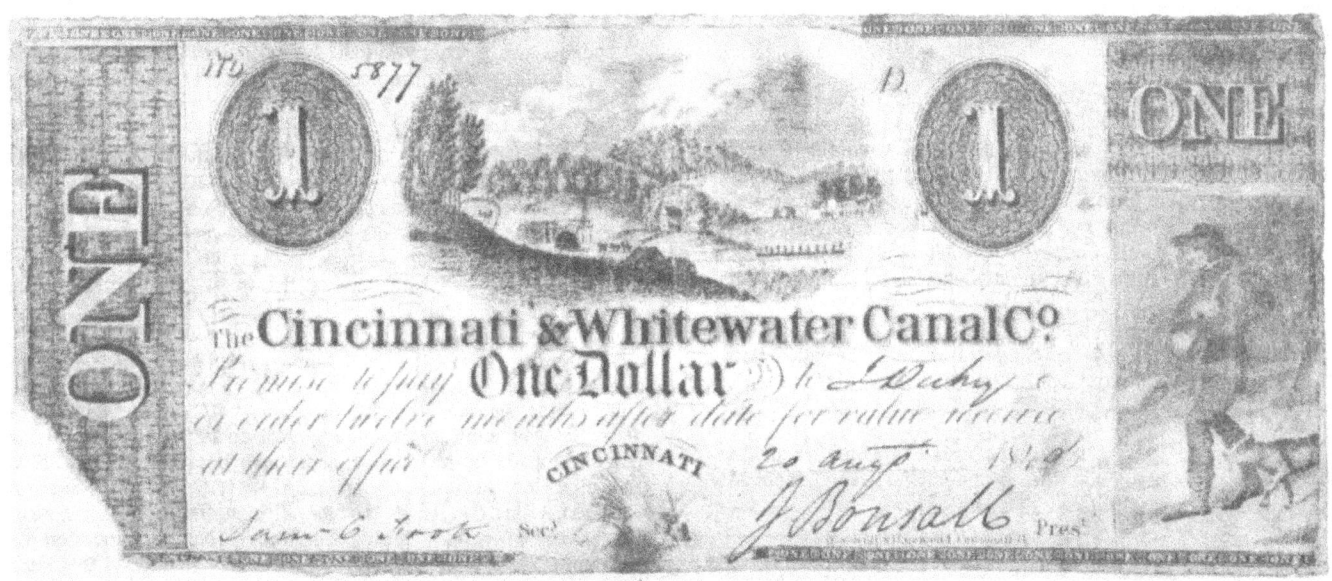

Cincinnati And Whitewater Canal scrip. Scene shows tunnel, canal boat and animals on tow path, and Harrison home at North Bend.

Chapter 13

RAILROADS COME TO MIAMI TOWNSHIP AND ITS BORDERS

The Ohio and Mississippi Railroad, the O&M, has the distinction of being the first to pass through North Bend. Now part of the Baltimore and Ohio system, it started to run through this region in 1854. The route from Cincinnati west followed closely the Ohio River, as well as the Whitewater Canal, out to Delhi--where a fine station was later built, on to North Bend and down along the river past Gravel Pit, old Fort Finney, Fort Hill and thence across the long bridge over the Great Miami to Lawrenceburg. This railroad bridge, an engineering feat in its day, was completed Jan. 26, 1854. Much difficulty was experienced in erecting this bridge due to quick sand in the river. The abutments and piers were laid on oakum. The following items, taken from the Independent Press, Lawrenceburg, tell of the opening of the new railroad:

Jan. 4, 1854. "The first locomotive passed over the bridge built by O&M Railroad Company."

Apr. 4, 1854. "An excursion from Cincinnati to Aurora took place celebrating the opening of the O&M Railroad. Passengers reached the terminus of the railroad below Mill Creek in carriages. James C. Hall, President of O&M Line, announced that fare from Lawrenceburg to Cincinnati is 60 cents; omnibuses take passengers from Mill Creek to any part of the city. The company will issue accommodation tickets which will sell in packages at about 40 cents per ticket."

The cars of the new O&M train were wide. Rails were laid 6 feet apart. This was known as broad gauge track. Normal or narrow gauge width between rails was 4 feet 8 1/2 inches, a measure introduced from England. Officials of the new O&M Railroad, hoping to do business with some of the eastern lines who were thinking big, laid their tracks 6 feet apart. (The variety of gauges, at one time 23 different ones were in use in the U.S., was a real nuisance. By 1886, the 4 foot 8 1/2 inch width became standard gauge.)

In 1853, the Indianapolis and Cincinnati Railroad, the I&C, later the IC&L, and still later the Big Four, had opened its first line from Indianapolis to Lawrenceburg. Its rails were of narrow gauge. In order to extend service to Cincinnati, an agreement was made with the O&M to install a third track on the O&M's tracks. Thus two railroad lines passed through North Bend to the city.

When the Whitewater Canal was abandoned in 1863, the I&C Railroad leased the canal bed and laid its tracks from Cincinnati through the canal and along the towpath, directly along side the O&M line. The track was also routed through the tunnel at North Bend. There the I&C branched off through Cleves and across the railroad bridge, constructed at the site across the Miami where the present bridge stands, and on over the Whitewater River to Elizabethtown.

Henry C. Lord, President of the I&C Railroad, and his associates built this new trackage to relieve their company of the payments of from $80,000 to $140,000 a year for the rental of the O&M line to Indianapolis.

On December 31, 1863, there were special excursion trains along the new main line of the I&C between Cincinnati and Lawrenceburg, a distance of 24 miles.

On the following day, January 1, 1864, a day of freezing temperature, the I&C Railroad also opened another branch service of 7 1/2 miles from Valley Junction to Harrison. So eager for a railroad, the people of Harrison had contributed $20,000 as a part of the cost of $100,000 for the little branch. Edwin Henderson, then a young boy reporter for the Cincinnati Commercial, joined the excursion that morning. A locomotive, tender and small day coach made up the entourage to Harrison. The day was bitterly cold. Men wore all shapes and sizes of shawls in an effort to keep warm. Two, woodfire stoves burned in the coach. The trip took from 8:00 A.M. to 10:00 P.M., whereas in ordinary weather it would have been made in a few hours. Train windows were broken by frozen limbs of overhanging trees along the line. Delays were inevitable due to freezing boilers of waiting trains along the tracks. The object of the day, however, was accomplished and the young reporter wrote his news account of the grand opening of the Whitewater Valley branch from Harrison to the city.

This railroad line was extended on into Indiana and became the Whitewater Valley Railroad. Harrison Junction became a well known stopping point to the residents of Miami and Whitewater Townships. Prior to the opening of this railroad to Harrison, the only transportation available had been daily omnibuses and canal boats. Notice of Harrison's transportation facilities appeared in the Independent Press, April 25, 1855:

"Harrison, O. Omnibus lines, 2 by turnpike; 1 omnibus to connect with the O&M railroad at North Bend."

The coming of the railroads to the region brought progress and rapid change. They also brought with them glimpses of a part of the world the inhabitants of the little villages had never seen.

North Bend, on Sept. 23, 1865, was the scene of great excitement, due directly to the passage of a railroad through the town. On that day, General U.S. Grant and his family came by train from St. Louis to North Bend. At the Bend they boarded the waiting Str. C. T. DUMONT, for the purpose of a formal reception with Cincinnati dignitaries, and departed for the city. David Rittenhouse, in his diary, noted that "U.S. Grant was at the Bend today."

In July, 1872, P. T. Barnum's show passed through North Bend along the O&M line, enroute for Aurora, Indiana. News items tell that people for miles around went to the Bend to watch the circus train cars go by. The Lawrenceburg Press reported the following news from Aurora:

July 25, 1872. "P. T. Barnum's show was in town. Pickpockets were everywhere. Folks rolled into town at 4 in the morning to see the show. An estimate of 10,000 strangers came to town and 11,000 tickets were sold by noon!"

The old canal tunnel at North Bend remained a part of the I&C Railroad route for over twenty years. The last passenger train to go through it went east on July 4, 1884. For some months after, it was yet used for freight traffic. Light Engine No. 59, going west, was the last engine through the tunnel. It is interesting to note that a glimpse of the arched roof of the old canal tunnel may yet (1969) be seen in Cleves.

Ironically, back in 1873 and 1874, there was concern voiced among the riders of the train cars to the city that the tunnel was unsafe, that it might cave in. Some passengers from Cleves and Lawrenceburg went so far as to ride wagons or omnibuses to the Bend and there board the trains, thus avoiding the tunnel. In April, 1874, M. E. Ingalls, Supt. of the I&C Railroad, had the tunnel examined by engineers. He issued a report stating that there was no foundation for the rumors that the tunnel was unsafe. He added that such reports were put out by a rival road. (Lawrenceburg Press, Apr. 13, 1874.)

The train tunnel was the scene of a catastrophe, however, on July 7, 1876. The story, entitled "Terror in the Tunnel," condensed from the Cincinnati Daily Times, was like this:

"Passengers--over 150 of them--on an accommodation train of the IC&L railway, which left the city from the Plum Street depot about 6 o'clock, experienced a sensation at the tunnel between North Bend and Cleves, which they will remember all their lives. It was raining hard when the train left the depot with 3 passenger coaches and a baggage car, and the rain continued to pour in torrents all the way out to the tunnel. There is a watchman stationed at the end of the tunnel. It is his duty to be out on the track on passage of all trains and he is also watchman of the tunnel. Having been in the tunnel a few minutes before, he gave the signal for the accommodation train to proceed on its way. The engineer had hardly entered the tunnel when he found that water from the hillsides and overrun culverts was pouring into the tunnel from the west end. He attempted to reverse the engine, but it was too late. The fires were put out by the water. The train slid to the center of the dark passageway, which is within a few rods of being half a mile long. Here there was found between 3 to 4 feet of water. It was dark as night, not a single lamp or match could be found. The water was rushing through the tunnel from the adjoining hillsides with fearful rapidity. The engineer knew that the fire in the furnace had been extinguished but he thought perhaps there was enough steam left in the boilers and 3 cylinders to carry the train through. He made an effort and pulling the throttle valve open gave the piston rods all the play they wanted. But it was to no avail, the fire had been extinguished and the steam in the boilers, cool and useless. There the ponderous machine stuck in the middle of the tunnel, refusing to move. There they were, 150 men, women and children, crowded into 3 cars, no light, and water rushing through with the noise of a cataract. There was a moment or two of terrible suspense and it was whispered that the lighting Omaha Express was due in a minute and would probably run in and make a total wreck of the accommodation. It was dark as pitch. Some one must get outside to signal the express train or there would be a fearful disaster. Quickly, a brave, daring fellow, whose name was not then learned, agreed to do his best. Throwing his shoes aside, he jumped into the roaring waters which had now reached a depth of 4 to 5 feet. After terrible exertion in both wading and swimming, he reached the mouth of the tunnel and on to the flag station. He was just in time, for in less than a minute the Omaha Express came thundering along. It was flagged and stopped. What an accident had been averted! After deliberation as to how to get the stranded passengers out, the Omaha Express engineer pushed a freight car, which had been standing idle on a side track, into the tunnel. The people were transferred from the accommodation to the freight car and then pulled out. The water by then began to subside but many were thoroughly wet. Yet there was no grumbling; everyone was too thankful. Soon the accommodation train was pulled out. Hundreds of carts of mud and dirt that had accumulated on the tracks had to be removed. It was no small undertaking. At 11 o'clock the Omaha Express was ready to proceed. It is a strange fact that no one was hurt, although Mr. Flowers, well known conductor, fell into the water twice and had to be rescued. Mr. G. W. Souders, who has resided in the vicinity of Cleves for 51 years, reported these facts to the newspaper writer, and stated he had never before witnessed such a storm as that!"

The Lawrenceburg Press, July 13, 1876, duly reported that the heroic fellow who had first swam out of the tunnel and caused the Express train to be flagged, thus preventing a fearful loss of life, was G. M. Welsh of Cleves.

Stations along the railroad lines often bore names of families who lived near the train stops, such as: Short's Station, Devin's Station, Griffith's Station and Pike's Station. Samuel Griffith, for example, gave land to the railroad company for the erection of a depot in North Bend not far from what is now known as the foot of Shady Lane. For maintaining this station, the Griffiths were given the lifetime privilege of riding the train, free of charge. Other train stops, such as Fort Hill, Gravel Pit and Valley Junction, were so named because of their geographical location.

The following newspaper items, gleaned from Cleves, Cincinnati and Lawrenceburg papers, and from a book about the O&M Railroad, written by Robert F. Smith--former mail clerk, tell the story of why trains sometimes ran behind schedule. The sites of each event are recognized by the names of the train stops or the geographical location along the route.

Jan. 2, 1856. Independent Press. "A locomotive of one of the O&M passenger trains 'jumped' into the canal near Lawrenceburg. No injuries. Had a time getting it out of the canal."

June 29, 1861. Vincennes Western Sun. "New bridge over the Miami is demolished. A severe gale passed over Lawrenceburg yesterday demolishing three spans of the new bridge of the O&M Railroad over the Big Miami. It will be several weeks before damage can be repaired. In the meantime freight will be transported to Cincinnati by boat."

The O&M Railroad bridge was again destroyed in September, 1866. Boats again brought passengers and baggage from Lawrenceburg upriver to Cincinnati. In October, a third rail was installed on the I&C track from Lawrenceburg to North Bend, in order that the O&M could run through.

The following is known as North Bend's "great train robbery:"

May 11, 1865. Seymour Times. "On Friday night, the express train that left Cincinnati on the O&M Railroad at 8 P.M. was thrown from the track by thieves at North Bend, by tearing up part of the track. Fortunately, nobody was hurt, but the train was immediately invaded and taken possession of by the robbers, and the passengers ordered to sit in their places whereupon they were required to disgorge their money and valuables, under the encouragement of loaded and cocked revolvers thrust into their faces. Over 100 men were thus robbed. There were about 15 or 20 in the gang. The safes of the Adam's Express Co. were blown open with powder and robbed. The scoundrels escaped across the river in skiffs, ready for the purpose, eluding pursuit. Twelve of them were since seen in Verona, Ky., where they were carousing defiantly and jubilantly spending their victims' money."

Gravel Pit, at the site of old Fort Finney, was also the scene of several railroad accidents:

Nov. 4, 1868. "Engine explodes at Gravel Pit. An O&M locomotive attached to a special freight train left Cincinnati at 6:25 Thursday evening in charge of Conductor Howe and Engineer Gardner. The train stopped at Gravel Pit, 18 miles below Cincinnati, for the purpose of taking on wood for the engine. Shortly after the train stopped, and while the wood was being stored in the tender, and the engineer was engaged in oiling machinery, the boiler exploded, killing the conductor, fireman and one boy who was standing near, outright, and wounded two other boys who were engaged in loading wood. The two wounded boys have since died.

The second poem was written by J. O. Speed, a lifetime employee of the railroads, and appeared in his book, Anecdotes and Tall Tales in Rhyme, 1962. Mr. Speed dubbed himself the "Pennyrile Poet," because he was born in the region of Kentucky where the pennyroyal plant flourishes. His wife, an early school teacher in Cleves, also wrote poetry.

WHEN RAILROADS WERE YOUNG

Lawyer Bruner was a-fuming
　At the slowness of the train
On which he was a rider
　During a red-hot campaign.
He was to make a big speech
　Down the line, some miles away,
And "the party's" hard-pressed workers
　Looked to him to save the day.

The conductor, losing patience
　As the critic kept on talking,
Suggested that he quit the train
　And end his journey walking.
"It would upset arrangements,"
　Said the irate Mr. Bruner;
"By this train I am expected;
　Should I walk, I'd get there sooner."

This account of the history of railroads in the region, together with the problems to which they were subjected, reveals that trains were prone to all the snags that steamboats encountered, perhaps even more. No wonder they frequently ran behind schedules. Nevertheless, the value of their contribution to the progress of that day can never be estimated.

The chief bane of the railroads were the frequent floods that washed out tracks and wrecked bridges. The next account should, therefore, tell something of the early local bridges.

Great Miami Bridge near Cleves. Ca. 1900.

★★★★★★★★★★

Railroad Nicknames

Trains frequently ran behind schedule which provoked the ire of waiting passengers. As a result of long waits, trains were often given nicknames that seemed to suit the situation of frustrated travelers. The C.C.C.& St.L., which ran through this region, was dubbed the "Can't, Cut'er, Cookie, Steam's Low."

Passengers on the commuters were also nicknamed, so recalls Steve Alling. The 6 AM crowd were the "workers"; the 7 AM travelers, the "clerks"; and the 8 AM riders, the "shirks".

Harrison Junction and Valley Junction Postal History
Postmasters and dates of appointments

Harrison Junction: Wm. W. Payne, Feb. 6, 1865; James Dowling, Sept. 28, 1865; Isaac Butler, Dec. 19, 1866; John N. Butler, Aug. 1, 1867; John Foley, Mar. 2, 1868; Joseph Cilley, Apr. 17, 1868; Wm. G. Rizzin, June 23, 1871. Name of station changed to Valley Junction, June 23, 1871.

Valley Junction: Jacob H. Hunt, Oct. 3, 1871; Reuben H. Warder, Oct. 21, 1872; John Walker, Apr. 28, 1874; Reuben Warder, Jan. 31, 1876; Thomas H. Hunt, Oct. 31, 1876; Charles A. Seals, Feb. 21, 1878. Discontinued, Mar. 6, 1879.

Elco Boys and Elco Street

The Elco Boys were a group from the Home City area who had a canoe club, in the 1910 era, on the Great Miami River just north of the horseshoe mill, opposite the mouth of Jordan Creek. They leased as their club house an old log cabin which dated from earliest times. That cabin, for many years the home of Edward Hughes, son of Ezekiel Hughes, washed away in the 1913 flood.

The Elco Boys socialized with a group of "bachelor girls" from Cleves, often entertaining them at their camp site.
The club took its name from one of these girls, Cleo Seibel McDonald. "Elco" was created from "Cleo".

Christie and Joe Burger, sons of Henry Burger, lived as young men on Washington Street, Home City (Sayler Park). They belonged to the Elco Boys Club. When Sayler Park was annexed to the city in 1911, all the street names were changed. Henry Burger, being the village street commissioner, marshal and lamp-lighter, had something to say about renaming Washington Street. At the suggestion of his sons, it became Elco.

Big Four Railroad depot at North Bend. Ca. 1900.

Chapter 14
BRIDGES AND FLOODS

Early toll bridge and railroad companies were incessantly plagued with damage and destruction to their bridges by flood, wind and fire. This region around the mouths of the Whitewater and Great Miami was, and is, known for its vast glacial deposits of gravel. Frequent floods in these valleys stirred up the river beds of gravel and sand and washed out bridge piers; strong wind storms undermined bridge foundations. Moreover, early bridges, many of them covered, were built entirely of wood and burned readily. With so many streams to cross, settlers in the region were greatly dependent upon their bridges, and when these were down travelers were forces to go many miles out of their way to reach their destinations. Therefore, a program of bridge repair and replacement was continually in progress or under discussion.

It is interesting to note among census records of the Miami Township area, 1850-1880, the number of men employed as stone masons, stone breakers and stone workers. Many of these were undoubtedly engaged in bridge building along the Miami and Whitewater Rivers.

The historic floods of 1883 and 1884 played havoc with bridges in the Ohio and Big Miami Valleys. These deluges put many railroad and highway bridges, on the local scene, out of commission. Steamboats once again were put into service, running from Cincinnati to Aurora where passengers there boarded trains on the O&M line. Coal flats, tied to trees at various landing points along the river, served as boat docks where steamers of the Cincinnati and Louisville packet lines picked up villagers and transported them to a terminal point near the mouth of Mill Creek. From there they were ferried in yawls to Eighth Street, where they found various horse-drawn vehicles waiting to carry them to their places of business in the city.

The 1884 flood resulted in a change of course for the Great Miami River. Prior to that time the channel had run closer to Cleves, nearer to the railroad tracks. A new channel, as we know it today, was cut by the force of the floodwaters and the river changed its route.

Previous floods had also caused changes in the Great Miami's course but none had brought about such a sweeping change as had the flood of November, 1847. The reminiscences of Ezra G. Hayes (1827-1919), told when he was 80 years old, found in The Hayes Family, edited by R. S. Hayes, tell of this change:

"The Miami River changed its course in the flood of Nov. 23, 1847, when it cut a new channel for itself through the valley and changed its bed. Formerly the river ran around by Hardinsburg, forming a loop called the Horseshoe Bend. The channel was deep enough to allow steamboats to go up as far as Hardinsburg when the river was fairly high. The farmers in the neighborhood loaded their flatboats with stock and produce for New Orleans and floated them down into the Ohio. (Hardinsburg, also known as Hardintown, was located between Elizabethtown and Lawrenceburg.)

"In 1847, my brother-in-law, Anthony Halberstadt, was living in the house at The Point, where mother and I lived three years. Father kept cattle at The Point and I stayed there part time. Also a man named David Whipple was there. On the afternoon of Nov. 23, the rain fell in torrents and the whole valley was submerged with the rain falling to the headwaters of the Whitewater and Miami Rivers. Water came like an avalanche, burying trees, buildings, cattle, haystacks and fences. The roaring of the thunder and lightning was terrific. We could hear acres and acres of land falling into the mighty current.

"After the storm subsided, the Miami was found to have changed its bed, having cut a new straight bed, and had left Hardinsburg two miles from the river. It was the most terrible storm I ever witnessed."

The 1913 flood, far more devastating than those of 1883 and 1884, brought about the greatest destruction of all time to the bridges of this region. (Although the 1937 flood was the flood of all floods, bridges at that time held firm.) Almost every bridge, with the exception of a few, were swept away in 1913. The CL&A Traction Line and Big Four Railroad Bridges over the Whitewater, near Valley Junction, were among those washed away.

Another to go out in the flood of 1913 was the B&O Southwestern Railroad Bridge over the Miami near The Point. Items from Lawrenceburg papers tell the history of this old bridge:

March 26, 1913. "This was one of the largest and oldest bridges on the B&O between Cincinnati and St. Louis. It was first built in 1852-1853 and cost the old O&M R.R. Co. $250,000. Much trouble was experiences getting a solid foundation on account of quick sand in the river bed. The abutments and piers were laid on oakum, the railroad company buying up all the supply that could be obtained."

Oct. 5, 1853. Independent Press. "The O&M Railroad Bridge is now being erected across the Great Miami. A serious accident took place there and many were hurt when the trusses of a span fell. Dr. J. Brower, attending surgeon, treated a number of men."

Jan. 4, 1854. "The first locomotive passed over the bridge built by O&M Railroad over the Miami. Built by McCullum and Brundage, under the direction of Francis Pruyn, Division Engineer of O&M Railroad, the bridge has 4 spans, each 210 feet long. The piers and abutments are the most substantial masonry laid with cement, and the bridge reflects great credit upon the engineer and contractors. On this occasion a 27 ton locomotive and tender with platform cars heavily ladened with cross ties passed over the bridge several times at all rates of speed, under 40 miles an hour, without causing the least creak or vibration."

Apr. 26, 1866. "The first pier of the O&M R.R. Bridge on the Indiana side at the Miami is in dangerous condition. The company is building a new one."

A flood of 1866 swept three spans of this same bridge away. Cost to the railroad company for rebuilding it was $300,000. The following news items tell more of this destructive flood and the havoc it wrought in this region:

Sept. 20, 1866. Union Press. "A dreadful equinoxtial rain storm swept by here. Many bridges on the I&C Railroad were injured and trains are not running regularly. The Whitewater Bridge on this road, between Cleves and Elizabethtown, is somewhat impaired so that trains do not run over it and all the bottom land is covered with water.

"The O&M Railroad is the greater sufferer. The Miami Bridge is entirely destroyed. The raise in the river undermined the piers to such an extent that they gave way and the two center spans of the bridge fell and were swept down the Ohio yesterday (Sept. 19, 1866), and the one on this side, as we go to press, was tottering. This will be a great expense to the railroad in the way of making connections by boat from Cincinnati to either Lawrenceburg or Aurora, besides rebuilding the bridge."

Oct. 11, 1866. "The O&M is transferring passengers to the I&C Railroad since the destruction of the Miami bridge. The company will have a third rail down on the I&C tracks from here (Lawrenceburg) to North Bend by next Saturday, when the O&M trains will run through. Success to so well managed a road."

Jan. 17, 1867. "The O&M Railroad is to rebuild its bridge during the spring and summer. The spans of the new bridge will be shorter than those of the old one, and the probability is that the new bridge will be entirely of iron."

May 2, 1867. "Messrs. Buckley and Gardner have given up the job of pile driving at the bridge and a gentleman named Wilson has taken charge of the work, in order for the bridge to be completed next fall."

Aug. 22, 1867. (An account of the work at the O&M bridge, mouth of the Miami, was given which told of the great number of men employed. All boarding homes in the region were said to be full.)

Dec. 9, 1867. "The O&M Railroad Bridge was completed and the first passenger trains commenced running over it."

David Rittenhouse of Mount Nebo, in his diary of March, 1868, noted that he had ridden to the mouth of the Miami to see the iron bridge.

The flood of February, 1883 was less damaging to this Miami River bridge, and the O&M line in general, than were previous floods, although the railroad was under water and out of commission for a time.

During the 1913 flood, one pier of this railroad bridge (by now called B&O Southwestern Railroad Company) was torn out but was soon replaced with a new span. The flood and ice gorge of 1918 did yet further damage.

Sept. 22, 1921. "Trains will soon be running over the new B&O bridge which spans the Miami near its junction with the Ohio. The floods of 1913 and 1918 played havoc with the other bridge at this location. It is believed the new structure will be flood proof." (See accounts "Railroads Come to Miami Township and Its Borders" and "New Life at The Point")

Back in 1913, the suspension bridge over the Whitewater at Harrison, Ohio, was also torn from its moorings and all communications to that community cut off. This bridge was below the site of the one burned by John Morgan's Raiders in 1863 during the Civil War. The history of this Harrison bridge is most interesting, although possibly typical of all bridges and bridge construction in that era. That history is pieced together here, in brief, from items of the Union Press and Lawrenceburg Press:

July 23, 1874. "Twenty years ago, in 1854, the first bridge at Harrison washed away. A wooden one was put up in its place about 1857. John Morgan's Raiders burned it down in 1863. An iron truss bridge was then erected and traveled over for the first time by county commissioners in December, 1865. The iron came from the establishment of T. F. Baker and Company in Cincinnati and cost only $12,000. This long iron bridge over the Whitewater, about 1/4 mile below Harrison, fell, crushing Jerome Johnson to death on July 14, 1870. For some time it had been deemed unfit for travel. County commissioners inspected it a short time ago and pronounced it unsafe but no warning signs were put up. No money could be spent to repair it until after election."

March 30, 1871. "Petitions were submitted asking Hamilton County Commissioners to aid in the construction of a new bridge over the Whitewater."

April 11, 1872. "We hear there is talk of building another iron bridge at Harrison. Hope it is only talk. Before the

Laying the CL&A traction line to Lawrenceburg through the Lost Bridge, over the Great Miami about 1899 Frank Franz, foreman, at far right. The bridge burned in 1903. (Picture courtesy of Edna T. Hayes.)

last bridge was built we protested at experimenting with people's money. People know that old fashioned wooden bridges are no experiment but a substantial reality. Iron bridges are subject to contraction and expansion from cold and heat. Iron bridges are made lighter than they should be. Let us have a good old wooden bridge at Harrison."

July 25, 1872. "A contract was signed for the erection of a bridge across the Whitewater near the village of Harrison; it is to be a single track with an 18 foot roadway. The expense is to be born equally by Dearborn and Hamilton Counties, each paying one-half."

July 23, 1874. "The bridge over the Whitewater River at Harrison is a fated bridge! Hamilton and Dearborn County Commissioners decided to put up a wire suspension bridge; $40,000 in work had been done when last Thursday, the cables broke and tumbled the whole structure into the river. J. W. Shipman, contractor, will have to stand the loss."

Another bridge was eventually built at Harrison and it, like many other bridges of the region, was swept away in the 1913 flood, the greatest bridge leveler of them all. Only two nearby bridges withstood the 1913 deluge. These were the Suspension Bridge, (first opened in November, 1869) over the Whitewater at Whitewater Park (later Long Island Beach), and the Miamitown Bridge over the Great Miami.

(Mabel Longnecker Herbert, a teacher at Harrison in 1913, had to ferry back and forth to school each day after the bridge went down.)

The Miamitown Bridge stood on the site of what was probably one of the oldest bridges in the entire region. The first bridge here was built in 1829 by a stock company which sold shares for ten dollars. This structure, along Harrison Turnpike, with partitioned roadway and footpath, was described in The Ohio Gazeteer of 1841 as having "two spans of 160 feet each." Floods never reached this bridge until 1884, according to the following item from the Commercial Gazette:

Feb. 1884. "From Miami (Miamitown) to North Bend the river reaches the hills. The Miami Bridge, never before touched by water, is half covered."

This old bridge was replaced in 1894 by a larger, one-span, camel-back bridge, which is yet seeing service today.

Whipple Lind, son of Thomas N. Lind of Mount Nebo, was one of the contractors who built this bridge. Although the approaches to this structure were washed out, along with much of the village of Miamitown in 1913, the bridge itself stood firm.

An account of the destruction of the bridges at Cleves during the 1913 flood was written by the late Judge Stanley Struble, illustrious citizen of Cleves, who served for 30 years in the Common Pleas Court of Hamilton County. Although born in Miamitown, where his father was an early day physician, Stanley Struble moved to Cleves in his youth and resided there all his life. (A fountain in front of the Miami Township Hall was dedicated, March 29, 1969, in his memory.) Judge Struble wrote several articles for The Valley Journal, a local newspaper which had its inception about 1930. One of his accounts tells of an episode which took place during the 1913 flood:

"Noah Clark and 'Happy' McDonald were heroes in 1913 during the historic flood. The Ohio and Great Miami Rivers had gone on a rampage of unprecedented fury. The lower parts of Cleves, south of Miami Avenue, were already inundated from backwaters of the Ohio. Then into

Lost Bridge under construction. This one-span bridge, the second at the site, replaced the earlier wooden bridge. This one went out in the 1913 Flood.

the region swelled the Great Miami with such force as to destroy both the Big Four Railroad and county bridges. The surging waters suddenly broke through onto Cooper Avenue, flooding homes and threatening their destruction. Within seconds the families of Capt. Jessup and Mr. Dean were caught by the flood and left stranded in their homes along Findlay Street.

"Soon the shore became lined with people bewailing the fate of their neighbors, trapped in those homes that might at any moment be worked off their foundations by the lashing waters.

"But Noah and 'Happy' became the men of the hour! They commandeered a truck and rushed to North Bend where they got boat and rope. I personally saw them rescue Capt. Jessup and his marooned family. It was a hazardous undertaking. With the crowds along shore looking on, the two men rowed their boat up the river and drifted with the current down to the Jessup place. They held onto a tree and manipulated the boat around the house to the side where the waters were quietest. From out a second story window stepped Captain Jessup and other members of his terrified family. Noah and 'Happy' then guided the boat with the current for nearly two miles until they found a safe place to land.

"The execution of the feat required both skill and courage. For their heroism, Noah Clark and Edward 'Happy' McDonald were later awarded Carnegie medals."

During this disaster of 1913, all communications were down. The Steamer J. R. WARE, setting an all time precedent, came up the Great Miami carrying supplies for the sunken community and tied up at the Cleves depot. Built in 1911, as a contractor's towboat, the Steamer WARE, herself, sank in the ice of 1918 at Manchester Island in the Ohio River. (Her hull and engines were later recovered and rebuilt into the Str. M. T. EPLING.)

The first bridge at Cleves was built about 1834 over the Great Miami along the crossing of the old State Line Road, which ran through the bottoms between Cleves and Elizabethtown. The course of the river took a different route than it does today. Trails branching out from along this road led to Miamitown, Valley Junction and Harrison and on across the bridge over the Whitewater. Before the coming of the Cleves bridge a ferry was operated near this site.

The Cleves Bridge Company was organized by the citizenry in 1833. Stock, at $50 a share, was sold, primarily, to residents of Miami, Whitewater, Green and Delhi Townships, although the bridge stood to benefit all who would pass over it. Names of many prominent pioneer settlers who purchased stock in the bridge company appear in a ledger found at CHS Library. It is interesting to note that the first six stock certificates were issued Nov. 13, 1833, to Joseph Garrison and the five descendants of William Rittenhouse. Both of these men had engaged in ferry operations along the Big Miami but they knew the necessity of building a bridge.

Tolls were charged to all who passed over the bridge, with the exception of stockholders. We wonder if the toll keepers at Cleves bridge had as much trouble collecting dues as the Lawrenceburg Bridge Company, as noted in the following item from the Western Statesman:

Mar. 1, 1833. "The Lawrenceburg Bridge Trustees invite those in arrear for toll to attend to the settlement of what is due with the toll collector, by paying cash or giving their note payable in 30 days. Two years have passed since the bridge was passable and a settlement ought to be made in some way. It is not the wish of the company to coerce by devising delinquent accounts in the hands of the magistrate. Those who do not pay must not think hard to find their bills in the officer's hands, John Saltmarsh, after Mar. 20, 1833. The above will be the case with all except stockholders. Signed, Jeremiah Phiney, Treasurer."

The Cleves Bridge Company functioned until 1870, at which time its directors, Peter Tebow, Otha Hayes, William T. Young, Edward Hunt and H. L. Howell, voted to sell and turn the bridge over to the management of Hamilton County Commissioners.

That old bridge was in use for 50 years, until it was destroyed by the ravages of the flood of 1883. That story was told in the Cincinnati Commercial Gazette:

Feb. 8, 1883. "For nearly 50 years the bridge over the Great Miami stood the tempest and the flood but now the venerable and useful structure is a thing of the past. The bridge was built by a stock company and a few years ago was sold to Hamilton County. The people in the western part of the county are seriously affected by the loss of the bridge and already are looking to the county for relief. we understand that authorities will visit the scene of disaster and carefully survey and make estimates of the cost to those acquainted with the old road bed from Cleves to Valley Junction. It is evident that a road bed above the high water mark is desirable. This can be secured with a small increase of distance and the expense would be inconsiderable. When our officials have examined the ground and considered the advantages of a roadway and bridge safe from the ravages of the floods so frequent in the Miami, we are confident that a change of route will be made."

Feb. 13, 1883. "Early in the progress of the rise of the waters in the Big Miami, the large bridge near Cleves was partially washed away. The commissioners estimate that to repair the bridge at its present location will cost the county about $40,000. If its present location is abandoned and a new bridge built at a point where it is believed it would stand against all floods, the expense will be double this sum. It would be better economy to build a bridge over at a point where it will have protection from the force of the waters than to repair it at its present location. A securer position is available where the structure would have the advantage of height."

The County Commissioners, divided in their opinions as to where the bridge should be rebuilt, delayed making a decision. Almost a year was lost while farmers and businessmen suffered for want of a bridge. The County Engineer reported in September, 1883, that it would be wise to build the Cleves bridge at another site, since the old bridge, owing to its location and exposure to a diagonal current, was always a bill of expense to the county. It was also noted that current in the river was already rapidly washing out a new channel.

The disastrous flood of 1884 moved in and settled the question. The Big Miami changed its course, cutting a new bed for itself and by-passing the channel where the old bridge had stood. A new iron bridge was erected in 1884 just north of the IC&L Railroad Bridge, which had spanned that site for over two decades.

Back when the Whitewater Canal was abandoned in 1863, the IC&L built its railroad from Cincinnati along the canal bed. At North Bend the route followed through the old canal tunnel, on through Cleves and over a bridge across the Miami, on the north end of town, where the present railroad and highway bridges stand. The railroad continued on beyond Valley Junction and over the Whitewater, where another bridge was built, on through Elizabethtown and thence to Lawrenceburg where the line was linked with the old section of the I&C, built back in 1853 from Indianapolis to Lawrenceburg.

The I&C Railroad Bridge over the Whitewater shared much the same fate as the other bridges in the region, as seen in the following items from the Union Press:

Apr. 6, 1865. "The Whitewater River, higher than in 1847, broke over its banks and swept away the trestle work of the I&C, just above Elizabethtown. Now business has to be done by O&M. A bad accident occurred here killing three persons, Aaron Bateman, George Sherrod and Wm. De Hart, engineer."

Aug. 3, 1865. "The I&C Bridge over the Whitewater was unsettled by rains and is unsafe for trains to pass over. The company is transferring its passengers to a special train on the O&M line to Cincinnati.

"While the bridge was being repaired a number of persons were hurt in an accident, and one lost his life."

A highway bridge was also built over the Whitewater around the same time that the first Cleves bridge was erected. This span, however, did not wear as well as the old Cleves bridge. It stood near the site of the later I&C Railroad crossing.

Oct. 19, 1865. "Since the destruction of the bridge over the Whitewater River, near Elizabethtown, the citizens of that portion of Hamilton County have been at great inconvenience in traveling toward Cincinnati. The commissioners for some reason have determined to build a bridge between the mouth of the Whitewater and across the Miami. The contract was awarded to McNairy, Claflin & Company."

On June 21, 1871, a severe rain and flash flood swept down the Whitewater and Miami valleys. Ezra Guard told of this storm in his diary, courtesy of Mrs. Eunice Guard Steele:

As it happened, Ezra, his sister, Angeline, and their father, Chalon Guard, left their home on Dugan Gap, Mount Nebo, that day, in their buggy and traveled to Moores Hill, Indiana, to attend Ezra's college graduation exercises. On their way home in the afternoon it began to rain. By the time they had reached Elizabethtown (then officially called Riverdale) rain was falling in torrents. The approach to Lost Bridge was inundated and the bridge over the Whitewater was impassable due to construction and repairs underway at that time. The Guards were forced to leave their horse and carriage, together with Ezra's trunk and school belongings, in the barn of a nearby farmer and cross the river on foot over the IC&L tracks, which they followed all the way to the foot of Mt. Nebo Road in Cleves. It was still raining. They climbed Rittenhouse Hill and at last reached home on Dugan Gap in a completely drowned state after midnight. What a graduation day for Ezra to have remembered! And to think his commencement oration that day had been entitled "To Be Living is Sublime."

In recalling the history of the bridges of this region, the legends of Lost Bridge must be told. This bridge over the Great Miami linking Mt. Nebo and The Point to Elizabethtown was first begun to be built sometime in 1865, near a site which had been used as a ford for around 75 years. The first bridge was built at the direction of Hamilton County Commissioners. Its piers were of stone, and the bridge-- itself of heavy timbers--was covered. Legend says it was an old Howe truss bridge of the early type with glass windows.

John Chamberlain of Vermont is said to have been the bridge contractor. While the span was under construction, Chamberlain boarded at the home of Job Hayes (1812-1887) on Mt. Nebo. The story is likely true. (Chamberlain resided at Delhi as early as 1869, and was among earliest members of a Union Sunday School, forerunner of Delhi Methodist Church, there. He was listed as engaged in repairing the IC&L Bridge across the Miami near Cleves, in April, 1874. The 1880 Delhi Township Census shows John V. Chamberlain as bridge builder. By 1887, however, he was occupied as superintendent of a coal mine. In spite of the foregoing information, there may have been two men of the name, possibly father and son, because Ford's History, 1881, lists one John V. Chamberlain buried at pioneer Berea Cemetery.)

The book The Hayes Family gives the year of Lost Bridge's completion as 1877-1878, but this is in error. A number of conflicting legends exist on the subject of how the bridge got its name; however, it seems to have been first identified as the "Big Miami Bridge" at Mt. Nebo or at Elizabethtown. Nevertheless, according to one little known story, the name "Lost Bridge" had its inception back in 1865, before it was even built. The legends are many but all carry threads of truth.

One of the best known legends tells that farmers of the area had agreed to make gravel fills at the approach from Elizabethtown upon completion of the bridge. For some reason, this was not done until a lengthy time after the bridge was built. So, as the story goes, the bridge, even though standing, was of no use--it was "lost"--to the community.

Minnie Matson Bonham (married in 1874), who was a young girl attending school at Elizabethtown during the years that the bridge was "lost," told of climbing up and down a ladder to get on and off the "unapproachable" covered bridge on her way to and from school. The fills were finally made, it is said, by Minnie's father, John B. Matson, and Chalon Guard (who died in 1873), with gravel and rock from the Matson farm, which was situated at the east end of the bridge.

News items gleaned from Lawrenceburg papers indicate that the approaches to both ends of the bridge were always in need of filling and that flooring and weather boarding rotted rapidly as a result of the endless floods of those times. Numerous references to this bridge over the Miami support the statement that it was standing as early as 1866. David Rittenhouse noted in his diary, Feb. 19, 1866 and Apr. 14, 1866, that he had walked down to the new bridge.

Nov. 11, 1869. "We (in Elizabethtown) noted that the Mount Nebo news items forgot to speak of a whiskey saloon that is a thriving condition at the east end of the Big Miami Bridge. Why don't they close the nuisance out?"

The Big Miami Stock Farm built Ca. 1875 by Joseph H. Hayes; A showplace of the township in its day, situated along Mt. Nebo Road, near Lost Bridge. The land, in early times owned by the Garrisons, is now a gravel pit.

Nov. 18, 1869. "Joseph H. Hayes has purchased the farm at the east end of the Big Miami Bridge belonging to Stephen W. Garrison who had his sale of farm utensils and is going west to settle."

Jan. 2, 1873. "The approach to the bridge on the west side of the river is very dangerous, especially now."

Feb. 20, 1873. "Looks as if we're going to have a better fill at the bridge. Bids were received at the Court House for making the approach to the end of the bridge in Whitewater Township. Matson and Flowers were lowest bidders, at 24¢ per yard."

May 1, 1873. "Matson and Flowers will begin 'fill' at the Lost Bridge soon."

July 17, 1873. "Doc Bonham thinks that 'Matson's Avenue' (near Lost Bridge) is one of the best driveways he ever saw. He ought to know, he often drives over it." (A. C. "Doc" Bonham was then courting Minnie Matson.)

Oct. 23, 1873. "The floor of Lost Bridge is in bad condition. Hope it will be fixed."

Dec. 4, 1873. "A contract for repairing the Miami bridge (in Mount Nebo notes) was awarded to A. B. Wamsley and S. H. Osborne for flooring and to Whitney (saw mill) at North Bend for weatherboarding."

Dec. 1873. John B. Matson, in a ledger owned by Mrs. John B. Bonham, stated that County Engineer Bowles passed by the road to look at the bridge. He noted that the river was rising. In an entry of Feb. 1874, Matson stated that he went to see Garrison about bridge matters.

Jan. 15, 1874. "The sureties on a bond accepted and approved by the County Commissioners Sept. 8, 1865 for making the fill at the lost bridge on the E-town Road have been notified to pay in for making said approach expended by the Board, on or before Jan. 20, or a suit will be commenced against them by the county solicitor."

Jan. 28, 1875. "Sam P. Bowles, County Engineer, was out taking a survey from the depot to Lost Bridge, preparatory to making a fill across the bottoms."

Aug. 5, 1875. "Flood. Between the E-town depot and the lost bridge is a sea of water."

Mar. 15, 1877. "Commissioners looked over the road at Elizabethtown with a view of making a fill through the low lands from the depot to lost bridge. It is needed by the traveling public."

Aug. 23, 1877. "The floor of the lost bridge over the Miami is in a condition that will cause loss of some of the traveling public unless it is looked after by authorities."

Oct. 1877. "The County Engineer and Commissioners examined Lost Bridge with view of reflooring it."

Dec. 20, 1877. "J. F. Wamsley has contract for replacing weatherboarding on lost bridge."

Feb. 1878. "Road leading to Lost Bridge is always bad."

It is evident that Lost Bridge was in use before 1878, but it is also evident that, with its western approach lying on such low terrain, it was frequently out of commission. This old covered bridge stood until 1903, when it was destroyed by fire and "lost" again. A ferry was operated here for a time until a new Lost Bridge was built. This one succumbed, too, to the 1913 flood:

Mar. 26, 1913. "A great property loss was the destruction of the bridge over the Miami at Elizabethtown. This magnificent steel bridge, the longest single span in the world, was crumpled up by the force of the water and now lies a twisted mass of steel beneath the waters of the river. This bridge had replaced the old wooden structure known as Lost Bridge which was destroyed by fire. The central span over the river was 586 feet in length."

(It is interesting to note that 'Hap' McDonald, who was to figure in an act of heroism in Cleves several days later, drove--his wife accompanying him--in his buggy down to Lost Bridge when the river was rising so rapidly and cut the cables across the bridge for the telephone company just before the bridge went out.)

Oct. 2, 1913. "There is no public road to the ferry and it is almost impossible to cross the river at Lost Bridge."

After the 1913 flood, Enos Hayes ran a ferry here over the Miami. His son, Jarvis, obtained a license to operate the ferryboat, and did so until a new bridge was constructed. When the new three-span, steel bridge was erected, replacing the one swept away in the flood, it was a foregone conclusion that it would be named Lost Bridge. That bridge, although "lost" beneath floodwaters innumberable times since, yet stands. Any wonder it is known as "Lost Bridge."

The following account gives still further explanation as to why the bridge was so named:

June 29, 1922. "When the commissioners were asked to build a bridge, they pointed to the great expense of building the approaches. The land owners on the west side of the river signed an agreement to make the approaches if the county built the bridge. The agreement was deposited in the engineer's office and while the bridge was being built the contract disappeared. There were no approaches made for a year or more, and the children from the east side of the river who came to school at E-town climbed up and down ladders 25 feet high. And how about the time the commissioners built a culvert about half way between the railroad and bridge which was 50 feet long and 10 feet high that cost $4,000, for a creek that ran across the road! Then they lost the creek and had to tear out the culvert. So you see the commissioners got "lost," the creek was "lost," and by fire the bridge was "lost." (Legend tells that the commissioners out on a survey trip to the bridge one day got lost and couldn't find the bridge.)

This next legend, "Why Was It Called Lost Bridge," written by Charles Wamsley of Zion City, Illinois, and appearing in the Lawrenceburg Press, July 2, 1922, may be the best version of all. It dates back the farthest:

"There was a petition circulated to build the suspension bridge across the Whitewater and one across the Big Miami at the same time. The county commissioners did not want to build both bridges, so there had to be a special act passed by the state legislature. Rev. B. W. Chidlaw, being in favor of the suspension bridge, went before the legislature and made a flowery speech, making the assertion that the bridge across the Big Miami River would be placed in the middle of a corn field and entirely lost and also would be 2 miles farther than the suspension bridge (miscalculating the distance). Then Abram Brower went to Columbus and explained to the legislature just the opposite of B. W. Chidlaw. Amzi McGill, then a member of the legislature, gave both bridges. So that is why it was called the Lost Bridge through the speech of Rev. Chidlaw. The road from Lost Bridge is not called the Gest Road but the Geist Road, for Casper Geist, who at the time of building was one of the county commissioners, 1865-1868." (Amzi McGill was Hamilton County Commissioner 1867-60; Casper Geist was Commissioner 1865-66. Mr. Wamsley, who wrote the legend, named Mr. Geist as Adam Geis, instead of Casper Geist.)

The foregoing legends and facts concerning local bridges give an overall picture of the problems that faced bridge builders and travelers of yesteryear. Today, the problems facing bridge builders and travelers are even greater. Bridges and highways cannot be built rapidly enough to meet the needs of the population. Travelers in this locality, however, will soon be introduced to a new route of travel when a new superstructure, in the making across the Ohio River just below the mouth of the Miami at a site where much of the early history of the region was laid, is opened. As Rev. Bushnell once stated it, "Advancement of any age or people is seen in the roads that are building," Viewed in this light, the new bridge, the latest on the local scene, is a physical sign of progress.

("The new bridge, in the building--near the mouth of the Great Miami, will be a key link in Interstate Highway 275, a circumferential route which will allow through traffic to completely by-pass the city of Cincinnati. Construction of four river piers was recently completed by Dravo Corporation. Each pier consists of two round columns connected by web walls, with the highest of the four rising 108 feet above normal water level. The unusual depth of foundation rock at one point--80 feet beneath the river's surface--required erection of one of the deepest cofferdams ever built in the Ohio to enclose the work site. The cellular structure was composed of eight steel sheet pile cells joined by connection arcs. Normally, river bridge piers are built inside rectangular single-skin cofferdams supported by steel bracing sets. This was the technique used for the other three piers, which were founded from 24 to 49 feet below water level." From the "Dravo Review," Fall, 1969.)

A new mode of travel was being introduced upon the local scene back at the turn of the century. It was the trolley, with its clang! clang! clang!, making a track into the villages and countryside. That story should next be recounted.

Chapter 15

TROLLEYS, STREET CARS AND BUSES COME TO RIVER ROAD

It was in 1900 that the Cincinnati, Lawrenceburg & Aurora Interurban Traction Line Company, better known as the CL&A, came into service in the down river communities. Prior to the coming of the trolley, residents of the area had ridden the commuter trains to and from the city. Anderson Ferry, site of the old toll gate, was the starting point of the new line. It was also the end of the street car line from Cincinnati.

The CL&A followed River Road out through Delhi, Home City, Addyston and North Bend. At North Bend the traction line followed the railroad tracks to Cleves Junction, near the crossing at Mt. Nebo Road. (The line had originally been laid up North Bend hill to Cleves Junction, but this section was rerouted, shortly after, through the railroad cut.) At Cleves Junction was built a small depot, which, incidentally, is yet standing along South Miami Avenue, and it is down behind this old depot that one can still catch a glimpse of the old canal tunnel. At this point the CL&A traction line divided into two separate routes. One route went out through the main street of Cleves, across the Big Miami River to Valley Junction, and on to Harrison, Ohio. (This route along Miami Avenue in Cleves was rerouted in 1923 to follow along the railroad tracks.) The second route, although of short duration, went to the foot of Mt. Nebo where it turned and followed along Brower Road, sometimes called Lost Bridge Road (now Miami View Road), to Lost Bridge, over to Elizabethtown and thence to Lawrenceburg and Aurora, Indiana.

Lost Bridge, being a covered wooden bridge, was a natural shelter for farm animals in cold weather. Crewmen along this trolley route frequently had to stop their cars, get out and chase mules and pigs off the tracks before proceeding. When this covered bridge burned in 1903, traction car service ceased along the Lost Bridge Road section of the line. Cars were rerouted through Cleves to Elizabethtown and on to Lawrenceburg and Aurora.

Mrs. Fannie Williams Hayhurst, resident of Addyston since its founding in 1889, recalls watching from a window of her dark bedroom on the evening of Good Friday in 1900, when the first traction car, no pushing and no pulling, glided past Addyston and over the Muddy Creek trestle. What a beautiful sight to her young eyes to behold the electrically lighted car sailing smoothly along in the night! Traditionally, her family had always gone to Cincinnati on the Saturday before Easter by train. She and her friends decided, instead, to ride the new electric car to Anderson Ferry, the end of the CL&A Line, and walk the rest of the way to the city. Upon deboarding at the ferry, the young ladies began the trek along River Road to Cincinnati, but on reaching Storrs (a railroad stop) realized they could never walk that far. They boarded a passing Sedamsville street car for the rest of the journey and did their Easter shopping in the city.

Crewmen who operated the CL&A Interurban cars in 1900 were: Charles Clotfelter, Dan Murphy, Ed Bixenstine, Harry Wells, John Hey, George Lyons, Robert Gruenemeyer, James Dore, Ray Trester, Dick White and Harry Meyers. George Bender was superintendent and master mechanic. President of the traction company was Col. John C. Hooven, a manufacturer of farm machinery at Hamilton, Ohio. He helped finance a horseshoe and iron company, in 1906, at what was then Berea, which, among other names, was known as the Phoenix Horseshoe Company. The community known for over a century as Berea was named Hooven, in 1927, in his honor.

Today, the Gulf Refinery, constructed in 1930, stands on the site of the old horseshoe mill.

A large brick car barn, for the storage and repair of the CL&A traction cars, and power house was built at North Bend opposite Marmet & Smith Coal Company, better known as "the coke ovens." That power house was only recently razed when the new highway was constructed.

The traction cars made frequent stops along the route. Each stop was numbered. Fare from Anderson Ferry to Delhi, at Zinn Place, Stop No. 17, was 10 cents. To Home City and Fernbank fares were 5 to 7 cents additional. Thrifty Home City residents walked to Delhi to board the trolley in order to save the nickel. The service, which continued until 1931, proved to be a great convenience to the community. Passengers inbound to Cincinnati boarded street cars at Anderson Ferry, where there was a nice waiting room that also housed a restaurant.

Records of the Cincinnati Street Railway Company's house organ, "The News," had this to say about early street cars:

"Cars of 1890, drawn by horses and mules, were not only short and small, but as uncomfortable as any means of transportation devised up to then. The seats were hard, wooden benches with long carpet-like pads for cushioning, used only during the winter months. Under ordinance these pads were removed between May and November.

"Coal oil lamps assisted those who cared to read while they rode. A quite frequent claim in those days was 'silk dress ruined by oil from lamps.' For heat, there was smelly straw, piled knee-deep for comfort. It not only gave off a stable-like odor but helped soil trailing skirts of female passengers.

"But even these were considered an improvement over the omnibus vehicle in use between 1858 and 1880.

"Go back with us to the year 1858, and stand for an hour in front of the post office, then located at Fourth and Vine Streets. You will hear the distant, low rumbling of wheels bumping heavily over the cobblestones. The thunder becomes louder as the source approaches, until it finally drowns out the other street noises. We turn and see coming toward us a large, wagon-like, horse-drawn vehicle resembling a stage coach and carrying 10 to 15 passengers. It is the first form of mass transportation in the city and it is known as the omnibus."

CL&A Power House, North Bend.

To River Road residents and passengers of 1880, the improvement of the horse-drawn car over the wagon-like omnibus was easy to see. However, from a driver of those new horsedrawn cars comes a different story, told in the Cincinnati Daily Gazette, April 20, 1881. In brief, the writer complained of the plight of the poor driver of cars on the mule line out to Riverside:

"He works 16 hours a day, in cold-blasts and rain without proper protection, not seeing his children except when they sleep. He puts up with the terrible jolting, wearing anxiety, and fearful racket of the route from 8th Street to Riverside in all kinds of weather. The loneliness of the life is awful. Let us have the good old-fashioned omnibus again."

About 1891, the horse-drawn car was replaced by the electric street car along River Road down to Anderson Ferry. "Fresh air" street cars, featured during the summer season, were open to the floor and boarded by a step which extended the full length of the car. Older residents today recall taking school and vacation-time excursions to the Zoo aboard the summer street cars. Fare on the cars from 1859 until 1919, sixty years, remained at 5 cents, by order of City Council. In 1919, fare was hiked to 5 1/2 cents a ticket and 6 cents cash.

The CL&A Traction Line service, begun in 1900, from Anderson Ferry west, was discontinued in 1931. Cincinnati Street Railway purchased the CL&A track and right of way beginning at the ferry out to Fernbank and extended the street car line to that point. Fernbank--once a part of Miami Township, along with Sayler Park and Delhi had been annexed to the city soon after 1910. This transportation service was wonderful for those along the street car route, but residents in the downriver communities west of Fernbank-- the corporation line, felt the loss keenly.

Street cars served the route to Fernbank until 1941, when they were replaced by gasoline motor coaches. Bus fare from Fernbank to Fountain Square was then 10 cents. About 1951, diesel powered buses came onto the scene, with service still ending at Fernbank.

Back in 1931, following the close of the traction line, North Bend, Cleves, Harrison and Lawrenceburg were virtually without public transportation. The use of automobiles was increasing but the cost was yet prohibitive for many people living in this period of great financial depression.

It was about this time that the late Bill Maurer of Addyston, a descendant of the Maurers who settled at North Bend in the 1840's, started a bus service from Cleves to Cincinnati. Although the service was often irregular and at times inadequate, it was--and still is--the only public transportation along the River Road route that the residents of Addyston, North Bend and Cleves have known since 1931. The route follows up through Delhi Hills to the city. This is the Ohio Valley Transit Company.

In 1948, Adrian E. Apswisch founded the Addyston to Price Hill Coach Line, which he operated until 1967. At that time he sold the line to Jerry Robbins, present operator. This bus line has proven a great service to those residents who live along Cleves-Warsaw Pike and in the Delhi Hills region.

Another line, Trailways Corporation, coming from Lawrenceburg, passes through Elizabethtown and Cleves and follows Bridgetown Road to the city. This affords service to passengers along that route.

Use of public transportation has declined sharply over the years; bus lines and railroad companies are facing financial crises. Highways are becoming clogged. Expressways cannot be constructed rapidly enough to meet the need. This is the age of the automobile. Even so, there are many persons yet dependent on and in need of public transportation.

What changes have transpired since North Bend's first travelers arrived by flatboat in 1789! Stage coaches, omnibuses, canal boats--pulled by oxen along a tow path, commuter trains, trolley cars, automobiles and air-conditioned buses have all made their way west along the Ohio River route. Old River Road, first laid out by Judge Symmes, has surely felt the wheels of progress move along it.

Anderson's Ferry, taken from the point on the Ohio where Gen. Morgan is said to have crossed in 1863. The building was the office and waiting room of the CL&A Traction Line at its eastern terminal. Ca. 1900. A toll gate once stood at this site on River Road.

Chapter 16

The Harrison Family In Fact And Fantasy: Cold Springs And Cold Springs Houses

The site of the home of General and Mrs. Harrison at North Bend was somewhere in the vicinity of the intersection of Symmes and Washington Avenues, probably on the ground where stands the cottage of the late William Morris. To the rear of the "Log Cabin" were orchards, gardens and stables, and on the farm were at least three fine springs.

Although much of General Harrison's land was either sold, lost or parceled out to his children before the time of his death in 1841, Anna Harrison continued to hold on to the North Bend farm. Her daughter, Anna, and son-in-law, William H. H. Taylor, together with their large family, lived with her at the homestead.

An interesting legend concerning one of the springs on the Harrison farm, and also a large oak tree growing near it, belongs to North Bend history. How much fantasy there is in the account is unknown, but the existence of the spring and oak tree is fact.

As is known, Charles W. and Hallie Stephens Caine built a home in the village in the early 1900's, on the hilltop behind the first council hall, along what is known as North Bend Hill. The land, on which the Caine home was erected, had been within the boundaries of the last part of the Harrison farm which Anna Harrison had retained until her death in 1864. From this high point was a good view of the village. On the Caine property was a fine spring near which grew an enormous oak tree, once estimated to have been over 400 years old. Legend told that slaves, conducted by the Underground Railroad to Ohio, had safely hidden in the spreading branches of "The Big Oak." It was also told that members of General Harrison's family, on errands to draw water from the cold spring on the hillside, rested or played beneath the shade of the giant tree. When a new roadway was being built through North Bend during the 1930's, the Caines succeeded in saving the legendary oak from being cut and had a plaque placed there. The old spring, at that same time, was walled in and could be seen by all who passed by. "The Big Oak" stood along the right side of the road, half way up North Bend hill, next to the retaining wall and steps until just a few years ago. A severe storm felled a great portion of it so it had to be cut.

It is also interesting to note that clay pipes were uncovered some years ago on the Calloway property facing Taylor Avenue, opposite the site of what once was the General's pear orchard. These pipes were believed to have once carried water from another of the cold springs on the Harrison farm down to "The Cabin."

One of the legendary springs of Wm. H. Harrison, not far from the site of the "Big Oak."

When the Harrison home burned in 1858, Anna Harrison went to live at the home of her son, J. Scott Harrison, at The Point, where she resided until her death. In the diary of David Rittenhouse appears the following entry:

Feb. 28, 1864. "Went to the funeral of Mrs. W. H. Harrison (she died Feb. 25); Rev. Horace Bushnell (blind pastor) preached the sermon; the text was Psalm 46, Verse 10; rode to the tomb on the cars, then took dinner at Mrs. Brown's." (Mrs. Sarah Brown was the widow of David J. Brown, brother to David Rittenhouse's mother. Brown was appointed postmaster at Cleves, Oct. 1851.)

It is appropriate at this point to relate something of Horace Bushnell (1802-1883), the blind missionary and beloved counselor of Anna S. Harrison and her family. His name is legend in pioneer annals; his influence was felt throughout the Miami and Whitewater Valleys. It was around 1830 that the young Presbyterian evangelist and teacher at Lane Seminary gathered together a congregation in Cleves and Delhi. By 1838 these two charges had a total of 41 members. Bushnell served as pastor in the Elizabethtown, Cleves and Delhi region for half-a-century, forty-five years of which he acted as missionary for the women's missionary organization of the Cincinnati area Presbytery. Two other ministers living during the same era bore the same name, Horace Bushnell. One was Horace Bushnell (1802-1876), the nationally known New England Congregationalist theologian and writer, who was born the same year as his Ohio Valley counterpart. The third man with the name was a son of the local preacher. This one, Horace Bushnell, Jr., also a lifetime minister, served a term in the Elizabethtown community, but went west in the 1870's and settled in Kansas. The elder Bushnell continued as a pastor here until his death at the age of 81. The Cincinnati Commercial stated on May 30, 1878, concerning the funeral of J. Scott Harrison, that Rev. Bushnell, old friend, blind and infirm, had preached the sermon from memory. His name surely belongs among accounts of fact and fantasy that relate to Anna Harrison and her family.

Back on Feb. 28, 1796, Judge Symmes in writing to an old friend in New Jersey had voiced concern about the man his daughter Anna--whom he called Nancy--had wed. (Intimate Letters of John Cleves Symmes, by B. W. Bond, Jr.) He stated:

"Nancy made rather a run away match of it, though she was married at my house in my absence. However, some people say she has married a worthy man. I hope I shall find him so. My greatest objection was that he was bred to no business, & therefore I can set him at none."

Judge Symmes' concern had been for naught. Although Anna Harrison had resided in a rugged pioneer setting most of her days and had been faced with endless family tragedies, she had had the abiding love of her husband, coupled with a strong religious faith, to sustain her throughout her life.

Henry Howe, writing in Historical Collections of Ohio, 1888, recalled his 1846 visit to North Bend, where he had spent several days with Mrs. Harrison and the Taylors. Of Anna Harrison, Howe recalled:

"The widow of General Harrison is distinct in my memory. She was of rather slender, delicate figure, with dark eyes and modest, quiet manners, then seventy years of age. She was born at Morristown, New Jersey, in the year of the Declaration of Independence, and soon after her mother died. Her father, Judge Symmes, then a colonel in the Continental army, was so anxious to place Anna with her grandmother, then residing at Southold, Long Island, that, when she was four years old, he assumed the disguise of a British officer's uniform, to enable him to pass through their lines with her on his way thither, a perilous undertaking. Incidents of that journey she remembered to her last days."

Historian Howe also included some lines of reminiscence written by Col. W. H. H. Taylor in 1888 to Henry Howe, in which the 1846 visit was recalled by Taylor:

"When you visited us at North Bend in 1846, Mrs. Harrison was there and you saw her at mealtimes. I was managing the farm for her. My first wife, her youngest daughter, and seven children were there. The day after your arrival, we walked down the Ohio River bank to an old blockhouse four miles below the Bend, of which you made a sketch; then we went a mile farther and took dinner with the Hon. J. Scott Harrison, father of the present President, then (1846) a lad of thirteen years of age.

"After dinner, in company with Mr. Harrison, we visited Fort Hill, which was on his farm, overlooking the three states of Ohio, Indiana and Kentucky. You examined the fort . . . The next day you viewed the ruins of Judge John C. Symmes' home on the Miami, the first settler of the Miami Valley, and father of Mrs. Harrison. You then left us and returned to Cincinnati. ("Yes; was carried thither by canal boat," noted Howe.)

"I send you a ground plan of the noted log cabin of 1840, in which I was living on July 25, 1858, when it was set fire by a she-devil of an Irish woman and burned to the ground; myself and my family getting out with our night robes only, leaving everything in the way of clothing, furniture, library and all the relics of 1840, of which we had a great many, and many that had been in the family for two hundred years."

Henry Howe also noted that W. H. H. Taylor had been an officer in the Civil War, a Colonel of the Fifth Ohio Cavalry, and that his two eldest sons, W. H. H. Taylor, Jr.--known as Harry--and John T. Taylor had served in the Union army. Col. Taylor, at the time he wrote to Howe in 1888, was State Librarian of Minnesota, his residence in St. Paul. An item from the Cincinnati Daily Gazette tells of Taylor's second marriage:

Nov. 10, 1879. "Col. W. H. H. Taylor of St. Paul, Minn., made a visit to Cleves. He claimed the hand of Mrs. Celia Anderson of Home City in marriage. All regret to part with the bride. Twice the Colonel was postmaster in Cincinnati, now State Librarian in Minnesota. Mr. Everett Anderson has been a member of the Colonel's family for some months and is much improved in health. He expects to enter the university next year."

There has been some question, over the years, as to where Anna and William Taylor actually lived after 1858, following the destruction of the "Log Cabin." It is known that the family suffered extreme poverty. Miami Township Census of 1860 listed Taylor as a clerk with 11 children. Letters written by Anna to her cousin--as well as brother-in-law, John Cleves Short, headed "Cold Springs," reveal something of their abject financial circumstances. Where this "Cold Springs" house was located is uncertain. There may have been two houses with the same name.

In her book West to Ohio, p. 196, Alta Harvey Heiser stated:

"William Taylor said he did not know what they should have done except for John Short's kindness and help after the homestead burned. They were fixed up in a house on the Harrison estate, but were in constant fear that there would be a buyer, who would wish to live in the house. William begged John to buy it and allow him to pay rent, which he promised to do promptly."

Except for the periods he served as postmaster of Cincinnati, two separate terms, and as an officer in the Civil War, Taylor was occupied as a clerk. In 1859 and 1860, he worked in the county clerk's office; in 1863, he was employed as a clerk for CH&D Railroad and boarded at a house on W. 4th Street in the city; in 1864, he was a clerk, boarding at Gibson House. He and his son, John, were real estate agents and auctioneers at 6th & Elm, in 1866, with residence in North Bend. (See Cincinnati Directories) Around 1867, the family moved to St. Paul.

The Miami Township census roll of June, 1860, offers one clue in that the names of the Taylor household appeared next to those of the Joseph Maurer family. The Maurers occupied a large strip of ground in North Bend, a short distance east of Indian Creek, near the railroad tracks and river.

A map of Hamilton County, dated in 1865, (drawn by R. C. Phillips, found at CHS Library) shows that Anna H. Taylor held two plats of land, one east of Indian Creek and the other, a very small tract, a short distance upstream from her brother's place at The Point. Whether the Taylors ever lived at the latter site is unknown. The family included: Harry, Lucy, John, Mary T., Anna C., Bessie, Fannie, Virginia, Jane H., Nellie and Everett.

Fannie Taylor Hendryx, daughter of William and Anna Taylor, in September, 1926, told members of the Mount Nebo Society that she had once lived in the "Cold Spring" house around the beginning of the Civil War and that the house had been built by one George Balsley.

Uncertainty as to which house was meant by the "Cold Spring" house has given rise, over the years, to confusion. Several legends surrounding the "Cold Spring" house and implicating the old William Harding-Jacob Young house in Cleves (recently razed when the Kroger Store was built) have evolved from this confusion. Legend also tells that the Col. Taylor family once occupied the Harding-Young home. For the reader to understand of this matter, some background information on several subjects must first be told.

Back in the early days of Cleves there existed a spring, known as the "Cold Spring," which legend tells never ran dry. Settlers from far and near came here for water in seasons of drought. A cottage which came to be known as "Cold Spring House" was built very near to the spring. This house, as recalled by Mrs. Alice Argo Struble, was yet standing in 1900, and was then painted red. She remembers it well because it lay on property acquired by her grandfather, Ebenezer Argo, which eventually fell to her family. The "Cold Spring" and "Cold Spring House" lay up the Argo pasture beyond where the Kroger Store now stands, near the intersection of Miami Avenue and Mount Nebo Road. The house and spring were reached by way of a dirt road from Miami Avenue. The road, designated as Cold Spring Street on the village map, had been officially platted many years earlier, although it was never developed. Bordering the Argo pasture was the Jacob Young place, which faced onto Miami Avenue.

Sometime during the early 1900's, the Strubles considered developing this land behind the Young place, building houses and laying out Cold Spring Street running off from Miami Avenue. From Cold Spring Street it was hoped to run a road through to Wamsley Avenue and eventually to have an outlet through to Harrison Avenue. Plans failed to materialize. Part of the proposed Cold Spring Street lay on the Jacob Young property. The Youngs declared that their deed stated that the road was originally intended solely for the right of way of the tenants of the Cold Spring House and not meant to be a public road.

This land which the Youngs and Argos had acquired had once been part of the Harrison estate. When the Harrisons were forced to give up their land, piece by piece, this section fell--after 1847--to the Shorts. A Hamilton County map of 1847 (drawn by Wm. D. Emerson and published by C. S. Williams & Son, found in the Hamilton County Engineer's Office) shows the land then unoccupied, no houses appear to have been standing on it, and it yet lay within the Harrison estate. A map of 1855 (presented by George Kattenhorn to Hamilton County, also found in the Engineer's Office at the Court House) shows the property to have been in the hands of John C. Short's sister and brother-in-law, Dr. Benjamin W. Dudley. The Dudleys lived near Lexington, Ky., never in Cleves. A later map of 1865 (drawn by R. C. Phillips, found at CHS Library) indicates the property was then owned by J. H. Magher & Gillison, possibly real estate developers. What type of dwelling lay on this land other than the Cold Spring House is unknown, but it is quite probable another house did exist near the site where the William Harding-Jacob Young mansion later stood.

William H. Harding and his wife, Margaret, purchased, about 1868, property fronting on Miami Avenue just north of the lane that led back to the Cold Spring. Harding operated the Washington Dining Saloon--a large restaurant--in Cincinnati. As early as 1857, he was listed in the Cincinnati Directory as proprietor of an eating house, or coffee saloon, on W. 6th Street; his residence was on Longworth Avenue. In the year 1869, his name first appears as a resident of "Clevestown." The 1869 Atlas of Hamilton County, by C. O. Titus, also shows him as occupant of this Cleves property. There must have been some type of place on the ground where the family lived while their home was being built or enlarged. Proof that the Harding home (or its major part) was not built until the 1869-1871 era, contrary to legend that it was standing in 1840 and that General Harrison made a campaign speech there, was found in items, as follows, from the Lawrenceburg Press:

Oct. 5, 1871. Cleves. "William Harding is having added to his residence a tower 40 feet high. When completed it will be the finest residence in Miami Township, except for Short's."

Dec. 1871. "The residence of Wm. Harding in Cleves is about complete. It is quite palatial."

Nov. 11, 1875. "Wm. Harding has one of the most beautiful residences in Hamilton County; still he is improving it, if such a thing is possible."

1876. "Mr. Wm. Harding is commencing sidewalks in front of his property in Cleves. No doubt when this is finished it will be a great improvement to our village."

The big, red brick mansion when completed was undoubtedly the showplace of the village. It had a mansard type roof, typical of the architecture of the Civil War era. A large carriage house stood in the rear of the residence. The Hardings had three daughters. It is quite possible that Mrs. Harding, herself, was a native of the Miami or Whitewater Township locality. Census records reveal the following information:

1870. Harding, Wm., 54; Eating Saloon Operator; b. in Ohio. Margaret, 45; Mattie, Lucy, Kate. (James Hickman, coachman; Lena Witenfelter, servant; John Hofman, gardener.)

1880. Harding, Wm., 66; Keeps restaurant; Margaret, 55; Kate A., daughter; Martha J. Hunt, daughter. Percy Pierce, 5, grandson; Martha Miller, 76, mother-in-law.

Other items pertaining to the Hardings appeared in the Lawrenceburg Press:

Nov. 18, 1875. "Mrs. Miller, widow of Thomas Miller of Elizabethtown, moved to Cleves where she will reside with her daughter, Mrs. Harding. (Martha Miller was the second wife of Thos. Miller of the pioneer Whitewater Township Millers.)

Jan. 6, 1876. "Miss Mattie Harding of Cleves was married at the residence of her father, Wm. H. Harding, to Mr. George Hunt, on Dec. 28, 1875."

Sept. 1876. "Miss Lucy Harding of Cleves, daughter of Wm. Harding, was married to Charles Campbell."

Mrs. Alice Argo Struble recalls going to Cleves School at the same time Percy Pierce, a Harding grandson, was attending. She also remembers well the beautiful Harding home, without a doubt the grandest ever built in Cleves.

Mrs. Lucy Hearn Creemer, "Mama Lucy," a lifetime resident of Cleves, lived near the Hardings in her youth. Born about 1870, she was named for Lucy Harding.

The Hardings occupied the palatial residence until about 1887. At that time Jacob M. Young (1828-1914) bought the home for $8,000. Legend tells that he bought the place with "Gold Rush" money. He and his brother, William T. Young (1815-1910), are said to have gone west long enough to strike it rich. The latter built a big home next to the Cleves Presbyterian Church, on State Street, which is now the headquarters of the American Legion Post. From the Lawrenceburg Press came these items:

Fall. 1872. "Wm. T. Young's palatial residence is nearly completed. A magnificent edifice, it has all the modern appliances and is built with a view to comfort. It will be occupied by the family of Mr. Young in about 4 weeks."

Oct. 24, 1872. "Wm. Young's fine residence is nearly completed as is George Welsh's fine residence, also."

William T. Young, known to the townspeople as "Uncle Billy," was born across the Big Miami in sight of the village of Cleves. (See Cincinnati Commercial Gazette, July 29, 1894) He moved to the village at a tender age and remained there all his life, living to the age of 95. He operated a general store. His brother, Jacob, known as "Jake," lived and farmed just north of Cleves, along Matson's Mill Road, now called East Miami River Road. He had acquired his farm around 1860 from his ancestor, William Young, pioneer settler in Miami Township. (The old Young farm home today is occupied by Arthur "Bud" McIntyre.) The Jacob Youngs had a daughter, Kate, and two sons, John and William. The family moved to the Harding home about 1887. From that time until about 1964, the Youngs and their heirs retained possession of the impressive residence.

By 1966, the once elegant Young home was in a deteriorating condition. So it was that the building was torn down to make way for the erection of a Kroger Store. Older residents of Cleves, particularly those interested in its history and legend, deeply regretted the razing of the house. It had stood as a reminder of the days long past.

It is said that Col. W. H. H. Taylor, son-in-law of General Harrison, and his family resided for a time in the Harding-Young home. Perhaps they lived in a dwelling on the property, one that the Harding's possibly occupied (or added to) while their big home was under construction around 1869-1871. Or perhaps the Taylors occupied the "Cold Spring House," standing not far from the future Harding-Young place. Mrs. Struble stated that the Young house was never called "Cold Spring House." If the Taylors did live on or near the site of the later Harding residence, it would have had to have been during the early 1860's. Anna H. Taylor died July 5, 1865, at the Columbus Water-cure, after a long and painful illness. She was buried at Congress Green.

Sometime about 1867, Col. Taylor moved the family to St. Paul, Minnesota.

Mrs. Betty J. Creemer Sizemore of Cleves states that she has a window pane taken from a back window of the Young house when it was razed. The glass is scratched with the names of several children which she believes are those of the Taylors. Mrs. Sizemore also recalls the stories of her grandmother, "Mama Lucy" Creemer, who knew the Hardings well. "Mama Lucy" told that large containers of delicious food prepared in the Harding restaurant in the city were regularly shipped out to the family home in Cleves aboard the evening train.

Because of the story, whether fact or fantasy, that the Taylors once lived in the old brick home with the mansard roof, another legend has arisen. It tells that the remains of President Wm. H. Harrison were brought to this home of his son-in-law, Col. Taylor, and lay in state there. History records that President Harrison's body lay in state, July, 1841, at Col. Taylor's home which was then located on Sixth Street in Cincinnati. Taylor had been appointed Cincinnati Postmaster upon election of his father-in-law, and had taken up residence in the city. (Details of the funeral may be found in the Cincinnati Gazette, July 8, 1841, at CHS Library, among the Harrison papers.) (See also the chapter "North Bend's Favorite Son.") Information given or written by someone unfamiliar with Harrison history appears in The Cincinnati Guide, Ohio Writers Project, 1943, on page 509. This article, which labels the old Harding-Young house as the Col. Taylor home and the place where President Harrison was laid out, has helped to perpetuate this legend.

Where the "Cold Springs" house--the one noted at the heading of Anna H. Taylor's correspondence--stood may never be known. Her mother, Anna S. Harrison, died in February, 1864, and her cousin, Judge John C. Short, who then held all of the original Harrison lands with the exception of the North Bend farm, died in March, 1864. Anna Taylor followed them in death a year later. The North Bend farm was then sold to Edward Woodruff, who had it surveyed and laid out into a village. Woodruff, himself, retained the parcel of land on which the legendary "Big Oak" grew.

The 1868 plat of the village of North Bend shows 42 lots bounded by railroad tracks on the south and west, Indian Creek on the east and Taylor Avenue on the north. Land north of Taylor Avenue up the hill to Harrison Avenue had already been sold by that time. Pear trees, remnants of the Harrison orchard, appear on the plat. A locust grove was indicated on the site now occupied by the United Methodist Church (E. U. B. Church). Beyond Indian Creek, the words "Subdivision of heirs of Anna H. Taylor" are shown. The plat clearly shows three springs in existence on the property along the hillside between Taylor and Harrison Avenues. Could the name of Anna Taylor's temporary dwelling, "Cold Springs," have been taken from one of these legendary water holes? The street Taylor Avenue was so called for this family.

It is interesting to note that a grandson of Anna H. Taylor, James B. Hendryx, who lived for a time around 1912 in Fernbank, the son of Charles and Fannie Taylor Hendryx, achieved notable success as a writer of both fact and fantasy. He did some newspaper writing but is best known for his numerous adventure stories. Several of these, the settings of which were generally in the far north country, were: Connie Morgan in Alaska, 1916; Courage of the North; Raw Gold, 1933; and The Yukon Kid, 1934.

The following account, although not specifically related to Harrison family history, holds interest on a local level. How much of it is fact and how much fiction is not certain:

The C. W. Caines once owned a punch bowl said to have had a history equally as colorful as the legendary "Big Oak" that stood on their property. An article of Jan. 1, 1931, Cincinnati Times-Star, stated that this punch bowl, with a 10 gallon capacity, then 137 years old, had been brought to Cincinnati by flatboat. As the story told, it once graced Yeatman's Tavern and from it were served such prominent men as George Rogers Clark, Aaron Burr, Lafayette and Andrew Jackson. The bowl, of English ware, was blue in color and decorated with Chinese figures. For many years the Caines displayed the legendary punch bowl at "Cliff View," their well known dining establishment with the magnificent view of the river at North Bend, just beyond Congress Green.

The old Eaton house on Harrison Avenue, now occupied by Eunice Guard Steele, situated on another site with a "million-dollar" view, holds an interesting history within its walls. Among the oldest buildings in this locale, it is safe to guess that Benjamin Harrison, while President, stopped here to visit his sister, Bettie Harrison Eaton. Bettie Eaton, with her physician husband, Dr. George Eaton (1820-1866), moved from Cincinnati to this place in 1853. Benjamin Harrison, himself, had lived for a time in the city with the Eatons while he attended law school. He maintained a close relationship with his sister.

Bettie H. Eaton was a woman of many sorrows. She outlived her husband and her five children, all of whom died in early life. Only one grandson survived her. Her oldest son, Scott Harrison Eaton--called Harry, became a physician like his father. He died at the age of thirty. Son George had a scientific mind and he achieved some success in the field of inventions. He, too, died at an early age, leaving behind a young widow and little son.

Bettie Eaton retained a clear memory until her death in 1904, and was clever at telling and writing of amusing incidents and anecdotes of the family. Having been born in 1825, she saw much of the Harrison history--of specific appeal to this region--unfold before her very eyes, including both the campaign of her grandfather and her brother. Some of her recollections appeared in an article in The Commercial Tribune, Sept. 19, 1897, written by Frances Langworthy Taylor. Excerpts of several of these anecdotes are copied here:

The name Benjamin was used again and again in the Harrison family. There were at least four Benjamin Harrisons of Virginia before the one who was Governor of that state and signer of the Declaration of Independence. Members of the Harrison family always referred to this Benjamin as "The Signer" in order to distinguish one from another. In connection with him, an amusing anecdote was related:

As the story goes, a descendant of The Signer concluded to become a member of the Daughters of the American Revolution (D.A.R.), and submitted her application to the society for examination. The dignified officer of the D.A.R. asked, "What ancestor of yours fought in the Revolution?" "I'm not sure if any of them did," replied the applicant. "No ancestor who fought in the Revolution!" said the officer, severely, "and you expect to become a member of the D.A.R.?" "Some of my forefathers may have been soldiers in '76. I haven't investigated, but," demurely she added, "one of them signed the Declaration of Independence."

In the case it seemed that the pen was mightier than the sword.

Bettie Eaton had in her possession, until her death, a gown which her mother, Lucretia Johnson Harrison (first wife of J. Scott Harrison), had worn to the Lafayette

Ball, held in Cincinnati in May, 1825, when Lafayette had honored the city with his visit. The Empire gown of silky India mull had a skirt of heavy embroidery, done by Bettie's mother's own hand. In 1897, Bettie Eaton stated that for herself she thought a woman, then, could not afford to occupy her mind with dress but should be able, on occasion, to go to her wardrobe and find a proper gown, placed there by some good fairy.

The Harrisons were close personal friends of the Beecher family. Bettie Eaton stated that Harriet Beecher Stowe, the novelist, was a guest in their home at North Bend on the night her brother Benjamin was born in 1833. (Harriet Beecher married Calvin Stowe in 1836.) Mrs. Eaton told how once when she was a child, Lyman Beecher, father of Harriet and the famous preacher, Henry Ward Beecher, visited her father's home. Looking at the great man in his big coat, little Bettie propounded the riddle to Lyman Beecher, "What animal do you think you look like?" Then she told Mr. Beecher, who insisted on knowing the answer, that to her mind, in his great coat, he looked "like a great bear," and he never saw her afterward without laughingly referring to the "bear story."

Upon her death in 1904, Bettie Eaton's prized possessions, including a scrapbook compiled by herself of clippings from newspapers that appeared in relation to members of the Harrison family, were willed to her relatives. Several years prior to her death, she had assembled a history of the children of the Harrison family and a manuscript of the Symmes family for Frank Willing Leach of Philadelphia, who wrote a history of the lives of the signers of the Declaration of Independence.

Lillian Stortz Eaton, widowed daughter-in-law of Bettie H. Eaton, resided in the Eaton homestead for many years. She gave piano lessons in the community and frequently played for school and church affairs. Mary E. Myers, daughter of John Myers (see "Role of the River")-- who had come to North Bend in 1839 on a coal barge and was given a home at The Point, lived there as a companion and housekeeper to Lillie Eaton.

When the Steeles bought the old Eaton place, around 1951, it was in an extremely deteriorated state, inside and out. They restored it to a cheerful and comfortable home. The view of the Ohio River from the old Eaton place is just as beautiful as the view from various sites along Cliff Road.

Every student who ever attended Taylor High School will recall seeing the statue of George Washington which stood in the second floor hall, but few will know the mystery that surrounds the source of this work of art. Legend tells that the statue was once commissioned by an organization in Cincinnati, but when completed was rejected because Washington was portrayed in a tunic. Somehow this object of art was set aside and eventually came into the hands of one of the men of Dr. George Eaton's family. Mr. Eaton, which one has not been learned, carried the statue to his home at North Bend. Some years after the demise of the Eatons, the house came into the possession of Charles W. Caine. Legend tells that the sculpture of George Washington was discovered in a corner of the house or barn, and that Mr. Caine's wife, Hallie Stephens Caine, president at the time of Cleves-North Bend Board of Education, presented it to Charles T. Young, superintendent of the schools, for display in the high school.

This writer was unsuccessful in learning anything further about the origin of the Washington statue or how the Eatons had obtained it. Perhaps a reader will be able to fill in the missing lines to this legend, or determine whether the story is fact or fantasy.

Drawn by Henry Howe in 1846.
RESIDENCE OF THE LATE PRESIDENT HARRISON, NORTH BEND.
Residence of President Harrison as sketched in 1846 by Howe.

The stories and legends behind the names of roads in this region make fascinating reading. A great number of them have interesting historical significance.

(Post-Times-Star, July 20, 1962. "Fiddlers Green Road gets its name from an old Indian legend. It concerns a fiddler whose playing brought a strange uneasiness across the countryside. The legend goes like this. The fiddler was inspired by the devil and his music caused pots and pans to jingle in the homes of settlers. When barns were built, timbers and beams rose in places under the stimulus of the music. The eerie sounds of the fiddler caused Tenskwatwa, Indian prophet, to leave his grave in a nearby cemetery. Then there was an explosion and the fiddling stopped. Thereafter, green lights would glow in the cemetery as Tenskwatwa searched for his grave.")

Author's Note: Tenskawautawan (meaning "open door"), known as "The Prophet", was the twin brother of the Shawnee leader Tecumseh. The Great Spirit was thought to be speaking through him; he urged his people to go back to old tribal ways.

The Harding-Young house, built in 1871, was the most elegant ever built in Cleves. It was razed about 1966 and the Kroger Store erected near the site. (Courtesy D. W. Collins.)

Chapter 17

GROWTH OF NORTH BEND AS A VILLAGE

After the death of Anna Symmes Harrison in 1864, the farm was sold and North Bend began to shape into a village. Edward Woodruff, proprietor of the land, platted the town in 1868. George W. Haire was its surveyor.

Ever since its settlement by Judge Symmes, the territory comprising North Bend included land anywhere along the river from Muddy Creek, east of Short Hill, down to The Point, up Indian Creek and over into Cleves. Places along the railroad came to be identified by the names of the families who lived at the stopping points, such as Short's Station, Devin's Station, Griffith's Station and Pike's Station. Other train stops and boat landings, such as Gravel Pit and Coal City, took their names from industries at those sites.

Samuel Griffith had acquired his property, running from the river back to the Warder line, from Eliza Carpenter in 1866. All of the land in this general region had once been a part of W. H. Harrison's estate. (Some of the earlier known proprietors of the land in this location east of Indian Creek and up to around Shady Lane included: Isaac Cooper, Jeremiah Goodrich, James Silver, William Markland, Moses Bussell, Abram Carpenter, Charles H. Gardner, John H. Smorzka, Mary Laird, John Cleves Short, George Winter, Joseph Maurer and undoubtedly many others.) Griffith granted a right of way through his land to both the O&M and IC&L Railroads. He gave a piece of ground for the erection of a station house. For this accommodation the railroad company granted to Griffith and his family, for as long as they lived and used the railway, the right of free transportation. Not far west of this site along the river there had once been a government landing where in earlier days canal boats often turned and unloaded. A tavern and store had stood nearby.

Lots in the newly platted village sold rapidly after 1868, and talk of incorporation soon arose, both in North Bend and in neighboring Cleves. Citizens of these villages met several times at Cleves Town Hall and engaged in heated discussion, pro and con, on incorporating the two villages as one. From the Lawrenceburg Press comes this item:

"Feb. 12, 1874. "Groups from Cleves and North Bend met at the Town Hall. Some are in favor of incorporating the two villages but some are against. North Bend's Dr. King believes in an independent village; Dr. Ewing and James Carlin (Cleves) spoke in favor of incorporating both villages."

The village of North Bend was incorporated for special purposes, August 25, 1874. In the first election in 1875, Samuel Griffith, Dr. Hiram M. Rulison and E. A. Woodruff were elected trustees. At a meeting in the IC&L railroad office, Griffith was elected president, John S. Conner, clerk and treasurer, and R. A. Warder, marshal and superintendent of streets. Shortly thereafter, a lot for school and town hall purposes was purchased.

Dedication of the new town hall and adjoining school house at North Bend took place in late October, 1877. Lawrenceburg Press recorded details of the ceremony:

Nov. 1, 1877. "Rev. G. T. Weaver opened the dedication ceremony with prayer; an address by Hon. J. S. Harrison was read by Wm. Disney; Rev. B. W. Chidlaw talked on the subject 'Improvements.' He alluded to the happy change that had taken place at the Bend especially in the mode of travel. Mr. Chidlaw referred to the old Steamer FOREST QUEEN and gave reminiscences concerning the boat and her landing at North Bend many years earlier (ca. 1851).

Mr. John S. Conner followed with a brief history of the village. Mr. Reuben Warder read a poem written by John James Piatt. Citizens of North Bend are jubilant over the new town hall. The marshal is now equipped with a full uniform."

Villagers were interested then, as now, in having good officers for their town and in taking part in its government, as indicated in the following items:

Mar. 21, 1878. "Dr. John King is a candidate for village trustee."

Apr. 10, 1879. "Dan Mahoney defeated Samuel Griffith for council; this was a close and exciting contest."

In 1880, there were 412 inhabitants in North Bend. The majority of the townspeople were engaged, in some capacity, in one of three occupations, namely, farming, railroading or coal dealing.

The coming of the railroad brought many new families out to North Bend, some of them quite prominent. Lovely homes, commanding beautiful views of the river, were built about the hilltops and outskirts of the village. The men of these families commuted daily to their businesses in the city and were met each evening at the train station by their house boys or coachmen, often dressed in tall hats, driving fancy carriages and high-seated hacks. The earliest IC&L depot stood at the foot of Symmes Street; the O&M stood a little to the west. After the tracks were raised to escape high water, the IC&L was moved to the foot of Harrison's Tomb.

Among the families who came to North Bend during this period of new village growth was John H. Morton, who lived in the home later occupied by A. E. B. Stephens, (opposite Taylor High School). John Morton was an attorney, associated with Samuel F. Cary, and real estate dealer. Several members of the family were teachers, one of whom, Mrs. Mary P. Morton, taught for a time at Fernbank School.

George V. Halliday was a manufacturer of safes. His children attended the public school at North Bend, unlike children of many of the other prominent families. Daughter Vernon Halliday served for a lengthy time as superintendent of the North Bend community Sunday School, and another, Mabel, played organ for church and school assemblies. After the Hallidays left the village and settled in College Hill around 1905, the C. E. Myers family occupied their large home until about 1911, when it was purchased by the congregation of St. Joseph Church for use as a rectory.

St. Joseph Church, North Bend's first church, had been built in 1886-1887, on Taylor Avenue, adjacent to the village school. It has remained the only Catholic church in all of Miami Township, and therefore has always had a large membership. For many years the St. Joseph congregation had a club house, known locally as "Tippecanoe Pavilion," overlooking the church and adjoining the parsonage lot on the hilltop. It was on the site of the pavilion that a new church was erected about 1960. Money for its construction was secured in a most unique way, primarily, through the collection, over a period of years, of Ohio sales tax stamps, for which the state gave refunds to charitable organizations. The old rectory, originally the Halliday home, has since been razed and a new one built in its place.

Although not classed among the "new" families in North Bend, the family of Dr. George and Bettie Harrison Eaton resided along Harrison Avenue in the home today occupied by Mrs. Winfield (Eunice Guard) Steele. This is undoubtedly one of the oldest residences in the area. The view from this place is magnificent! Bettie Eaton, daughter of John Scott Harrison, settled at this site about 1853.

Richard Henry Stone (1822-1908) was another prominent man who settled, in the late 1870's, in the village. He had come with his parents from Va. to this region in 1832. Stone was an attorney, civil engineer and public official of note. He served in the Ohio Legislature, 1852-53, and as Hamilton County Clerk of Courts, 1858-1861. His sons, Richard Henry and George W. were attorneys--with offices in the city; Obed W. was a clerk. (1880 Census) Daughters Cora and Fannie were music teachers and played an important role in the organization of a Sunday School in North Bend. These ladies donated a library and organ to the village school. The Stone residence stood almost opposite of where the high school now stands. The family, a most refined one, moved to Clifton around the turn of the century.

John S. Conner, Judge of the Hamilton County Court of Common Pleas, built a home opposite Harrison's Tomb. He served as president of the first North Bend Board of Education, 1876, and for him the first public school was named.

W. A. Davidson, attorney, whose dwelling was on the site of the later North Bend Inn, John J. Piatt, poet and consul to Ireland, and Murat Halstead, editor of The Cincinnati Commercial, all lived, at one time, along Cliff Road. (See account of J. J. Piatt, elsewhere) Cliff Road in earlier days was called Taylor Road, since it was an extension of Taylor Avenue out of the village. The bridge joining Harrison Avenue to Cliff Road was not built until 1875.

Across Indian Creek, up Ohio Avenue and along Sunset Avenue--parallel to River Road--stood many fine homes. Dr. Hiram M. Rulison, early (1860's) physician of the community, resided here. He had a hand in delivering many of the babies born in that day. Dr. Rulison's daughter, Pauline, and son, H. M., were listed as school teachers in the Miami Township Census of 1870.

Dr. John King, prominent Cincinnati physician and medical college professor, resided on Sunset Avenue with his daughter and son-in-law, General and Mrs. Charles W. Karr. (See brief biography, elsewhere, of Dr. King.) Both Dr. King and General Karr were active in the government of the new village. Charles Karr's ancestors had been among the very earliest settlers in Miami and Whitewater Townships.

Of Charles W. Karr the Cincinnati Daily Gazette reported:

July 25, 1879. "Charles W. Karr, late Adjutant General of the State, mentioned as possible office of Recorder in Hamilton County, will be presented before the convention. He was a plow boy in 1861, hero of many battles, and efficient Adjutant General on Governor Hayes' staff, honest, tried and faithful."

Nov. 29, 1879. "The home of Prof. John King was the scene of the wedding of Gen. C. W. Karr to the professor's daughter, Miss Libbie Piatt. The ceremony was performed by Rev. R. E. Hawley (Presbyterian).

Shortly after Dr. King's death in 1893, his house burned. The Karrs took up residence along Cliff Road on the site which was to become the location of the renowned Cliff View Inn, operated by Charles W. Caine.

Col. David W. McClung, who had wed Anna Carter Harrison, daughter of the General's son, Carter Bassett Harrison, held many public offices in Cincinnati, including surveyor of the U.S. Customs House, secretary of the Board of Elections, and U.S. Internal Revenue Collector. Earlier he had served as a principal and superintendent of public schools in Hamilton, Ohio, where he had edited the Intelligencer for a time.

The McClungs came to North Bend soon after 1881, and resided along Sunset Avenue until about 1899. At that time they moved to Fernbank where Col. McClung served several terms as mayor. They were loyal workers and teachers in the Cleves Presbyterian Church. McClung was an 1854 graduate of Miami University. His account "Miami in the (Civil) War" appeared in a diamond anniversary volume published in 1899.

Of Col. McClung the late Emma Stumpp Speed spoke very highly; she treasured his teachings and words of advice. He once said to her: "Emma, always dress in a way that folks will remember you, not what you wore." On another occasion he suggested that if she would like to see a real President she might go to the train station in North Bend at a certain time. Emma went to meet the train, as Col. McClung had suggested, and there saw former President Benjamin Harrison and his wife (Mary Dimmick Harrison, his second wife) disembark at the depot. The travelers were whisked away in a buggy to the McClung home, located on Sunset Avenue.

The widow of Carter B. Harrison resided with the McClungs until her death at North Bend in 1893. Married in 1836, she was left a widow with a small daughter in 1839.

Dr. John A. Warder, who had come to North Bend in 1855, resided on a large farm overlooking the Ohio. His home was reached by way of a lane from Sunset Avenue up the hill. Dr. Warder first built a frame house which was replaced in the 1870's by a grand stone residence resembling an English country house. The magnificent stone work was said to have been done by a Mr. Pessler, a stone mason from Home City. The Warder driveway was, in early days, planted in persimmon and evergreen trees. Indian Creek ran through this estate. After the Warders vacated their homestead, about 1906, and from that time until around 1923, a number of families occupied the house, including the Hortons, Suits, Grimeses and Emersons. The L. Arthur Perkins family purchased the farm from the Warder heirs in 1923, and have remained there since. (An account of the life and work of Dr. Warder, a most interesting man, is given elsewhere in this volume.)

Another who settled, during the 1870's, in this Indian Creek-Sunset Avenue region was Martin Breining. His descendants yet live in the surrounding communities.

The Samuel Griffith residence, a large and stately one, in later years occupied by the Tyler Gleasons who operated a chicken hatchery there, stood (and yet stands) along River Road, west of the road we know as Shady Lane. (Shady Lane was called by this name as early as 1884, perhaps before.) Here was the railroad stop, Griffith's Station. Descendants of Griffith, Mrs. Ella Burdge Walker and Mrs. Florence Burdge Stuewe, live in the Sayler Park-Delhi Hills region.

Joseph Maurer and his wife, both from Baden, Germany, settled in North Bend sometime before 1850. Their land lay east of the Griffith place, around the foot of Shady Lane, fronting on the river. As early as 1847, and as late as 1869, a schoolhouse stood along Shady Lane, not far from River Road, the only known school building in North Bend during that period. It was probably closed about 1870, when Burr Oak School at Sekitan, near Silver's Creek, was opened. (See chapter "Short's Station, Sekitan and Addyston"). Until 1875, when a school was established at North Bend village, these early schools, the ones on Shady Lane and near Silver's Creek, served the River Road region from North Bend up to Muddy Creek. The little schoolhouse on Shady Lane, later used as a Sunday school--conducted by the Warders, eventually became a dwelling. This early school was situated near the Warder or Maurer property.

Samuel Griffith home along River Road at Griffith's Station, North Bend. Ca. 1890. Yet standing, this was a grand house in its day. (Picture courtesy Ella B. Walker.)

Farther up Shady Lane, beyond the Warder and Maurer lands, resided the William W. Brawley family, who also settled there before 1850. They were well educated people One of their sons, Marcus, became a physician.

Something of North Bend's early inns and stores must be told, although the "something" actually known is little. Cooper's Tavern, mentioned in a document at CHS Library, dated 1814, (see chapter on "Indian Creek") stood near the eastern side of Indian Creek, close to where later the coal yard was established. This was among the earliest taverns in Miami Township, and in Hamilton County, for that matter. Isaac Cooper's tavern is also named in an account found in the Cleves Area Sesquicentennial Book, edited by Walter W. Harrell, which states that this inn stood there as early as 1793. Dr. Stephen Wood, pioneer physician, ran a store at North Bend back in the 1797-1800 period, possibly later. Supplies for his business were delivered by boat from Cincinnati. James Ogden kept a general store, well stocked, during the 1835 era, as indicated in his ledger in the hands of D. W. Collins. The site is not known. In the region east of the Harrison homestead and farm, along the river front, in 1847, stood Smorzka's Tavern. (Note* This name is found spelled in many ways, Smoskey, Smoska, etc.) This inn may have come onto the scene during the building of the canal, or it may have stood on the site of Cooper's Tavern. John H. Smorzka, who lived in North Bend as early as 1841, owned a parcel of land a little west of where Samuel Griffith later settled. According to a map of 1847, "Smoskey's" Tavern stood next to Gardner's Store. Charles H. Gardner, merchant in the 1850 Census, was likely the proprietor. Smorzka was no longer running a tavern in 1850, but Moses Bussell, 50, born in Kentucky, (U.S. Census 1850) was then innkeeper at the site. (Bussell had settled in Miami Township as early as 1820. He also had a son Moses.) It is not known how long "Pappy" Bussell, as his descendants refer to him, kept his tavern at North Bend.

As late as 1890-1900, a delapidated old inn, the subject of mystery and legend, stood near the North Bend coal yards. Residents of that day were told that, in earlier times, this inn was purported to have been a refuge for run-away slaves. But, as legend went on to tell, the proprietor of the inn was a southern sympathizer who locked up the refugees and notified their masters of the slaves' whereabouts, thus collecting a nice profit for his endeavors. Legend also related that the inkeeper, for his cowardly deeds, met a tragic end. How much truth there was to this tale has not been learned. Nevertheless, boys who delivered newspapers around North Bend in the 1880-1900 era, always hesitated to go near the place, repeating the tale, handed down to them, that "those who stopped at that inn were never heard from again! Around 1897, Job H. Malson was proprietor of a hotel and saloon on Cincinnati Avenue, then called "Fifteen Mile House."

Whether "Fifteen Mile House" was the same old tavern shown on the map of 1847, or Bussell's Inn of 1850 and later, is unknown.

For some reason, no one can explain why, the immediate neighborhood around the eastern end of the coal yards came to be called the "Pig's Ankle." And, just as much a mystery, the community lying downstream, just below North Bend and Harrison's Tomb, was known as "Hamburg." The place was being called by this name as early as 1875, and was still familiarly referred to as such until at least 1940.

Some of the known businesses established or in operation in North Bend during the 1870's included:

Whitney's saw mill, with which Jerry Hudson was associated, and Howell's saw mill.

Two large coal elevators were in operation. Stone and Company elevated 15,000 bushels of coal per day and furnished employment for 50 or 60 hands, in 1871. Coal sold for 25¢ a bushel, delivered. Mr. Gates also had a coal elevator.

Reynolds Ice Company (Stone Lake Co.) was very important to the community. (See full account of this in chapter "Indian Creek.")

Wm. C. Mitchell, son of John Cleves Short's second wife, Mary Ann Goodrich Mitchell Short, lived for a time on Harrison Avenue and along Cliff Road. In 1873 he built several fine residences in the village. An enterprising citizen, he engaged in brick making. The Mitchell Brick yards suffered heavy damage in the 1884 flood.

Eugene Burns and Thomas Sullivan ran saloons.

A general store was owned by J. B. Kessner and W. M. Cooper, in 1874. Blackberries were being sold for 3¢ a quart back in July, 1876.

Ezra Bussell was agent for the newspaper The Evening Star, in 1872. Printed in Cincinnati, it cost 10¢ per week.

The North Bend Hotel was being run by S. B. Hayes in 1871. Soon after that time, Joseph and Sarah Garrison bought it and operated it until it burned. The hotel stood on the site of the present Fisher home.

Several organizations and civic groups sprang up about the time the village was platted and incorporated. One of the first was North Bend Masonic Lodge No. 346, chartered Oct. 18, 1864. J. C. McCullough became first worshipful master.

A unit of The Sons of Temperance was organized in Cleves in January, 1866. Both of the communities of North Bend and Cleves had need of a temperance movement. Saloons always outnumbered grocery stores. Results of this action were noted in a letter to the editor of the Union Press:

Feb. 15, 1866. "In Cleves, (and this would surely have applied to North Bend, as well) a town widely known as an awful hard place on account of intemperance and all the lawlessness growing out of the evil, there has been a remarkable change since the organization of The Sons of Temperance in the town. About 3 weeks ago, the division was organized. Out of 7 'doggeries' that were in the place, 4 have died. Heaven bless the temperance men of Cleves."

Aug. 1872. "Newly elected officers of Sons of Temperance are: A. R. Lind, James Carlin, Eliza J. Wamsley, Rev. A. Garrison, Jacob Balsley, Wm. Wiggins, G. M. Riggin, Frank Carlin, J. M. Young, Arnold Van Ausdall, John Young."

The temperance movement in Cleves was without a doubt supported by citizens of North Bend. Women of the community also organized, in 1874, a "Women's Whiskey War." One newspaper would declare that "the recent temperance movement was a success," while the next edition would report news that proved otherwise. That war has never been won.

Henry V. Horton acquired a parcel of land around the corner of what is now Ridge and Harrison Avenues, about 1865. He was associated with the well known temperance advocate Samuel F. Cary, an attorney and a national officer in the Sons of Temperance. (Sam Cary was a brother of Dr. Freeman G. Cary, founder of Farmer's College.) Henry Horton was listed in 1869 as Grand Scribe, Sons of Temperance. The 1870 Miami Township Census noted that he was a publisher. Horton undoubtedly played an important role in the early Sons of Temperance movement in the community.

Miami Township Building and Loan Company was organized in May, 1881. Board of Directors on May 26, 1894 were: Col. T. J. Truitt, Thos. A. Darby, Cal Harlan, A. E. B. Stephens, Geo. Loew, Capt. C. D. Dowling and John Flinchpaugh.

That residents of the area enjoyed educational and cultural pursuits is evidenced in the following notes:

From the time of its founding in 1866, many members of the community actively participated in the Miami and Whitewater Pioneer Association. (See chapter on this society.)

March, 1872. "Dr. King delivered a lecture at Cleves."

Aug. 14, 1873. "The Cleves Horticultural Society was organized with Dr. Royal Struble, president, and Martin Harrell, secretary. Meetings are held at the Town Hall. Dr. C. W. Skidmore will talk on 'preventing ravages of the potato bug.'"

Oct. 29, 1874. The Cleves Literary Society, called the Cleves Lyceum, was organized. E. Argo, James Bogart and W. B. Welsh were appointed to draft the constitution and by-laws. The club's purpose was mental improvement and cultivation of a taste for literature. The group also entertained with musicals.

North Bend also had its Literary and Dramatic Society. From the Cincinnati Daily Gazette came this item:
Apr. 3, 1880. "The North Bend Literary and Dramatic Society will give their 11th and last entertainment of the season at the Town Hall. A drama, "Above the Clouds," will be performed. The cast includes: Mr. Grossman, Mr. Logan, Mr. Argo, Mr. Matson, Mr. Grimsley, Mr. Woodruff, Mr. Morton, Miss Rulison, Mrs. Woodruff, Miss Logan and Miss Devin."

Apr. 13, 1878. "Prof. Robert Warder lectured at the Town Hall on the 'metric system.'"

Mar. 21, 1878. "The Historical Society met at the Town Hall in North Bend, where John S. Conner gave a lecture."

Back in 1887, North Bend's population was 500. Its officers were:
Mayor, George W. Chambers; Clerk-Treasurer, James B. Matson; Marshal, Henry D. Graham; Trustees, George W. Chambers, Charles W. Karr, W. J. Hayes; Road Supervisor, George Eaton; Postmaster and Justice of the Peace, James B. Matson.

In a copy of "The Commuter," June 1890, was the following statement:
"The North Bend board of trustees met June 18, 1890, and passed an ordinance consenting to the separation of Coal City and Addyston from North Bend, in order that they might incorporate as a village."

In that action, North Bend's wide territory was diminished. Addyston then became a village.

In 1891, North Bend was incorporated as a hamlet. After that, Thomas J. Truitt, Frank Kumpf, Jr., and C. W. Karr were elected trustees. Truitt was chosen president, and T. A. Darby, clerk-treasurer.

It was about this time that gas lights came to North Bend. In May, 1894, James Carroll was appointed lamp inspector. In 1897, Alexander Wiles was official lamp lighter.

Persons who conducted businesses or professions in the village during the era 1887-1893 included:

Barber, Jacob Brunson; Beer Agent, Frank Kumpf, Jr.; Blacksmith, John Zapf & Co.; Boarding Houses, Mrs. Joseph Garrison, Richard A. Bunnell; Carpenter, U. N. Moak; Coal Dealers, W. C. Harrell, North Bend Coal & Coke Co., and Marmet & Smith; Dress Makers, Mary Maurer, Mary Elvord; Fishermen, John Clark & Son; General Stores, C. W. Caine, Clement Dowling & Hannah Sullivan; Grocers, Anderson W. Hayes, Joseph Maurer, Mathias Blank; Ice Dealers, Stone Lake Co., Music Teachers, Cora Stone, Fanny Stone, Lillie Eaton; Physicians, Dr. John King, (Dr. O. J. Wood came in 1895); Saloons, Ellen Burns, Reuben Rudisell, Mrs. T. Sullivan, John W. Gaines, Bernard Sheridan, Richard Bunnell; Saw Mills, Wm. Whitney, Peter Wycoff, Henry D. Graham; Tailor, Wm. H. Engelbrecht; Wagon Maker, John Zapf & Co.; Wooden Shoe Maker, Lambert Dues.

The original North Bend council hall and jail, built in 1877, adjoined the first school on the same lot. (Earlier, that lot is said to have been the site of an old barn, used as a U.S. Government commissary during the military expedition at North Bend in 1862.) Pupils on their way to and from school could see the vagrants who happened to be "locked up."

The jail was frequently occupied. The reason for this was that, in 1881, 110 bee-hive coke ovens were constructed at North Bend Coal & Coke Company. Hobos gathered around this place at night and slept on top of the ovens to keep warm. Their presence created a menace to the village, for there was much drunkenness and begging from the townspeople. Noise and vulgarity followed their confinement, and this made for disturbances to the school, adjoining the jail.

By 1897, school attendance was increasing. At a joint meeting of the board of education and hamlet trustees, a resolution was passed by which the hamlet trustees released all claim on the school property, with the proviso that the board of education purchase a suitable lot for hamlet purposes. A lot was purchased on Taylor Avenue for $250. To this site the council chamber and jail was moved, away from the school premises. School-girls Nell Morgan (Garrison) and "Nettie" Truitt (Hayes) watched with excitement the day the jail was pulled away with horses down Taylor Avenue.

This new jail and town hall site was to serve as village headquarters until August, 1954. At that time a new minicipal building, housing fire station and post office as well, was appropriately dedicated, with Ohio Governor Frank Lausche in attendance. Curtis Smith, Jr., who set an all time record in terms elected to the office, was then mayor of North Bend. The new hall was built on ground that had once been General Harrison's pear orchard. (The old hall is now occupied by Joe Spraul, Jr.)

It was in 1905, that North Bend was officially incorporated as a village. The first officials were:

Mayor, C. W. Caine; Clerk, G. W. Yancey; Treasurer, D. W. McClurkin; Council, H. G. Carr, J. C. Malson, L. C. Cady, Joseph Ake, William Morgan and Jason Long; Marshal, Thomas Pierson.

It was also in 1905 that the United Brethren Church was organized. For many years, prior to that time, a community Sunday school had functioned in the village. In 1868, Dr. Hiram M. Rulison, an Episcopalian, had organized the first Sabbath school, which met for a time at Whitney's saw mill, just west of the B&O Railroad station. Dr. Rulison served as superintendent for about ten years. Saw-logs were the first pews. About 1877, the Sunday school began to assemble in the new school building and town hall, just erected.

Evidence that North Bend was engaged early in Sunday school and church activities of an ecumenical nature is seen in the following items from the Lawrenceburg Press:

Sept. 11, 1873. "Rev. M. Baker is the new Methodist minister of North Bend Circuit." (The North Bend Circuit took in the greater part of Miami and Green Townships.)

July 9, 1874. "Rev. B. W. Chidlaw addressed a large audience at Whitney's saw mill in the cause of forming a Sabbath school."

Aug. 6, 1874. "Robert Warder addressed the people of North Bend at the saw mill on the subject 'Prodigal Son.'"

Nov. 5, 1875. "A concert was given at Cleves Presbyterian Church for the benefit of the Episcopal Mission Church of North Bend."

Mar. 21, 1878. "The Mite Society met at the home of Samuel G riffith."

Apr. 4, 1878. "Miss Maude MacKenzie took part in the Methodist Episcopal Sunday School held at the town hall. Miss Lillian A. Stortz is organist and teacher."

May 13, 1879. (Cincinnati Daily Gazette) "North Bend Episcopal Society contributed a gift of $103.83 to Cleves Presbyterian Church debt on the parsonage. Cleves hopes to give practical expression of gratitude sometime to North Bend."

Nov. 29, 1879. (Cincinnati Daily Gazette) "Episcopal services are held every Sunday in the town hall. Rev. Mr. Sturgis, rector of the Church of the Resurrection at Fernbank, is in charge."

Rev. Charles Sturgis served as pastor to both the North Bend and Fernbank Episcopal congregations. The Sunday school was under the supervision of the Warder family, but when Rev. Sturgis left, sometime after 1880, for another charge, the community Sabbath school was abandoned.

Shortly thereafter, Anna Warder, assisted by Cora Stone, reorganized the school. Miss Stone later became superintendent, assisted by Irving Street, son of Rev. Street of the Cleves Presbyterian Church. In 1883, Fanny Stone was elected superintendent, and she served in this capacity until 1895. Average attendance during this period was 70. Children came from all classes and denominations, a few of them being colored.

Miss Vernon Halliday succeeded Fanny Stone. The school sent pictures, charts and teaching materials to Belle Morgan Lippert, a former member of the school, then a missionary in Africa. D. W. McClurkin followed Miss Halliday as superintendent and continued in this position for several years.

After the organization of the U. B. Church in 1905, the congregation met at the public school until a church was completed. Within the cornerstone, laid in May, 1911, were placed the following items: a Bible, church papers and historical sketch, some daily newspapers and several 1911 coins. Oliver Swisher, engineer and school teacher, drew the plans for the church building and superintended its construction. It cost $6,000. With its completion and dedication in May, 1912, the village then had two churches. Clara Gray and Ernest W. Volz have the distinction of being the first couple wed in the new church.

In May, 1916, a most interesting souvenir booklet was issued by the U. B. Church, which had been edited by Charles R. Coulthard and J. Everett McClurkin. In addition to history of the church, this booklet contained a general history of the North Bend community. (That booklet has served as an invaluable source to this writer.)

All through the years, this church has held annual Christmas programs and entertainments, as well as Hallowe'en parades and parties, to which all of the community has been invited. In Dec. 1925, the primary grades of the Sunday school entertained with "Christmas at Jolly-ville Junction," while the young people enacted "The Bethlehem Pageant." The church has been most fortunate in having many musically talented members, and as a result has had a minor claim to fame in its magnificent choirs.

In 1955, on the 50th anniversary of the organization of the U. B. Church (by then the Evangelical United Brethren Church, and now the United Methodist Church), another booklet was prepared, chiefly, through the efforts of Willard Hayes, Sunday School Superintendent. This was a resume of the church history up to that time.

The churches of North Bend have played an important role in the life of the village. In keeping with the new ecumenical movement, all churches of the Cleves-North Bend vicinity joined in a united Thanksgiving service at St. Joseph's Catholic Church in 1967. This was the first such joint service of the two faiths in the history of the community.

Back in 1914, a census reading showed North Bend's population then to stand at 557, a growth of only 57 since the 1887 census. However, included in this new population figure in 1914, were two additional businessmen who had firmly established themselves in the town. To omit these persons from North Bend's story would make its telling incomplete. They were W. W. Taylor and Joe Spraul.

W. W. Taylor had first started in business as a flour merchant, about 1900, going on to become a dealer in groceries, hardware and building supplies. By 1914, he had added the sale of automobiles to his wares. His business occupied the corner which later became the Horton Brother's Grocery, today the Morris Brother's Market. An advertisement of 1916, tells of the W.W. Taylor business:

"Automobile accessories; call me up; I will quote you prices on anything that can be bought; see our Ford animated weekly films at Pastime Theatre on Saturday evenings and Ivy Theatre on Tuesday evenings; let me demonstrate a Ford or Maxwell to you."

In 1926, the new high school was named for W. W. Taylor, first president of Cleves-North Bend Board of Education. This man remained active in affairs of business and community until his death in the 1950's. 'Round North Bend his name has become legend.

Along with W. W. Taylor was another whose name is also synonymous with North Bend. He was Joe Spraul, all-time favorite of children because he operated a confectionery. In the early 1900's, Joe kept store in the building along side the Big Four Railroad tracks, last occupied by Hopping's grocery. He later moved his business to the big building once owned by saloon keeper Bernard Sheridan. Spraul's ice cream parlor occupied one end of the building and a barber shop, the other. This corner became a year-round loafing place. A sign board over Joe's door back in 1916 revealed that "large orders for picnics and socials" was his specialty. His ice cream parlor was to remain a town landmark for nearly half a century, open for business until his death in the late 1950's. Above the glass counters, incasing every variety of penny candy, was mounted a great stuffed eagle. This "old bird" caught the eye of all who ever entered Joe's parlor.

Another man, of outstanding moral character, who also left a significant mark in the annals of North Bend, although of a more recent era, was Manning R. Moreland. The value of the contributions he made in his many years of service to the community, both as a Sunday school teacher of young people and as a member of Cleves-North Bend Board of Education and Hamilton County Board of Education, can never be estimated. He belongs among the ranks of John Warder, Hiram Rulison, John S. Conner, the Warder, Stone and Halliday sisters, Tom Truitt, Hallie Stephens Caine and the endless parade of those early day pioneers and citizens whose highest hopes were for the betterment of mankind!

Although the population of the village, proper, has remained at a virtual standstill since the early 1900's, 620 now in 1969, many persons also dwell on the outskirts beyond the corporation limits. Their mailing address is North Bend, and the post office in the little town serves their needs.

Something of the history of North Bend's Post Office and mail service should be told. The post office has been in every way--from earliest day to the present--as important to the welfare and progress of the village as flat boats, roads, grist and saw mills, schools, churches, canals, bridges and trains.

From The Intimate Letters of John Cleves Symmes and His Family, edited by B. W. Bond, Jr., we note that Judge Symmes, himself, was greatly dependent on, and concerned with, the mails:

Feb. 28, 1796. "Northbend." In writing to friends in New Jersey, Judge Symmes told of the slowness of the Post Office. He stated that he had to go to Cincinnati to pick up mail and send letters there for mailing.

Jan. 1804. Judge Symmes instructed his grandson, John Cleves Short, to write to him and to "always seal the sheet you write on, for if you put a wrapper on it, it comes to double postage; one sheet a yard square pays but 12 1/2 cents, but 2 pieces of paper no bigger than your two hands pay 25 cents."

The Ohio Gazeteer of 1817, and 1818, by John Kilbourn, described North Bend in this way:

"North Bend--name of the settlement on a northern bend of the Ohio. Here is a post office and a thriving circumjacent settlement."

Another mention of North Bend's early post office is found in Ford's History of Hamilton County, p. 290:

"New Haven P. O. (near Harrison) was established in 1826. The mail was received in saddle bags by horseback post from North Bend once a fortnight."

The business area along River Road east of the Harrison estate was once known as Mechanics Row. A postal station bearing that name was established March 22, 1833, with James L. Ogden as postmaster. Bondsmen for this post office were Robert Glass and Joseph Rittenhouse. It is known that Ogden operated a general store in this region so the mail was likely handled in his store. The station was discontinued Jan. 21, 1835.

For some years in North Bend's history, the mailing address for the town's inhabitants was Cleves, and the mail had to be picked up there. Duties of the early postmaster were varied. Often he handled the mails as a sideline in his general store or tavern. He frequently served as agent for newspapers. Judging by the following news item, he must also have run an employment agency:

May 24, 1833. Western Statesman (Lawrenceburg). "An engineer wants a situation. A letter addressed to G. B. at Cleaves (sp.), Ohio, will meet with attention."

An official application for a post office to be called "North Bend" was entered Sept. 6, 1872. Edward S. Keeler was recommended as the first postmaster. Keeler at that time was the authorized agent for IC&L Railroad, having been transferred from the Elizabethtown depot a short time before.

According to information obtained from the National Archives and Records Service, Washington, D. C., the post office at North Bend was officially established Jan. 26, 1874. Postmasters and dates of appointments were as follows:

Edward S. Keeler, Jan. 26, 1874; R. S. White, Feb. 5, 1874; Frank O. Gates, July 12, 1875; Cullum A. Wright, Dec. 10, 1878; James B. Matson, Dec. 17, 1885; Sarah A. Garrison, Jan. 14, 1887; Hannah Sullivan, Nov. 20, 1896; Mary E. Hayes, Dec. 29, 1900; Leslie E. Hayes, Mar. 30, 1914; Mary E. Hayes, Sept. 5, 1919; Anderson W. Hayes, July 15, 1927; J. George Loew, Aug. 20, 1927; Mrs. Daisy Zulager, Sept. 14, 1928; Miss Jessie Dell, Jan. 13, 1942.

North Bend's post office has been located at several different places. Postmistress Sarah Garrison, "Aunt Sarah" as she was familiarly known, kept the post office at her hotel until it burned. The hotel, built around 1870, was called North Bend Hotel. It stood on the site where Bernard Sheridan later built a fine home, now occupied by Lawrence Fisher. After the hotel fire, "Aunt Sarah" handled the mail from a small room in her next home, directly in back of the former hotel, on Washington Avenue.

(Sarah Ann Garrison was the daughter of James Leonard who settled in North Bend prior to 1850. The Leonards occupied land along River Road, east of Indian Creek, near the Maurers. In 1852, Sarah wed Joseph D. Garrison, early ferry operator, and they set forth with a company heading west to seek gold. In those days it took 5 or 6 months to reach California by wagon train. Only travelers with iron constitutions survived the journey. Many are reported to have died of fever and cholera along the way. The Garrisons, it is safe to say, were of sturdy stock. In her later years as postmistress, "Aunt Sarah" must have had some interesting tales to tell of her adventures out West during the Gold Rush. (See "It Happened 'Round The Point.")

For a time, around 1904, the post office was housed in the store building close to the Big Four Railroad Station, last occupied by Hopping's Grocery, which was razed when the new highway went through the town. The late John Zapf, Jr., told this writer a humorous story related to this post office. It seems, so the story goes, that the pigeon-holes of the tall mail shelves were well marked and easily seen through the big glass window of the store front. Thomas Truitt, respected citizen of the village, lived then on the hilltop overlooking the site and had, at certain seasons of the year, an unbroken view down to the post office. Tom Truitt owned a pair of binoculars, much admired by the villagers, which had such powerful lenses that he could walk out on his porch and look through these glasses over the hill to the post office and see whether or not he had any mail in his box, before making the trip down the hill.

Sometime after that, the post office was returned to the same house on Washington Avenue, where Sarah Garrison had once tended the mail, with Mary E. Hayes as postmistress. The office remained here for a number of years, until around 1934, when it was moved across the street to the old C. W. Caine store building. Here was located the North Bend Post Office until 1954, when the new municipal building, on Taylor Avenue, was completed. Mrs. Cordia G. Walters, appointed as acting postmaster following Miss Jessie Dell's quarter of a century of competent service, effeciently dispatched the mails here for several years. Charles "Chick" Lehring only recently, Oct., 1969, succeeded her to the office.

(Directly opposite North Bend in Boone County, Kentucky, stands the historic Cave Johnson plantation home dating from 1796. It is interesting to note that for many years a descendant of Johnson kept a small post office on the farm. It was, humorously, called "Weneda" Post Office, so relates Richard C. Crisler, grandson of the man who kept the post office and present occupant of the historic house. That office ceased to exist with the coming of rural free delivery. Mr. Crisler, in reply to this writer's query as to whether that place was ever called North Bend, Kentucky, stated he had never heard it spoken or seen it written as such.)

Rural free delivery service was launched in this part of the county sometime around 1902. Early rural carriers on the Cleves route, established in 1902, included: Erastus B. Hayes, Anna R. Hayes Yancey, Banning Hopping and Oliver Troxell. North Bend's rural mail delivery service, started in 1905, today, encompasses the region up Shady Lane, over Mt. Nebo and through Dugan Gap, down and around Brower Road, and across Lost Bridge to Elizabethtown, which has not had a post office since 1919. (Elizabethtown had a post office continuously from 1820 until 1919.) The late John Zapf, Jr., carried mail over this rural route for many years. Robert Anderson is today's rural mail carrier.

Along with postal service, telephone service has been an important feature in the life of the community. Telephones were introduced to the region August 31, 1905, with the opening of an exchange located in Cleves. There were then twenty-two subscribers in the area. The site of that first exchange was in the residence of Mina Hearn, on record as the first telephone operator. The house stood on the west side of Miami Avenue, one block south of State Road (now the location of the Highland Center building). This home was later occupied by Jennie Rittenhouse and her daughter, Mina Rittenhouse (Wood), both of whom also served as telephone operators. In February, 1913, facilities were expanded to serve the, then, 163 customers living in the Cleves, North Bend, Miamitown, Valley Junction, Hooven, Taylor's Creek and Elizabethtown communities. The exchange was moved, in 1925, from the Rittenhouse home to the second floor of Bundy's Restaurant, located on Miami Avenue just south of Cleves Avenue. It remained at this location until December, 1951, when the area was converted to the dial telephone system. Mrs. Gertrude Bevens Chris holds the record, 30 years, for having served the longest as telephone operator at the Cleves exchange.

Equally as important to the villagers as the telephone was the coming of electricity. This feature was introduced into the homes of North Bend and Cleves about 1918. Gas lamps were replaced by electric street lights.

Today, we are inclined to take for granted our marvelous postal, telephone and electric service, forgetting that our forefathers had none of these.

Back around 1960, a new highway, by-passing the villages of Addyston, North Bend and Cleves, was completed. It became the Three Rivers Parkway. A number of longtime residents of the towns along the route of the new thoroughfare were forced to vacate their homes, in order to clear a path for Progress. New approaches leading to Harrison's Tomb and Brower Road were also constructed.

Around 1959, there was a study and discussion among businessmen and village officials of Addyston, Cleves and North Bend concerning the possibility of merging these towns of Miami Township into a new city. Although the case for consolidation presented distinct advantages such as combined water, sewage and police service, the paper city failed to emerge. Each village yet operates alone, but not without the cooperation of one another.

What a glorious heritage is North Bend's! Howard Morris, a man concerned with holding fast to North Bend's heritage, is now mayor. In a recent statement to The Cincinnati Enquirer, Mayor Morris said that his goal was "to see the village a better place to live."

This nation was founded and the Miami country settled by men who had a clear purpose, a common goal, that of a better way of life. Since North Bend was charted back in 1789, and platted in 1868, much has transpired within her borders. Countless persons have come and gone, making notable contributions along the way. Progress has been made. But the chief goal, then as now, that of making the town a better place to live, the world a better place to live, has not changed. It is the highest aim that man can set forth, the only compass that will keep him on course. We must hold fast to this heritage!

As John Scott Harrison stated, to the newly organized Miami and Whitewater Pioneer Association, back on Sept. 8, 1866:

"We should not forget the service of the brave men who macadamized with their blood the highway to this land of 'milk and honey.' It is our duty to preserve the good name and fame of these worthy ancestors."

****

North Bend village officials in 1912: Mayor, T.F. Mahoney; Clerk, Edw. Hearn; Treasurer, Thos. A. Gleason; Marshal, Wm. Weirman; Councilmen, Frank Franz, John Geier, Dennis Gleason, John Dell, George Chris and Patrick Burns.

****

Enquirer, June 29, 1931. Gulf Refinery: "The huge refinery of Gulf Oil Co. is nearing completion at Hooven, near Cleves. In connection with the refinery there is being built a river transfer station at North Bend. The plant includes stills, cracking plants, 128 large storage tanks for gasoline and other oil products."

Gulf's river terminal at North Bend was installed for the purpose of supplying gasoline, with a fleet of tank barges, to towns along the Ohio and Kanawha Rivers. (This action was responsible for bringing this writer's father, Capt. Vernon K. Byrnside, with the Campbell Line steamer "FAIRPLAY", to settle at North Bend.) Establishment of the refinery also caused an influx of many families of Gulf employees from Texas and Louisiana to take up residence in the general locale.

Chapter 18

INDIAN CREEK

Indian Creek, for over a century and a half, played a unique role in the history of the North Bend community. This creek, at one time a sizeable stream, flowed down through the farm of General Harrison, where it emptied into the Ohio. A bridge spanned the creek near its mouth.

Among Harrison papers at the CHS Library is a memorandum of William H. Harrison, dated Nov. 13, 1830, stating that L. and A. Bump had worked on the bridge at the mouth of Indian Creek. Lawson and Ansel Bump had settled in Miami Township around old Fort Finney as early as 1820, possibly sooner.

On Indian Creek General Harrison erected a large stone mill. Judge Symmes, himself, had operated a grist mill on the site, so legend tells, in the earliest years of settlement. Up the creek the General is said to have built a dam, the water of which was used to turn the wheels of a woolcarding mill*, believed to have been among the first in this part of the country.

(*A document found at the CHS Library indicates that Harrison very possibly operated a woolcarding mill, in view of the fact that he and a group of Cincinnati men entered into a seven year contract in 1814, "as co-partners for the improvement and increase of a stock of American and Merino sheep." The experiment was to be conducted on the Harrison lands. Boundaries of the land in the North Bend and Cleves region were stipulated and agreements with the tenants of the various tracts stated in the document. Persons and places named in this contract included: Congress Green, Bellamy--a shoemaker, the grave yard pasture, Bingle's field, Barnabas Strong, Hutchinson's Mill, the place called "the burnt chimnies," State Road, Moke, Indian Creek, Cooper's Tavern, Ebenezer Tutle, Stephen Wood, Goodrich, Thomas and Logan's field. The partners in the company were given "the right of way to and from the sheep fold through the tract called Congress Green, herein before reserved, and also a right of way from the road crossing Indian Creek to the house formerly occupied by Thomas.")

(Author's note: The place called "the burnt chimnies" was undoubtedly the site of Judge Symmes' home which had burned in 1811. Legend tells that his mansion was called The Chimneys. The home stood near the intersection of the present Mt. Nebo Road and Symmes Street in Cleves.)

The waters for operating the woolcarding mill were also harnessed to turn the wheels of the Harrison grist mill. When water levels permitted, barges of grain were pulled from the Ohio up Indian Creek to the mill. Legend also tells that it was here General Harrison made gin or cider.

In another document among the Harrison papers at CHS Library, dated during the summer of 1828, Wm. H. Harrison stated that:

"Mr. Henderson will be down to see about the mill race but he has no instrument to level the race; Mr. Hodge can do it very well with a common water level."

When Dr. John Warder later bought the tract of farm land through which Indian Creek flowed, he hauled the old Harrison millstone up to his new home site. That millstone may be seen, today, lying along the driveway of the Perkins home. As late as 1900, a great portion of the old mill walls, built entirely of stone taken from the bed of Indian Creek, were yet standing. Some of the window frames and casings, put together with wooden pegs, could yet be seen. That spot was long the favorite swimming hole and haunt of the local lads.

A sketch of the wreck of the old mill appeared in the Cincinnati Commercial Gazette, May 13, 1894, with the following by-lines:

"The cider-mill, whose product played a conspicuous part in the Presidential election of General Harrison, is now one of the most picturesque ruins in Hamilton County and undoubtedly its history is more familiar than any similar relic of the first half of the century surviving in the county."

Some time after 1860, the waters and pond of Indian Creek were put to still another use. A dam was built and an ice cutting business was established which grew, through the years, into an immense operation. In early days it was known as Reynolds Ice Company, owned and operated by some of the family of Lucy Este Reynolds, granddaughter of General Harrison. Crystal Lake was the name given to the pond. Later, when the business changed to a Cincinnati based operation, it became known as Stone Lake Ice Company. Still later, in 1895, the business was renamed Silver Lake Ice Company.

Items from the Lawrenceburg Press tell of North Bend's early ice business:

May 24, 1877: "The ice pond struck a leak causing Mr. Reynolds, the owner, considerable uneasiness, compelling him to draw off water in order to repair it. It was a beautiful lake and will take time to refill it."
Jan. 10, 1878: "Reynolds, the North Bend ice man, is shipping ice to the city."
April 4, 1878: "No ice stands in Reynolds ice house on Crystal Lake this summer."

Two large ice houses, three stories high, were built near to the railroad tracks. Behind what is now North Bend United Methodist (E. U. B.) Church stood the horse-power house. During cold winter months ice in great blocks was cut with a saw-like plow and floated to shore. From there it was pulled to the insulated ice houses, where it was packed between layers of straw, to retard melting. In this manner ice could be kept until the heat of summer. How early this business started has not been learned. However, in his diary of June, 1867, David Rittenhouse noted that he had gone to Cleves for ice and that his sister, Susan, had made ice cream. Another news item of Dec. 26, 1872, stated: "Denizens are engaged in putting up ice, now of the best quality."

Ice, frozen from Indian Creek waters, was peddled by horse and cart to the surrounding neighborhoods. Train cars carried it great distances beyond North Bend. For many years G. W. Chambers was superintendent of Stone Lake Ice Company. It is safe to say that countless wooden ice cream freezers, packed with ice from Crystal Lake--and later Stone Lake, were cranked by enthusiastic young hands at the then popular church socials.

There are some folks who best remember Indian Creek, not for ice making, but for ice skating. A small pond, or "nook," was always reserved for skaters. The bigger pond was in this way kept clear of persons who might otherwise contaminate the ice with tobacco juice or other foreign debris.

In early days, so it seems, everyone--young and old--loved to skate. To quote the older generation, "Winters were colder in those days and there were greater opportunities for skating and sleigh riding." When conditions permitted, teachers often dismissed school early so that pupils could go skating. Edna Truitt Hayes was one teacher who enjoyed ice skating as much as did her scholars. She recalls skating, as well as tobogganing, with her pupils while teaching at Berea and Locust Grove (Bond Road) Schools in Whitewater Township, 1901 to 1907.

Fishing was an equally popular sport. The following item, supporting this claim, was gleaned from the Cincinnati Commercial Gazette, May 21, 1894:

"A gay fishing party took possession of Stone Lake ice pond. A number of young ladies and men of the community were present."

In the early 1900's, Edward Sullivan developed the pond into a larger fishing lake and eventually built a tavern and dining spot along the eastern bank. Later, during the early 1920's, the lake was drained and a ball field laid on the grounds. From earliest days there had existed a strong rivalry between the baseball clubs of North Bend and Cleves, and throngs turned out at the site of the old skating and fishing pond to cheer the players on to victory. It is interesting to note that as early as 1869, Cleves had a ball team called the "Blue Stockings." In the late 1920's, Chester Argo acquired the property from the Sullivans and once again set up a fine fishing resort, naming it Lake Edward. (The stout timbers from the dismantled grandstand that had stood at the old ball park were put to use in the foundation of John Bonham's barn on Mt. Nebo, now the Vernon Byrnside property.)

John S. Conner School, the oldest section of which was built in 1877, on what is said to have been General Harrison's stable, overlooked Indian Creek and Crystal Lake-- and still later Lake Edward. The water was frequently shallow but ofttimes dangerously deep. The sermon "Don't go near the pond" was preached with regularity to all North Bend pupils. Even so, there were--and are yet--many who could tell a humorous tale of how they had played hooky and gone skating or fishing on the pond.

LaFreda Cady Arnold tells that children were instructed to go directly home after school and get permission before returning to the skating pond. Ignoring the rule, in order to save time, she and one of her pals hid their ice skates outside in the school toilet (the convenience of that day) and hurried down to the pond when class was dismissed. And, who should catch them but their favorite teacher, Stella Heintz! Miss Heintz's disapproval was worse than the paddling she inflicted.

In addition to the many pleasant and humorous memories concerning the pond, there is one which will be recalled with sadness. A tragedy took place at the lake a week before Christmas in 1938. Two little Hayes brothers drowned when the sled on which they were riding broke through thin ice. It was a sad Christmas for the North Bend community.

Today all evidence of Indian Creek's historic past has been swept away. In the interest of progress, the construction of the new super-highway, Route 50, as well as flood control, the lake was drained about 1960. Scenes of water wheels turning, corn grinding, ice cutting, skating and fishing are only memories. The stream, by yesterday's standards, flows in a mere trickle.

★★★★★★★★★★

North Bend's "Black-eyed Dulcinea" Identified

At the Aug. 3, 1872 gathering of the Miami and Whitewater Valley Pioneer Association, S.S. L'Hommedieu, a former president of Cincinnati Pioneer Association, identified the lady whose sparkling eyes had caused the substitution of Cincinnati for North Bend as Queen City of the West. The lady, then in 1872, was alive and nearing her 90th year. She was Mrs. Strong, widow of Major, then in 1789 captain, Strong. L'Hommedieu noted that she made annual visits to the home of Cincinnati pioneer Reese E. Price, where he had seen her, and he assured the audience that her eyes sparkled still. (See Cincinnati Commercial, Aug. 4, 1872)
*Author's Note: This revelation is interesting but the age given for the lady makes the story doubtful.

★★★★★★★★★★★★★★★★★★★★★★★★

Miami Township Officials

Apr. 10, 1879: (Cincinnati Daily Gazette)
Trustees: Caleb Flinchpaugh, Dem.; Jos. Garrison, Dem.; Fred Stumpp, Rep.; Treasurer: C. A. Wood, Dem.; Clerk: John Hamilton, Ind.; Assessor: Jesse Herron, Dem.; Constables: John Peace: Jas. Carlin, Dem.; A.R. Lind, Rep.; Constables: John Balzer, Dem.; Eli Moak, Greenback; Peter Cooper, Dem.
1887 Election:
Trustees: Peter Minges, J.C. Hearn, Thos. Guard; Clerk: Phil Zondler; Treasurer: Chris Riehle; Constables: C.C. Runyan and U.N. Moak.
1902 Trustees:
Thos. A. Gleason, John Begley and Wm. Harrell. Thos. Truitt was a notary public.
Miami Township population in 1880 was 2,317.

The elegant Short Homestead once stood on grounds now occupied by Monsanto Company, at Addyston. The house was built by Judge John C. Short for his bride, Betsy, the daughter of Wm. H. Harrison.

Chapter 19

Short's Station, Sekiton And Addyston

The present village of Addyston comprises what once were the sites called Sekitan, Coal City and Short's Station. Until 1891, this region was part of the wide corporation of North Bend. The coming of the railroads in the 1850's and 1860's stimulated the growth of the area. The Cincinnati and Whitewater Canal had passed through here.

Coal City came into being after a large coal elevator was located there. Coal towed by barge from West Virginia and Pennsylvania mines was unloaded at this terminal point for distribution by local dealers or transferred to railroad cars and shipped westward.

Sekitan, the name given to the settlement adjoining Coal City on the west, was a Japanese word meaning "coal." However, Harry C. Dick, who lived there as a lad and attended Burr Oak School, recalls that Sekitan was an Indian word translated to mean "woods and water." (This writer was unable to find the word recorded among glossaries of Indian tribes. However, the word "Sakiegan," meaning "lake" in Chippewa dialect, is found in Indian trader John Long's Journal, 1768-1782.) Sekitan was the post office address for Coal City.

A tract of land lying between General Harrison's place and Muddy Creek, in the Sekitan region, was owned, in early days, by Judge James Silver (1766-1822). James Silver had come to the North Bend settlement with Judge Symmes and had married the latter's niece, Elizabeth "Betsy" Thompson, on June 12, 1798. Silver family tradition states that "Betsy," the judge's niece, rode to North Bend from New Jersey by horseback. There she met James Silver, then a judge in Hamilton County Court. They were wed at the home of William H. Harrison, Anna Harrison being a cousin of the bride. James Silver served three consecutive terms as associate judge, expiring during his third term. His widow, Elizabeth Silver (1777-1849), resided in the area later called Sekitan. The creek running through the property was known as Silver's Creek. When Addyston was founded, the road called Silver Creek Road was officially recorded, 1889, and named for the Silver family. Several references to the Silvers are found among letters of John Cleves Symmes. Some members of this pioneer family were buried at Congress Green Cemetery.

During the Civil War era, this area had two railroad stops, Devin's Station and Short's Station. The former was on the property of Amanda B. Devin, a Harrison family connection, whose son, Augustus Devin, figured in the horrible grave robberies at Congress Green Cemetery in May, 1878. Short's Station stood near "Short Hill," (sometimes written "Shorthill"), the stately residence of Judge John Cleves Short along the Ohio.

John Cleves Short, son of Peyton and Maria Symmes Short, was a grandson of Judge Symmes. He married his first cousin, Betsy Bassett Harrison, daughter of William H. and Anna Symmes Harrison, and built, in 1817, a fine home in the eastern end of the North Bend settlement, near the mouth of Muddy Creek. The home, which stood on land given to Betsy Short by her father, was called "Short Hill," after the ancestral home in the East. It came to be regarded as the most elegant home ever built in Miami Township. (Author's note: The Harding-Young house and the Warder place must also be mentioned in this category of the most elegant.)

In an account "River-Shore Tramps" by John Uri Lloyd, taken from John James Piatt's Hesperian Tree, is the following tale, recalled by an old Boone County resident:

"At Fernbank was the home of Judge Short who owned a power of land and a lot of negroes. He built an outside chimney to his house and left two big holes through opposite sides, which extended into the fireplace. The negroes used to stick logs of wood into the fire from outside the house. A very convenient chimney."

John Cleves Short studied law in the office of Judge Burnet. He entered public life, was elected judge of the Common Pleas Court of Hamilton County in 1820, and later served in the state legislature.

As the years passed, Judge Short came into such a position that he was able to acquire more and more land. He took over much of the farmlands formerly held by General Harrison and members of his family. (The Harrison heirs turned over land to him for much needed cash, feeling that they were keeping it in the family.) After Betsy Short died in 1846, Judge Short married, in 1849, Mary Ann Goodrich Mitchell, a widow with one son, William C. Mitchell. By this marriage were two sons, John Cleves, born 1850, and Charles Wilkins, born 1851.

It is interesting to note that Jeremiah Goodrich and his wife, Milcha, parents of Mary Ann Short, were early settlers in the North Bend community as early as 1814. The family lived in the region east of the Harrison homestead, along the river, not far from what is now the foot of Shady Lane. (Griffith-Burdge family papers, courtesy of Mrs. Ella B. Walker.) Among Harrison papers at CHS Library is a memorandum showing that land was conveyed by John Cleves Short to Jeremiah Goodrich in 1823.

A study of old letters and maps reveals the extent of Judge Short's land acquisitions, much of which was formerly held by the Harrisons. Certain tracts Short and his brother and sister had inherited as their share of their grandfather Symmes' estate. Sections of the lands were owned--for a time--by his brother, Dr. Charles W. Short, and his sister, Anna Maria Short Dudley, who had wed the eminent surgeon and teacher at Transylvania College, Dr. Benjamin W. Dudley. These families resided in the vicinity of Lexington, Ky., and Judge Short, so it appears, looked after and sold their lands for them.

Until around 1855, a great tract upstream from the John Scott Harrison place, embracing the River Road, Dugan Gap and Cliff Road area--along and overlooking the Ohio--where the Guards, Fagalys and Yanneys later had farms, was in the name of Benjamin W. Dudley. A record among Harrison papers at CHS Library, dated 1825, states that Gen. Harrison asked John C. Short to secure permission of Dr. Dudley, on behalf of a group of men, to be allowed to cut timber from his land for use in building a steamboat below the Bend. A map of 1855 shows that Dudley also owned, at least for a time, a parcel of the former Harrison estate in what is now Cleves, at the foot of Mt. Nebo Road and Miami Avenue, where Kroger's Store now stands. On this site, in early days, was a large spring, known for miles around as "Cold Spring." Legend tells that in dry seasons settlers from far and near came here for water. A cottage, which came to be known as "Cold Spring House," stood near the spring. This house, as recalled by Mrs. Alice Argo Struble, was yet there in 1900.

According to the map of 1847, Dr. Charles Wilkins Short, brother of Judge Short, owned a tract along the Ohio east of "Short Hill," across Muddy Creek. A residence stood on the site in that year and this building is believed to be the same brick house, now painted white, standing on this location near River Road, today, behind the lumber company. It is generally accepted that Judge John C. Short built this home. Legend says that the house was never completed, that the original plans called for wings to be added. A former resident of Fernbank, a Mr. Bailey--now deceased, is said to have once seen (or had in his possession) the old plans of the house. (This information was from Mrs. Mabel Herbert of Fernbank.) Who first lived in the place and why it was unfinished remains a mystery. This home is among the oldest yet standing in the entire region. Maps dated after 1847 show the land to have been part of the John C. Short estate. It was possibly occupied by tenants on his place.

(This writer, in an effort to learn the identity of the builder of the house in question, contacted a descendant of Dr. Charles W. Short. The lady, a granddaughter of Dr. Short, was familiar with her family history but knew nothing of the old home.)

Near this old mystery house, on the same lot, was a cottage which, legend tells, served as the Short's private chapel back in the days before a church existed. The original part of this cottage is yet standing next to the Fernbank Lumber Company. It would not be recognized as a former chapel for it has undergone much change in its basic structure through the years. Since Fernbank Church was built in 1877, this chapel would have existed earlier. The 1870 U.S. Census reveals that two preachers, C. T. Crum and T. W. Sanders, resided in the Short home with Mrs. Short and her sons.

At the time of Judge John C. Short's death at "Short Hill" in March, 1864, less than two weeks after the death of his aunt Anna Symmes Harrison, the Short property included 2200 acres of farmland and orchards lying around Muddy Creek, North Bend and The Point, much of which was leased or rented. His estate also included an extensive library totaling 2,741 items of books and paintings.

Dr. John H. F. Thornton, resident of Cleves, whose wife was Mary Harrison (1808-1842), sister of Betsy Short, was appointed executor of the Short estate. Edward Woodruff, Probate Judge who handled the Short affairs, very soon afterward acquired the Anna Harrison farm and platted the village of North Bend.

Judge Short's widow, Mary Ann Short, died in 1871, and his older son and namesake, John Cleves Short, unmarried, died May 4, 1880. In hopes of finding more about the "mystery house," this writer searched death records on John Short, Jr. His death date was learned from Spring Grove Cemetery. Cincinnati newspapers, Daily Gazette and Commercial, found at CHS Library, revealed the following facts:

Young John C. Short died by his own hand, of poisoning, 1/2 mile from the family residence in the house used as the Short brothers' office. Other persons named Newbrough were dwelling in another part of the house when the tragedy occurred. Near neighbors were Col. Skinner, John Long, Mr. Magnus and J. F. Thornton, a relative who had charge of much of the Short estate. Drs. John Campbell and John M. MacKenzie of Delhi were summoned to the scene. Short, then only thirty years old, was an extremely sensitive, painfully shy, melancholy and quiet person. Illness in childhood had left him nervous and largely dependent on his mother and younger brother. He was 6 1/2 feet tall and was playfully called "Long" Short. Jesters knew not what anguish this caused him. His physical development made him feel out of place in society. Life became a burden. Being the older of the brothers, John was willed, by Judge Short, the homestead, "Short Hill," but due to his infirmities its management was left almost entirely to Charles. The brothers acted as one; they maintained an office together in the city, boarded the train together daily at Short's Station, and resided together. (Charles, wed to Mary Dudley in 1872, had several children.) Possessions of each were estimated at over a million dollars. John had contributed bountifully along with Charles in building, in 1877, the beautiful Episcopal Church in Fernbank, in memory of their parents; however, it was decided to have "that last sweet and solemn farewell" pronounced at the old family residence. He was interred in the family burial ground, in sight of the homestead. Pallbearers included: George Eaton, H. W. Woodruff, Dr. Louis Worthington and R. H. Warder.

The Short brothers owned the St. James Hotel in the city and held considerable stock in the CCC&St.L Railroad and were tie agents for the railroad. Charles was educated as a lawyer and dealt in real estate. He operated several businesses including the Southern Ohio Brick and Tile Company at Coal City. It was he who laid out the village of Fernbank in the 1870's, a part of which lay in Miami Township.

Near neighbors of the Shorts at the Fernbank settlement and Short's Station in 1880 included: J. F. Thornton and P. L. Dudley, both Short family connections; Wm. Newbrough; Sara Vanblaricum; N. E. VanTyne, life insurance agent; Wm. A. White and John Long, railroad clerks; Thomas Green; Col. Fred Skinner, correspondent for a newspaper; C. F. Vent, book publisher; Edw. P. Wilson, railroad freight agent; and George E. Whiting, organist at Music Hall.

(At this point it is interesting to tell of George E. Whiting who figured in Cincinnati's early music history. It happened that in 1877, a remarkably fine organ was built for the new Music Hall. In January, 1878, George Whiting, a prominent Boston organist and composer, was engaged to play for the May Festival and for a series of concerts. Whiting also was employed as a professor at the College of Music. In May, 1883, after five successful years at the College, a grand farewell concert was tendered for Prof. Whiting at Music Hall, attended by 2500 elite of the city. (Miami Township Census of 1880, George Whiting, 37, organist at Music Hall, Cincinnati, and Helen, 35.) Whiting resided somewhere in this locale for a time.)

Charles W. Short resided at "Short Hill" until around 1887. About that time he built a fine home in Fernbank next to the Episcopal Church. The other Short house, the brick house in question, was sold to Col. Edw. P. Wilson in 1897. Sometime around 1899-1900, the C. W. Shorts left Fernbank, moving to Cincinnati. The March family then occupied his new home next to the church and reside there still.

On the slope behind "Short Hill," near where old Addyston School later was built, was once the early burial ground of the Short family. Some of the gravestones and remains were removed from this site to Spring Grove in 1902; other graves were removed about 1930. One Addyston schoolgirl of the 1920's recalls that she often stayed after class to help the teacher wash the blackboard and clean erasers. The best way to clean the erasers--so the pupils found--was to dust them on the tombstones nearby.

Around this old cemetery and Addyston School, in early days, were remnants of apple trees. A legend grew among the school children which told that "Johnny Appleseed" had planted the trees. While it is possible that John Chapman did plant the apple seeds, it is more likely that these trees were what remained of Judge Short's extensive orchards, referred to in historical accounts.

Also somewhere along the railroad near Short's Station was Short's Grove, a picnic ground which came into being during the 1860's. The I&C Railroad sponsored affairs here, transporting picnickers from all over the city. In his diary of June, 1870, David H. Rittenhouse noted: "The family went to Short's Grove to a Sangerbund." The Cincinnati Daily Gazette of July 9, 1879, recorded that Delhi Methodist

Sunday School would hold a picnic at Mr. Short's grove. This picnic grove may have been located on ground now known as River Park.

(A humorous legend concerning the Short family and a unique source of some of their wealth may be read in the chapter "The West End of Cincinnati," by J. J. Piatt.)

A large part of the Short estate, including the old residence of Judge John C. Short, "Short Hill," was purchased in 1889, by industrialist Matthew Addy.

Matthew Addy had come to Cincinnati from Canada in 1857. At the outbreak of the Civil War, the South, of necessity, began to develop its iron industry. Cincinnati, at the beginning of the war, had many pro-slavery sympathizers and thus was able to carry on a rich trade with the South. Matthew Addy, who had entered the iron business, soon made the city a principal market for southern iron.

The late Harry Hale, in The Cincinnati Enquirer column, "Suburbs of Cincinnati," wrote:

"Addy bought land and established Addyston in 1889, building that year the Addyston Pipe and Steel Company, using iron from Alabama and Tennessee in its output. He named the place after himself, it was Addy's town.

"For many years Addy's plant was the largest one of its kind. A great industrial future was predicted for Addyston and the community bragged that the place would be another Pittsburgh. The eastern corporation line of North Bend was drawn in and part of that much-too-extensive village corporation was added to Addyston."

From "The Commuter" newssheet of June 28, 1890, a paper printed in Home City for the benefit of riders on the commuter trains, was the following item:

"The North Bend board of trustees met at the mayor's office June 23rd, and passed Ordinance No. 237, consenting to the separation of Coal City and Addyston from North Bend, in order that they may incorporate as a village."

Incorporated in 1891, Addyston was a little industrial town of houses built along River Road and the two railroad lines. Frank Nevitt was first mayor; Frank M. Ware, clerk; S. Enos Kelch, treasurer; and Sherman McDaniel, marshal. George W. Benjamin was first postmaster of Addyston in 1889. (Thomas B. Williams was appointed postmaster at Sekitan in 1885. This office was discontinued in 1933.)

Postmasters have included: (Sekitan) Thos. B. Williams, Geo. C. Markland, Henry G. Carr, John J. Maloney, James T. Coghlan, John M. Diller, Jos. M. Shane, Charles L. Kelley, John M. Dick, Earl Cain, Martha A. Jackson.
(Addyston) Geo. W. Benjamin, Albert B. Ryon, Mary W. Cliff, John M. Fury, Walter J. Fury, Raymond Richards, Ross E. Benter and Orpha Geeding.

Coal City, Sekitan and Short's Station had a population, in 1887, of about 500. Almost overnight the number soared, reaching 2,000 by 1891. Then, the new Addyston Pipe and Steel Company employed 1,000 workmen.

Occupations and businessmen of Addyston and Sekitan during the 1887-1893 era included:

Bakery, Charles A. Honaker; Barbers, John T. Johnson, Louis Bookwalt, Silas Hawkins, Pritchard Cinnamon; Basket Maker, Martin Eckstein; Blacksmiths, Harvey Dick, John Thompson; Boarding Houses, Ella Pierson, Rebecca Currier, Frank Lohrer, Amanda Devin, Charles Seitz; Boots and Shoes, Christ Blum, Brick Company, C. W. Short, President; Bricklayer, Page Sortwell; Cooper, Andrew Lipps; Confectioner and Billiards, H. G. Carr; Dairy, Louis Myers; Dress Makers, Julia and Kate Maurer; General Store, A. B. Ryan, Schroyer Bros., J. M. Diller, C. W. McFee, Thomas B. Williams; Grocers, Mathias Blank, Joseph Maurer, Nathan Hazen, J. W. Davis, C. S. Long; Hotel, Palace Hotel; Painter, John England; Pattern Maker, H. C. Lambert; Pharmacist, C. A. Brooks; Physician, F. I. Black, (J. B. Hanna, ca. 1900); Saloons, Louis Kohus, Frank and Wm. Blank, Samuel Bowman, John Kyle; Saw Mill Sawyer, W. S. Wycoff; Stone Mason, Charles Seitz; Wagon Maker & Blacksmith, E. F. Kelch; Wooden Shoe Maker, Lambert Dues.

Many residents of Addyston and Fernbank were employed in some way at the Pipe Foundry. Others were occupied at the coal yards and elevators or engaged in farming. William Shane and sons, whose address was given as Short's Station, farmed.

Burkhardt Schmaltz, a brick burner in 1891, was a veteran of the Civil War. He had the distinction of living to be the oldest soldier of the G. A. R. in Miami Township. Every Decoration Day he went to Maple Grove Cemetery and participated in memorial services. He came to be recognized by hundreds of Miami Township school children who annually marched through Cleves to the cemetery. Burkhardt Schmaltz kept his zest for life until his death in November, 1946.

During the period of Addyston's founding several churches were organized, including the Methodist, St. Andrew's Episcopal and Baptist Churches, both white and colored congregations.

The Methodist Church was established on River Road in 1888. While the church was being built, Sabbath School was conducted on Sunday afternoons in the old Burr Oak School. Pastor in 1891, was Rev. George Easton.

The First Baptist Church (Colored), organized in 1889, was located on River Road. This church, like the other three churches of Addyston, continues to this day.

The Addyston Baptist Church met for a time as a Sunday School in the old Burr Oak School. In 1899, this church was officially organized. The first chapel was located along River Road, west of the present council hall, and served as the church until about 1927. A Baptist Church was built in 1928, near the first Addyston school. This building was again replaced in 1966, by a larger house of worship.

St. Andrew's Episcopal Church was established Sept. 2, 1889, officially named Dec. 12, 1890, and the parish house built in 1891. This church was associated as a parochial mission of the Fernbank Church of the Resurrection. Misses Kige and Beeson were early deaconesses. (St. Andrew's now functions as a diocese mission and is independent of the Fernbank Church.) During the depression years, the Lower River Nursing Association was established by the Episcopal Diocese with a clinic at St. Andrew's Parish House. The late Eleanor Tromey served the Addyston and Lower River community as a visiting nurse for 28 years, retiring in 1952. Three years before her retirement she had the distinction of being elected first woman member of Addyston village council. The Lower River Nursing Association, still housed at St. Andrew's, is now a member of the United Appeal agencies. Back in the days when the church was first built, the road running past it was called Plank Road. Beautiful oak trees lined the street to the outskirt of the village.

(*Just beyond Addyston along Plank Road and around the intersection of Old Hillside Avenue was once a platted settlement, according to maps of the 1840-1860 era, called Ervina. The place lay where the borders of Miami, Green and Delhi Townships meet. Efforts to learn more of Ervina have been fruitless. No mention of it has been found other than on old maps. Is there a reader who knows something of Ervina?)

Back in the early 1890's, Norwood, Ohio, celebrated the laying of its first water mains. In the dedication program booklet, honoring that event, was an advertisement which stated that the Addyston Pipe Foundry had furnished the cast-iron pipe for the Norwood job. In those days Addyston Foundry supplied most of the pipe used for water and gas mains in this section of the country. The huge foundry made pipe in sizes from 4 to 74 inches in diameter.

Sometime in 1898, a flag raising ceremony took place at the Addyston Foundry. The "Girls' Brigade," a drill team from North Bend Village School, directed by Hallie Stephens Caine, was invited to take part in the program. As a special treat the group was afterwards taken to the "Lagoon," an amusement park at Ludlow, Kentucky. The drill team returned to North Bend aboard the Str. LEVI J. WORKUM, a packet boat that plied between Petersburg, Ky., and Cincinnati, picking up stock and produce at landings enroute. The WORKUM was owned by the Freiburg and Workum Distillery at Petersburg and was used chiefly to haul their product. She carried a whiskey barrel between her smokestacks as her trademark. The "Girls' Brigade" was photographed aboard the WORKUM as she landed at North Bend. Mrs. Edna Truitt Hayes, a schoolgirl member of that 1898 drill team which performed at Addyston Pipe Foundry, has a copy of the picture.

The Steamer Levi J. Workum, packet boat, landing at the "Lagoon" Amusement Park at Ludlow, Ky. On top deck is seen the "Girls' Brigade" Drill Team from North Bend Village School, with their leader, Hallie Stephens Caine. 1898. (Ferry boat in foreground.)

During the early 1900's, when business at the foundry was booming, school lunch hours lasted for an hour and 45 minutes. Sylvia Whitney Stephens, Addyston teacher from 1906 to 1911, recalls that the reason for this was to allow pupils time enough to carry dinner pails to their menfolk at the foundry. The entire village virtually revolved around the work at the pipe company.

At a gathering in Elizabethtown in September, 1925, J. Oury Tebow of U.S. Cast Iron Pipe and Steel Company spoke of the improvements his company was doing for the village of Addyston, which included a new road and railway depot.

The old residence of Judge Short, and later C. W. Short, continued to be used as an office building for as long as Addyston Pipe Foundry was in operation. The plant eventually closed down and the property lay idle for some time. In 1951, Monsanto Chemical Company purchased the foundry and developed it into what is now a giant plastic manufacturing concern.

It is interesting to note that James Albert Green, close friend of Matthew Addy--the man who founded Addyston, an employee in the pig iron brokerage business of the Matthew Addy Company, wrote the book William Henry Harrison: His Life and Times. This volume was published in 1941, the 100th anniversary of the Inauguration and death of General Harrison.

A road bearing one of the most curious-sounding names in Hamilton County leads into Addyston. It is Fiddlers Green, which begins at Bridgetown Road and runs until it becomes First Street at Addyston's corporation limit on the north. Several legends exist as to the name's origin. A "ghost-fiddler" is said to have once played his wild and eerie strains over the greens of Delhi and Green Townships. Somehow the fabled fiddler was associated with a mysterious green light that was said to have glowed on certain nights from the little cemetery adjacent to Mt. St. Joseph grounds. Henry Darby, buried in that pioneer graveyard, is reputed to have been the legendary fiddler. (The first Henry Darby came to Ohio in 1818, says Miss Alice Darby of Sayler Park, whose ancestors, the Greens, Mayhews and Darbys, all settled in the Delhi Township area. Delhi Township Census of 1820 lists Henry Darby. Alice Darby knows nothing of the legend.) Cecil Hale, radio personality and member of Mt. St. Joseph College faculty, wrote and staged, in 1963, a play, "The Legend of Fiddler's Green," based on the fact and fantasy surrounding the myth of the "ghost-fiddler." For many years, the name of this road, inspired by a legend, reached by passing through Addyston, has provoked interest and curiousity.

Addyston, like North Bend and Cleves, took on a new look when the new highway, Route 50, skirting the town, was built. Upon its completion, avenues leading to the new roadway were named in honor of five former mayors. These were: Al Dinning, James Grigsby, William Gray, Frank Baker and Perry Stoneking.

Addyston, like many other small villages of today, is losing population annually due to inadequate housing. The population now totals 1306. Officials of the town are coordinating their efforts toward bringing about some program that would draw people into the community. A doctor and drug store are badly needed. The slopes and hilltop areas have excellent Ohio River views and could be developed into desirable residential sites.

Mayor of Addyston today is John Calvert. He recently stated: "If my four years as mayor accomplish nothing else, I want to bring more housing to this community."

Village council meetings continue to be conducted in the old town hall, which was once old Burr Oak School. The hall of today, however, bears little resemblance to the school or council chamber of yesteryear; it is a thoroughly modern building.

Something of the history of Addyston's schools must be told. Let's look back again to a hundred years ago, when Burr Oak School was young.

Chapter 20

BURR OAK AND ADDYSTON SCHOOLS

By 1870, a schoolhouse stood in the region of what became known as Sekitan, not far from the early day residence of Elizabeth Silver. This was called Burr Oak School. Burr Oak School at Sekitan must not be confused with Burr School at Zion. The latter was named for the Burr family, early settlers in that region.

Burr Oak School originally had 2 rooms in the basement level, facing out toward the creek, and 2 rooms above. In later years when the building was converted to the Addyston council hall, two more rooms were added, making it a 3 storied building. After the village of North Bend was laid out in 1868, but before a school was established there in 1875, some boys and girls attended classes at Burr Oak.

Known teachers and principals of the 1880-1895 era at Burr Oak and Addyston included: Granville Beckwith, Eva Kirgan, John A. Heizer, William S. Lanthorn, Miss Faust, and Virgil Henderson. These were all teachers of Harry C. Dick, now of Cleves.

The first Addyston School, a red brick building, was opened about 1892. At that time Burr Oak School was closed. Several years later, however, when the foundry was booming, an overflow of students at the new school caused Burr Oak to be reopened and used for 6 or 8 more years. Teachers at Burr Oak during that period of reopening included: Arthur E. Moak, Bertha Brater and Edith Suit (Young). There were no doubt many others.

Teachers known to have taught at Addyston during the 1900-1905 period were: Virgil Henderson, A. E. Moak, Anna Marie Brawley, Charles B. Bonham, George P. Wood, Alice L. Bell, Edna Truitt (Hayes), Bertha Brater, Hattie Carl, Miss Bennett, Miss Avey, Nellie Gregg, Sylvia Whitney (Stephens), Charles T. Young, Edith Suit (Young), Cora Wiles (Flowers), Christine Breining and Royal S. Hayes. There were undoubtedly others whose names have not been learned.

Virgil Henderson came to Addyston as a teacher in 1893, and with the exception of a few years around 1896-1898, when he taught at Burr (Zion-Miami Heights) School, he remained close to 25 years. After that time he assumed the principalship of Boys' Special School in Cincinnati, a school for wayward boys, where he also served for nearly 25 years. Virgil Henderson was highly respected as a teacher. Bertha Brater, Edna Truitt Hayes, Charles T. Young and Sylvia Whitney Stephens, all of whom became lifetime teachers, secured their first teaching experiences under Schoolmaster Henderson. A mark of Virgil Henderson's success at handling delinquent boys was that in the years after his retirement he was continually visited and remembered by his former students.

Addyston School's first commencement class in 1900 included three boys: Frank Dick, Austin Conley and Alfred Richards.

The class of 1901 had seven graduates. They were: Mabel Fanny Williams (Hayhurst), Virginia A. Schroyer, Bessie B. Kyle, Rebecca Gately, Everett E. Hayhurst, Thomas A. Nixon and Oscar Brater. Fanny Hayhurst recalls well her 8th grade commencement. Each of the four girl graduates was surprised with a bouquet of flowers from their teacher, Charles B. Bonham, a thrill never to be forgotten by the young ladies. (Charles Bonham, older brother of the late John B. Bonham of Mount Nebo, was an extremely promising young man, college-educated, who died in early life.)

Among later, longtime Addyston teachers were: George P. Wood, Sewell G. Chance, Cora Wiles Flowers and Bertha Butler.

The old red brick schoolhouse was in use until about 1938. A new school building was under construction when the historic 1937 flood swept into Addyston, submerging the foundation and prolonging the school's completion. This building housed eight grades and continued to do so until about 1960, when the new Three Rivers Junior High School was opened. At that time, 7th, 8th and 9th grade boys and girls from throughout Miami Township were transfered to the new junior high school. Several years before this time, Cleves-North Bend School District had been renamed Three Rivers School District.

Addyston's older scholars began to attend Taylor High School in North Bend in 1926. Prior to that time, students-- those fortunate to do so--attended high school at Home City or Cincinnati. Several went to Union High School which was conducted from about 1920 to 1926 in the John S. Conner School at North Bend.

Meredith Hitchens, a native of Addyston who served for a time as Addyston School principal and also as village mayor, 1952-1956, became superintendent of Three Rivers School District following the death of John Brannon in 1965.

Old Addyston School, opened in 1892, was used until 1937. Virgil Henderson was Principal when this picture was taken in 1903.

★★★★★★★★★★

Early Schools Around Harrison, Ohio

An account of early schools of Harrison was given by James Wiley, April 19, 1866 in Union Press, Lawrenceburg. Wiley stated that his father had settled near Harrison in 1804, and that he knew a part of the customs of the times. Quote: "I will give you our educational facilities. We had a cabin of round logs some 18 by 20 feet, hewed puncheon floor and door of pieces riven out of oak longer than the boards with which the building was covered. This was all well enough but our teachers were far behind our houses. They seldom were advanced in Arithmetic to the Rule of Three, and they had an area of about the size of our Sectional Township to form a Winter School, and two terms was all a boy or girl could have to get a finished education, as it was termed. Now what must be thought by the students of this day (1866) of the characters of men and women of that day and time? It produced men and women who far excelled those of present day in all the real worth in building up a wilderness into a fruitful country."

Chapter 21

NEW LIFE AT THE POINT

By the time of the death of John Scott Harrison in 1878, there was no property left in the family name. Chief landowners around The Point were Charles W. Short and Abram Brower.

Abram Brower, eldest son of Dr. Jeremiah H. and Hannah Mills Brower, was born in 1822 on his father's farm at Elizabethtown near the Whitewater River. His mother was a descendant of the Mills family who had come to The Point from Elizabethtown, New Jersey, about 1790.

As a young lad Abram heard much talk of his ancestors' experiences with the Indians in that region. John R. Mills had come to North Bend as a surveyor for Judge Symmes and was wounded by Indians while out with a surveying party. Records show that he was a tax collector in Hamilton County in 1801. Isaac Mills, Abram's maternal grandfather, was involved in an Indian skirmish near Fort Hill, soon after 1790, where Capt. Hugh Dunn had erected a stockade. Indians had tried to steal Capt. Dunn's horses and destroy the stockade.

(Mills is named in Cist's Cincinnati in 1841, in a news item copied from an early issue of The Western Spy:
April 17, 1802. "An Indian was killed on the Ohio, below the Great Miami, near Isaac Mills' residence."

Isaac Mills had married Hugh Dunn's daughter, Elizabeth--also born in Elizabethtown, New Jersey, and contracted, in 1801, for 100 acres of ground in Whitewater Township, just then opened for settlement. Mills is credited with platting Elizabethtown and naming it for his wife, as well as for the familys' home town in the east. With such an ancestral heritage, young Abram Brower came to love the land around Elizabethtown and The Point.

(Isaac Mills was first postmaster of Elizabethtown, Whitewater Township, when it was established in 1820. The post office carried the name Elizabethtown until Aug. 30, 1867, when it was changed to Riverdale by the P.O. Department in order to avoid confusion caused by the existence of another Elizabethtown in the state. James W. Leek was appointed postmaster of Riverdale. The name, however, never took hold. The townspeople objected vehemently. They submitted petitions signed by persons living all around Ohio and Indiana and were successful in having the name Elizabethtown restored in August, 1871.)

In addition to having such noteworthy ancestors on his mother's side, Abram Brower had equally illustrious forebears on his father's side. Both his father, Jeremiah H. Brower (1797-1866), and his grandfather, Abram Brower (1775-1865), practiced medicine in the Elizabethtown and Lawrenceburg locality and in numerous ways made outstanding contributions to the community. Their accomplishments should be recorded.

Dr. Abram Brower was born in New York and practiced medicine there until 1817, at which time he brought his family west and located in Lawrenceburg. He took pride in the fact that he had cast his first vote for President George Washington, in his second term of office, and had voted in every election thereafter, casting his last ballot for Abraham Lincoln. (Cincinnati Gazette, Oct. 1864) He organized the first Sunday School known in Lawrenceburg in 1819, and, along with Dr. Ezra Ferris, served among its first superintendents. (Union Press, Jan. 1865) At his death in 1865, at the age of 93, Dr. Abram Brower was the oldest physician in Dearborn County.

Jeremiah H. Brower, son of Dr. Abram Brower, who had come to Lawrenceburg with his family in 1817, at about the age of 20, not only achieved prominence as a physician and surgeon, but was an outstanding leader in school, church and community activities at large. Some insight into his character and occupation may be gained from the following items taken from early Lawrenceburg newspapers. They serve to further illustrate to what a heritage our subject, Abram Brower, had been born.

May 18, 1825. NOTICE. Dr. J. H. Brower, having returned from New York, has resumed the practice of his profession in Elizabethtown and the adjacent country. Having furnished himself with a complete assortment of surgical instruments, he is now prepared to attend to the operative part of that branch of the profession and respectfully solicits the patronage of the public. (Indiana Palladium, Lawrenceburgh, May 20, 1825)

June 20, 1832. Dr. J. H. Brower has removed to Lawrenceburgh and offers professional services. (Western Statesman)

Jan. 1833. Dr. J. H. Brower was elected a director of the Lawrenceburgh Library Company. (Western Statesman)

Feb. 8, 1833. NOTICE. Dr. J. H. Brower will attend to the practice of dentistry in all of its various branches. (Western Statesman)

April 19, 1833. SCHOOL NOTICE. Lawrenceburgh School to be opened April 22 in the room over the bank for instruction of pupils in English, geography, composition, mathematics and Latin. References: Thomas Shaw, George H. Dunn and J. H. Brower. (Western Statesman)

May 17, 1833. Dr. J. H. Brower informed the public that there was danger of a cholera epidemic, that several cases existed near the mouth of the Miami. (Western Statesman)

July 26, 1833. Lawrenceburgh High School will meet in the basement of the Presbyterian Church. Parents are invited. Z. Casterline, Principal. J. H. Brower, M.D., trustee. (Western Statesman)

June 27, 1851. Dr. J. H. Brower is president of the organization of Sabbath Schools. Superintendents and teachers will hold a celebration July 4th. The Declaration of Independence will be read, on that occasion, by Col. W.H.H. Taylor of North Bend. The Whitewater Brass Band will play. Dr. Brower is marshal for the day. (June 27 and July 3, 1851, Independent Press)

Jeremiah Brower's name appears again and again, throughout the years, as the attending surgeon at all kinds of accidents, especially railroad accidents. It is evident that he had the interest of mankind in his heart.

Feb. 2, 1865. J. H. Brower is president of the Soldiers' Relief Society. (Union Press)

Aug. 2, 1866. Dr. Jeremiah H. Brower died Aug. 1, 1866, at the age of 69. His voluntary services as a surgeon in the Army was evidently the cause of the long illness and death. (Union Press) (His survivors included a daughter, Martha, and sons, Dr. Isaac, Henry and Abram.)

Abram Brower (1822-1911), who eventually came to acquire great tracts of land in the region of The Point, had attended school in Elizabethtown as a very young lad. His first teacher was Alfred J. Cotton. In the latter's book,

Cotton's Keepsakes, written in 1858 at Dearborn County, Judge Cotton described his pupil as a "promising lad." Cotton also noted that Abram later served, for a time, as clerk in his court in Lawrenceburg.

Abram's mother had died early in his childhood. Dr. J. H. Brower, with his responsibilities as a physician, was unable to completely care for his children and school them at home, so he placed young Abram at Cary's Academy (forerunner of Farmer's College) in College Hill, where the boy boarded and was educated.

Several years later (1832), Dr. Brower moved from Elizabethtown to a home in Lawrenceburg, where his son Abram rejoined him. Henry Ward Beecher, young pastor at Lawrenceburg Presbyterian Church from 1837 to 1839, resided many months in the Brower home. The young minister became a tutor to Abram, which resulted in a strong attachment between the two. This experience formed the basis of Abram's wonderful command of Greek and Latin and his knowledge of the classics.

Shortly thereafter, Abram Brower entered Miami University. Upon completion of his studies and admittance to the bar in 1843, he practiced law in Lawrenceburg in the office of Ezra G. Hayes, where he later became a partner. The two men had known each other as children, having played together at Elizabethtown where Abram's mother's people, the Mills, had lived. Brower served as clerk, for two years, of the Circuit Court of Dearborn County (Independent Press, Aug. 1, 1851), and took part in the Debating Club. In 1854, he moved to Cincinnati, gained admittance to the Ohio bar and engaged in practice there for a half a century.

Brower had married Susan Dunn in Lawrenceburg. After her death he married Josephine P. Craft. The family settled, in 1861, at Riverside in a beautiful home along River Road, a spot especially known in those days for its fashionable residences and scenic view. (This home was razed about 1905 to make way for the Big Four railroad yards.) Three daughters and a son were born to the Browers.

Brower had long been a worker in the Episcopal Church. With Charles W. Short, John S. Conner and the Warder family, he helped to found the Church of the Resurrection at Fernbank, the chapel of which was built in 1877, by Short, as a memorial to his parents, John Cleves and Mary A. Short. Brower served as a warden of the church for 40 years.

About the time when Addyston was being developed, when Charles W. Short, himself, left his stately residence, "Short Hill," and settled in Fernbank, Abram Brower also moved, about 1889, from Riverside to Fernbank. He built an immense home along what was then, Commercial Avenue, facing the railroad and river, several doors west of the Sayler estate, "Forest of Arden," where Arden Station was located. The old Brower residence, extremely Victorian in appearance and embellished with much "gingerbread," is yet standing along River Road, and is now being used as an apartment house. At the time of Brower's move to Fernbank, he and Short, who controlled vast acres of land around The Point and North Bend, were among the largest landholders in the state.

It was sometime after 1850 that Abram Brower began to invest in farmland near his birthplace and in the region of Fort Hill. The country round about, in those days, was also known for good fox hunting. Little by little Brower increased his holdings until his lands embraced 2,000 acres. In 1876, he was listed among the heaviest taxpayers in Miami and Whitewater Townships. As time passed he gave more and more attention to the management of his farms, gradually withdrawing, in a large part, from his law practice. The outdoor life agreed with him. Almost every day he boarded the O.&M. train at Riverside, and later at Fernbank, and rode along the river out to Gravel Pit, the site of old Fort Finney.

Gravel Pit and Fort Hill were early O.&M. Railroad stops along the Ohio between Pike's Landing and the John Scott Harrison place. The former derived the name from the extensive gravel deposit which was opened for the ballasting of the railway tracks in the 1850's. The O.&M. Railroad had bought ground, rich in gravel, from Brower with the agreement that after the company finished using the gravel, the land would revert back to him. Gravel Pit's only claim to fame in history appears to have taken place in September, 1862, during the threatened siege of Cincinnati by Gen. Kirby Smith, when a battalion of "Squirrel Hunters" was ordered there to guard a ford across the Ohio.

An old boarding house, erected sometime when the railroad was being laid, stood for many years near Gravel Pit. Census records of the 1860-1880 era show that many of its occupants were stone workers and railroad laborers. Early owner of the place was Thomas Slammons (or Slemmons). The Bumps, among the earliest settlers at The Point, and the Buckinghams lived closeby. Herman Burke, railroad laborer, also settled here, and his son, Dan, later became section boss of the railroad workers. The O&M (later B&O) operated a tie yard at the site, and Gravel Pit became a kind of colony for railroad work crews. Benjamin Cave, whose descendants yet live around Cleves, resided in the Finney region in those days.

The railroad stop at Gravel Pit was known by this name until sometime about 1888. When it was learned that another place called Gravel Pit existed in Ohio, the name was changed. Someone, probably an official of the railway line, conceived the idea of calling the stop "Brower" for the gentleman who owned the land where the station stood, and who most often was the only regular passenger boarding and deboarding there. For a time the station was called 'Brower," but this displeased Abram Brower. As legend tells, he rode the train down from Fernbank each day to oversee the management of his farms and dairy. As the train approached the station, the conductor lustily called out, "Brower," meaning the name of the stop. Hearing his name being bellowed out through the train disturbed Abram Brower. It seemed to him that the conductor was rudely addressing him. A short time later, the name of the stop was changed, appropriately, to Finney because of its nearness to the site of the old fort.

Upon the death of Abram Brower in 1911, about 700 acres of land around The Point--encompassing Fort Hill and the Harrison home--was put up for sale. Because of the sentiment and history attached to the locality, heirs of Brower stipulated that the ground should not be broken up but must be sold in one tract. In the meantime the family, his three daughters, continued to operate the farmlands under the management of the Henry Winter family, who had been in the employ of Abram Brower for many years and throughout several generations.

Chris Winter had come to the region from near Lawrenceburg before 1870 to work for Brower. His son, Henry, after attending school at Gravel Pit (Finney) soon found himself, likewise, in Brower's employ, farming and dairying. Shortly after his marriage, Henry Winter moved into the sturdy farmhouse earlier occupied by Abram Brower's brother, Henry, who had operated the dairy farm.

(While Abram Brower's brothers, Henry and Isaac, played no important role in the history of The Point, it is interesting to note something of their occupations.

Henry Brower as a young man had gone west to Nevada and California, as did many young fortune and adventure seekers of that day, where he remained until 1867, returning then to Lawrenceburg. Soon after that time he superintended a lead mine in Wisconsin, which was jointly owned by him and Abram in partnership with a white lead company of Cincinnati. (Lawrenceburg Press, Jan. 25, 1872.) In 1872, he married and sometime thereafter brought his bride to the dairy farm at Gravel Pit, where the couple lived in a home built for them by Abram. Henry managed the dairy farm for his brother for about nine years; after that time he once again moved west.

Although little has been learned of the second brother, Dr. Isaac Brower had a most interesting career. He also had gone west to California as a young man. In May, 1852, he journied back to Lawrenceburg to visit with relatives, returning to California by way of the Isthmus several months later. (Independent Press, June 2, 1852; July 28, 1852) Isaac then went to the Fiji Islands where he served as American Consul, not returning to Lawrenceburg again for twenty years. (Lawrenceburg Press, May 9; June 27, 1872.)

Henry Winter later moved his family, about 1898, into the old John Scott Harrison home to look after the place and to manage the Brower lands. Abram Brower always reserved for himself two downstairs rooms of the Harrison home, one for an office and the other for a bedroom--in the event that bad weather kept him from returning by train to Fernbank.

Not far from the Harrison home was another big farmhouse, built in the 1870's by Sanford F. Tuthill, a lumber dealer. Tuthill used the very best of materials in this home. He operated a 100 acre farm and employed many hands. This place was later occupied by the J. A. Angevine family, and still later by Clarence Coleman, who sold it to the Columbia Gas and Electric Company about 1923. After that time this home and farm was rented, the Tekes and Mitchells being among the occupants. That big farmhouse is yet standing. This farm, along with several others bordering closeby, has been under the management of Charles B. Winter ever since Columbia Gas and Electric Company purchased the ground and located its plant near The Point.

Henry Winter's son, Charles Brower Winter, was born in 1887 at Gravel Pit near the site of the railroad tie yard and the future creosoting plant. He was named for the only son of Abram Brower, Charles M. Brower, attorney, who died in 1905, at the age of 36. Young Charles Winter attended school at Finney, never having but a few classmates. His teachers included Morgan Wamsley and Fanny Hayes. Upon completing the 8th grade and passing the Patterson examination, Charles attended, for one year (1905-1906), Miami Township High School, which was conducted at John S. Conner School in North Bend. Oliver Swisher was his teacher. The high school, only operated for three years, was then discontinued. Charles then went to O.M.I. (Ohio Mechanics Institute) in Cincinnati, graduating in 1910.

Charles joined his father in the care of the Brower lands and the historic Harrison home. He became proficient and wise in the area of farm management. In time he also became an authority on the subject of Indian relics, those types found over the legendary grounds where he had tramped and plowed since childhood. His collection of Indian artifacts, today, is among the finest in all the country.

The following item is copied from the Lawrenceburg Press.
Sept. 20, 1911. "Fort Hill. Henry Winter and son, Charles, while excavating at Fort Hill recently uncovered the skeleton of an Indian. A tomahawk and other relics were found beside it."

After marriage, Charles Winter brought his bride to reside in the old Harrison home, the same place where Benjamin Harrison had earlier brought his bride. Here, their daughter was born. Charles, also called "Dick" by intimates, continued to manage the Brower lands. Several years later the family moved into the farmhouse first occupied by Abram Brower's brother, Henry, which overlooked the recently (1917) established creosoting plant. There they live to this day.

It was in 1917 that the Brower sisters sold 30 acres of ground on the broad, flat, lower level bordering the Ohio, along the B&O Southwestern Railroad, for the erection of the plant for creosoting railroad crossties. Close to the new plant, in site of old Fort Finney and the gravel pit, a group of cottages were built to house some of the families, several of them colored, who came to work there. The need for a new road to the region of The Point had--by this time--begun to be sharply felt.

Access to Finney and Fort Hill had never been good by roadway. As late as 1887, the post office address of those residing around Gravel Pit and The Point was given as Lawrenceburg, Indiana. It was easier to reach, or make contact with, Lawrenceburg, via the O&M Railroad Bridge over the Great Miami, than North Bend. Teachers for Finney schools had always been hard to secure because transportation posed such a problem. In addition, several of the old schoolhouses had stood on the lower bank, near the site of old Fort Finney, and were in constant danger of being flooded. For many years the only road from North Bend to The Point was the old River Road, laid out close to the river in the days of John Cleves Symmes, which ran from the mouth of the Miami to the "Meeting House" in Cincinnati. Even after the coming of the railroad, this old pathway was retained below the tracks along the original bank. From North Bend down as far as Dugan Gap (Note: Dugan Gap ran from Mount Nebo down the hill to the river road), River Road was fair as a wagon road in dry weather, but from there to Finney and the Harrison home it was little more than a dusty, deeply rutted, trail, frequently washed out by floods. As early as 1894, possibly sooner, the trustees of Miami Township urged Hamilton County Commissioners to relocate the old River Road, commencing at the southwestern line of the hamlet of North Bend and going to the mouth of the Big Miami, laying it above the railroad tracks. (Cincinnati Commercial Gazette, June 5, July 19, August 18, 1894.)

Time passed and little progress was made on the subject of relocating old River Road. Finally in 1912, grading on a new county road, designated as Brower Road, was begun on a higher level, above the tracks. News items from Lawrenceburg Press tell of this proposed highway:

April 3, 1912. Finney. The proposed pike from North Bend to the Angevine farm and thence to Lost Bridge near E-town is going to be built as rapidly as possible. It is understood that the Hamilton County Commissioners are favorable to a bridge over the Miami and a pike connecting Lawrenceburg with the Hamilton County road. It is stated that the B.&O. Southwestern Railroad wishes to straighten its tracks in front of the Brower house and will build a road bridge as part of the cost of straightening. Many years ago there was a road along the river from Aurora to the Miami; a ferry located there cared for travelers in crossing the stream. There are advantages to a road.

Aug. 21, 1912. Dugan Gap-Mount Nebo. Grading on the new road is almost completed to Dugan Gap.

Nov. 6, 1912. Finney-Fort Hill. Next March the Hamilton County Commissioners will let the contract for building a pike from North Bend paralleling the B.&O. R.R. to Fort Hill, thence around its base and up the hill to connect with the Dugan Gap Road. If a bridge were built over the Miami and a road made leading to Lawrenceburg, there would come trade between Lawrenceburg and the territory around Mount Nebo.

As fate would have it, however, the devastating 1913 flood came along and abruptly destroyed most of the ground work, laid the previous year, of the new road. Severe losses caused by the flood left the county without funds to continue work on the road.

Several years passed during which little further was done toward relocating the old River Road. At Finney the condition was particularly bad because it was necessary to cross the railroad tracks and follow down along the ancient wagon trail to the mouth of the river.

When Central Creosoting Company negotiated to buy the Brower land for the erection of the new plant in 1917, they naturally did not wish the old road to continue to run through their property. On behalf of the Brower estate, attorney Milton Sayler appealed to the Hamilton County Commissioners to change the proposed site of Brower Road--dedicated five years earlier but not yet improved--from along the B&O Railroad back to the hill for a distance of about two miles. (Lawrenceburg Press, Oct. 18, 1917.) Since a roadway situated on higher ground than originally planned in 1912 was obviously needed, as proven by the disastrous 1913 flood, the request was granted. The Brower sisters donated land and right of way required for the new section of road, at the same time setting aside a plot of ground along the proposed roadway for relocating Finney schoolhouse, which had just been rebuilt about 1916. (See account of schools at Finney and The Point, at end.)

Near the site of the school was a creek which ran from the hilltop down to the Ohio. Although shown in the Hamilton County Atlas of 1914, Miami Township, as "Kinney Creek," it must have been intended to read "Finney Creek." Mr. Charles Winter, however, recalls that he never heard the creek called by any other name than "Dark Hollow Creek." At any rate, the latter name would have been more intriguing to the school children who waded through it.

The forces of Nature once more stepped in and the building of Brower Road was again delayed. The historic flood and ice gorge of 1918 wrought tremendous damage to railroads and bridges. Repair of these took precedence over road building. Nothing further had been done to Brower Road when, in 1923, the Columbia Gas and Electric Company (sometimes listed as Union Gas and Electric, and later as Cincinnati Gas and Electric) purchased the Brower estate amounting to about 1300 acres and including the prehistoric fort and Harrison homestead, as a site for the company's second electric generating plant.

Electricity was gradually replacing gas lighting throughout Cincinnati, and an extensive house wiring program was being conducted, creating a need for additional generating facilities. Electricity had come to the villages of North Bend and Cleves about 1918.

The following item, copied in brief, tells of the building of the plant: (Commercial Tribune, Nov. 23, 1923; Lawrenceburg Register, Nov. 29, 1923)

Power Plant, Miami Fort Station. Union Gas and Electric Company of Cincinnati are to build a $15,000,000 plant at the mouth of the Big Miami. 1200 acres were purchased from the Brower estate. The building will begin the first of April, 1924. The object of the new plant is to supply the growing demand for electric current. The Brower farm was chosen out of a number of prospective locations because of its advantageous setting, adequate water and rail. The B&O runs within a few feet of the proposed location of the plant. It will be possible to transport coal cargoes from West Virginia coal fields at a reduced cost. It is estimated two years will be required for completion of the plant. "Miami Fort Station" is the name chosen.

The most urgent need of the Columbia Gas and Electric Company, following purchase of the Brower estate in 1923, was to get that long delayed road established down the river to the plant. The only really accessible route by automobile was from North Bend up past Congress Green and out along Cliff Road to the head of Dugan Gap hill. Here workers at the new power plant parked their cars and walked to the site of the construction. The first move was to improve Dugan Gap Road over the hill. Harry Burns, county road engineer, laid out this old worn pathway so that cars could ascend and descend it. Only one vehicle, however, could ever travel it at the same time and gas tanks had to be full ascending the hill. This roadway came to be called "Burns Hill," after the engineer, by the workers at the power station. A local newspaper described the new road over Dugan Gap as "a real boulevard." At the top of the hill, Dugan Gap Road continued on to meet Brower Road, which circled Fort Hill.

Use of Dugan Gap Hill as a roadway for automobiles was short lived, however, for several years later the road and hillside around it caved in. Fortunately, the new Brower Road was in use by that time. Old Dugan Gap Hill, nevertheless, did come into use again, although just as a foot path, when all routes to Columbia Park were cut off by water during the 1937 flood.

Random items from Lawrenceburg Press, 1924 to 1927, tell of the progress of the road and power plant construction:

Feb. 6, 1924. Mount Nebo. The Union Gas and Electric Company have distributed their poles from Lost Bridge along the road to the south side of Andrew Jackson's farm, intending to extend the lines on to their site for the location of their power plant along the Ohio, at the mouth of the Miami just east of Fort Hill. They have made surveys from their site for a direct line. On this line they propose to set up steel towers on the farms of Ezra G. Guard, James Stoneking, Essie E. Yanney, Louis Guard and others.

Mar. 20, 1924. Mount Nebo. The demand for homes in the neighborhood of the "Miami Electric Plant" is increasing daily, as the weather improves, so that men can be assured that their employment will be steady. Parking grounds for autos at Dugan Gap is already at a premium.

Apr. 3, 1924. Mount Nebo. Hamilton County engineers are surveying the road between Jim Stoneking's place (corner of Dugan Gap and Brower Roads) and running around Fort Hill to the new electric plant. There is talk of it being a concrete road.

Jan. 29, 1925. Fort Hill (A map of the proposed road and bridge across the Miami near Fort Hill was shown.) (A bridge was never built.)

Sept. 1926. Mount Nebo. The new Brower Road is beginning to look like it will be ready for travel inside of 12 months. The concrete will be completed to Lost Bridge from the Stoneking place in 15 days. It will be one of the most wonderful roads in Ohio, 20 feet wide and encircling the skirt of that pre-historic old fort.

Cleves and North Bend School Board has contracted

with the owner of a school bus to transport the children from Columbia Park to North Bend.

Mount Nebo Road has been resurfaced.

Sept. 1927. New Brower Road (first proposed and dedicated back in 1912) is ready for travel.

As the newswriter stated, Brower Road was truly one of the most wonderful roads in Ohio in that day. Since its opening, hundreds of cars have daily passed over it to the plants and factories established in the region of The Point. (Since the coming of the creosoting plant, now Koppers Co., Inc., Forest Products Division, and the power station, several other industries have located along Brower Road including the Southern Nitrogen Company, now called Kaiser Agricultural Chemicals, a fertilizer company, and American Bitumels, an asphalt products industry, now called Chevron Asphalt Company.)

The new electric power transmitting unit, standing at the foot of the ancient Indian fortification and within sight of the old brick farmhouse--boyhood home of President Benjamin Harrison, was dedicated in December, 1925. One of the country's pioneer stations, designed for the complete use of pulverized fuel and the reheat cycle, it was at that time one of the most efficient plants in the world. Originally slated to be called "Miami Fort Station," it came to be better known as "Columbia Power Station." This probably had much to do with the fact that the little village established there was called Columbia Park. However, on Dec. 1, 1948, the plant was officially named "Miami Fort Station," the name chosen back in 1923.

The dedication at Columbia Power Plant took place Dec. 10, 1925, with special ceremonies continuing over a four day period. Brief notes taken from Lawrenceburg Press tell of the outstanding events:

> The mammoth Columbia Power Plant will open at old Fort Hill with a dedication on Dec. 10th. Miss Virginia Junggren, daughter of the General Electric Company engineer who designed the turbine installed in the power plant, is to open the throttle turning the steam into the units. Charles P. Taft will then throw the switch, releasing the energy of the station into the distribution lines of Columbia System.
>
> A program is being planned for 50,000 visitors during the 4 day period. Motor cars and special train coaches on the B&O will conduct round trips on those days for the low fare of 50¢. There will be a tour through the new village site and an inspection of the club house and homes built for the use of the families of the men who will work here.
>
> The Columbia Park tract covers 1400 acres and is approximately three miles long.

Prior to 1923, this land along the Ohio downstream from North Bend to the location of the new power station had never been greatly developed. Woodlands mingled with a few farms were all that existed. The railroad tie yard and creosoting plant had drawn some newcomers to the place. Other inhabitants for the most part were engaged in farming.

In order to induce skilled employees of the electric company's older West End Power Station in Cincinnati to transfer to this isolated location, housing had to be provided. So it was that a unique village was established, comprised of 37 homes, a one-room schoolhouse, a grocery store, a community building--designated particularly as a Sunday School--and a large club house. Of these buildings, the grocery and schoolhouse burned when the village was yet young. The club house provided sleeping rooms and boarding accommodations for single men and transient employees of the power plant. In addition, this building also housed a little post office, a two-lane bowling alley, kitchen, dining and drawing room. The club house was most attractive. Throughout the years that followed, the drawing room was frequently the scene of business meetings, dinner parties and even, wedding receptions.

The Cincinnati Gas and Electric Company retained ownership of the village, naming it Columbia Park. Roads, water supply and sewage system were established and maintained by the company. This was a beautiful little community with a peace lending atmosphere, initially untouched by civilization. Columbia Park's first settlers arrived in the fall of 1925. The late Joseph H. Heimbrock, chief engineer of Miami Fort Station for many years, stated, soon after the village was originated, "In name only is the site new; historically speaking, it is one of the oldest as well as richest."

The following account, headed "New Village in Hamilton County Holds Election," appeared in the Cincinnati Times-Star, Dec. 24, 1926:

> "Columbia Park, the community built for employees of the new Columbia Power Station, went to the "polls" Thursday night and chose their councilmen.
>
> The incident marked the first election in the little village since its completion and formal opening last Dec., 1925, when the huge power station was dedicated.
>
> The village is divided into three areas, and the clubhouse counting as the fourth, resembling the wards in Cincinnati. The name of every resident in each area was placed on the ballots in the primary for nomination.
>
> Immediately following the circulation of the notice about a week ago, candidates formed platforms and began campaigning. Many amusing platforms were presented to the voters. For instance, one candidate advocated a street car system.
>
> Others were in favor of greater cooperation in the community and furtherance of social activities and community spirit. Three men who were elected advocated the erection of a church to take the place of the community house, which has served the residents both as a moving picture showhouse and a place in which to worship.
>
> Those elected to the council are: Joseph H. Heimbrock, Frank Gibson, Frank Brooks, Edward Kidd, F. M. Stoddard and Earl Mason. The first meeting will be conducted next week and a mayor selected.
>
> C. W. DeForest, vice president of the Union Gas and Electric Company, and D. S. Brown, in charge of all the company's power stations in the Cincinnati district, will act as councilmen, ex-officio.
>
> The population of Columbia Park has reached the total of 168 men, women and children. All of the men living in the village are employed at the power station.
>
> After the election was finished the villagers took advantage of the occasion by having all the voters participate in a Christmas celebration at which bowling, billiards, music and luncheon constituted the entertainment."

Joseph Heimbrock served as the first mayor, and the late Jessie Glatting acted for many years as Columbia Park's postmistress. A very old Negro man known to everyone only as Jasper, who dated himself way before Civil War times, was custodian at the club house. All of the children in the village knew Jasper and treated him with the greatest respect.

Columbia Park Post Office was officially established and Joseph H. Heimbrock appointed postmaster, Jan. 17, 1927.

From the book "Presbyterianism in the Ohio Valley, 1790-1940": A Presbyterian Church was officially organized Mar. 21, 1927, at Columbia Park, the location of the power station. It had a brief existence, with no building available, and disbanded Feb. 15, 1932.

Cecil Irwin was long active in the community Sunday School and taught Bible classes there as long as the school existed. Many of the villagers attended churches in North Bend and Cleves.

Before the power station was completed and just after it commenced operations, coal was supplied by railroad until river facilities were installed. Then, the Ohio River Company--formerly the Philadelphia and Cleveland Coal Company--began to ship fuel by barge from West Virginia mines down the Kanawha and Ohio. Ever since that time the same company has transported the mountains of coal burned at Miami Fort Station in the production of electricity. Generating capacity has increased as the station, through the ensuing years, has been enlarged and improved.

In the shadow of that old Indian fortification, Columbia Park's children grew up. Theirs was a playground--a happy hunting ground--all their own. They tramped footpaths over the mound, built tree houses and dug holes in search of Indian artifacts. They swung on grape vines and hoarded buckeyes. They camped out on a point which had served as an Indian lookout centuries earlier. In the coals of their bonfires they roasted potatoes. They knew where the sweetest raspberries vined, the biggest walnuts dropped and the hardiest bittersweet grew. They learned where the yellowest buttercups bloomed and the shyest violets hid.

Bordering the little village were family garden plots and strawberry patches. Closeby was a tennis court and baseball diamond. Hoops attached to telephone poles at several street corners evidenced the popularity of basketball. Throughout its years of existence the village produced a bumper crop of athletes for the teams at Taylor High School.

In the beginning years, before the little white schoolhouse burned, the younger children attended primary grades in Columbia Park. Older grade pupils rode the bus to classes at North Bend and Cleves. Starting in 1926, all students of high school age throughout the entire Miami Township began to attend Taylor High School. The little Finney School, although standing along Brower Road at not too great a distance from the new village, and open until June, 1932, could not accommodate the Columbia Park grade school children.

Finney School had the distinction of being among the last one-room schools conducted in Hamilton County. Its last teacher was Raymond Fisher. The following account, copied from Lawrenceburg Press, March 16, 1934, and Cincinnati Times-Star, March 6, 1934, tells of both the school and the teacher, a 1928 graduate of Taylor High School:

"A University of Cincinnati student was slain in Arabia. He was on a trip around the world. The State Department got the official report. Belief is expressed that tribesmen might be responsible for the death of the daring college man.
Raymond Fisher, 24, son of Mrs. Josephine Fisher, who was killed last week by Arabs on the Euphrates River, 120 miles south of Bagdad, was well known around Cleves. (He was a nephew of the Ray Robisons.)
Fisher was touring the globe at the time of his death. He was shot in the head and his companion shot in the abdomen.
Prior to his graduation he was principal teacher at Finney School near Cleves, the only remaining one-room school in Hamilton County. He taught the entire school of some 15 pupils ranging through all grades. His "tooth brush" drills for the children were an innovation there and highly enjoyed by the youngsters. The novelty of the one-room school and the devotion of the children to their sole teacher was the subject of a school page article nearly 2 years ago (1932). The school has since been absorbed by the Cleves-North Bend School District." (March 2, 1932, Times-Star)

It was a sad day to see the little old Finney School close, but even sadder to learn that its last teacher had so tragically lost his life. (An account of the schools that have existed around Fort Finney and The Point, together with what has been learned of the teachers, will be found at the end of this article.)

It came to pass that during the late 1950's, maintenance of the village of Columbia Park was posing serious financial and sanitation problems. The homes and streets were in need of repair. The estimated cost required for the Cincinnati Gas and Electric Company to comply with new countywide water and sewage regulations far exceeded the evaluation of the buildings. After thorough deliberation, company officials concluded that Columbia Park had served its original purpose. Its further existence was no longer deemed necessary. Following a specified date, the dwellings were dismantled, midst loud protests and moanings from those fortunate enough to have lived in the "story-book" village. A few of the houses were purchased intact and moved by rollers to scattered vistas upstream along the Ohio, where they were set on new foundations. In these homes a glimpse of the extinct village of Columbia Park, in existence less than thirty-five years, may yet be seen around North Bend.

During the years of Columbia Park's existence, the old Harrison home, standing on the property of the power company, was occupied by a steady flow of tenants. From time to time patriotic societies voiced concern over the neglect of the historic home and urged that it be purchased by the state and restored for posterity, but no action was ever taken on this issue. By 1959, the building was determined beyond repair and ordered dismantled along with the village of Columbia Park.

The following pertinent news item appeared in The Cincinnati Enquirer, Oct. 20, 1959:

"Local members of the D.A.R. recently had the foundations pulled out from under them.
The D.A.R.'s Cincinnati Chapter had ordered a bronze marker for the boyhood home of Benjamin Harrison, 23rd President of the United States.

With plans to place the marker with appropriate ceremony, the women all of a sudden found that the old brick residence was torn down last summer, unbeknownst to them.
The Harrison homestead was on the property owned by Cincinnati Gas and Electric Company. The home was torn down for safety reasons. Beyond repair, the mortar was completely gone from the bricks, making the historic building a hazard."

It is interesting to note that Caroline Scott Harrison, who had come to this old house as a bride of Benjamin Harrison in 1853, later served as first president general of the D.A.R., founded in 1890, in Washington, D. C., while her husband was President.

Back in 1931, C.G.&E. Co., in a step initiated by Joseph Heimbrock, gave to the City of Cincinnati the 113 acre site encompassing Fort Hill (Miami Fort), so that this monument of a prehistoric race could be preserved as a park for the people of Ohio. The park, however, was never developed.

As early as 1912, James Albert Green, author of the fine biography of William Henry Harrison, advocated in the "Optimist," a magazine published by the Cincinnati Business

Men's Club, that a park be erected at Fort Hill. At that same time he urged that improvements be made at Harrisons's Tomb.

In those days when little thought was being given to preservation for future generations, James A. Green and Joseph Heimbrock were already looking ahead. The latter spent much time in scientific study of the ancient mount. According to an article by Frank Grayson in The Cincinnati Times-Star, April 19, 1933, it was stated that Joseph Heimbrock had unearthed many of the tools and weapons of the Mound Builders.

It was not until 1968, that this ground, together with additional land totaling 685 acres, was officially turned over by C.G.&E. Company and the City of Cincinnati to the Hamilton County Park District for the purpose of creating a fourth county park. Citizens and civic groups contributed over $100,000 to the Park Board to enable purchase of surrounding land needed to connect parts of the park already acquired from C.G.&E. The U.S. Army Corps of Engineers, who recently established a marina along the Great Miami within the park area, also contributed a large parcel of ground. Long range plans are now being made for development of the park, which now includes 1,010 acres. The hilltop area of the park overlooking the confluence of the Ohio and Great Miami Rivers was once the lookout of a great Shawnee war chief, "Bluejacket." From this historical reference "Shawnee Lookout" was selected as the name best suited to the new park. To older residents of the locality, however, the place will always be Fort Hill.

(An account of Chief Blue Jacket may be found in The Frontiersmen, a historical narrative by Allan W. Eckert. Blue Jacket was a white man captured in his youth by the Shawnees, his name having been Marmaduke Van Swearingen. He came to adopt and love the ways of the Shawnees and to despise the white men for their treatment of the Indians.)

An archaeological survey and excavation was conducted at Miami Fort during the summers of 1965 through 1968. Directed by Fred W. Fischer, University of Cincinnati instructor in anthropology, the dig was sponsored jointly by the Miami Purchase Association, Cincinnati Museum of Natural History and University of Cincinnati, and was a part of the university's summer school program. The program was continued during 1969.

In a lecture to the Three Rivers Historical Society, July 9, 1967, Fischer stated that findings at the archaeological survey indicated that the earliest inhabitants of the region were of the Early Woodland period. The Middle Woodland group (1 A.D. to 600 A.D.), however, was responsible for constructing the fort, ca. 270 A.D., (150 years more or less) as determined by radio-carbon tests. Inhabitants of this period lived in permanent villages, hunted and cultivated the soil.

Artifacts found at the fort will be kept for the present at University of Cincinnati. If a museum is built at the park, in the future, the articles will be placed there. Mr. Charles B. Winter has already been invited to place some of his wonderful collection of Indian relics there, should the museum become a reality.

"Hamilton County Park News," Nov. 1967 issue, reported that rangers had sighted a large buck, a doe and two fawns in the Shawnee Park area. The paper further stated:

"This wild natural area offers a refuge for these wild deer and if not molested will remain as permanent residents. Every effort should be made to encourage and protect these beautiful animals."

Ours is a heritage to be treasured and preserved. The coming of the deer, symbolic link to the past, is a sign of hope that new life will continue to appear at The Point and a promise that something of the glorious heritage of these surroundings will be preserved for the generations to come.

Fort Finney, 1785, drawn to scale by T. Marshall Rainey, architect of Cincinnati, based on the description of Major Ebenezer Denny in his military journal. Denny stated that the fort was square, with two-storied block houses located in each corner, each one being 24 x 18 feet. The curtains (stockade fence) were 100 feet long, constructed of pickets 13 feet long and planted four feet deep. A building, measuring 18 x 24 feet, was located between the east and west walls to house the army contractors' stores and Indian goods. In the center of the north curtain was a small but strong magazine building. A council house, 60 feet long and 30 feet wide, was also provided nearby.

✯✯✯✯✯✯✯✯✯✯

Elizabethtown Postal History
Postmasters and dates of appointments

Elizabethtown: Isaac Mills, Aug. 10, 1820; Jos. Lewis, May 27, 1835; Isaac M. Dunn, Sept. 12, 1839; Jas. Thompson, Feb. 12, 1840; Solomon F. Rodman, Oct. 19, 1841; Chas. Mills, May 23, 1842; Nat'l C. Clark, Mar. 16, 1848; Powell D. Clark, June 1, 1849; Amos B. Dunn, June 10, 1850; Wm. J. Clark, July 19, 1852; Isaac D. Mills, Nov. 26, 1852; Wm. P. Rees, Jan. 13, 1858; Thos. H. Hunt, Feb. 10, 1858; Isaac D. Mills, Nov. 4, 1858; Sam'l Runk, Oct. 9, 1860; Mrs. Susan M. Bonham, May 12, 1862; H.K.W. Smith, Aug. 22, 1866; David E. Avery, Dec. 11, 1866; Jacob Andres, Aug. 1, 1867; *office name changed to Riverdale.

Riverdale: James W. Leek, Aug. 30, 1867; Mrs. Lucinda M. Dunn, Mar. 14, 1870; Jos. H. Miller, Apr. 19, 1870; *name changed back to Elizabethtown, May 19, 1870.

Elizabethtown: Ezra G. Hayes, Oct. 19, 1874; Geo. T. Devore, Feb. 2, 1876; Andevoon B. Wamsley, Aug. 2, 1876; Wm. J. Clark, Dec. 18, 1876; Geo. Gun, July 25, 1877; Moses B. Lake, Aug. 20, 1877; Frank F. Guard, Apr. 26, 1889; Otto C. Pope, July 20, 1893; Frank Guard, Aug. 7, 1897; Frank B. Lake, Oct. 5, 1901; Hannah W. Hayes, June 22, 1906; Harry J. Sykes, Dec. 30, 1907; James B. Radcliffe, Oct. 15, 1915; Bonnie M. Gibson, Jan. 23, 1917. Office discontinued, Mar. 15, 1919. Mail to Cleves, RFD. Address now is R.R. 1, North Bend.

Chapter 22

SCHOOLS AT THE POINT AND FINNEY

In the days before the first log schoolhouse stood at The Point, boys and girls who lived in the scattered cabins round about undoubtedly got their first lessons, a bit of reading and writing, in the light of the wood fire at the feet of their parents.

The earliest known school in the region was a little log house built by John Scott Harrison, near his home, where his children, together with several nephews and nieces and neighboring boys and girls, attended. Tutors were hired to come to The Point, live in the Harrison home and see to the education of the children. One of the early tutors was Joseph Porter, later president of Yale. Another was Thomas N. Lind, known to have been a favorite of Benjamin Harrison. Families who were fortunate enough, like the Harrisons, sent their older children to boarding schools.

However, most of the scholars who lived in this general region went up to Mount Nebo School. The Mount Nebo neighborhood was more thickly settled than The Point and had had good schools even in the earliest days. For the 1848-1849 school year, Thomas N. Lind, Mount Nebo teacher, sent school bills to a number of parents, many of whom resided in the region of Finney, Fort Hill and Goose Pond, including the Wamsleys, Bumps, Whipples, Garrisons and Hayeses. It was evident to see from the list that scholars traveled long distances to school. Charles B. Winter relates that his mother and several other relatives, at one time, went over the hill to Mount Nebo School.

Mr. Winter recalls hearing or knowing of at least seven sites where school was once conducted in the Gravel Pit-Finney region. The first of these early day schools was said to have stood on top of the hill above where the asphalt company now has a parking lot. Here some of the Harrisons are said to have attended. No written record has been found of a school in this location but the story seems quite probable.

Another known school (Site No. 2), a two-story stone building, the remains of which may yet be seen within the barn on Charles Winter's place, existed during the 1850-1870 era. (The 1869 Atlas shows the location of this school on Abram Brower's property.) The cellar part of the building was divided into two rooms. Here was a spring where stock was watered and milk cooled. Overhead was a one-room school. Mr. Winter recalls hearing his Uncle Jimmy Buckingham (b. 1839, U.S. Census) tell of attending this school and seeing whiskey being made in the cellar. Children of the Bingle, Cady, Myers, Bevens and VanGorder families, who farmed for John Scott Harrison, were sent here.

It was at this school, in the early 1860's, that Harry VanGorder and Harriet Cady met as children. Harry is said to have gone home from school on his very first day and said, "The prettiest little curly headed girl goes to school." It was love, for both, at first sight, and after 60 years of marriage they were still in love, so wrote their daughter, Mrs. Nellie VanGorder Blackford. Mrs. Blackford cherishes some "award for merit" cards which her parents earned at that Gravel Pit school.

Sometime after Abram Brower acquired the property, a large dairy barn was built right over the spring house and site of the old (No. 2) school.

The next Gravel Pit-Finney school (Site No. 3) stood on the lower bank, below the O&M Railroad tracks, near to where the creosoting plant was later built. It was frequently flooded. (This school is shown on the 1884, Moessinger and Bertsch, map.) Charles Winter's father, Henry (b. 1859, U.S. Census), attended classes here in the 1870's. When excavations were being made, preparatory to building the creosoting plant in 1917, the foundation of this old school at Gravel Pit was uncovered.

It was possibly in this school at Gravel Pit (No. 3) that Ezra G. Guard taught from about 1870 to 1872. At that time Ezra was a young man attending Moore's Hill College, Indiana. During his last year of school (1870-1871) he learned that Gravel Pit, over the hill from his home, needed a teacher. Somehow, Ezra managed to teach and at the same time keep up with his studies so that he was able to graduate with his college class, June 21, 1871. The subject of his graduation oration, interesting to note, was "To Be Living is Sublime." Upon graduation he returned to teach for another term at Gravel Pit. Chalon Guard, Ezra's father, owned the farm at the top of the hill bordering the Abram Brower place. The Guard home, now a part of Shawnee Lookout Park, faced out onto Dugan Gap Road. In those days there was much travel up and down Dugan Gap hill, to and from the river and railroad. Ezra usually caught the O&M train at Pike's Station when going to college.

James B. Matson (1855-1913) was teaching at Gravel Pit School (No. 3) in March, 1873. He had attended Mt. Nebo School, as had Ezra Guard, and was fortunate in being able to go on to Hughes High. His family lived on a big farm near Lost Bridge. A Matson family journal tells that Jim, in February, 1874, rode to school in the city on "the accommodation," catching it at Elizabethtown and paying 80¢ a round trip. Jim was a correspondent for Lawrenceburg Press during this era, contributing news items from the Mt. Nebo, Lost Bridge, Finney, Goose Pond and Elizabethtown locale. In 1880 he married and moved to North Bend where he taught school and served as postmaster. He continued on to Cincinnati Law School, graduating with the class of which President W. H. Taft was a member. Jim later lived in Home City and was one of chief sponsors of changing the name of that village to Sayler Park. He was active in the Mt. Nebo Society, returning frequently to the scenes of his boyhood at Mt. Nebo and Finney.

Around 1878, a Mr. Proctor taught at Gravel Pit. Charles Winter recalls hearing his Uncle Jack Winter speak of this teacher, although nothing further has been learned of him.

In 1880, John River was the teacher at Gravel Pit. He boarded at Charles White's place. (1880 U.S. Census)

A.E.B. Stephens of Cleves taught there about 1881. He often walked to his charge or hopped an O&M freight train at North Bend and rode down to Gravel Pit.

Sometime before 1887, another schoolhouse (No. 4) was built, this one on somewhat higher ground than the preceding school, although yet below the railroad tracks. Here Stanley Struble taught for a short term, around 1889, just before he left to study law at Oberlin College.

From 1890 until about 1901, Morgan Wamsley was the Finney schoolmaster. The Wamsley family lived upriver a short distance, near old Pike's Station, and "Morg," as he was known, walked back and forth to school each day. He probably held the all-time record for teaching the longest period at Finney.

Morgan Wamsley was followed by a woman teacher, the first known at Finney. She was Fanny Hayes (Shrader) who taught from around 1901 to 1907, also a long term for a teacher to remain.

Other teachers of this era included: Charles Gant, Miamitown, ca. 1907; Ed Smith, Harrison, who boarded at the Angevine farm, ca. 1908; Bud Betscher, Emma Betscher, John C. Lacy and Edgar Stratton. Since it was a problem for teachers to reach Finney, they usually stayed just about a year. Ed Smith, for example, chose to transfer to Mount St. Jo after his term ended because he was able then to ride the traction car from Harrison to his school. Nevertheless, Finney proved to be a good training ground for many successful teachers and civic leaders.

About 1914, Finney schoolhouse (No. 4) burned. Charles Winter recalls that he was plowing that day and saw the building go up in flames. For a time after that no school was conducted at all until classes were temporarily resumed in the old railroad building at the tie yard. This makeshift schoolhouse was site No. 5. Arthur Jones taught here in 1915.

A new school was built (Site No. 6) below the railroad tracks about 1916, where classes were taught until the creosoting plant was constructed. Then (1917) the daughters of Abram Brower gave a plot of ground (Site No. 7) along the present Brower Road to where the school building was moved on rollers. Although it was actually the sixth school building, it stood on the seventh known site where Finney and Gravel Pit schools had been conducted. Teachers of this era included: Alice Bratton, Helen Guard, Fern Yanney (English), Elmer Schubert and Margaret (Mrs. Louis) Wood.

Fern Yanney (English) resided along Cliff Road, not far from Dugan Gap Hill. Each day her mother drove her down to Finney School in the family buggy. After consolidation of the schools of the district, Fern Yanney taught art in several of the grade schools for many years.

(Autograph books or friendship books, once called memory books back before the turn of the century and especially treasured for their beautiful penmanship, are yet popular among school children today. This writer still cherishes in her memory the line that Miss Yanney wrote in her autograph book back in the 6th grade: "May fortune never smile on you but laugh right out.")

Another known school site was in Columbia Park. When the village was established in 1925, a little white frame schoolhouse was built for primary grade pupils, kindergarten through second grade. Most of the families who moved to Columbia Park then had very small children. The older scholars were bussed to school in North Bend and Cleves. This little school burned, in the 1930's, when the village was yet new.

Finney School, located on site No. 7, had a significant claim to fame in that it was among the last of the one-room, eight grade schools to remain open in Hamilton County. Conducted until 1932, it was made up of about 15 pupils ranging through all grades. Raymond Fisher, 1928 graduate of Taylor High, had the distinction of being Finney's last teacher. This young man was later murdered by bandits in Arabia while on a trip around the world in 1934. (See Times-Star, March 6, 1934.)

Finney School was featured in an article in the Times-Star, March 2, 1932, in which it was stated that it was the last rural, one-room, eight grade school in the county.

Finney schoolhouse, yet standing, now serves as a comfortable dwelling.

(Author's Note: I am indebted to many persons and numerous sources for information about the Gravel Pit and Finney schools. Mr. Charles B. Winter, who has lived in the region all his life, was of invaluable help and I am grateful to him.)

(It should also be noted that a very early school existed in the region of the "big bottoms," in the Elizabethtown area, called Bonhams' Schoolhouse. This school, named by Judge Cotton in his book, was conducted by Aaron Bonham and his wife, Sarah Guard Bonham. Aaron R. Bonham (1792-1866) was a son of John Bonham who came from Pa. to North Bend in 1796. The family soon settled in Whitewater Township, building the second log cabin west of the Whitewater River in the place where Bond's Mill later stood. Aaron served in the War of 1812, and in 1815 wed Sarah Guard, daughter of Alexander Guard, one of the first settlers around The Point.)

★★★★★★★★★★★

Early Schools of Whitewater Township

In days before the land west of the Miami was for sale, a number of squatters located in the area of the present Lost and Suspension Bridges. Education, even then, was considered so vital that a log schoolhouse was built near the site of the latter bridge. Not a board, nail or pane of glass went into its structure. The building was raised in one day of timbers and a few sheets of oiled paper (for windows) with the help of strong arms, sharp axes, a frow and an inch augur. Billy Jones was installed as schoolmaster (winter of 1799) with the Testament and Dilworth's Speller in the hands of his scholars. He was paid $4 a month and boarded 'round. The second school was built near Elizabethtown and of a more pretentious style of architecture and furnishing. The days of saw mills and nail factories had dawned; carpenters and masons could be employed. In this house Wesley Clark taught a good school of an advanced grade. Master Clark ruled with the rod, but the authority of goodness and love held it in an even hand and used it with sound discretion. (B.W. Chidlaw in "Early Times", and Ford's History, p. 404)

Another school located 1/8 mile east of E-town, near the state border, was built by James Blackburn. Isaac Polk taught here 1807 to 1809. James Grubbs, born in 1805 in Lawrenceburg Twp., told of attending his first school here in the Hayes-Miller neighborhood. That school was a rude, round-log cabin. (History of Dearborn and Ohio Counties)
*Author's Note: A complete history of Whitewater Township's schools should be written.

Former site of Elizabethtown Female Institute, Ca. 1853-58. Once a drovers' inn, the brick structure, yet standing, was erected Ca. 1831 by one of the pioneer Hunt family. It was also used as a temporary school, 1860-61, by Western Female Seminary (now Western College) after that school burned.

Chapter 23

EARLY SCHOOLS OF MIAMI TOWNSHIP AND THE TEACHERS WHO GUIDED THEM

Records concerning the very earliest schools of Miami Township are few, yet it can be stated with certainty that schools, conducted in pioneer homes or in log schoolhouses, whether taught by parents or by boarding teachers, did exist.

Settlers of the Ohio Valley were no ordinary men. Many among their ranks had had good educations. Spelling and arithmetic books, along with the Bible, were inseparable accompaniments of the rifle and plow. It is interesting to note that John Cleves Symmes, himself, in early life, had engaged in teaching school.

Legend tells that Cincinnati's first school, in 1790, was taught by Benjamin Griffith aboard a flatboat which was made fast to a tree by a grapevine.

Earliest-day teachers boarded 'round, their pay was little and often collected in the form of farm produce. Books were scarce and paper expensive, so the latter was used sparingly. Quill pens were fashioned from stiff goose and wild turkey feathers; ink was made from juice of pokeberries or oak galls. There being no blotters, pupils dried ink by sprinkling sand on their papers. Individual hand slates were used. There were no writing tablets, fine maps or comfortable desks in those days. Scholars sat upon rough benches. Older pupils helped the teacher by tending the fire and filling the wood box and water bucket.

Sarah Armstrong at 7 1/2 years of age was indentured in 1818 to William Rittenhouse, pioneer settler on Mt. Nebo. The indenture agreement particularly stipulated that Rittenhouse was to teach Sarah, or have her taught, to read and write.

While the majority of children of early Miami Township settlers received their meager educations under most irregular conditions, some families, more financially able, hired tutors to live and instruct in their homes. In this category was William H. Harrison, who placed great emphasis on schooling. At heavy expense and personal sacrifice, he saw his children, particularly his sons, educated.

A Cincinnati newspaper account of Oct. 3, 1920, tells of the benevolence of the Harrisons concerning schooling in their home:

"In 1814, General Harrison resigned his commission in the army and returned to North Bend. There were no schools in North Bend and as Mrs. Harrison employed a private tutor for the education of her own family, she invited many other children to take advantage of her home to learn the three 'R's'."

Around 1816, Cincinnati historian Timothy Flint made a trip down the Ohio and Mississippi and later wrote a book of recollections of the journey. In the account he tells of spending several days at the residence of General Harrison, delayed there by a storm, where he was received with hospitality. He stated, "Harrison has a copious fund of that eloquence which is fitted for the camp and for gaining partisans." Flint also wrote of listening to the Harrison children recite their lessons in geometry.

Legend tells that William Bebb, later Governor of Ohio during the Mexican War, was a teacher at North Bend at the residence of General Harrison in 1826. Bebb became a follower of Harrison, aligning himself with the Whig party. He was an eloquent speaker. Elected governor 1846 to 1848, he did not favor the war with Mexico. The Bebb family, related to Ezekiel Hughes, were among the Welsh pioneers who settled in the Paddy's Run region, around New Haven and Shandon, between the Whitewater and Great Miami Rivers, shortly after 1800. (See the book Saga of Paddy's Run by Stephen R. Williams.)

It is interesting, at this point, to tell of another who lived in this same general region who also became a Governor, Ohio's fifth. He was Othniel Looker who settled in Crosby Township, Harrison, Ohio, in 1804. Prominent in county affairs, he was elected to the general assembly. Upon the resignation of Governor R. J. Meigs in March, 1814, Looker, then speaker of the senate, became acting governor. He filled the office for eight months and was succeeded by the duly elected Governor Thomas Worthington. Looker returned to his farm at Harrison and later served, for many years, as Associate Judge in Hamilton County Common Pleas Court. The Village Historical Society at Harrison is presently planning to restore the early home of Othniel Looker.

(The major event during the brief term of Acting Governor Looker was his call for 500 militia volunteers in August to join an expedition under General Duncan McArthur against Indians in the Chicago area.)

It is interesting to know that this locality contributed two governors to Ohio, one of whom, Bebb, had been a young educator, first at Oury's schoolhouse in Whitewater Township, and afterwards, ca. 1826, at North Bend. Bebb also conducted a private school near New Haven on his father's farm. This was in the days before free public schools came into existence.

Nathan Guilford, Harvard educated, who came to Cincinnati in 1816 to practice law, was an early advocate of free education for the masses. He was elected to the Ohio Senate and succeeded in having a law passed requiring all people who owned property to pay a tax to support common schools. Because of this act the first free school in the Northwest Territory was opened in Cincinnati in 1829. For many years demonstrations and flower parades were conducted in the city to draw interest and win support for common, or public, schools.

Early school examinations were conducted orally. Parents and friends were urged to visit the schools and witness the lessons and recitations. These public examinations were not given--as one might guess--to keep pupils "on their toes," but were held for the purpose of stimulating interest in the cause of education. The custom existed for many years, in rural as well as in village schools.

From the Cincinnati Chronicle, May 12, 1838: "Common Schools. The annual examination of the public schools of this city is now in progress. It is hoped that as many citizens as can find time will attend. It is due to the cause, the teachers and the pupils, that they should do so."

From the Cincinnati Chronicle, Jan. 12, 1839: "The School House. More than 1000 school houses have been erected in the state during the last year. It speaks a language for Ohio which cannot be misunderstood. It is the language of intelligent progress which must equal that of physical development, to preserve us from the corruptions of all former peoples. The school house is, indeed, not everything but around it nearly everything valuable will cluster. The apt and efficient teacher will soon find his way to it, the parent will regard him as a necessary adjunct of his own government, and the child connects the idea of his school with that of early sports and joyful accessions to knowledge and happiness."

Where the first log school at North Bend actually stood is unknown. However, one is known to have existed in the region of what we now know as Shady Lane, not far up from old River Road. This school was in use in the 1840's, possibly sooner, and was still being used in the era of 1870. (Some pupils from the North Bend locality are known to have attended school at Burr Oak. See chapters "Short's Station, Sekitan and Addyston" and "History of Addyston Schools.")

The village of North Bend was platted in 1868, on grounds of the original Harrison homestead and farm. The first known school in the village was conducted at the Seiter cottage on Taylor Avenue, opposite the present school, in the early 1870's. That house was later owned by Joseph W. Garrison and presently by Robert Taylor. Nell M. Garrison recalls that the home, before remodeling, had a partition in the back room dividing the space into two cloak rooms. Joe Garrison's mother once attended sewing classes in this place in early days. Maude McKenzie of Delhi was among the early teachers in this school.

The first North Bend schoolhouse was built in 1877, with the village council hall and jail along side it on the same lot. At times this created quite a stir because pupils could look in at the prisoners as they walked to and from school.

(In 1881, coke ovens were built at North Bend Coal Company. Tramps and vagrants of all kinds congregated at the coal yards, sleeping at night on top of the ovens to keep warm. Begging, pestering the North Bend residents and drunkenness resulted from their presence, so the jail was usually filled to capacity with these "visitors." When the jail and council hall was later moved to another site, in 1900, along Taylor Avenue, all the school children gathered around with great excitement to watch the building being pulled by horse and sleds to its new foundation.)

Sam F. Logan was the first principal of the new North Bend School in 1877. He shortly afterward went to Westwood School where he was in charge a number of years. In August, 1883, he served as president of the Hamilton County Teachers' Institute, and Morgan Wamsley, a teacher from Cleves, was secretary of the organization.

Will Harrell (later of Cleves), Eva L. Kirgan, James B. Matson and Max Braam were among North Bend's educators of the 1880's. The story of Max Braam must be told; it is unusual.

Maximilian Braam, who served as village schoolmaster from 1886 to 1888, was a native of Holland. Born in 1850, he came to Cincinnati at the age of 24 with little more than a carpetbag in hand, but with a great thirst for learning. North Bend was his first teaching position. Braam rented a small cottage (in later years the home of the late Mrs. Mary Gray and Floyd Bingle) near the school for $7 a month, where he lived with his wife and baby daughter, Florence. The Braams were extremely frugal people.

Max Braam began to teach biology at Hughes High School in 1904, where he remained until 1921. For over 30 years he attended night classes at University of Cincinnati. He spoke many languages fluently; studied astronomy, botany and chemistry; loved to garden and compose poetry. His friends marveled at his never-ending enthusiasm in his quest for knowledge. At his death in 1931, at age 81, he was the oldest student at the university. At that time he was only a thesis away from his doctorate degree, for which he had been working on the subject "The Dialects of Zeeland."

Upon Max Braam's death, the city was surprised to learn he had left a bequest of $10,000 to be used for purposes of park beautification. How could this man have saved such a sum?

A committee was appointed and counseled to use Max Braam's bequest wisely. In due time a project worthy of this humble teacher was selected. A tract of ground in Mt. Airy Forest was landscaped and planted with numerous varieties of azalea. It was called the Max Braam Arboretum, in memory of this man and his wife. Today these azalea gardens, when in bloom each spring, present one of the loveliest sights to be seen in our Queen City. There a plaque to Max Braam is displayed.

Back on Oct. 5, 1887, a "Sacred Pilgrimage" was conducted at the tomb of William H. Harrison. People from all over the city attended. North Bend's talented schoolmaster, Max Braam, composed a number, entitled "Tippecanoe," for his scholars to sing on this grand occasion. The words of the composition extolled General Harrison.

Legend tells that Max Braam, ever grateful for his good fortune in this country, never forgot his little home village in Holland. He frequently sent money to the school there specifying that it be used for the children for a celebration with treats and dancing in the street.

How fortunate were those school children of North Bend back in 1887 to have had a man of Max Braam's stature for their teacher.

Ambrose Everett Burnside "Buzz" Stephens was principal of North Bend School from 1890 to 1892. His assistant was Miss Jessie M. Hunt of Valley Junction, (who became the mother of Delhi's Willa K. Butterfield). Schoolmaster Stephens, who had come to Cleves about 1876, had taught at Gravel Pit (Finney) and Cleves Schools. He entered the field of politics and became mayor of Cleves in 1891; deputy treasurer of Hamilton County, 1892-1898; deputy County Clerk, 1901-1911; Clerk of Courts, 1911-1917; elected Representative to Congress, 2nd Ohio District in 1919. In this position, A.E.B. Stephens was instrumental in securing an appropriate monument at the tomb of President Harrison.

Prof. Stephens was succeeded as North Bend's principal by his sister, Hallie E. Stephens (later Mrs. Charles W. Caine). "Miss Hallie," as she was affectionately known by many, has become a legend in North Bend school history.

Prior to her coming to North Bend, Hallie Caine had taught music around the area, at Berea and Jordan. Her father, S. Kyle Stephens, was a versatile teacher in the Berea and Elizabethtown region for a number of years. He was particularly known for his singing schools. He directed his classes and played on his violin for accompaniment. His daughter, Hallie, doubtless got her inspiration from him.

Hallie Caine came to North Bend in 1892, and remained as principal until 1909. The influence of her years at the school was felt for decades afterward. She wanted her pupils to learn, but above all she wanted them to enjoy learning. She is known to have done much "missionary" work among the needy students.

"Miss Hallie" was great for promoting school plays and musical entertainments. Parents were frequently invited to visit the school on Friday afternoons to hear their children recite, take part in spelling bees or play the piano or mandolin. Often Hallie Caine pumped away at the organ while her scholars sang. She kept a rocking chair in the classroom, in which she frequently rocked while listening to lessons. (Today's teachers might take note.)

During the era of the Spanish-American War, Hallie Caine organized a girls' drill team which was called the "Girls' Brigade." Uniforms of long skirts and middy blouses were worn by the girls and their leaders. Sabers, flags and even

The Girls' Brigade drill team of North Bend Village School, directed by Hallie Stephens Caine, 1898. Picture taken in front of original school.

North Bend Public School, June, 1901, showing addition to the front of the building. Renamed for John S. Conner, in inset.

brooms were carried over shoulders and used in the drills, depending on what suited the occasion. "Miss Hallie" wore a Teddy Roosevelt, "Rough-Riders-type," wide-brimmed hat with her uniform. While drilling her "brigade" in martial time, the leader displayed such enthusiasm that the "troop," itself, was infected by her enthusiasm. The routines being clever, the "Girls' Brigade" was invited to participate at flag raisings, dedication ceremonies and parades.

Hallie Caine's enthusiastic approach to teaching was also contagious. She inspired others to want to teach just as she did. Among her pupils who became dedicated teachers were Edna Truitt Hayes and Cora Wiles Flowers, both members of the "Girls' Brigade." (See "History of Mt. Nebo School" for sketch of Edna Hayes' teaching experiences.)

Until around the turn of the century, the majority of teachers of rural and small village schools had completed only the eighth grade in common school. Those who had had the benefit of both high school and college education were rare. A scholar, upon completion of eighth grade, graduated from school after passing the uniform Boxwell or Patterson examination. (Since there was little uniformity in lessons taught among the schools of that day, these tests helped to determine a pupils's standing.) Anyone desiring to teach could qualify by securing a teachers' certificate. This was obtained by going before a board of county examiners and submitting to a long oral test. Most young teachers who secured their teaching credentials in this way then furthered their educations by studying with tutors or by going to normal schools for summer courses. In those days there was National Normal University at Lebanon, Ohio, where many local teachers attended. This school closed about 1916. In earlier times, Oyler Teachers' Institute existed near Harrison, Ohio.

Back in 1901, North Bend School was enlarged and the name changed to John Sanborn Conner School, in honor of a man who had worked faithfully on the first school board (1876), and had done much to further education in the village.

John S. Conner (1844-1911) had settled at North Bend around 1874, where he built a home adjacent to Harrison's Tomb. A graduate of Woodward High School and Dartmouth College, he had attended Cincinnati Law School and had been assistant solicitor of Cincinnati. John S. Conner served as judge of Hamilton County Common Pleas Court from 1882 to 1887. At North Bend he was a most distinguished citizen.

Dedication of the John S. Conner School was held April 12, 1901. The affair was publicized and announcements stated that traction cars would run from Anderson Ferry every half hour. Notable personages were present to take part in the ceremony. John James Piatt and his wife, Sarah M. Piatt, celebrated poets of North Bend, read original verses they had composed for the occasion. John B. Peaslee, Ex-Superintendent of Cincinnati Schools, gave the address and Judge Conner responded in appreciation of the honor accorded him. School children, directed by Principal Hallie Caine, sang a rousing new composition entitled "Hurrah for the Schools of Ohio," written and published by Cincinnatians W. H. Venable and A. J. Gantvoort, in 1898. (Prof. A. J. Gantvoort was at one time a resident of Harrison, Ohio.) The number was well received. This rallying song, dedicated to school teachers, came to be known and sung by thousands of Ohio boys and girls. (See "John James Piatt, North Bend Poet.")

Pupils who attended John S. Conner School between Sept., 1901 and May, 1904 included:

Bradley (Pearl); Breining (Mary, Christine); Burke (Frank); Cady (Anna, Henry); Clark (John); Garrison (Edgar, Marie); Gray (Clara, Myrtle); Halliday (Nellie, Clifford, George); Hayes (Charles, John, Frank); Hopping (Arthur, Bessie); Horton (Oliver, Chester); Kern (Crystal); Loew (Charles, Minto); McIntyre (Hallie, Archie); Malson (Nellie); Maple (Bonnie); Morgan (May, Nellie); Newell (Rebecca); Reock (Frank); Rittenhouse (Stephen, Rosa); Roselle (Cyrus); Rountree (Jessie); Schrader (Ida); Souders (Stella); Steele (Stella, Leo); Stephens (Corrine, Maude); Stoneking (Jessie); Suit (Edna, Edith, William, Mabel); Sutton (Josephine); West (Ruby); Wickman (Albert); Wiles (Leonard); Wilson (Chester); Wood (Alfred); Yancy (Clifford); York (Joe, Katie, Mary); Zapf (Leroy, Margaret, Re)

Situated directly behind John S. Conner School was a pond, formed by the waters from Indian Creek. At times this was shallow but often it was deep, thus creating a safety hazard for the school. Pupils often played hooky and went fishing or ice skating at the creek. Although they were instructed to go directly home after school and secure parents' permission to ice skate, some of the more daring pupils hid their ice skates in the outhouses, so they would lose no time in getting down to the pond when school was dismissed. Some former pupils can yet recall paddlings they received for disobeying the rule.

Board of Education members of North Bend School in 1898 were: Sam P. Suit, president; James Hopping, clerk; and George Loew, treasurer.

Graduates of North Bend Intermediate School in 1898 were: Laura Halliday, Fanny Hayes, Edna Truitt and Cora Wiles.

In the year 1902, a public spirited citizen of North Bend, Thomas J. Truitt, noted that no flag waved at Harrison's Tomb. He took it upon himself to raise the money for a 63-foot flagpole. This he had installed at the memorial site. In response to the project, Hallie Caine and her husband donated a flag in the name of the John S. Conner School pupils.

Among the known teachers who assisted Mrs. Caine during her tenure at North Bend were:

Adah Smith, Rose Struble, James Shaw, Jr., Anna Francis, Mary E. Meurer, Fanny Hayes, Anna Cady, and Myla Schrader.

Hallie Caine remained at North Bend until about 1909, at which time she was succeeded by Royal S. Hayes. She left a lasting mark on the community and later served a number of years on the Cleves-North Bend Board of Education.

Known teachers at North Bend grade school during the 1910 to 1925 period included:

Royal S. Hayes, principal 1909-1912, Florence G. Carter, Mary Jane White, B. H. Gaines, Stella Heintz, Lucille Stratton, Charles Gant, Nell Kraus and doubtless many others.

In the year 1916, B. H. Gaines was principal. Misses Mary Jane White and Stella Heintz were assistants. Enrollment that year reached 136. World War I had created a need for teachers and it was during this period that many married women returned to teaching, a custom previously frowned upon.

John S. Conner School teachers of the 1925-1940 era were:
Edna T. Hayes, Ruth Scnardine, Norma Welsh Fineran, Ina Seiving Garrison, Bernice Vane, Mildred Wood Robison, Okla Miller Calloway, Florence Taylor, Marian Story Petrick, Mildred Sipes, Mildred Gieringer Bauer, Fred Ramsey (principal 1934 to ca. 1944), and special teachers, A. E. Bollinger, music; Edith Suit Young, penmanship; Fern Yanney English, art; and Robert Morgan, physical education. William Moore succeeded Fred Ramsey as principal. Mrs. Mary Gray and Mrs. Thelma O'Shaughnessy were in charge of the lunch room for many years.

Miss Ruth Schardine, native of Miamitown, who taught at North Bend School many years, and then at Taylor High in the 7th and 8th grades until her retirement, recalls several Harrison relics kept on display in the Conner School office. There was a section of a log, supposedly hollowed out for use as a water pipe--said to have come from a Harrison spring, a brick and a hinge, the latter thought to have come off of a door of the Harrison stable, which had once stood on the site of the school. One of the Harrison springs fed a well in the school yard from which, Miss Schardine recalls, the school once used the water.

North Bend Public School was modernized in 1931, according to an article, as follows, in the Cincinnati Times-Star:

"Contracts have been let by Cleves-North Bend Board of Education on improvements for John S. Conner School on Taylor Avenue. Several departments will be added to the institution to modernize and fire proof. The cost will be $50,000. New sections will include a playroom, kindergarten, rest rooms, library, kitchen and dining room. New plumbing and heating together with a ventilation system will be installed. The school now includes 6 rooms and an auditorium. A radio system will be placed in the building so that each classroom can have a loud speaker. The school is a unit in the County Board of Education and is being enlarged to take care of the growing list of pupils in that section of Hamilton County." (This was the second addition to the school which was built in 1877.)

The Cincinnati Gas and Electric Power Station had been erected at Columbia Park and the new Gulf Refinery just completed at Hooven, causing an overnight growth in the population throughout all of Miami Township. With the consolidation of the schools of the district, and a high school built, a number of rural schools were gradually closed and the pupils transferred to North Bend and Cleves. (For further insight into the growth of the schools see the histories of Finney, Addyston and Mt. Nebo Schools.)

The history of the high schools at North Bend must be told but it is necessary first to go back in time and tell something of the story of Cleves village schools and those in rural areas of Miami Township.

Cleves had a common school as early as 1847, built, so legend tells, on ground set aside for the purpose by William H. Harrison when he platted the village in 1818. A brick schoolhouse, yet standing, was erected on this site but whether or not it was the first school to stand there has not been learned. This old brick building may yet be seen in the block between North Miami Avenue and Skidmore Street, behind Joe Labelle's business place, not far from the old council chamber and jail. Classes were conducted at this first known schoolhouse until 1871, when a new common school was opened on College Street behind the Miami Township Hall.

Legend also tells that an even earlier school was conducted in Cleves in the Laird home, said to have been built around 1837, probably by Andrew Laird (1840 census) and his wife, Mary. This house, among the very oldest in the town, occupied by the Milton Thompson, Sr., family for many years, is located on Laird Street. Mrs. Thompson recalls that many years ago a very old man named George Edson told her that he and members of his family once attended school in the front room of her house. The story seems quite logical because the U.S. Census of 1880 shows one E. A. Edson, then 38 years old, dwelling on Laird Street. If he were born ca. 1842, he (and brother George) might well have attended school in the Laird home, possibly before a school was built on the schoolhouse lot. The 1860 U.S. Census shows that Mary Lewis, age 22, a school-"marm," lived in the home of Mary Laird, age 70. Whether classes were then being held in the Laird house, or whether School-"marm" Lewis was teaching at the common school is unknown.

After the first brick schoolhouse was abandoned as a public school in 1871, it became a school for colored children. Where the colored boys and girls had attended before that time has not been learned. It is known that a colored church existed by 1865, so it is possible that a school was conducted there. Colored children from around Miami Township went to classes in the old public schoolhouse until 1888, at which time they took their rightful places in the new public schools.

References to this school and another colored school in Whitewater Township have been found in Lawrenceburg Press and Mt. Nebo records:
Nov. 14, 1872. "Morgan Wamsley has secured the colored school at the township hall in Whitewater Township and has commenced teaching there this week."

Feb. 1873. "W. B. Jones has been engaged to teach the colored school in Cleves, beginning Feb. 24th." (Mt. Nebo, where Prof. Jones had previously taught, was forced to close for a brief period due to a lack of funds.)

Feb. 27, 1873. "The colored school under Prof. Jones was discontinued until Monday due to so much sickness with measles."

1877. Wm. C. Ely will teach the colored department of Cleves at a salary of $1.75 per day."

Old treasury records of Mt. Nebo School Board show expenditures of tuition for five colored children who attended school at Cleves in 1885-1886.

In 1887, Miss Linnie Sanders of Cincinnati was a teacher at the Cleves Colored School, probably the last year it was open. After that time colored boys and girls are found in the public schools.

The names of several teachers, gleaned from numerous sources, who taught before 1871 in the first known Cleves school have been found. Based on fact and legend, it may be assumed that Mary Laird, herself, and Mary Lewis, school "marm," were among the earliest teachers. It must be remembered that very few families lived in Cleves in the year 1847.

Elbert Bogart, a most capable man, is known to have taught here and in the Zion area. His wife, Eva Fagaly Bogart, was also an early teacher around Miami Township and Miamitown. Several of the Bogart's children later taught school at Cleves. Elbert Bogart showed talent as a writer of verse; some of his poetry was published in magazines of that day. One poem, entitled "I Look For Thee," was published in Sartain Magazine in 1852, when the author was only 20 years old. Many early postcard views of Cleves, found in the scrapbooks of older families, were printed and sold by Mrs. Eva Bogart in the 1890-1900 era.

Emma Newton, who married James O. Tebow in 1868, is known to have taught school at Cleves during the Civil War period.

William B. Welsh is believed to have taught school at Cleves around this time. He was one of the organizers of the first Hamilton County Teachers' Association in 1867. During the 1869-1870 era, he was principal at Mt. Nebo, which then had a good size school. Welsh became mayor of Cleves in 1875, when it was first incorporated, and served again in that capacity in 1887.

Godfrey Clause, Mt. Nebo teacher from 1859 to Jan. 1866, came to Cleves in 1866.

John Wesley Dunn taught at Cleves during the 1860's. It is interesting, at this point, to present a brief sketch of the life of this longtime teacher of Miami and Green Townships:

In the year 1835, John Wesley Dunn with his widower father and three little brothers left Ireland and came to Cincinnati, settling near Cheviot. Death soon took the father of the four motherless lads. The Dunn boys were placed in different homes as was the custom of those days. John had the good fortune to find a home with Dr. Barrus Agin, who encouraged him to study for an education, and to teach school, which he did in the rural and village schools of the area. He had the honor of being granted the first Five Year County Teachers' Certificate, which was a much coveted prize in those days, by the Hamilton County Board of School Examiners. Four of his five children followed him in the teaching profession.

John W. Dunn wed Elizabeth Silver (1843-1901) of Zion, Miami Township, descendant of Judge James and Elizabeth Thompson Silver, pioneers in the North Bend settlement of John Cleves Symmes. Elizabeth T. Silver, herself, was a niece of Judge Symmes.

John Dunn was an early teacher in the Zion (Burr School) area. By his late daughter's statement, he was teaching at Cleves in 1866 when she (Margaret) was born. (The late Margaret Dunn Walton, who lived to be 100, was a teacher at Cleves School around 1890-1891.) The John Dunn family later moved, around 1880, from the Zion community to Dent, Green Township. Dunn's son, Jesse K. Dunn, became a lifelong teacher and principal in the rural schools, the House of Refuge (a school for delinquent pupils), and in the Cincinnati Schools.

The following item from Lawrenceburg Press gives the identity of the 1869 teachers at Cleves School:

Dec. 2, 1869. "Prof. R. N. John and his two assistants, Misses (Eliza) Wamsley and (Anna) Cassady, are at work and performing valuable service to the youth of the village." (Anna Cassady was daughter of Dr. George Cassady; Eliza Wamsley was the daughter of Samuel Wamsley, blacksmith. Eliza's sister, Anna, and brother, Morgan, were teachers in the area at this same time.)

"Cleves has a good public school," stated Sidney D. Maxwell in 1870, in his book Suburbs of Cincinnati.

Before the coming of the railroads in the 1850's and 1860's, the population of the village of Cleves was small. The 1830 U.S. Census listed only 22 heads of households in the town in that year. A great part of the land now situated in Cleves was, until after the death of Anna Harrison, a part of the Harrison estate. By the late 1860's, the village was growing, creating a need for a larger schoolhouse.

So it was that in 1871, a new brick school was built on College Street, behind the Town Hall, opposite where the United Methodist Church now stands. The following items (Lawrenceburg Press) tell of the new school:

Oct. 12, 1871. "The new schoolhouse in Cleves, a spacious and well arranged edifice, will open Monday. A corps of good teachers is employed. Cleves will be blessed. There are now 3 spacious halls in town, besides the school."

Dec. 7, 1871. "Cost of Cleves School was about $10,000."

Apparently Charles Phares of Harrison was the first principal in the new school in 1871.

July 25, 1872. "Charles Phares of Harrison was re-elected principal of Cleves School. Appointed assistants for the ensuing year were Misses Anna Cassady and Eliza J. Wamsley.

Feb. 6, 1873. "Our new schoolhouse leaks like a riddle. It is very strange that the honorable Board of Education of Miami Township would fritter away $10,000 in erecting a leaky structure."

April 17, 1873. "Jacob Balsley was elected director of the school board."

July 17, 1873. "John Dunn was employed as principal of our school. He is a gentlemanly principal." (Dunn had taught earlier in the old school during the 1860's. Around 1877-1878 he taught at Valley Junction.)

June 18, 1874. "Mr. John W. Dunn, Miss Fanny Lind and Miss Bray, in charge of the three departments of

Cleves Public School, had a school picnic at a grove on State Road near Cleves." (Possibly at Matson's Grove)

July 23, 1874. "A contract for building a stone wall west of the schoolhouse lot has been awarded to Rininger & Barker at $2 per perch."

June 24, 1875. "W. B. Jones was elected principal of Cleves but he will not accept."

Sept. 16, 1875. "G. W. Powell, formerly of Hamilton, is principal at Cleves. 170 pupils attend. Assistants are Misses Anna Cassady and Fannie Lind. Owing to increase in attendance the board decided to hire another assistant for this year."

Dec. 9, 1875. "Changes have been made at the school. Dr. Royal Struble is now principal." (He was an early physician around Miamitown.)

Mar. 2, 1876. "Prof. Stephens will be a teacher of a singing school in Cleves."

May 25, 1876. "Prof. S. Kyle Stephens was appointed principal of the public school for the ensuing year at $4 per day. Eight teachers of Miami Township were before the examining board."

Dec. 28, 1876. "The little ones of the Cleves Public School gave an exhibition at the Town Hall. They sang, declaimed and were amusing."

Apr. 26, 1877. "Thomas N. Lind (son of A.R. Lind) is clerk of the school board."

May 3, 1877. "Mr. J. L. Trisler made application for Cleves School."

Fall of 1877. "W. B. Jones is principal in Cleves School at a salary of $3.25 per day."

(W. B. Jones' brother, Irvin Jones, was a teacher in the Fagaly (District 7) and Zion Schools during the 1873-1875 era. For more about W. B. Jones see "History of Mt. Nebo School.")

Apparently Professor John M. Grimsley came to Cleves in the fall of 1878, where he remained for several years before going to Fernbank School.

July 1, 1879. (Cincinnati Daily Gazette) "Cleves School Board re-elected the present corps of teachers with the addition of Miss Helen Guard of North Bend. Mr. Grimsley is in charge. There are four teachers. It is the first time since the place was incorporated (1875) that a principal had a chance of serving two years successfully." (Royal S. Hayes, later a teacher himself, and editor of The Hayes Family, stated that he had been a pupil of Prof. Grimsley at Cleves and noted that he was a fine teacher.)

A private school was conducted at Cleves in early days, during the 1860-1870 era, although little has been learned of this. It was known as Mrs. Ewing's school, and possibly was conducted in the house that stands directly opposite the former Bright Motor Company (lastly Seaver Ford Agency). It is said that a private school was once conducted in this place. At one time, as early as 1850, Dr. Richard H. Ewing, physician, and his brother, William C. Ewing, merchant, resided in Cleves. Dr. Ewing practiced around the community for many years, left the neighborhood for a time, and returned in the early 1870's. He and William C. Ewing were brothers of Sarah Rittenhouse Lind, the wife of Thomas N. Lind, early Mt. Nebo teacher and Methodist preacher. Fannie Lind (Pratt), daughter of Sarah and Thomas Lind, is said to have attended Mrs. Ewing's private school and once taught there. She was a teacher at Cleves Public School during the 1873-1880 period. Fannie L. Pratt later wrote and presented several interesting papers for the Mt. Nebo Society Reunions.

An item from Lawrenceburg Press mentions Mrs. Ewing's school:

Jan. 13, 1876. "Miss Leah Hayes of Mt. Nebo is attending Mrs. Ewing's private school in Cleves."

(Elizabethtown, nearby, has a minor claim to fame in the field of private school education. Back in 1854, the elite Elizabethtown Female Institute was established, in charge of Rev. C. E. Babb and his sisters. The private boarding school, housed in an elegant brick structure, provided through the generosity of townsmen Thomas and Jacob Hunt, yet stands today. During 1857-1858, twenty-eight young ladies were enrolled in the college, among them Mary Lewis of Elizabethtown, and Martha Chidlaw and Adeline M. Jameson of Cleves. The seminary functioned until about 1859. It may have been the aforesaid Mary Lewis who was the schoolmarm residing in the home of Mary Laird, Cleves, in 1860. Those who served on the Elizabethtown seminary's board of trustees included: Joseph Lewis, president; A. E. Bonham, secretary; J. P. Haire, treasurer; Jacob Hunt, George W. Haire, and J. H. Bonham of Elizabethtown; John Noble, Cleves; Rev. C. E. Babb and Rev. B. W. Chidlaw.

It is interesting to know that the old Elizabethtown Female Institute played a small role in the history of Western College for Women at Oxford, Ohio. As it happened, Western Female Seminary was founded at Oxford in 1853, with Miss Helen Peabody as president. On Jan. 14, 1860, that school suffered a fire which destroyed its building. In order to continue as an educational institution the trustees rented a house at Elizabethtown, the site of the former seminary. There the "middle" class of twenty-five students who had gone to their homes after the fire assembled in Sept. 1860, and carried on a year's work under Misses Walker, Gow and Mills. In the fall of 1861, they returned to Oxford where a new seminary had been built. The school later assumed the name Western College.

The commodious brick building, formerly the Elizabethtown Female Institute, was purchased around 1867 by Silas Van Hayes from Wm. P. Rees, a Hunt descendant. It has remained in the same family ever since, Mrs. Bessie Hayes Matteson being the present owner.

A former resident of Elizabethtown, 109-year-old Mrs. Kitty Bonham Harvey of Minneapolis, Kansas, recently figured in the news, nationally, when she was awarded a degree from Western College. As the story goes, Mrs. Harvey was born Kitty Bonham at Elizabethtown in 1860. Her father, Aaron E., died when she was a year old and her mother, Narissa Olmstead Bonham, wed Rev. Horace Bushnell, Jr., in 1865. Kitty recalls a regiment of Union soldiers passing through E-town during the Civil War. The troops were treated by the women of the village to a chicken dinner which was cooked in the big kitchen of her grandmother Charlotte Hunt Bonham's house. One soldier asked Kitty to give him a kiss for his little girl back home, which she did. She's wondered all these years if he ever got back to his little girl. While Kitty was a student at Western Female Seminary, in 1878, ill health forced her to leave school. Shortly after, she went west to join her mother and step-father. Out west Kitty married and has remained ever since. A Wichita newspaper recently published an interesting account of her life, administrators at Western College learned of it and chose to confer a degree upon Kitty Bonham Harvey--93 years after she had entered what was then Western Female Seminary. How incredible to find a woman yet living in 1969 who was born in

Elizabethtown the very year that that school had temporarily conducted its classes there. (This writer wrote to and heard from Kitty Harvey.)

Back at Cleves in December, 1875, another kind of school was established by Morgan Wamsley. This was a night school for the benefit of young men who could not attend public school. The name of Morg Wamsley appears again and again as a teacher in Miami and Whitewater Townships. He also taught at Industry (Delhi) School. Wamsley served on the Cleves council and was for many years director of Hamilton County National Bank, Cleves.

The second known Cleves Common (public) School, opened in October, 1871, housed eight grades. This building of two stories had six class rooms and two large halls. A big, pot-bellied stove stood in each room with a coal scuttle along side. A water bucket, with dipper, was conspicuously placed in a corner of every room. Cloak rooms, having numerous pegs, or hooks, held the wraps of the scholars. This village school was quite an improvement over the rural schools of the township. Classes were called to order with the ringing of a bell by the teacher. Scholars studied from McGuffey's readers--in use for nearly 50 years--and Ray's arithmetics-- in use for about as long. Writing was considered as important as the other 2 R's, reading and 'rithmetic. Most early-day teachers, men as well as women, wrote in beautiful Spencerian script. Daily exercises in writing were conducted with the use of penmanship pads and charts, and all pupils, holding pens and wrists correctly, rhythmically made ovals and push-ups to the count of the teacher. Creator of the penmanship copybook best known in this area was Platt Spencer. On each writing pad was stated Platt Spencer's purpose:

"Plain to the eye and gracefully combined,
To train the muscle and inform the mind."

Today, there is a generation which does not know that the McGuffey readers have probably had more influence on Americans than any other book outside of the Bible. These books were storehouses of fables, mottoes, proverbs, "Memory Gems," and quotations. They taught a stern code of honor, loyalty, and the rewards of virtue, industry and honesty. There are also those who think of McGuffey only as a book, never as a man. Yet, there is probably no man who played such a vital role in shaping the destiny of this nation as William Holmes McGuffey, who stuffed education into a saddlebag and carried it out to meet the needs of the people. (See Out of the Midwest, by Frank Siedel.)

(Concerning McGuffey it is interesting to Miami and Whitewater Township history to note that Benjamin W. Chidlaw related that while a student at Miami University (ca. 1835), at Professor McGuffey's request, he made a copy, for publication, of the manuscript of the first McGuffey Primer. For the task he was paid $5. (From The Miami Years, by Walter Havighurst) Chidlaw later resided at Berea (now Hooven), having wed the daughter of Ezekiel Hughes. He was minister at Cleves Presbyterian Church and an ardent worker in the American Sunday School Union. (See The Story of My Life, by B. W. Chidlaw, 1890.))

Boys and girls who attended school around the 1850-1880 era received Reward of Merit cards or certificates. These fancily embellished testimonials were presented as compensation for good work. They are prize collector items today.

A kindergarten was conducted by a Mrs. Wallace, ca. 1880, near the Cleves railroad station, so recalls Mrs. Alice Struble.

The building of the canal and railroads brought many persons of Irish and German nationality to the vicinity. Many

Cleves School, the second known schoolhouse, Ca. 1900. This was opened in 1871 and burned in 1926. It stood across from the Methodist Church.

of these people were of the Catholic faith. For a time during the 1870's, a Catholic school was conducted in a building behind what is known now as "Bundy's," opposite the Cleves theater. A Catholic kindergarten was also said to have existed in the community in the early 1880's. Prior to that time classes were conducted in private homes. As transporation means improved, some pupils were sent to Delhi to the Catholic Church and school located there.

Known teachers of Cleves Common School in the 1880's included:

John M. Grimsley, Helen E. Guard, Mollie Carlin, Sallie Westcott, A.E.B. Stephens, Stanley Struble, Will Harrell, Virgil Henderson, and Miss Lou H. Godley. Since this was a large eight grade school, four teachers were usually employed during this period.

Mollie (Mary) Carlin taught primary grades at Cleves and records attest she was "the favorite" of many. She had a lovely voice and participated in the music, literary, and dramatic societies so popular in that day. In 1884, she wed A.E.B. Stephens, a fellow teacher at Cleves, who later taught at North Bend.

Stephens, who with his family had come to Cleves about 1876, taught at Gravel Pit (Finney) around 1881. His father, S. Kyle Stephens, taught in Elizabethtown and Berea. A.E.B. Stephens, better known as "Buzz," entered the field of politics, became widely known, and was eventually elected Representative to Congress, 2nd Ohio District, in 1919. He remained in this office until his death in 1927. His sister, Hallie Caine, became equally well known as principal of North Bend School.

Helen E. Guard was an educator who probably held the all-time record for teaching at more schools in the Miami and Whitewater Township area than any other. She is recalled as a capable woman and excellent teacher.

Lou H. Godley was of a prominent Harrison family. She later became a school superintendent.

Stanley Struble taught for a time at Mt. Nebo, Cleves and Finney before attending Oberlin College. He began the practice of law in Cleves in 1896 and later gained prominence as a Judge in the Hamilton County Courts. It is interesting to note that while at Cleves School he taught Alice Argo in the 3rd and 5th grades. He taught her so well that she became his bride in 1895, upon her graduation from Hughes High. The Argo family were pioneers in Cleves. A fountain in memory of Judge Struble was dedicated at the Miami Township Hall on March 29, 1969.

William Harrell served as principal, off and on, over a period of about twenty years, at North Bend and Cleves village schools. He often tutored students who desired to go beyond 8th grade, before high schools were introduced, and assisted scholars in securing teachers' certificates. At North Bend he taught for several years before 1886; he was principal at Cleves from 1886 to 1893, and again from 1898 until around 1906. Harrell left Cleves to teach at Cincinnati First Intermediate School and from there to Boys Special School, where he became quite successful at handling and disciplining delinquent boys.

Virgil Henderson graduated from Moore's Hill College about 1886, and came to Cleves for his first assignment. From there he went to Addyston, for a few years around 1893, then to Zion (Burr) around 1897-1898. He returned to Addyston where he was in charge for many years. After that time, he assumed the principalship of Boys Special School, Cincinnati school for wayward boys, remaining until he retired at the age of 70. (A certain sign of his success as a teacher was that after his retirement old pupils continued to come to visit him at his home in Cleves.)

Teachers at Cleves during the 1890 era were:

Will Harrell, Margaret Dunn Walton, Helen E. Guard, Leslie Struble, William Flinchpaugh, principal from 1893 to 1898, Elizabeth Bogart, Marcia Cassady Hughes, Anna Chrisman, Emma Stumpp Speed, Flora Myers and Lydia Myers.

Salaries of teachers of the 1880-1900 era amounted from around $42.50 to $50 a month, roughly $2.25 to $2.50 a day. Principals of village schools received a little more, sometimes as high as $4 a day. W. B. Jones signed a contract to teach at rural Zion School in 1874 at $52 a month. Teachers in rural schools often paid janitors or older pupils several dollars a month to help build fires and carry water. Coal sold for about 10¢ a bushel and was purchased by the school board along with tin cups @ 7¢, and desks @ $3.25.

Pupils walked good distances to school so they carried lunch pails. (Tin lard buckets were popular for this.) At recess they played jacks, jumped rope and played hide-and-seek. There were hills on both sides of Cleves School so sled riding was enjoyed in winter. Girls, in those days, often wore aprons over their dresses to keep them clean longer. (Mabel Graham Hayes, a schoolgirl at Cleves in the 1890's, told of these recollections.)

Good scholarship was encouraged as much then as now. The names of those pupils who had excelled on examinations in their respective classes in Cleves School were published in Feb. 1896, in the Cleves Review, local--short lived--newspaper, edited by D. B. Sherwood. Grade levels of classes, in that day, bore letters rather than numbers. Honor scholars named in the paper were:

Advanced grade, Emery Shaw; A grade, Ethel Forbes; B grade, Viola Rosencrans; C grade, Harry Newell; D grade, Eddie Hearn and Hattie Newell; E grade, Johanna Clark; F grade, Willie Sonnenday and Willie Vetri; G grade, Maude Stephens; H grade, Mabel Graham.

The "Pledge of Allegiance to the Flag," written by Francis Bellamy, was first published Sept. 8, 1892, in the magazine "Youth's Companion," in connection with a national public school celebration of Columbus Day in October, 1892. (400th anniversary) It would be safe to say that Miami Township school children were taught the "Pledge to the Flag," and that demonstrations in patriotism were encouraged, an example of which was the "Girls' Brigade," organized by Hallie Caine at North Bend. Boys and girls are known to have participated in annual pilgrimages to Harrison's Tomb.

Popular pastimes at the turn of the century included parades, train rides, singing schools, taffy pulls, spelling bees, going "hickory nutting," piano recitals, ice skating, picnics, ice cream and strawberry socials, and trips to local and county fairs, among these Carthage Fair, Dearborn County Fair, Harvest Home Fair in Green Township, and the annual Miami and Whitewater Valley Pioneer Picnic at Whitewater Park. Entire classes of scholars are known to have taken steamboat excursions on the Ohio. In that day, and for many years to come, trips to the Cincinnati Zoo were annual attractions for school children.

Board of Education members of Cleves School in 1897 were:

J. O. Smith, president; F. S. Blocher, clerk; C. A. Wood, treasurer; Thomas Cassady and S. W. Cooper.

Graduates of the Cleves Intermediate School that year were Linnie Flinchpaugh and Charles T. Young.

William H. Flinchpaugh, schoolmaster from 1893 to 1898, was followed by Will Harrell who returned to Cleves for a second time as principal. When Harrell left Cleves School in 1906, he was succeeded by D. S. Richards who acted as principal for several years, from 1906 to 1909.

In 1909, there came a young man to Cleves to teach 7th and 8th grades and serve as principal, who was destined to become a most influential educator in the district. He was Charles T. Young, a product of this very school.

Charles Young had graduated in 1897, in that class of two. He then rode the commuter train to old Hughes High, located in that day at Fifth and Mound Streets in the city. In an interview with Mr. Young in 1954, this writer made notes of his school days recollections at Hughes High, as follows:

Classes lasted from 8:10 AM to 1:20 PM. There was a full schedule with no extracurricular subjects. During the period he attended Hughes, an outside building was erected for physical education classes. Early basketball was a "rough and tumble" game, with no rules except to get the ball into the hoop. One team wore handkerchiefs around their arms to distinguish their side from the other players. Boys and girls homerooms were separate. Pupils carried their lunches, but on occasion a lady prepared sandwiches on a counter in the Hughes High cellar. There were no tables or seats, so everyone huddled around eating in an awkward manner. There was no bell system for changing classes, only a gong on the 2nd floor. The janitor resided in the attic. The school had no brick walkways, no yard nor grass, and tanbark was strewn over the ground to keep students out of the mud. Even though the school lacked many of the conveniences of the present day, Hughes High, in its time, had much to offer its scholars. (A new Hughes was opened in 1910.)

In 1903, Charles Young began his teaching career at rural Jordan School, also known as Maple Grove and Sub-District No. 6 School, located north of Cleves, off of East Miami River Road, on Cilley Road (now Buffalo Ridge Road). A school had existed at this site from earliest times, as indicated on old maps. The ground for the school was originally given by a pioneer family and specified to be used for school or religious purposes only. The school drew students from around East Miami River Road, once called Matson's Mill Road, and up along Jordan Creek. Morgan Wamsley was principal of Jordan in the 1873-1874 era. He had 35 scholars. (Lawrenceburg Press, Nov. 20, 1873.) Hallie Stephens Caine had taught there for a time before going to North Bend in 1892. Jordan School, a one-room building, remained in use until the mid 1920's. The old schoolhouse was razed about 1941. Mr. Arthur Sheckler of Cleves has the bell from old Jordan, or Maple Grove, School.

In addition to Jordan School, two other schools which once existed in Miami Township must be mentioned. These were Fagaly School, along Buffalo Ridge Road, near Gum Run Road, and Burr School, at the corner of Zion and Bridgetown Roads. Schools had existed at these sites, or in a general proximity, from earliest days. Each was named for pioneer settlers of Mt. Zion, the present Miami Heights area. The Fagalys, along with the Flinchpaughs, were organizers of the United Brethren Church in the vicinity. This church is said to be the second oldest of that denomination west of the Alleghenies. Zion U.B. Church, now Zion United Methodist, is located at Zion and Zion Hill Roads. (A school called Flinchpaugh School also existed in the Taylor's Creek neighborhood in early times.) Samuel Burr, who had acquired a large tract of land in Miami Township in the area of Zion and Dog Trot Roads, was an early Hamilton County teachers' examiner, ca. 1835. His settlement was once known as Burr's or Burr District.

Fagaly School was founded around 1850 by Emanuel Fagaly and other members of his family. The road running past the school in early days was called Fagaly and Bogart Road. This school was featured in a Caroline Williams sketch in the Cincinnati Enquirer, Sept. 8, 1940, and was counted among the last of the one-room schools in the county. In October, 1941, former teachers and pupils of the little school held a final reunion and homecoming on the school site. Fagaly School closed shortly thereafter when the new Miami Township Rural School was completed. This is now known as Miami Heights Elementary School. A room in the school was dedicated as the Fagaly room.

Burr School was known by the name as early as the 1860's, possible sooner. David H. Rittenhouse, in his diary in 1868, mentioned attending a caucus meeting at Burr schoolhouse. Being located on Zion Road, it was also known as Zion School. A still earlier school building stood in this general region in 1847, but it was located along what is now known as Shady Lane, just a short distance off of State or Bridgetown Road.

John W. Dunn and W. B. Jones were among teachers at Burr, or Zion, during the 1860-1870 era. From the Lawrenceburg Press comes this item:
Nov. 27, 1873. "The first term of Zion school ended. Maggie Rogers, George Hearn and Royal Hayes obtained prizes for spelling."

Royal S. Hayes was born on Mt. Nebo in 1867, the son of Mahlon and grandson of Job Hayes. The family moved soon after to Zion where Royal acquired his early schooling. He eventually became a teacher at Addyston and North Bend, before joining the Cincinnati School system. In 1929, his book of pioneer history and genealogy, The Hayes Family, was published. At the time of his death at the age of 94, Royal Hayes was working on a history of the Zion-Miami Heights region, with emphasis on the people who once lived there. (As a young boy his Zion neighbors included such figures as Dr. John Thornton--General Harrison's son-in-law, and John H. Matson (1804-1877), son of Isaac Matson who had come to North Bend with Judge Symmes about 1790. John Matson's son, Isaac B. Matson, achieved prominence as a Judge of the Probate Court of Hamilton County from 1873 to 1885.) As far as is known, Royal Hayes' history of Zion has not been published. Judging from his book about the Hayes family, his writings on early Miami Heights most surely would be of tremendous value to the overall history of Miami Township. In Roger Miller's column, "On the Cuff,"

Western Hills Press, March 1, 1957, it was stated:
"Mr. Hayes followed the original ownerships of the (Zion) Miami Township School site through Symmes, Oliver Spencer, Sam Burr, William Burr and John Schinkal, who sold the initial six acre tract for Burr School in 1848. He has traced the movements of many pioneer Miami Township families whose names are familiar throughout the western county--Markland, Wood, Fagaly, Flinchpaugh, McGee and Hearn."

Professor Virgil Henderson taught at Burr about 1898. He was followed by David W. Gwaltney in the 1899-1900 era. The latter came to Cleves from Indiana as a young man and taught in the Miami and Whitewater Township schools for 20 years. He later worked in the county treasurer's office, served as mayor of Cleves for 12 years, and as justice of the peace of Miami Township for 30 years.

Charles R. Coulthard (1872-1961) taught at Zion School for a number of years, ca. 1905 to 1912. A lifelong schoolmaster, he served for 50 years, 33 of them in the Cincinnati system. It was he and Everett McClurkin who, in 1916, compiled a Souvenir Book of North Bend, Ohio, issued by the U. B. Church, which included an interesting history of the area.

In later years Burr School consisted of two, one-room buildings, one for housing first through third grades, the other for fourth through eighth grades. When Jordan School was abandoned in the 1920's, its scholars were sent to Burr. In 1935, the seventh and eighth graders of Fagaly and Burr districts began to attend school at Taylor High. These rural schools remained in use until replaced by Miami Township Rural School on Bridgetown Road, not far from Shady Lane.

(A better account should be written by one familiar with the history of these rural schools, Fagaly, Burr and Jordan.)

Back in 1906, after three years as schoolmaster of rural Jordan (Maple Grove) School, Charles T. Young went to Addyston village school where he taught under Principal Virgil Henderson. While there he worked with Bertha Brater and Sylvia Whitney Stephens, two fellow teachers with whom he was to share a lifetime association. The three of them studied together for their teachers' examinations during the long lunch periods at Addyston. (Boys and girls there were given 1 hour and 45 minute breaks for lunch in order that they might have time to eat and also to carry dinner pails to their menfolk at Addyston Pipe Foundry.)

In 1909, Charles R. Coulthard, Principal of Zion School, was president of Hamilton County Teachers' Association, and Charles T. Young, newly appointed principal of Cleves, was treasurer.

Charles Young remained as principal of Cleves from 1909 until 1920, at which time he went to John S. Conner School to organize a township high school. During the 1909-1920 period, many men and women conducted classes at the school on College Street. It would be impossible to learn all of them but the list included:

Will Harrell, Helen E. Guard, Ada Smith, Elizabeth Bogart, Anna Chrisman, Flora Myers, Jessye F. LaBoiteaux, D. S. Richards, Edith Suit Young, Hallie McIntyre Landon, Charles T. Young, Myla M. Wood Robinson, Marcia Cassady Hughes, Mary M. Pouder, Nellie McGee Jacobs Rankin, Irene D. Hague, Nan Hopping McCullough, Pearl Ringwald, Cora Rittenhouse, Hazel Stratton, Fern Yanney English, and Edna McCormick.

Edna McCormick succeeded Charles Young as principal in 1920. She retained the position until 1923, when she resigned to go to Norwood to teach. Miss Halliday of Lebanon succeeded her.

The date May 2, 1926 goes down in Cleves School history because that was the day the schoolhouse burned to the ground. Fortunately, it happened on a Sunday morning when no one was in the building. Excerpts from the Cincinnati Enquirer tell of the catastrophe:

May 3, 1926. "Flames swept Cleves School. Three volunteer firemen were hurt: Harry Cassidy, fire chief; Lester Hoffman, and Royal Jones, school janitor. Cheviot Fire Dept. also responded. Loss was estimated around $25,000. The two story building, more than 50 years old, housed grades 1 through 6. The 7th and 8th grades attend the new Taylor High School. Arrangements will be made to send the 300 children to the high school. Cleves Methodist Church and the residence of John Stephens just across College Street were saved only by heroic work. The only thing saved from the fire was the school telephone carried out by Edward McDonald, who won the Carnegie medal and $500 during the 1913 flood for his bravery in saving a life during high water."

Following the fire, pupils were sent to Taylor High, just opened a few months earlier, in January 1926, and to John S. Conner School. Known teachers of Cleves classes during this era were:

Cora Wiles Flowers, Edith Suit Young, Alice Rector, Lillian Amos Mears, Sylvia W. Stephens, and Jessie Wolcott. There were, undoubtedly, others.

Charles Young had meanwhile become superintendent of the Cleves-North Bend School District, and was in the process of consolidating all of the schools in Miami Township. Population was soaring and rural schools bulging. Old Cleves School, even though built in 1871 and outmoded in many respects, could not have burned at a more critical time.

Nevertheless, Mr. Young proved then his ability as an administrator. He took the matter in hand and by Monday morning had the Cleves scholars placed in the high school and grade school at North Bend. This temporary measure lasted for three years, until a new Cleves School was opened on North Miami Avenue. From the Lawrenceburg Press:

Jan. 3, 1929. "The new $100,000 Cleves School building is taking form and beginning to show that it is a thing of beauty. The school children are making progress at Taylor and North Bend."

When Cleves School was completed in 1929, it was truly a thing of beauty. Principals of the school since that time have included:

Edith Young, Ralph Atherton, Ray Hutchens, Jessie Wolcott, who had a record of lengthy service in that place from 1928 to 1963, and David Sisson, present principal.

The school carried the name Cleves School until 1954, when it was fittingly changed to Charles T. Young School, in honor of the man who had served the community for fifty years, 1903-1953.

An appropriate dedication exercise took place at the school, May 23, 1954, presided over by Earl J. Jenkins, Superintendent of Cleves-North Bend Schools. Fred Pontius, long-time (30 years) mayor of Cleves, gave the welcome. Other participants included:

Frank Crow, president of Cleves-North Bend School Board; Manning Moreland, president of Hamilton County School Board; Mrs. Jessie Wolcott, principal of Charles T. Young School; Charles B. Crouch, superintendent of Hamilton County Schools; Judge Otis Hess, Court of Common Pleas; Rev. S. E. Bruner, Methodist Church; and Rev. Dean Montgomery, Presbyterian Church. Taylor High Band, under direction of Milton H. Dockweiler, played; Cleves School choir, led by Anne Dunston, sang. John and Steven Young, grandsons of the honored educator, presented a spade and trowel.

Faculty of the school in 1954 included:

Jessie Wolcott, principal; Emma Harms, Luella White, Norma Fineran, Belle Moreland, Nancy McCullough (a long-time teacher), Geneva Calvert, Margaret Heil, Anne Dunston, Muriel Mahoney, Margaret Rothenbush, Lenora Steele, Dorothy Wintersteen, Fern Seibel, Kathryn Schwing, Lula Kemp, Milton Dockweiler, Patricia Kennedy and Robert Meador.

Among the many who served as teachers at Cleves was Bertha Brater, a legend to all who ever called her "Teacher." She had received her early education at old Fernbank grade and high school, graduating from Home City High. For a time she attended Normal University at Lebanon. She taught at Burr Oak, Addyston, "new" Addyston and Cleves, where she remained until her retirement in 1953. Like Charles T. Young, she also taught in the community for half-a-century. Countless other teachers with the same sense of dedication as Bertha Brater have given years of service to Cleves and Miami Township.

(Another teacher worthy of note was William Matson Chidlaw (1870-1968), descendant of the pioneer Matson and Chidlaw families. Although never a teacher in Miami Township schools, he was a lifetime resident of Cleves. Born near Berea, the grandson of Rev. B. W. Chidlaw, William learned his ABC's at historic Berea school. His son, Ben, recalls his father telling that, in periods of severe weather, all the neighboring farmers took turns hitching up their farm wagons and carting the youngsters to the schoolhouse. In early life his family moved to Cleves. William attended old Hughes High and Miami University, graduating from there in 1891. While a scholar at Miami he was left halfback and captain of the college football team when it played its first game against the University of Cincinnati in 1888, starting a classic rivalry. William Chidlaw taught in Delhi Township and later served, for 23 years, as principal of Sayler Park School. His son, who gained national fame, is USAF General Benjamin W. Chidlaw, Retired, former commander in chief of the Continental Air Defense Command. Born in Cleves, Ben Chidlaw attended Cleves Public School. The subject of his 8th grade commencement recitation in 1914 was "The Cumberland.")

For many years Miami Township was without a high school. Pupils fortunate enough to do so, rode the trains to Cincinnati to attend Woodward or Hughes High Schools. During the late 1890's, Will Harrell conducted some advanced classes at Cleves Common School for those who wanted to study beyond eighth grade.

In 1901, Oliver Swisher started a high school at Berea. The first class of 6 or 8 pupils was carried on right in with the grade school. High school, or advanced school, was conducted here until June, 1904, at which time Swisher moved to Elizabethtown to supervise a high school there during the 1904-1905 term. Some scholars from the Cleves and North Bend area attended and graduated from high school at Berea and Elizabethtown during this period. The coming of the CL&A traction cars in 1900 was a great boon in many ways--but especially to education.

Oliver Swisher was a man of tremendous ability. He had taught for many years in the Whitewater Township schools, was also an engineer and contractor for a time, and later became an assistant superintendent in the Cincinnati School system. He and his daughter, Luella Swisher Hayes, longtime postmistress of Hooven, are credited with naming that village in 1927. (Although the region had been known as Berea since shortly after 1800, no post office had ever been established until 1927. Another town in Ohio was named Berea, so a new name had to be found. Hooven was chosen.)

A high school called Miami Township High School was started in September 1903, in the John S. Conner School building. Miss Leonarda Goss was principal for two years. In 1905, she transferred to Elizabethtown High School, exchanging places with Oliver Swisher, who came to North Bend for that year. Pupils from around Cleves, Mt. Nebo, Finney and Zion attended high school here. Miami Township High School lasted for three years, 1903 to 1906, and from that time until 1920 there was no high school. Pupils continued on to Home City, Hughes or Elizabethtown High Schools. Principal at the latter school for about 20 years was James B. Radcliffe.

During the period 1906-1920, there was quite a heated controversy in the community as to where a high school should be located.

In 1920, Charles T. Young organized a district high school, again housed in the Conner School building. It was known as Miami Township Union High School. Designed along the plan of a full four-year program from the start, the new high school had one pupil in its senior class in 1920-1921. The first graduation class in 1922 consisted of two persons, Thelma Kelly and Okla Miller (Calloway). The latter went on to become a longtime teacher at Conner School and was especially knowledgeable on the subject of American Indian lore.

From the Lawrenceburg Press:
May 11, 1922. "The various boards of education of Miami Township are making an effort to organize the whole township under one board of education in order that a first class high school may be maintained as the Miami Township Union High School."

Among the teachers at Union High School from 1920 to 1926 were:
Charles T. Young, math and science; Laura Matson Bridgeman, science, sociology and home economics; Esther Schuerman, English, history and French; Edna Riley, Latin and math; Hazel Winston, Latin and government; Lucille Scudder, English, history and French.

The class of 1925, comprised of 13 girls, was the last class to hold commencement in the Conner School auditorium. A new high school was then under construction. (Miss Helen N. Dick, 1925 graduate of Union High, helped this writer to set the record straight. Mrs. Margaret K. Frankenhauser loaned her graduation program.)

Union High School classes continued to be held at the North Bend School until Jan. 6, 1926. On that day the beautiful new brick high school, grades 7 through 12, was opened on Harrison Avenue, North Bend. It was named in honor of W. W. Taylor, president of the first Cleves-North Bend District School Board. (Legend tells that some persons favored calling the school William H. Harrison High, because the site was originally a part of General Harrison's farm.)

From The Archaeology of Hamilton County, Ohio, by S. F. Starr, (p. 98), comes the following item of interest:
"Taylor High School in North Bend is built over the site of an archaic (Indian) village. The number of burials which were found when the school was built, and the material in many local collections testify to the richness of the site. Although the skeletons were not saved, the stemmed points, drilled shell disks, rough pestles, and bannerstones are all typical archaic artifacts."

A flag raising ceremony was held at new Taylor High School on Jan. 10, 1926. The occasion was unique in that the flagpole which originally stood at Harrison's Tomb, the one secured through the efforts of Tom Truitt back in 1902, was brought to the new high school. The erection of a tall new Harrison monument in 1924, had rendered the "little" 63-foot pole obsolete, but only temporarily. This pole was re-installed in front of Taylor High. At the flag presentation ceremony Edna Truitt Hayes, daughter of Tom Truitt, appropriately told the history of the "transplanted" flagpole. That pole yet stands, today.

On May 2, 1926, Cleves School burned. With Charles Young now at the helm of the schools, order was quickly restored out of the chaos resulting from the fire. The school children were placed in classes at the new Taylor High and Conner grade schools in North Bend, where they remained until a new school was completed in Cleves in 1929.

High school age students from all over Miami Township were enrolled at Taylor High. Several rural schools, Maple Grove (Jordan) and Mt. Nebo, were abandoned. Jordan pupils were sent to Burr School. Pupils of 7th and 8th grade standing from the Burr and Fagaly district began to attend Taylor High in the fall of 1935. These latter schools remained open until replaced by Miami Heights Elementary School. Addyston School continued to maintain 8 grades until the Three Rivers Junior High was built in 1960. Finney School continued as a one-room, eight grade school until 1932, among the last of the rural schools in Hamilton County in this category (8 grades under one teacher). Raymond Fisher, a 1928 graduate of Taylor High, had the distinction of being the last teacher here. He was killed in Arabia in 1934, the victim of bandits, while on a trip around the world.

Shortly after it opened, Taylor High also began to accept tuition paying students from Hooven and Elizabethtown in Whitewater Township. Pupils from these areas continued to attend Taylor for many years, until Cleves-North Bend District no longer had space to accommodate them. For a time a high school was conducted at Miamitown. Students of this region now attend William H. Harrison High School at Harrison.

Scholars from South Road, Taylors Creek and Dent Schools in Green Township also began to attend Taylor High in 1937. After the district could no longer accept them, students from the Green Township area were enrolled at Western Hills High, continuing to study there until Oak Hills High was built.

With the consolidation of the Miami Township school district and the building of Taylor High School, Charles T. Young (1883-1956) became superintendent of the schools of Cleves-North Bend School District. From the time that he began his teaching career back in January 1903, in a one-room, eight grade school, known as Jordan or Maple Grove, until his retirement in 1953, Mr. Young's highest aim was better education for all pupils. To know him was to respect him. He had the ability to walk into almost any classroom and take over where an absent teacher had left off, whether the situation called for conjugating Latin verbs, directing music classes or reading from Shakespeare. His handwriting was of a beautiful Spencerian type and could quickly be identified on the inside covers of hundreds of school text books which he had personally labeled "Property of Cleves-North Bend Schools." Scholarship came first with Charles Young, and no other, between 1903 and 1953, achieved a better record of progress for his school district than did he.

In one matter there were some who thought Charlie Young dictatorial. He insisted that all pupils in the school district march in the annual Memorial Day parade. Even though this was a legal holiday, teachers were instructed to bring their record books and take attendance. School buses picked up boys and girls as on any regular school day, dispatching them at the foot of Mt. Nebo Road and S. Miami Avenue in Cleves, where parade positions were formed. By Charles Young's rule some pupils were forced to be patriotic whether they wanted to or not. Looking back, in the face of today's mounting record of indifference and delinquency, we venture to guess that those "parade dissenters" of yesteryear may now agree that Mr. Young's rule wasn't such a bad one after all. (It must be stated, however, that the majority of scholars of the district dearly loved the annual parade and would have been sorely dissappointed had they not been able to march. It is one of the most pleasant recollections of many "old scholars.")

Upon Charles Young's retirement in 1953, Earl J. Jenkins, principal and science teacher at Taylor High since the school's founding, assumed the responsible position of superintendent of Cleves-North Bend School District. The community held tremendous respect for Earl Jenkins.

On May 23, 1954, Cleves Public School was renamed Charles T. Young School for the home-town educator who had devoted a full half-century to teaching in Miami Township. It was an honor well deserved.

Sylvia Whitney Stephens, who began to teach at Addyston in 1906, and studied with Charles Young and Bertha Brater during the long lunch periods, has also charted up quite a record herself. She taught over a period of 60 years in the Miami Township District. After many years at Cleves School, she went to Taylor High in 1947 to teach math and science in 7th and 8th grades, where she remained until retirement in 1966. Even though she has formally retired, Sylvia Stephens still accepts substitute teaching assignments. She has many hobbies, among them hooking rugs. Like Grandma Moses, Mrs. Stephens has also taken up painting pictures in her golden years.

To write of all of Taylor High's outstanding teachers would take a book. In the never ending parade of dedicated men and women who have taught--and are still teaching--there, continuously for a quarter of a century or longer, these names stand at the head of the list. A chapter could be written about each:
Earl J. Jenkins, A. E. Bollinger, S. U. Sisson, Maye DeLay Wright, Edna G. Balsley, Helen N. Dick, Milton H. Dockweiler, John E. Brannon, Ruth Reisinger, Ruth D. Schardine (North Bend and Taylor), Sylvia Stephens (Cleves and Taylor), and, of course, Charles T. Young.

One day back in 1930, the question as to why Taylor High had no school song was raised in Albert Bollinger's 8th grade music class. Then and there, two girls of the class were chosen to write such a song, Dorothy Robison (Knight) to compose the music, and Mary Bell Clark (Euchs), the words. The girls left the classroom to work on their composition and were back within thirty minutes, song in hand. The result was "Here's To Dear Old Taylor," a rousing number that has since been learned and sung by thousands of boys and girls--and "old grads." "Here's To Dear Old Taylor" has remained at the top of the hit parade for 39 years, the best known tune for miles around.

Albert E. Bollinger taught music classes in the Cleves-North Bend District for many years. He introduced the finest musical selections from opera and operetta and from the best of composers. Many older persons, once pupils of Mr. Bollinger, attribute their appreciation of music to their former singing teacher and are grateful to him for their introduction to music.

Another in the music field, who must not go unnamed, is Milton Hill Dockweiler, instrumental instructor and band director of Taylor since September 1935. Patience has been his number one virtue throughout these many years. He has encouraged countless boys and girls to play instruments and enjoy music, thereby helping them to lay foundations for happier and fuller lives. Milton Dockweiler's name is synonymous with Taylor High.

John E. Brannon (1914-1965) was another home-town lad who came to teach in his own high school in 1937. He succeeded Earl J. Jenkins as principal of the school in 1953, upon Mr. Young's retirement. Upon Mr. Jenkins' retirement, John Brannon assumed the role of superintendent in 1963. His sudden death in May 1965, was a tragedy for the school and community. Meredith Hitchens, assistant superintendent at that time, also a product of Taylor High, stepped up to superintendent.

The name of the rapidly growing school district was changed in 1956 from Cleves-North Bend District to Three Rivers District. The erection of the beautiful Three Rivers Junior High in 1960, relieved, at least temporarily, the space problem. Taylor High School has undergone several major building expansions since the school was erected back in 1926. A large addition, including a fine library and cafeteria, has just recently been completed. Offices of the Three Rivers Board of Education will soon be housed in the former Kiwanis Youth Lodge which stands on the site of the old Cleves school on College Street.

In 1969, Raymond H. Sisson and Harold Fisher, both "old Taylor boys," were re-elected president and vice-president of Three Rivers School Board. Hugh Williamson of Cleves, who was president of Hamilton County Board of Education for seven years, resigned in 1969 from the board on which he had served since 1956. The community was honored to have been represented by him.

A Taylor High School yearbook, THISO MEMOIRS, has been published annually since shortly after the school was founded. In these annuals may be found a proud record of the school's growth and progress over the years.

(*Author's note: Because of the apparent lack of records concerning early schools of Miami Township, this writer was prompted to learn what was available and to set the facts down for future generations. It is believed that some records of the old Cleves schools may have burned in the school fire of 1926. Few records exist before that time. Many persons, names too numerous to mention, have helped me in this labor of love. I studied old census records, perused old maps, gleaned early newspapers, searched libraries, read books pertaining to the area, and copied school programs which friends made available to me. Several loaned diaries. I am certain there were those who thought my project a real waste of time. I pestered my old friends, those willing to reminisce for me, unrelentingly. I wrote letters by the score. How encouraging were those responses, which came almost by return mail, stating, "Delighted to help!"
It has not been my intention to cover the entire history of the schools of the township. Any omissions of names of longtime teachers in the district has been unintentional. It was, obviously, impossible to give a biographical sketch of each named. Records of the district kept by both the schools and school board give a detailed history since consolidation. My account, even though incomplete, may give to the reader of the future some picture of early schools of the region and the characters of the teachers who guided them. A better account should be written by one familiar with the early

schools of the Zion and Miami Heights area. Perhaps one day more records of old Miami Township schools will come to light.)

LEST PUPILS FORGET

A Code of Rules to be observed in the common schools of Ohio was adopted in 1830:

1. Scholars must keep hands, faces and clothes clean.
2. Scholars must not stop or loiter on way to school.
3. Scholars must make no unnecessary noise.
4. Scholars must obey their teachers and rules of the schools.
5. Scholars must attend closely to studies.
6. Scholars must not study aloud.
7. Scholars must not talk or whisper to each other.
8. Scholars must not leave seats without permission.
9. Scholars must always speak the truth.
10. Scholars must not quarrel or injure each other.
11. Scholars must not use profane or indecent language.
12. Scholars must be polite and respectful in their conduct to everyone. (Schools of Cincinnati, by John P. Foote)

LEST TEACHERS FORGET

The following rules for teachers were posted by a New York principal in 1872:

1. Teachers each day will fill lamps, clean chimneys and trim wicks.
2. Each teacher will bring a bucket of water and a scuttle of coal for the day's session.
3. Make your pens carefully. You may whittle nibs to the individual taste of the pupil.
4. Men teachers may take one evening each week for courting purposes, or two evenings if they go to church regularly.
5. After ten hours in school, the teachers spend the remaining time reading the Bible or other good books.
6. Women teachers who marry or engage in unseemly conduct will be dismissed.
7. Every teacher should lay aside from each pay a goodly sum of his earnings for his benefit during his declining years so that he will not become a burden on society.
8. Any teacher who smokes, uses liquor in any form, frequents pool or public halls, or gets shaved in a barber shop will give good reason to suspect his worth, intentions, integrity and honesty.
9. The teacher who performs his labors faithfully and without fault for five years will be given an increase of 25 cents per week in his pay providing the Board of Education approves.

(Copied from Ohio Retired Teachers Association Quarterly, (ORTA), September, 1961.)

*This writer will welcome any information the reader can supply or suggest concerning early schools of the area.

★★★★★★★★★★

Oury's: School and Post Office

Oury's, named for pioneer James Oury, was an early settlement in Whitewater Twp. It was located in the area now known as Kilby Road, north of Hunt's Grove and Dry Fork. An early school, Oury's School, was conducted here; Wm. Bebb taught here ca. 1825. Oury's Tavern (1847 map, Wm. D. Emerson) stood along this route of the Whitewater Canal. Oury's P.O. was established Dec. 16, 1830, with Jas. Oury as postmaster. Possibly the office was housed in the tavern. This station was discontinued in Nov. 1856.

Old Mt. Nebo School, built Ca. 1853.

Representative occupations of Whitewater Township, other than farmers and laborers, from 1850 Census

Whitewater Township, including Elizabethtown & Miamitown: Blacksmiths: Jos. Bunnell, John Ingersoll, Rob't Lind, J. G. McCullough, Joshua Gibson, Wm. Randell, A. Lawton, Rob't Hopping; Carpenters: Thos. and Absolem Crale, S. C. and A.H. Smith, Wm. Shaw, Jos. VanCleaf, Wm. Rosencrans, Michael Cox, Henry Scott; Coopers: Hugh Barnes, Paul Baxter, Jas. Bellows, Lafayette Bunnell, Jas. Chambers, Wesley Higgins, Michael McCormick, Tubal Wiles, Rob't Winens, Richard Porter; Clerk: Philip Taber; Gardener: John Hill; Grocer: Chas. Brook; Harness Maker: A. Graff; Merchants: J. W. and Geo. Taber, J. B. Farmer, A. B. Dunn; Miller: Isaac Baughman; Ministers (Methodist): Penninus Rosencrans, Wm. Crawley; Omnibus Drivers: A. P. Cleaver, John Couch, John and Wm. Johnson, Matthew Richey (all resided at Galbreath's Tavern); Physicians: C. C. Little, Thos. Francis, John Hughes, Walter Clark; Pilot: Amos Bolender; Saddler: Jos. Lewis; Saw Millers: Eli Holliday, John Cox; School teachers: M. L. Best, Stephen Holmes; Shoemakers: Jas. Beard, Wm. Smith; Speculator: David Bonham; Surveyor-Engineer: Sam'l Herrider; Tailors: Henry Farmer, Alvin Wheeler; Tavern Keepers: John Galbreath, Emon Bishop; Wagon-makers: Chas. Yanders (? sp.), Lot Holliday, Caleb Hopping; Weaver: Wm. Spears.

*Note: Whitewater Twp., then in 1850, included an area which became part of Harrison Twp. in 1853.

Berea Chapel, built in 1822, on ground donated by Ezekiel Hughes. The building was dismantled in 1927.

Chapter 24

HISTORY OF MT. NEBO SCHOOL: AN ACCOUNT OF A RURAL SCHOOL

"Who among us does not recall the days spent going to school at "Tick Ridge," "Coon Hollow" and other familiar landmarks known as the "Little Red School House?" They were simple, about 40 x 80 feet, 3 or 4 windows, black board, long bell rope. In the center stood an old "burn side" stove which in winter was kept red hot, roasting the pupils who sat near it while the ones farther away shivered in their seats. Here, the men and women who made America learned their 3-R's."

From Ohio Builds A Nation, by Samuel H. Stille.

The history of Mt. Nebo School is very likely typical of all rural schools of the 1832 to 1927 era. The schoolhouse, along with the church, served as the social and information center of the rural community. The school building was used as a meeting place for the general public, for farmers and politicians alike. Exhibitions, oyster suppers, ice cream socials, strawberry festivals, temperance lectures, singing schools and spelling bees were conducted at the country schoolhouse. Parents and neighbors were often encouraged to visit the school, to hear programs of recitation and witness oral examinations. This was done for the purpose of arousing interest in the cause of education. The rural schoolmaster, who boarded 'round, was highly respected and was frequently a leader in social activities and charitable endeavors.

The Mt. Nebo area, first called Rittenhouse Hill, had schools from earliest days, conducted by young men who rotated a term in one rural school and a term in another. Teachers of rural schools frequently contracted to teach for three month periods, or 65 days. Since a schoolmaster taught all eight grades in one room, the frequent changes undoubtedly benefited the scholars as well as the teacher. A boy or girl would have missed a great deal if he had had the same teacher for all eight years. In order that pupils might help with the planting, schools were often dismissed early in spring. Many students attended school irregularly and it was not uncommon to find scholars older than their teachers.

Established as a one-teacher, eight-grade school, the earliest known school on Mt. Nebo, a log house, said to have been built in 1832 by John Wright, was located in the middle of the pasture on the Job C. Hayes farm. (Miami Township Census of 1830 shows a John Wright did live there.) Job Hayes had purchased the schoolhouse lot in 1838 from Philip Moak, who had originally bought it from William H. Harrison. Younger children on their way to and from school were often frightened by the farm animals, so legend tells. Mahlon Hayes (b. 1842), son of Job, received his early education in the public school right on his father's farm. The log school also served for a time as a Campbellite Church.

Among the teachers at that first log school was Thomas N. Lind, who is said to have tutored in the Harrison family. He was also a Sabbath school teacher. How early Lind taught at Mt. Nebo is unknown but it is certain he taught there in 1848-1849, for he sent "school bills" to parents of his scholars. Knowing from the names of these families in what areas they lived, it is easy to see what great distances pupils walked to school. Those who received bills in 1848-1849 were:

John Osborn, Moses B. Wamsley, John Holland, Henley Smith, Harrison Rittenhouse, Samuel Wamsley, Job C. Hayes, P. Miller, Stephen Wood Garrison, James Conner, Sarah Jane Rittenhouse (widow of Jos. Rittenhouse, who wed Thomas Lind, the schoolmaster, in Dec. 1848), Mrs. A. M. (Abigail) Hall, L. Bump, James T. Hayes, George Moak, David Whipple (who then lived on the Hayes farm at The Point), Chalon Guard, M. Shotts, Stephen Wood Rittenhouse, and Philip Moak.

Dr. Reese P. Kendall (b. 1828) stated in his book, Pioneer Annals of Green Township, that he taught on Rittenhouse Hill during 1849-1850. Since he lived in Green Township he passed John Rybolt's sugar camp each day coming and going to school.

Job C. Hayes (1812-1887), on whose lot the first known schoolhouse stood, built a big stone house along Mt. Nebo Road, which was in later years owned by James Horton, A.E.B. Stephens and last occupied by Albert Brunner before it burned around 1956. The old home was situated in close proximity to the pioneer Mt. Nebo cemetery. Job Hayes' brother, James T. Hayes, Jr., father of Erastus B. Hayes, built a large brick house which was later occupied by the Henrie family and last by the late Andrew Jackson. This place, erected ca. 1840, yet stands along Brower Road not far from Dugan Gap Road. (The Dugan Gap area was known as Howard's Hollow in earlier days.) Interesting to Mt. Nebo School history is that this home, while occupied by James Hayes, once served for a time as a school. Legend tells that some of the families had a "falling out" and set up their own school at the Hayes place.

The second known Mt. Nebo School, a frame one, was built about 1853. The old log building them became a blacksmith shop operated by Henry Eckman. Who the first teacher was of this school has not been learned. Ezra Guard, born in 1849, started to Mt. Nebo School in 1855, and his first teacher was Hampton Tomlinson, a local preacher. Other teachers named by Ezra Guard in his family papers included Mr. Hartpence, Mr. Holt and Mr. Heaton.

S.D. Sanford is said to have taught the Mt. Nebo School for 65 days from July to October, 1858, which fact shows that school was sometimes conducted in summer, possibly because teachers could be secured then.

Godfrey Clause kept the school from 1859 until January, 1866. Susan Rittenhouse, who attended Miami University, substituted for Mr. Clause occasionally during 1865. The Rittenhouse family have an old hand bell which Professor Clause, who resided next door to them, rang to call his classes to order. (This bell was later used to call the Mt. Nebo Society to order.) From Mt. Nebo School, Mr. Clause went to Cleves to teach.

Joel Holt, a "supply" teacher in the district, succeeded Godfrey Clause.

William B. Welsh (1828-1896) taught at Mt. Nebo in the 1869 era. Along with G. Clause, George Welsh and G. W. Oyler (of Storrs School), William Welsh aided in the formation of a Hamilton County Teachers Association in 1867. Purpose of the organization was "to promote the progress of education and mental discussion."

(It is interesting to note that G. W. Oyler, named above, had earlier operated Harrison Institute, or Oyler College, on Harrison Pike, east of Harrison. The expense of erecting and equipping that teachers' academy, about 1856, was borne by the family of Oyler, graduate of Farmer's College. Many local people got their teacher's training at the Institute. Capt. William Jessup, grandfather of Walter J. Harrell, attended the Institute in 1858. G. W. Oyler went on to become a well known teacher in both Hamilton County and Cincinnati schools. Oyler School in the city was named for him.)

William B. Welsh was principal at Mt. Nebo when the school presented a Christmas exhibition Dec. 30, 1869.

According to an old program, which had belonged to Minnie Matson Bonham, about 30 scholars took part in the exhibition. Those pupils bore one or another of only eight names, Hayes (in the majority), Matson, Welsh, Lewis, Guard, Bussell, Garrison and Skinner. Schoolmaster Welsh became the first mayor of Cleves when it was incorporated in 1875, and served in that capacity again in 1887.

W. Bracken Jones commenced teaching at Mt. Nebo in October, 1871. In March, 1872, the schoolhouse caught on fire but owing to Prof. Jones' alertness the fire was extinguished with little loss. During the summer of 1872, the building was repaired, new floor and seats installed, long needed. Mr. Jones resumed teaching again in October, 1872. He began to edit a school paper called "Mt. Nebo Palladium" which he soon turned over to the management of the scholars. The paper included readings, rhetorical exercises and songs.

Lawrenceburg Press carried several interesting school-related items in the Mt. Nebo news during this period:
Oct. 24, 1872. "Job Wamsley walked to school, 2 miles to the schoolhouse, beginning in 1863 and went for 3 years without missing a day. Who can beat that?"

Nov. 7, 1872. "Minnie Matson started to school in 1863 at the age of 6, and went 4 years without missing a day and lived a mile from the school. She has the teacher's certificate that will bear her out."

Mt. Nebo School was forced to close February, 1873, due to a shortage of funds. With the school closed some pupils enrolled at Cleves. Mr. Jones continued to hold spelling schools, occasionally, at the schoolhouse. However, on February 24, 1873, Prof. Jones was engaged to teach the Cleves Colored School. (This was being conducted in the old Cleves School building, as the new school on College Street had been opened in October, 1871.) For a time Mt. Nebo had no school, but not for long.

School reopened on April 7, 1873, with Miss Fannie Lind as teacher. She was the daughter of Thomas N. Lind. After a 9 week term school closed for the summer.

Ezra Guard taught during the year 1873-1874, at $2 per day. Born just over the hill on Dugan Gap, Ezra had attended school here as a lad. One of his early teachers, Joel Holt, took an interest in him and encouraged him to go to Moore's Hill to college in September, 1867. Holt tutored him in Greek and Latin to better prepare him for college. To reach Moore's Hill each term, Ezra walked over the hill to Pike's Station where he boarded an O&M train. Upon return from school, when the weather was bad, he could usually count on Lewis Bump to haul his heavy trunk up Dugan Gap Hill with his wagon and team. Ezra Guard graduated from college in 1871, a great accomplishment for a country boy in that day. His commencement oration was entitled "To Be Living Is Sublime." He taught for a period at Finney (Gravel Pit) before coming to Mt. Nebo in 1873. Ezra later served many years as clerk of the Mt. Nebo Board of Education, Special District No. 4. He was one of the founders, in 1905, of the Mt. Nebo Society.

J. L. Trisler, efficient teacher at Mt. Nebo during 1874-1875 lectured at Cleves Town Hall, June 3, 1875. He later served many years on the Hamilton County Board of Examiners, supervising tests given to prospective teachers and overseeing Boxwell and Patterson examinations given to eighth grade graduates.

C. Heaton, of Moore's Hill, Indiana, was at Mt. Nebo in November, 1875.

During the 1876-1877 era, Prof. W. B. Jones returned to teach and much progress was reportedly made.

Prof. Alfred Butler, quite talented musically and known for conducting singing schools, taught on the hill from September, 1877 to December, 1877, resigning then due to illness. Miss Leah Hayes filled in during the month of December, 1877.

Prof. Heaton was once more engaged in January, 1878.

S. K. Stephens is said to have taught at Mt. Nebo for a short period around this time. From here he went to Berea and Elizabethtown. He was musically gifted, conducted singing schools, and encouraged his scholars along this line.

W. B. ("Brack") Jones returned to the hill for another two year period, 1881 to 1883. His mother being a Wamsley, he had many kinfolk in the Miami Township locale. Born at Kentland, Indiana, he attended Normal School at Rushville, following service in the Civil War. He married Alice A. Silver whom he met while she was his pupil at Burr (Zion) School. (Alice Silver was a descendant of Judge James Silver who had come to the North Bend settlement with John Cleves Symmes. Silver had wed Betsy Thompson, niece of Judge Symmes.) Prof. Jones also taught at Hunt's Grove and Cleves before moving to Mt. Healthy.

Stephen H. Hayes was principal at Mt. Nebo for the year 1883-1884.

Paul L. Guard succeeded Hayes in 1884, teaching for one year.

Royal (Roy) Struble supervised the school from September, 1885 to December, 1887. The father of Stanley, Rose, George and Leslie, he had earlier been a practicing physician around Miamitown and Cleves.

Stanley Struble took over the school from his father in January, 1888, teaching until June of that year. During this era he also taught at Cleves and Finney. Shortly thereafter he departed for Oberlin College, graduated and began to practice law in Cleves in 1895. He subsequently became a prominent judge in Hamilton County Common Pleas Court.

Helen E. Guard served at Mt. Nebo for the school year 1888-1889. During her lifetime she taught at about every school in Miami Township, in addition to those at Berea and Elizabethtown.

Bailey G. Guard taught for two years, 1889 to 1891. He also instructed at Elizabethtown in later years.

William Flinchpaugh, principal for two school years, 1891 to 1893, came to the hill from Elizabethtown School. He later went to Cleves and from there to Home City, where he taught many years.

Arthur E. Moak was in charge at Mt. Nebo for four years, 1893 to 1897. From there he went to Burr Oak and Addyston. Moak was elected mayor of Cleves in 1901.

Sewell G. Chance first came to Mt. Nebo in the fall of 1897, remaining until June, 1900. He had previously been employed at Elizabethtown and Whitewater Park Schools. From the hill he went to Addyston where he remained a number of years. His school records were kept in exquisite penmanship. Chance was an early member of the Mt. Nebo Society. His only son, Oliver G., became a promising physician in the locality. In 1935, the young doctor tragically contracted spinal meningitis from a patient and died. Sewell Chance caught the disease from his son and also died, several days later.

For many years David H. Rittenhouse was a most efficient treasurer of Mt. Nebo School District No. 4. From his old records have been gleaned some interesting facts about the school, its pupils and its financial operations. The information no doubt is similar to accounts of other rural schools of that era.

Teachers of the late 1800's were paid $2.50 a day. Common expenditures went for cleaning the well at the schoolhouse; a bunting flag; desks (@ $3.25); and tin cups (@ 7¢). Coal was purchased from many local tradesmen (Marmet & Smith Co., Harrell & Co., Suit & Caine, Wm. Gibson) for about 10¢ a bushel. Thomas Guard, president of the board of education for a time, was paid $4.20 for repairing the school bell. In 1902, a flag pole was purchased for $2. The Mt. Nebo School board paid to the village of Cleves tuition for five colored pupils to attend the colored school there, 1885-1886. (It was shortly after this time that the colored children took their rightful places in the Cleves Public School.) Effa Moore's tuition for 1896 ($8) was paid to Cleves.

Herbert Rittenhouse passed the Boxwell examination in 1901, entitling him to participate in the Boxwell Commencement at John S. Conner School, June 7, 1901. On that occasion Herbert gave a recitation and was presented his diploma by Judge Conner, for whom the North Bend School had only recently been named.

Pupils enrolled at Mt. Nebo during the period 1897-1901 included:

Acra (Edgar, Henry, Edith, Laura); Barnes (Cynthia, Lee, Everett); Bennett (Raymond, Edward, Nora Ralph); Carr (Norma); Dressel (Etta); Eckles (Clarence); Fenney (Charles); Graham (Blaine, Thomas, Susie, Ethel, Edna, Edward, Sanders); Hayes (Howard, Jarvis, Evan, Etta, Mildred, Russell, Mark); Henrie (Allen, Dan, Will, Clarence, Cora); Holden (Lillie); Lucas (Clay, Nora, Lula); McIntyre (Edith, Archie, Olive); Moreland (Manning); Morrison (Leslie); Nugent (James, John, Susie); Parmer (Maud); Peak (Lula); Pierson (George, Florence); Pitzer (Fannie, Gerturde, Mabel); Rittenhouse (Herb, Cora); Rudisal (Harry, Hazel, Mamie); Russell (Francis, Kirby); Shallenberg (Wil, Nellie); Smith (Robert, Sadie, Ethel, Clara, Clif, Wilbur); Stoneking (Jessie, May); Taylor (Alpha, Stanley, Addie, Kennet, Hazel); Teaney (Lula, Clara); Vincent (Elbers, Florence); Waldrige (Sylvia, Clyde); Young (Charles, Ruth, Lula).

Berea School in 1906. This school, the second on the site, was built about 1850 and burned about 1910. It stood near historic Berea Chapel and cemetery. (Picture courtesy Edna T. Hayes)

The quality of Mt. Nebo's teachers was remarkable considering the fact that it was a country school with little to offer young teachers except hard work.

Daniel W. Gwaltney (1861-1934) taught from the fall of 1900 to around June, 1906. He was a later longtime mayor of Cleves and holder of county offices. Gwaltney was the last president of the old Miami-Whitewater Pioneer Association.

Alta McKinney (Baker) of Elizabethtown followed Gwaltney at Mt. Nebo where she served two years, 1906 to 1908. She wrote several extremely interesting papers for the Mt. Nebo Society. In 1907, she read her paper "Former School Days at Mt. Nebo," in which it was noted that:

Pupils of the early 19th century attended school in a crude log house. Desks were fastened to walls around the room and large pupils sat at benches drawn up to these desks with their backs to the teacher, whose desk was in the corner. Primary scholars sat near the middle of the room around the stove. There was no bell and for many years no blackboard. Children came from all directions and great distances; often the young ones rode on the backs of older brothers. Some pupils attended until they were 24 years old. Frequently the bigger boys were unruly, making it difficult to secure teachers.

Alta McKinney presented a second paper to the Society's reunion in 1908, which was an account of early Mt. Nebo history. (This latter report, printed in Lawrenceburg Press, Sept. 1931, has been of great benefit to this writer.)

In 1907, a combined graduation program was held at Miami Township Hall for students of Alta McKinney, Mt. Nebo; Richard Simmonds, Blue Jay; and Charles R. Coulthard, Burr. One Mt. Nebo scholar, Manning R. Moreland, graduated that year. He went on to become one of the most respected citizens of the Miami Township community. He later served for many years as president of both Cleves-North Bend School Board and Hamilton County School Board. Manning lived, as a boy, in the old Job C. Hayes house.

Hallie McIntyre (Landon) taught for a year, 1908-1909, following which time she went to Cleves School. She lived near the foot of Mt. Nebo hill and walked to and from school each day. When it rained, her neighbor, Martin Harrell, hitched a buggy up to his old white horse and drove Hallie to and from Mt. Nebo.

Nell McCauley succeeded Hallie Landon in 1909. She remained a year, possibly two.

S. G. Chance returned to the hill during the 1912 era and it has not been learned how long he remained this time.

The second known Mt. Nebo schoolhouse, a frame one built back about 1853, was used continually for nearly 65 years, an outstanding record in itself. Finally in 1917, it was replaced by a red brick building, constructed within sight of the old one. Mrs. Mabel Howard Hann was the first to teach in the new schoolhouse, the third one known, when it opened in the fall of 1917. During that year she and her family resided in the old frame school, nearby. Mrs. Hann had few pupils during this era. Who followed her has not been learned, but it is likely her successor was S. G. Chance.

Mr. Chance was back at Mt. Nebo by the fall of 1920, possibly before, and remained until June, 1921, when he accepted a position at Elizabethtown.

Miss Edith Boland, of Valley Junction, came to the hill in the fall of 1921 and remained two years. (In November, 1923, she became Mrs. Jennings Pope.)

In the spring of 1921, J. Howard Hayes and his family moved to the Big Miami Stock Farm to assist in its management. His father, Enos Hayes, was no longer able to care for the farm alone. So it was that when, in 1923, no teacher could be found to take over Mt. Nebo School, W. F. Sizelove, Ass't. County School Superintendent, implored Mrs. J. Howard (Edna "Nettie" Truitt) Hayes to take the position.

Edna "Nettie" Hayes became Mt. Nebo principal in 1923 and remained there until the school was closed in June, 1927. In 1923, there was an enrollment of 18; in 1924, 22 pupils attended the rural school.

It was during this era that Cleves-North Bend School District was in the process of being consolidated by Superintendent Charles T. Young. A high school (Union High) had been started in 1920 at John S. Conner School. During this same period the big electric power station was under construction (1924-1925) at Finney, which was drawing many newcomers to the area. Every available house and room in the Finney, Brower Road, Lost Bridge and Mt. Nebo region was rented to workers at the new plant. Mt. Nebo's little country school was bursting at the seams. To add to the general confusion of the school system, Cleves School burned in May, 1926. In the emergency pupils from there were sent to the newly opened (Jan. 1926) Taylor High School and over to Conner School as a temporary measure which lasted until 1929, when a new schoolhouse was completed in Cleves. By the fall of 1927, it appeared that Mt. Nebo's prospective enrollment would reach 40, far too many for one teacher to handle in an eight-grade, rural school.

So it was that historic Mt. Nebo School was closed. Founded as a one-teacher, log school back about 1832, it had remained a one-teacher school all those years until 1927. Howard Hayes signed a contract to transport Mt. Nebo pupils by bus to school at North Bend. (Howard Hayes had attended Mt. Nebo School in his youth. Starting in 1927, he drove the school bus over the same route, transporting boys and girls to Cleves and North Bend schools, for 27 years, a noteworthy record in itself.) Edna Hayes, who had the distinction of being Mt. Nebo's last teacher, was employed at Conner School.

The story of Edna Hayes' experiences as a teacher is unique. It is worthy of being recorded. As a girl she had attended North Bend Village School, had passed the Boxwell examination, and graduated in 1898. For her commencement exercises she had recited "Battle of Lookout Mountain." Col. D. W. McClung had presented her diploma. Having been inspired by her teacher, Hallie Stephens Caine, Edna had acquired a thirst for learning and a love for school. Perhaps she had also acquired this deep interest in school from her father, Thomas Truitt, who, as a young man following service at Andersonville during the Civil War, secured a teacher's license. Dated Oct. 19, 1868, Tom Truitt's certificate was engraved with this significant heading: "Common schools--the hope of our country."

There was no high school in the community in those days, but at Cleves Common School Principal William Harrell conducted advanced classes for those who cared to study beyond eighth grade. (Some students attended Hughes High School in the city, riding the commuter trains, but it was a great distance for young people to travel each day.) So it was that Edna, "Nettie" as she was better known--her middle name being Winette, walked to Cleves where she studied physical geography, algebra, ancient and medieval history. In her second year, Mr. Harrell coached her in bookkeeping and principles of psychology. There was little time for individual instruction; she had to do much study on her own. "Nettie" was also tutored some by Oliver Swisher, then a teacher at Berea, who conducted an irregular sort of high school where advanced subjects were taught.

By June of 1900, "Nettie" Truitt was 15 years old and Will Harrell considered his special pupil quite prepared to go to the city and take the teachers' examination. In those days the examination was a long one, part of it given one month and the second part the next month. Because of her youthful appearance, Schoolmaster Harrell cautioned "Nettie" that, before taking the test, she must make herself look older and suggested that she pile her hair upon her head and lengthen her dress, already worn long in those days.

She passed her teachers' examination easily. But, since she was so young, and in order to satisfy any doubts that some might harbor as to her qualifications, Mr. Harrell suggested that she repeat the examination. Again she passed the test, and yet has those certificates to prove it.

On August 13, 1900, "Nettie" Truitt turned sixteen, and on the day after Labor Day she began to teach her first class at Addyston School, at a salary of $42.50 a month. (The coming of the large pipe foundry, ten years earlier, had caused the school population to soar.) At the end of the year (1901), the school board was low in funds and was unable to retain all eight teachers, so "Nettie" was not rehired.

(While at Addyston, she had met another young teacher, Bertha Brater, who lived just outside the village along Plank Road (now Cleves-Warsaw Pike). Miss Brater was to become a life-long teacher in the community, teaching for half-a-century.)

During that summer, 1901, "Nettie" learned that Locust Grove School on Bond Road (near Elizabethtown) in Whitewater Township, a one-room school, was in need of a teacher. Full of enthusiasm she agreed to try the position, which had recently been held by Charles Bonham, 1898-1899, and John Smith, 1899-1901.

(Locust Grove School was mentioned in the writings of Judge Alfred Cotton in 1858, as being near Bond's Mill where he got his grinding done. The school was undoubtedly among the early ones of Whitewater Township.)

The rural school in 1901 had few of the advantages of the village school. But Edna Truitt brought to Locust Grove the customs and habits of North Bend School, those inspired by her former principal, Hallie Caine. She encouraged more participation is lessons, in programs and entertainments; she conducted spelling matches, sled riding parties and arranged picnics at the school year's end; she observed holidays in the classroom and made a genuine effort to show interest in her pupils.

Rural Locust Grove School, on Bond Road, Whitewater Township, Ca. 1901. Martha Cilley with horse and buggy in foreground. Schoolhouse, yet standing, is used as a dwelling. (Picture courtesy of Edna T. Hayes.)

"Nettie" found willing learners among her scholars and this quickened her enthusiasm. One of her students, Ray Robison, older than she, applied himself and went on to study telegraphy. He became a highly respected citizen in the Miami Township region, later serving for many years on the Cleves-North Bend Board of Education. Another of her older scholars, a nineteen-year-old girl from Kentucky, who had had little previous opportunity for study, stayed on to graduate from Locust Grove, a real accomplishment for such a person in those days.

To reach Locust Grove School, "Nettie" rode the CL&A traction cars, new to the region, from North Bend to Cilley's Crossing near Valley Junction, Stop #116. From that point she walked or bicycled the 2 1/2 miles to the schoolhouse. She stored her bicycle in the Cilley barn. In inclement weather Mattie Cilley drove her in the family buggy to Bond Road.

"Nettie's" salary was set at $50 a month but with the chronic shortage of school funds in those days, she did not always collect a full pay. Out of her salary she paid $2 a month to a janitor to start a fire in the stove on cold mornings. Older students helped wash blackboards and carry water.

Here at Locust Grove Edna Truitt remained for three rewarding years, genuinely appreciated by her pupils and the rural community as a whole. While there she had more than proven herself capable of handling a one-room, eight-grade school.

From Locust Grove "Nettie" went to historic Berea, in 1904, another rural school, where she taught another three years, resigning in 1907 to be married. Among her fondest memories of Berea were the winter sleigh rides and ice skating parties with her pupils and the good fellowship and hospitality she enjoyed in the neighborhood. The first school at Berea was said to have been conducted in Berea Chapel, which was built in 1822 on ground donated by Ezekiel Hughes-- first owner of the land. Several years later, a log schoolhouse was built near the chapel, adjoining pioneer Berea Cemetery. This log school burned in 1849, and was replaced in 1850 by a two-room frame building. This second schoolhouse--where "Nettie" Truitt taught--burned around 1910. Old Berea Chapel, which had a unique history, itself, was dismantled in 1927.

When "Nettie" Truitt later returned to teaching at Mt. Nebo in 1923, as "Nettie" Hayes, she had had the benefit of her experience at rural Locust Grove and Berea Schools. Few teachers of the 1920 era cared to take the responsibility of a one-room, eight-grade school.

From Mt. Nebo she went to Conner School and later served as principal. During those years of teaching she studied at night and took university classes in summer until she had acquired a life certificate. In 1935, "Nettie" accepted a position as principal at Elizabethtown. There she stayed for twenty years, until her retirement in 1955, evidence that she liked her work and that her work was approved by the people of Elizabethtown. Until the last day of her teaching career in 1955, "Nettie" Truitt Hayes retained that same enthusiasm she had carried with her to that first class back at Addyston in 1900, when she started as a newly certified teacher of sixteen. She yet cherishes her minor claim to fame, that of being last teacher at Mt. Nebo's one-room, eight-grade school.

(It is interesting to note that Mrs. Hayes' son, Robert Truitt Hayes, has earned for himself a genuine claim to fame in the field of art, both regionally and nationally. In 1965 and 1966, he was among a group of American artists chosen to represent U.S. in the International Exposition at Monaco. A native of North Bend, Bob Hayes now resides in Westwood. In his youth he attended old Mt. Nebo School, with his mother as his teacher.)

(The following item, interesting to North Bend history as well as to Bob Hayes, appeared in the Times Star, Aug. 20, 1935: "The Str. OTTO MARMET burned at Raymond City Coal Co. wharf. Robert T. Hayes had just completed a water color of the boat in July for Dennis Gleason, the North Bend manager of the coal company." Water and boats remain the favorite subject of Bob, even today.)

★★★★★★★★★★★

Peter Tebow House at Elizabethtown

Uriah and Martha Tebow settled in Elizabethtown shortly after 1806. According to Mr. Tony Collins, who is most familiar with the history of this locality, the Tebow family originally came from the region of Alsace-Lorraine to Cincinnati, but legend tells, after seeing the drinking and immorality in the city decided to move farther west. Peter Tebow (1802-1868), son of Uriah, built a big house which may yet be seen at the right of the highway approaching Elizabethtown from Cleves. This place once served as a drovers' inn on the turnpike from Indiana to Cincinnati. On the third floor of the house was a ball room with sliding doors; on the top deck Peter Tebow is said to have placed a telescope. The Tebow home is also believed to have been a station in the Underground Railroad. There are a number of other old homes still standing in the Elizabethtown area with histories equally as interesting as the Tebow house.

Another Artist Once Resident of North Bend

Cordelia A. Plimpton, widow of Florus B. Plimpton-- longtime co-editor with Murat Halstead on the Commercial Gazette, was a Cincinnati artist of merit. She resided for a time, ca. 1894-95, at North Bend in the home now occupied by the Frank Crows. Her son, Lucien, was an architect.

One of the first school buses of Cleves-North Bend District, 1927. J. Howard Hayes, driver of the 30-passenger vehicle, operated the Mt. Nebo route for 27 years.

Chapter 25

JOHN ASTON WARDER (1812-1883)
Physician, Naturalist And Horticulturist

John Aston Warder ranks as one of the most illustrious citizens in the history of North Bend. He was completely dedicated to mankind.

Born in Philadelphia in 1812, the son of Quaker parents, Jeremiah and Ann A. Warder, John Warder absorbed a deep interest in nature in his father's house, where Audubon and other naturalists were often visitors. He graduated in 1836 from Jefferson Medical College and shortly thereafter married Miss Elizabeth B. Haines.

In 1837, Dr. Warder located in Cincinnati and began his practice of medicine. During his residence in the city he was not only an enthusiastic member of his profession but a public-spirited and energetic citizen, as well. He was greatly attached to Cincinnati's public schools and served for a number of years on the School Board. He gave much time and labor to the problems of hygiene and sanitation in the schools. He studied aspects of school construction, methods of instruction and educational systems. He worked diligently to introduce the best and most advanced ideas in the schools. Dr. Warder had the distinction of serving on a committee on whose report the first public Cincinnati high school was founded in 1847. This free high school was established in the basement of a German church. (Woodward and Hughes, sister high schools, began their existence on the same day in September, 1851.)

From the Cincinnati Chronicle, July 21, 1838:

"Dr. J. A. Warder offers his professional services. Office at the Newport Ferry, corner of Ludlow and Front Sts., Cincinnati."

John Warder maintained his interest in the Medical College of Ohio, holding the chair of chemistry and toxicology, 1854-1857. He was an active member in many scientific societies. In 1839, he was a curator and treasurer of the Western Academy of Natural Science and later served as president for five years. He was a charter member of the Cincinnati Society of Natural History, of which he was president, 1870 to 1875.

Dr. Warder was appointed, in 1843, to the Entomology committee of the Hamilton County Horticultural Society to study insect depredations on fruit and shade trees. This was the first such society in the Northwest Territory. It is very likely that he was acquainted with General Harrison, since both men were active in agricultural associations. Dr. Warder is said to have attended the President's funeral service and burial at North Bend.

Warder was a practical landscape gardener and helped in the establishment of Spring Grove Cemetery. As early as 1850, he suggested and designed a park system for Cincinnati and helped popularize flowers, lawns and trees for decorations of homes and parks. In this role he imported trees and shrubs from far corners of the world. In 1853, he enriched botanical science by his description of the CATALPA SPECIOSA, as a separate species.

Most of his writings pertained to botany and practical forestry. His scientific study "American Pomology-Apples," published in 1867, was the result of 16 years of investigation. The subject of forestry was dear to his heart and in this field he became a national figure. Dr. Warder was one of the organizers of the Ohio State Forestry Association and served as president of the American Forestry Association. In 1873, he was U.S. Commissioner to the Vienna Exposition and there submitted an official report on forests and the forestry movement in this country.

It was in 1855, that Dr. Warder gave up his practice of medicine and moved to North Bend. There, from the widow of President Harrison, he bought a farm to which he gradually added until he possessed 325 acres. He established a grand home, a type of English manor house, which is yet standing today. It was built of stone, hauled from the bed of Indian Creek, and timber, found on the farm. The home was surrounded with model gardens and orchards. The Warder farm may justly be called the first fruit experiment station of the Middle West and the first forestry station in the United States.

Dr. John A. Warder's home, overlooking the Ohio at North Bend, as it appeared in 1900. This English manor-type house, built Ca. 1870, was occupied by the L. A. Perkins family from 1923 to 1969.

Dr. Warder and his sons planted trees and shrubs of unusual species. Today, the many varieties of trees planted over a century ago stand as monuments to his useful life. Among those trees were tamaracks. When the Perkins family acquired ownership of the farm in 1923, the tamarack standing on the point overlooking the Ohio had grown to such spreading proportions that they chose to call their new home "Tamarack Farm."

John Warder also found time for civic affairs. In 1860, he participated in the first Harvest Home Festival at Carsons's Grove (Cheviot), Green Township. That celebration continues, to this day, to be an annual event. He was also a member of the Miami & Whitewater Valley Pioneer Association.

Dr. Warder's family was active in the early village life of North Bend. Daughters Anna and Elizabeth devoted much time to the work of an Episcopal sponsored Sunday School, long before a church building existed. After the Fernbank Episcopal Church was built, the Warder women organized a Sabbath School there. When the village of North Bend was organized in 1875, Robert A. Warder was elected marshal and supervisor of streets. He also participated in the work of the Sunday School. The following news items tell of his work:

"Robert Warder addressed the people of North Bend at Whitney's Mill on the subject "Prodigal Son." (Aug. 6, 1874, Lawrenceburg Press)

"Prof. Robert Warder lectured at the town hall on the "Metric System." (Apr. 23, 1878, Lawrenceburg Press)

"Prof. Robert Warder's removal to Philadelphia is a loss to our church, Cleves Presbyterian. He was our Bible class teacher. On Wednesday the Sunday School expects to have a picnic at Parlor Grove, going on the Str. MINNIE which leaves North Bend at 8." (July 1, 1879, Cincinnati Daily Gazette)

Robert Warder was later a professor at University of Cincinnati. Another son, Reuben Haines Warder, became Superintendent of Cincinnati Parks. In 1901, he went to Chicago to assume the same role in that city, and died there in 1907, a bachelor. Elizabeth Warder married John H. Vorhees, and their son, Warder Vorhees, became an attorney. Others of the Warder family were Jane, John and William. The North Bend farm was occupied by them until about 1905. From that time until 1923, when the Perkins family acquired the Warder estate, a number of families lived in the home, including the Charles Hortons and Sam P. Suits.

Reuben H. Warder also served as postmaster at Valley Junction for several terms during the 1872-1876 era, shortly after the name of that station was officially changed from Harrison Junction to Valley Junction (June 23, 1871). Warder succeeded Dr. Jacob H. Hunt as postmaster. (Of the latter it was noted in Valley Junction news: "Dr. Hunt meets expectations when the mail bag is left for the doctor to deliver.") Reuben Warder also operated a hominy mill at that place during the same period.

Dr. John Warder--it must be known, along with Superintendent of Cincinnati Schools John B. Peaslee, played an important role in the founding of School Arbor Day, April 27, 1882. On the same day that the Memorial Authors' Groves were planted in Cincinnati, the Royal Forest Academy of Therandt, Saxony, the most renowned forestry school in the world, planted--on the "Cincinnati plan"--a grove of one-hundred catalpa (CATALPA SPECIOSA), and dedicated it to Cincinnati Arbor Day. The trees were sent by Dr. Adolph Leue, Cincinnati naturalist, from Dr. Warder's farm at North Bend. The CATALPA SPECIOSA was a purely American tree, described and named by John Warder, and the occasion was its first introduction into Europe.

Among those from the North Bend locality who served on Arbor Day committees in 1882 were: Judge John S. Conner; Judge Isaac B. Matson, then Probate Court Judge; Mrs. Bettie Eaton; Mrs. D. W. McClung, daughter of Carter B. Harrison; Dr. John A. Warder and his son, Reuben H. Warder. Altogether, it was a proud day in the history of North Bend.

John A. Warder passed away July 14, 1883, and was buried beneath the soil he loved at Spring Grove. (Otto Juettner, in his book Daniel Drake and His Followers, 1909, stated that Dr. Warder rests at North Bend.) With his lifetime record of service, it is easy to understand why he ranks among the foremost men who ever lived around North Bend, and around the entire United States, for that matter.

The late Emma Stumpp Speed of Cleves, wrote an account of her childhood recollections of the Warder apple orchard. It appeared in The Valley Journal, May 1, 1952. She entitled her story "A Famous Neighbor."

"Few people residing now in this section have remembrance of John Aston Warder, the distinguished pomologist, who lived a number of years on a small farm within the precincts of North Bend.

"Mr. Warder was born in Philadelphia, Jan. 19, 1812, of Quaker parentage, and died July 14, 1883, at the age of 71. He was a physician by profession which he continued to follow after moving to Cincinnati. His great love for and interest in fruit raising, particularly apples, induced him to purchase the picturesque hill-side farm, a portion of which he planted in apples of the best and newest varieties, those promising the highest desirability. When they grew and fruited, his orchard became the Mecca for school children hereabout, of whom may we mention Kate and Sue Jessup and myself. We recall with utmost pleasure those apple-hungry raids on the Warder orchard, at that time cared for by his sons, four surviving him, one of whom we were apt to encounter in the orchard, and who admonished us to 'pick the best on the ground.'

"John Aston Warder soon became known as a famous pomologist and was accorded many honors. He was president of the Ohio Horticultural Society and for many years served as secretary and vice-president of the Ohio State Board of Agriculture. His book on apples became a worldwide authority."

REUBEN H. WARDER

Reuben Haines Warder was honored by the Cincinnati Park Board in 1929, when a tract of land used for nursery purposes was named in his memory. The Reuben Warder Nursery of 40 acres was located in Winton Place. A letter telling something about Warder was written by Charles T. Greve, Cincinnati historian, and sent to Irwin M. Krohn, president of the Park Board. Excerpts of the letter read as follows: (Times-Star, Sept. 7, 1929.)

"He died in Chicago, Dec. 26, 1907. He had held for six and one-half years the position of secretary of Lincoln Park Board and superintendent of Chicago parks. He was superintendent of Cincinnati parks from 1893 until 1899.

"He was the son of Dr. John A. Warder, a national celebrity of his time and president of the American Forestry Association. His biography is contained in Appleton's Cyclopedia of American Biography. Dr. Warder wrote many books and pamphlets with regard to trees and woody plants and botany generally of this locality. Reuben Warder was a zealous advocate of park extension and also of tree planting in streets and avenues of the city. He is said to have caused the planting of trees on Madison Road. In Chicago he is credited with the rehabilitation of Lincoln Park and the North Side parks. I have always felt a great interest in the suggestion made by him in his report for 1898 (p. 1254 in the volume of Cincinnati annual reports) with reference to the improvement of the river front.

"My own acquaintance with Warder came through his membership in a most remarkable organization known as the Hengstenberg Lunch Table, which met for lunch at a little restaurant on Third Street. During the years 1884 to 1889, I met with this group. Mr. Warder was one of the most active spirits in the conversation at the table. Many distinguished men lunched at this gathering. An annual meeting was held, usually at the Zoo, at which poems and papers were read and songs sung, which record was made each year in a booklet. A complete set of these is owned by Mr. James who said that they were rarer than the first folio of Shakespeare.

"Reuben Warder, in the judgment of those who have been interested in the development of our city, was one of our most valued citizens."

(Author's note: How interesting to note that a North Bend resident of 1898 was then thinking along the lines of riverfront improvement for the city.)

(*July, 1969. Ownership of the Warder-Perkins place changed.)

Chapter 26

JOHN JAMES PIATT, NORTH BEND POET

Several Piatts migrated to North Bend with Judge Symmes. The family was numerous and of high intellectual reputation. One John H. Piatt, a Cincinnati banker, was praised by President-elect Wm. Henry Harrison for his sound banking developments in the city. Another Piatt, Captain Jacob Piatt, Revolutionary officer on the staff of General George Washington and original member of the Society of Cincinnatus, lived at "Federal Hill" in Petersburg, Kentucky, opposite Tanner's Creek, near Lawrenceburg. From this family came one who is well known in the annals of North Bend. He was John James Piatt.

John J. Piatt made his mark primarily in the field of poetry. His wife, Sarah Morgan Bryan Piatt, was also an authoress of note. His writings illustrated new modes of life upon his generation. His were poems for posterity. Several of these, "The Lost Farm," "The Pioneer's Chimney," "The Mower in Ohio," and "Riding to Vote," may be found in his book Idyls and Lyrics of the Ohio Valley.

Piatt was born March 1, 1835, in an Indiana village, James' Mills, now Milton, in Dearborn County, not far from the Ohio border. Until 1845, the Piatt family lived on the farm at Milton and John James attended school at Rising Sun.

In his book The Hesperian Tree, Piatt wrote of going to the post office at Rising Sun in 1843, to get a magazine, the May issue of "Grahams," in which he saw a facsimile of Henry Wadsworth Longfellow's signature for the first time. His interest in Longfellow began then and continued throughout his life. He began to write verse at the age of fourteen.

When he was ten, the family moved to the region of Columbus, Ohio. Young John stayed for a time with his Uncle Charles Scott, publisher of Ohio State Journal, where he learned something of the printer's trade. It was during this period that Ohio passed from the pioneer stage to an atmosphere of industry and wealth. These changes were reflected in the young poet's verses.

The first literary venture of Piatt was published in 1860, a work written in association with William Dean Howells and entitled Poems of Two Friends.

In September, 1858, John James Piatt had the unique experience of being seated on a train beside Abraham Lincoln. Lincoln was enroute to debate with Stephen A. Douglas, and Piatt at first mistook him for a clergyman. The privilege of having sat and eaten with the great future President was appreciated by him more in later life than it was at the time it happened.

Piatt submitted poems to George D. Prentice, editor of the Louisville Journal, and in time became a member of the editorial staff, as well as confidential secretary to Prentice. It was here that he met, and later married, Sarah Morgan Bryan, whose verse was being published by Prentice.

In 1861, Piatt was appointed, by S. P. Chase, a clerk in the Treasury Department. The young Piatts lived in Washington, D. C., and during this period became acquainted with many famous men, among them Lowell, Whitman and Longfellow.

After the work in Washington was terminated in 1868, the family made its abode at North Bend, Ohio. From 1869 to 1878, Piatt was affiliated with The Commercial, working both in Cincinnati and Washington. Murat Halstead, who later resided at North Bend with his daughter, was then editor of that newspaper. (Halstead's granddaughter, Jean Davidson, later married Piatt's son, Cecil.) Piatt occupied, during this same period, positions of clerk and librarian in the House of Representatives. Later he worked as money-order clerk for the Cincinnati Post Office. Work was drudgery for him but he had his family to support. (1880 Census shows he was clerk in Post Office.) It was also during this era that Piatt's poem "Snow Falling" appeared in McGuffey's Fifth Eclectic Reader. Hundreds of school children of that day memorized it.

The Piatts lived at two different locations outside the village of North Bend. It is believed that they first lived for a time in a little frame cottage near the end of Rittenhouse and Cliff Roads. The property had earlier been owned by members of the Harrison H. Rittenhouse family. Sometime soon after 1870, Piatt built a home overlooking the river on Cliff Road, closer to Congress Green, (where the Robert Horton home now stands). Piatt, at the same time, retained the property at the corner of Rittenhouse Road, along the Cliff. The new house, it is said, was frequently shaken by passing trains along the O&M Railroad at the foot of the hill. Piatt walked up and down the hill each day to catch the train to Cincinnati.

The Piatts erected a small observation platform with a gabled roof at the edge of the cliff, where they found quiet and inspiration while composing verse. Called "The Lookout House," it was built by a Mr. Glenn who worked at the "cokeovens." On Sunday afternoons, persons for miles around walked to "The Lookout House" to view the river and the beautiful Boone County farmlands. (A good picture of the Piatt house is found in a booklet, "Along the Line," published about 1900 by the CL&A Traction Company. Postcard scenes of "The Lookout House" were also printed during that era. Miss Cora Rittenhouse has copies of these.)

On July 4, 1874, the eldest son of the Piatts, Victor--then about ten, was killed as a result of a powder explosion at their North Bend home. The young boy and several playmates had the powder in a bottle and were using it to fire off a small toy cannon. The bottle burst into fragments, one of which struck Victor, severing the jugular vein and causing instant death. The funeral service was read by Rev. B. W. Chidlaw at the residence. (Lawrenceburg Press, July 9, 1874.)

Bob Baker, early Mount Nebo resident and playmate of the Piatt children, who lived in Cleves to a very old age, was blinded as a child. He attributed his blindness to this same accident in which Victor Piatt was killed.

Mrs. Edna Truitt Hayes has among her possessions a little toy cannon which had been given to her elder brother by the Piatt children sometime before they went to Cork, Ireland in 1882. Whether this was the toy cannon that figured in that tragic accident is not known.

Another of the Piatt children, probably Donn, died sometime during the period 1880-1882. The graves of two children were located on the Piatt property, across from their home-- away from the river, and over the hill. The site was enclosed for many years by a red picket fence.

The 1880 Census listed the children of John J. Piatt, 43, and Sallie M. B. Piatt, 42, as Marion, 18, Don, 13, Fred 11, Guy, 9, Louis, 5, and Cecil, 2. (Victor had died in 1874.) The family was named on the census roll next to John S. Conner, who resided near to Congress Green.

From 1882 until 1893, Piatt served as U.S. Consul to Cork, Ireland. (It was a custom during this era to patronize the arts. Washington Irving went to Spain and England; James Russell Lowell also went to Spain and England; W. D. Howells to Italy; Bret Harte to Germany; Piatt to Ireland. Hawthorne had his custom house appointment. These positions allowed leisure for writing.)

On School Arbor-Day, April 27, 1882, students all over Cincinnati planted trees in honor of American authors. Maple trees were planted by scholars of Third District School in the names of J. J. Piatt and Mrs. S. M. B. Piatt, North Bend poets, who then were in Ireland or enroute there.

On April 7, 1883, Honorable John J. Piatt, Consul of U.S. at Cork, Ireland, wrote a letter to John B. Peaslee, Supt. of Cincinnati Schools. He expressed pride that trees had been planted in honor of Mrs. Piatt and himself. He wrote, "What a happy thought it was to set school children throughout Ohio to planting trees. The trees will, I dare say, rise up and call you blessed! I write this looking out on the pleasant waters of the River Lee; but they are not so pleasant to our sight as those bright waters in front of our door at North Bend."

While in Ireland, the Piatts met with another tragedy. Their little son, Louis--then nine, drowned in July, 1884.

Upon returning to the U.S. in 1894, the family again took up residency at North Bend, in their home near the later site of North Bend Inn. Sometime around 1900, a fire severely damaged this house. The Piatts moved back to the frame cottage at the end of Rittenhouse Road, which they enlarged and remodeled to resemble an Irish country house. (This is the house on Rittenhouse Road which local people most frequently recall as the Piatt home. The other home--rebuilt after the fire--was occupied for sometime by the Smedley family. This latter place was razed when James Walsh, son of Nicholas Walsh of Walsh Distilleries, built a lovely home on the site. The place is now owned by Robert Horton.)

The Piatt family spent their later years in quiet retirement. It was quite common to see them huddled under umbrellas, as protection against the sun, sitting out along the cliff, in view of the river, meditating and composing poetry. Daughter, Marion, called "Birdie," played piano and also wrote for magazines and newspapers. The late Birdie Rittenhouse Welsh, whose family lived across the road from the Piatts, was named for "Birdie" Piatt.

Sometime around 1902, Thomas Truitt of North Bend hauled to the Piatt place a great deal of stone which was used in remodeling the home, the first part of which had been built by the Rittenhouses. Piatt, as a mere poet, had no money to pay for the stone so he paid Truitt with a bushel basket full of copies of his recently published books The Hesperian Tree.

The Hesperian Tree, of which there were several volumes, 1900-1903, was made up of a variety of poems and essays. Included in the books were works of a number of local persons, such as William C. Cooper, Edith C. Cooper, William Harrell and Bettie Harrison Eaton.

Noted works of the Piatts included Poems of House and Home, Pencilled Flyleaves: A Book of Essays in Town and Country, The Children Out-Of-Doors: A Book of Verse by Two in One House, and countless others.

For eight years before his death, which occurred at his winter residence in the city, J. J. Piatt was editor of Book Reviews column in The Cincinnati Enquirer, as well as a contributor to the Atlantic Monthly, Harpers and other magazines.

Piatt died in 1917 at the age of 82. He had been permanently injured three years earlier in a carriage accident (a runaway horse) a short distance from his North Bend home. Daughter Marion's death followed soon after. In 1919, Sarah M. B. Piatt, widow of the poet, who had achieved considerable note herself as an author, passed away at the home of her son, Cecil, in New York. Sons Frederick, U.S. Consul to Edinburgh, Scotland, Guy and Cecil survived her. Guy Piatt continued to occupy the home on Rittenhouse Road until at least the mid 1920's.

The Lookout House, built by J. J. Piatt, overlooking the river from Cliff View.

The "Piatt place," which has changed hands numerous times since the Piatt occupancy, remains one of the most charming of the old homes around North Bend.

One of John J. Piatt's best known poems was "Snow Falling." It first appeared in 1879 in McGuffey's Fifth Eclectic Reader.

SNOW FALLING

The wonderful snow is falling
Over river and woodland and wold;
The trees bear spectral blossom
In the moonshine blurr'd and cold.

There's a beautiful garden in Heaven;
And these are the banished flowers,
Falling and driven and drifted
Into this dark world of ours.

The settings of many of Piatt's poems, some of those written while he lived at North Bend, will be familiar to those readers who know the place and surroundings where the author resided. One in particular, "Walking to the Station," reflects the thoughts of the poet, himself, describing his walk past the old graveyard with blackened names on the stones (Congress Green) on his way to the train station.

* Note: Material for this account was gleaned from the following sources:
The Poets and Poetry of the West by Wm. T. Coggeshall, 1860, Follett & Foster Co., Columbus, Ohio.
Ohio State Archeological & Historical Quarterly, Vol. 45, 1936, a biographical sketch of John James Piatt by Clara Dowler, pp. 22-26.
Thoughts and Experiences In and Out of School, 1899, by John B. Peaslee.
Cincinnati and Lawrenceburg newspapers.
Miss Cora Rittenhouse and Mrs. Edna Truitt Hayes.

Chapter 27

THE WEST END OF CINCINNATI
by John James Piatt

(The following account appeared in the Commercial Tribune, March 19, 1899, under the heading "Points of Historic and Scenic Interest Along the Route of the New Electric Road Which Has Been Authorized by the County Commissioners." The article was introduced thusly:

Utilitarian as the electric street car line may seem, it has nevertheless been the means of bringing the residents of crowded cities to a fuller appreciation of the beauties of the country surrounding their municipality. This is especially true of Cincinnati, and now that there is to be a long, interurban car line down the Ohio River from Cincinnati to Lawrenceburg, Ind., the manifold beauties of the scenery along the matchless river will become familiar to those who have never suspected that such beauties existed so close to home.

To describe the scenes, the old mansions, the beauty of the views and the many quaint bits of landscape along the river, one should have the pen and mind of a poet; and the Commercial Tribune feels itself fortunate in having secured to write this description the famous poet and author Mr. John James Piatt, whose article follows. Mr. Piatt writes not from a hasty trip through the section he describes, but from a long acquaintance with it, for he has lived in the midst of these scenes many years. (Excerpts are taken from his account and anecdotes.)

"Cincinnati is fortunate in its environment . . . Go in whatever direction one will, he finds an outlet into places of wonderful rural beauty and healthful air . . .

"But, somewhat singularly, it might seem, one of the most attractive outlets of Cincinnati--what we may call the West End--has been comparatively unrecognized and neglected . . .

"Cincinnati may be said to have had its first impetus from its West End. The first military station in the early occupancy of Southwestern Ohio was a blockhouse built eighteen miles below town, at North Bend, in the autumn of 1785-- three years before the regular settlements at Columbia, Losantiville and North Bend . . .

"There was a time, forty or fifty years ago, when the West End of Cincinnati became the fashionable quarter--when Storrs, Sedamsville and Riverside attracted people on pleasure bent for evening and holiday amusement and relaxation. There was then a race track on the bank of the Ohio at Riverside and the lower river road (long since fallen into the tide) was the fashionable drive. There were not a few attractive country residences in that neighborhood.

"But there were discouragements for people who were inclined to be "stepping westward." As late as 1860, the Whitewater Canal and the O&M Railway--which did not seek to accommodate suburban dwellers--were the only means of egress, except by private carriage, for the people living ten or fifteen miles down the river. The canal boat was pleasant enough, doubtless, to such as took no note of time, save from its loss (but they could hardly ignore the mosquitoes). People who did not fancy such transportation had to drive, and west of the city the roads were bad enough, even in the summer months. When the CI&L Railway was established, and occupied the bed of the canal, it helped matters, considerably, but there was not sufficient disposition to give easy commutation rates, etc . . . Meanwhile good roads were provided in all directions for the people seeking the high places overlooking the city, street car lines were routed back of the city, and the popular western tendency was diverted to Walnut Hills, Mt. Auburn, Clifton and the suburbs toward Dayton. The great current of the wealthy and well-to-do moved. Good school facilities, too, were denied to those who, for various reasons had preferred to live below the city in the westward current of the Ohio.

"There has been other drawbacks, preventing the development of the West End. At Trautman's Station there was established between thirty and forty years ago, a certain factory, for many years known as "Si Keck's Fertilizer." (Note*It was also better known as the "stink factory.") It was not a welcome homeward companion in the cool of the summer evenings. It was a faithful one, however; it met and followed one home, and would not let him go, even then . . . Our down the river people didn't feel grateful, I fear, to Mr. Keck.

"There were several attractive stations, twenty-five or thirty years ago, between Cincinnati and North Bend--Southside, Delhi)previously from some manufactory established there many years ago, known as Industry), Home City and Fernbank. These have grown more attractive year by year. One should not omit to mention St. Joseph's, a Catholic Institution which makes so handsome a feature on the hilltop to people going up and down the river near Rapid Run.

"Home City, when I first knew it, was especially interesting to me, personally, having been the place of residence at an early day of Col. William Piatt (an uncle, by the way, of the late Major Gen. E.R.S. Canby). Some tall cedar trees there marked the site of his old home, where Lafayette visited. Col. Piatt was on especially friendly terms with Gen. Jackson, on whose staff he served at the Battle of New Orleans. Gen. Jackson once presented him with an Arabian horse which had been sent to the President by some Oriental potentate. Col. Piatt, a bachelor, is said to have prized this Democratic gift horse so highly that he kept him and had him fondly groomed in the back parlor of his Home City mansion, which long since has disappeared.

"Less than half a mile from Fernbank is, or rather was, Short's Station, now Addyston. Here one begins to touch the historic neighborhood of North Bend. The large, palatial home of Judge Short (John Cleves Short), son-in-law of General Harrison, is still standing. An uncle of Judge Short was U.S. Minister at Paris shortly after the establishment of our Government. His commission, signed by Washington, used to hang on the wall in Judge Short's library, where I saw it about twenty years ago. A singular and somewhat romantic story of this Minister Short was related to me last year by a relative of the family. During the Reign of Terror a lady came to see Mr. Short (a bachelor) at his Legation, asking for a private audience and telling him that her life was in peril, implored him formally to marry her, in order that she might save her life by claiming protection which marriage to him would give and so escape from Paris. She was a lady of rank and wealth, the story goes, and begged him so persuasively that Mr. Short finally consented. After the legal ceremony, the object of the Franco-American alliance being accomplished, the lady having saved her head from the guillotine, she went her way. It is said, however, that she was grateful for the service and that some of the wealth of the Short family was derived from that international alliance, the lady having attested her gratitude by a large bequest to her proforma American husband.

"The Short residence remains intact and is used for the offices of the steel and pipe works, and the beautiful grounds are sadly disfigured by the shops and the output of the foundry, and there is clamor of forges by day and electric flame by night.

"One of the most beautiful country places is the fruit and horticultural farm of the late Dr. John A. Warder, with the handsome stone house built by him twenty years ago on the wooded hilltop overlooking Sekitan Station. I do not think I have ever seen more lovely landscapes as I have seen from this place where Mr. R. H. Warder, so well known in Cincinnati, privately and as Commissioner of Parks, resides.

"At the original North Bend, the home of General W. H. Harrison, and the headquarters of the great Whig party of 1840, little remains except the Tomb, a stone's throw back of which is the old burying ground known as "Congress

Green," on the town plat made by Judge John C. Symmes, whose ambition was to have his Miami City become what Cincinnati now is, the capital of the Ohio Valley. What lovely views the eastward slopes of this old graveyard give of the Upper Ohio, winding to the southeast toward Delhi!

"I believe all of the old hard-cider apple trees which remembered Gen. Harrison, when I first visited North Bend, are gone. Perhaps one or two old pear trees near the site of his famous "log cabin" are still extant. And half a mile back of the old homestead on land to the Warder estate in the valley of Indian Creek are the ivy-draped ruins of Gen. Harrison's stone mill and distillery, built in the first quarter of the century, some time before he was sent as U.S. Minister to Bogota. Judge Symmes had built two stone mills there previously. Just eastward of the Whig "log cabin," Indian Creek has been dammed to form a pond for making ice for twenty-five years past. The coke ovens just above, whose fires light up the night with a magnificence truly infernal, are not an unmixed blessing. In their cheerful precincts they make a flying cloud of smoke and soot all day.

"Across the river in Kentucky and below North Bend as far as the Great Miami are several points of historic interest, including the site of Fort Finney, Fort Hill and "Goose Pond," whither flocks of sportsmen are just now thronging after flocks of wild ducks."

****

Downriver Postal History, 1851 to 1911
Postmasters and dates of appointment

Home City: Aaron Lyon, July 28, 1851; Abel Childs, Sept. 13, 1852; Stephen Maxon, July 16, 1853. Discontinued, Oct. 14, 1854. Mail to Delhi.

Home City office re-established: Alvin G. Clark, Jan. 15, 1890; Sam'l W. Carpenter, May 11, 1893; Thos. B. Calloway, May 6, 1895; Walter B. Calloway, Dec. 17, 1896; Mrs. Anna M. Brauer, Dec. 15, 1897. Name changed to Sayler Park, 1909.

Sayler Park: Anna M. Brauer, Aug. 4, 1909. Discontinued, Dec. 31, 1911. Mail to Cincinnati.

Industry: John Kennedy, July 28, 1851. Station changed to Delhi, 1854.

Delhi: John Kennedy, Oct. 14, 1854; Peter Zinn, June 20, 1856; James Todd, July 12, 1856; Chas. Herman, Mar. 18, 1857; P. Zinn, Apr. 5, 1858; Alfred M. Cook, Nov. 30, 1861; P. Zinn, Mar. 19, 1864; Mrs. Rosalia E. Best, Dec. 9, 1870; Wm. J. Applegate, July 30, 1872; John Drucker, May 8, 1883; Sam'l H. Goodin, Feb. 4, 1884; Sam'l W. Carpenter, May 4, 1885; Moses L. Andrew, Apr. 22, 1889; Frederic N. Moore, Feb. 7, 1892; Edw. R. Stephens, Sept. 26, 1894; Harry R. Enoch, Mar. 31, 1899; Louis A. Haber, Nov. 17, 1899; Geo. Bascom, Apr. 17, 1901. Discontinued Dec. 31, 1911. Mail to Cincinnati.

Fernbank: Elizabeth Haire, Apr. 3, 1888; Asenath S. Forman, Sept. 8, 1893; Linda L. Fitch, Jan. 28, 1898; Theodore C. Snowdon, Apr. 13, 1899; Wm. E. Wynne, Sept. 21, 1907. Discontinued, Dec. 31, 1911. Mail to Cincinnati.

South Bend: Chas. M. Trautman, June 22, 1874; Adam Linkersdoerfer, July 3, 1878; Station name changed to Trautman, 1880.

Trautman: C. Trautman, July 30, 1880; A. Linkersdoerfer, Feb. 21, 1881; C. Trautman, Nov. 7, 1881. Discontinued, July 18, 1883. Mail to Cincinnati.

Anderson's Ferry: Wm. D. McClurkin, Dec. 22, 1890; Granville C. Wiswell, Dec. 9, 1892. Discontinued, June 22, 1896.

Chapter 28

Recollections Of The Campaign Of 1840

(Written expressly for The Hesperian Tree, by Bettie H. Eaton)

Back in 1899, John J. Piatt requested Bettie Harrison Eaton, daughter of John Scott Harrison and granddaughter of Gen. Wm. H. Harrison, to write of her personal recollections of the campaign of 1840, for inclusion in his book The Hesperian Tree. Bettie Eaton complied with the request. From her interesting account the following lines are copied:

"You give me a very difficult task when you ask for my personal recollections of the campaign of 1840, in which my grandfather, General William H. Harrison, was elected President. To recall the events of sixty years ago, without some data, is not an easy thing to do. Memory is not always a reliable artist, although her pictures seem to glow with brighter and more enduring colors the further they are hung from our present vision.

"So many of the events of that campaign are matters of history, that I need not record here, and my 'personal recollections' may not prove as interesting as you expect them to be . . .

"As I stood on one of the beautiful hills which encompass North Bend, and looked on the sleepy little hamlet at its base, with not very pleasant surroundings, the kaleidoscope of Time presented a very different picture to my view. I saw a home dear to my childhood, with its blossoming apple-orchard rich in its promise of the coming fruit, the wide-spreading meadows, sweet with the odor of new-mown hay, and the dear old house ('the log-cabin' it was called), with its ample rooms, and wings outstretched as if to take to its fostering care all who needed refreshment and rest. Notable men and women were entertained there--Henry Clay, Daniel Webster, Thomas Ewing, Tom Corwin, the famous "Wagoner Boy," and many others. It was in this house that Ex-President Benjamin Harrison was born; and on the night of his advent Harriet Beecher Stowe and her scholarly husband were guests, and they were much surprised to be told, at the breakfast-table, that a new member had been added to the family."

In her account Bettie Eaton tells that in 1840, she, some of her cousins, and a number of other Cincinnati girls were at a boarding school in Steubenville, Ohio. While there she attended a political convention in Pittsburgh at which time she met Gov. John Tyler of Virginia, whose name was second on the Whig ticket with that of her grandfather.

Mrs. Eaton wrote that before she left home her father told her he hoped she would not put on airs, or let her head be turned by the honors being paid to her grandfather-- it would be in bad taste and unbecoming to a lady.

She recorded the following anecdote which she often heard her father relate, illustrative of the strong feeling that existed between the political parties of her grandfather's day.

"In former years it was the custom, as steamboats passed North Bend on their way up and down the river, to fire a salute in honor of "Old Tippecanoe." On one occasion when General Jackson, in one of the floating palaces, was on his way to his Inauguration as President, the captain of the boat, no doubt knowing the politics of both Generals, did not like to observe the custom without the sanction of his distinguished passenger. He went to him, and said: 'General Jackson, we are about to pass North Bend, and it is our custom to salute General Harrison as we pass. Shall I give him one?' 'Old Hickory' knitted his brows and after a few moments hesitation, said, 'Yes; give him two for his military services; but d--n his politics.'

Bettie Eaton wrote of conventions, band-wagons, glee clubs singing Whig songs, delegations visiting North Bend and of dinners to many guests. On one occasion she and her cousins were entertained in Wheeling at a luncheon. It was at this time that President-elect Harrison was passing through the city on his way to Washington for the Inauguration. The granddaughters had the opportunity to spend part of the evening with him. Mrs. Eaton recalled that all the buttons of his coat were missing, having been cut off by souvenir hunters. General Harrison told his granddaughters to be good girls, to apply themselves closely to their studies, and when they had graduated they could come to visit him at the White House. But alas! That time never came.

"My grandmother did not accompany her husband. Her health was delicate, the journey an arduous one, as the mountains had to be crossed in a stage-coach, the weather at that season was inclement, and her physician (Dr. Thornton), who was also her son-in-law, was not willing that she should take the risk. It was arranged that her son, John Scott Harrison, should escort her to Washington later in the spring. That journey was never taken. Man proposes, God disposes."

"The family at the White House comprised the President; his daughter-in-law, Jane Findlay Harrison, the widow of his namesake son, and her two sons; her aunt, Mrs. Findlay, (wife of General Findlay); her cousin, Miss Eliza Ramsey; Mrs. Lucy Singleton Taylor, the President's niece, and her two sons; Mr. Henry Harrison, of Berkeley Virginia, the President's nephew; and Montgomery Pike Harrison, a grandson, who was also a grandson of General Zebulon Pike, who was killed at Little York, Canada, in the War of 1812, and whose only child, Clarissa Harlowe Pike, married General Harrison's eldest son, John Cleves Symmes Harrison. The old Pike homestead stood on the banks of the Ohio River, in Kentucky, two and a half miles below North Bend. My uncle had six children, and I used to visit these cousins quite often in my childhood, and was always interested in a large British flag which Mrs. Pike often exposed to the sun and air to protect it from depredation of moths. It was captured from the British by General Pike's troops, and when his body was sent home, it was draped over his casket, seemingly a triumph even in death. My cousin, Montgomery Pike Harrison, graduated at West Point with honor several years after grandfather's death, and was killed by the Indians while with his regiment in the far West . . .

"In June following my grandfather's death, a committee was appointed to go to Washington and bring the remains back to North Bend . . . The lovely (burial) spot was selected by my father and Colonel Charles S. Todd, an old army friend and aide-de-camp of my grandfather in the War of 1812 . . ."

*Note: The foregoing material was copied from "A Far-Backward Look at North Bend: Memories of Sixty Years Ago" by Bettie Harrison Eaton, October 1, 1899. It appeared in The Hesperian Tree, A Souvenir of the Ohio Valley, Edited by John James Piatt, Published by John Scott & Co. Three Rivers Elm, North Bend, Ohio. Vol. I, Ed. 2, Copyright 1900, by John James Piatt.

★★★★★★★★★★

Dec. 2, 1825, Indiana Palladium, Lawrenceburg: Wood Wanted. Those of our subscribers who live near town and who wish to pay for their papers in WOOD are informed that a few cords would be very acceptable at present. Editors.

Chapter 29

JOHN KING, PHARMACOLOGIST, MEDICAL WRITER AND TEACHER

Another one-time, prominent citizen of North Bend was Dr. John King (1813-1893). Together with William S. Merrell, he was the greatest analytical pharmacologist in the history of medicine in Cincinnati. Of Dr. King, Otto Juettner had the following to report in Daniel Drake and His Followers:

Born in New York City, Jan. 1, 1813, John King was a grandson of the Marquis La Parte, Lafayette's friend and comrade. His parents being in comfortable circumstances, John had a thorough classical and scientific education. He spoke and read French and German. He was a mechanical genius and in his leisure hours learned the art of engraving. He was a good amateur musician and tried his hand successfully at the art of playwright. At the age of twenty-five, he graduated in medicine from Wooster Beach's medical school in New York. After graduation he devoted many years to practical work as a botanist, pharmacologist and chemist. In 1851, King became a teacher in Cincinnati Eclectic Medical Institute and taught its classes until the time of his death, which occurred in North Bend, Ohio, in 1893. He was held in almost idolatrous veneration by his students.

Not only did John King work extensively in the field of pharmacology, but he was also a voluminous writer. His greatest work was the "American Dispensatory," 1855. He published text books on the subject of obstetrics and gynecology.

Dr. John King resided in a fine home in North Bend, east of Indian Creek, along Sunset Avenue. His daughter, who had married Gen. Charles W. Karr, attorney, lived with him. Sometime around the period of Dr. King's death in 1893, their home burned. The Karrs then moved to Cliff Road to a home on the site of where later Cliff View Inn was built. General Karr and Dr. King were both active in the government of the village of North Bend.

John Uri Lloyd, a protege of Dr. King and author of Stringtown on the Pike, wrote a book entitled The Right Side of the Car, a symbolic sketch, in tribute to the memory of his friend and teacher. The proceeds from the sale of the book were used to erect a monument over the grave of the great pharmacologist at Maple Grove Cemetery, near Cleves, on June 16, 1901.

★★★★★★★★★★

Miami Heights, east of Cleves, is to have an observatory erected by the Cincinnati Astronomical Society because the sky is clearest there. The observatory will be built of granite from the old Cincinnati Chamber of Commerce Building. (Law'burg. Press, March 16, 1916.)

★★★★★★★★★★★★★★★★★★★★★★★★★★★

Dry Ridge Postal History

Dry Ridge was located a mile west of Bridgetown at the junction of Taylor's Creek Road and the Ebenezer Church and school house, now Mack. Known postmasters were: Wm. McConnell, July 9, 1838; Wm. B. Biddle, Feb. 18, 1842; Enoch W. Carson, Mar. 29, 1844; Wm. H. Markland, Mar. 7, 1855; P.O. discontinued Sept. 3, 1875; Re-instated Jan. 29, 1883 with Geo. P. Hodge as P.M.; discontinued Jan. 7, 1884. Mail sent to Delhi.

Chapter 30

WILLIAM COLBY COOPER PHYSICIAN AND WRITER

A biographical sketch of William C. Cooper, teacher, physician and author of Cleves, appeared in the book Daniel Drake and His Followers, by Otto Juettner (1909). From that account the following is taken:

W. C. Cooper of Cleves, Ohio, ranks with the foremost literary men in the medical profession. He was born at North Bend, Ohio, in 1835. He had no school advantages whatever because his father, as he put it, "maintained a dead level of impecuniosity through all the son's minority." The son's love of knowledge and study triumphed over all difficulties. The years of his childhood and adolescence were spent amid all kinds of manual and menial work interspersed with many a long-night-vigil over books which he managed to borrow or buy. When he was twenty years of age, he had qualified himself to take charge of a little country school. He rapidly rose in the profession of teaching, and after twelve years was the principal of a high school. At this time he began to study medicine under J. M. Scudder. In 1867, he graduated from the Cincinnati Eclectic Medical Institute, practiced for one year in Mt. Carmel, Indiana, and for twelve years in Indianapolis, where he edited a small journal, the "Medical Review." In 1880, he took up permanent abode in Cleves, Ohio. For fifteen years he was W. E. Bloyer's associate in the editorial management of the "Medical Gleaner." In this capacity he attracted attention by his vigorous idiomatic English and his quaint originality of thought. His book "Tethered Truants," containing many of his essays, sketches and poems, reveal Cooper's power as a word-painter, a sharp and forcible critic and observer and, in no small degree, his gift of delightful humor. His book "Immortality" is a philosophic product in which Cooper appears as a hopeful agnostic. His views on the philosophy of medicine are contained in his "Preventive Medicine." In later life he lost his sight and hearing, but his mind remained remarkably clear.

Dr. Cooper was much admired by the townspeople of Cleves. His poetry, which dealt with familiar subjects, appealed to the average citizen. Dr. Cooper's daughter, Edith, to whom he was devoted, was also a writer of verse. After her untimely death, he published, in 1902, a book of her works, entitling it "Poems of Edith Caskey Cooper." In this book Dr. Cooper named some of the girlhood and young womanhood friends of Edith, among them Rose Struble, Anna Chrisman and Sallie Westcott--all of whom were teachers. Mollie Carlin was named as Edith's first teacher at Cleves School, then located on College Street. Special praise was given to Anna Chrisman for her self-sacrifice and devotion to his daughter during the last months of her life.

It was a popular custom to write verses for friends back in those days when Edith C. Cooper (1873-1901) lived. In her collection of poems there are several dedicated to friends on their wedding days, to her parents, and one--in the form of an acrostic--to her friend Elizabeth Bogart, Cleves teacher.

Elizabeth Bogart, whose parents, Elbert and Eva Fagaly Bogart, were descendants of pioneer Miami Township settlers, came from a bright family of scholars and teachers. Elizabeth, herself, taught at Cleves from about 1890 to 1907, and was long remembered with affection by her pupils. Her brother, George Henri Bogart, became a newspaperman, for a time editor of the Brookville, Indiana, Democrat. Elizabeth Bogart befriended young Edith Cooper, who was an invalid for many months before her death. Following the death of the young woman, Miss Bogart penned a verse called "Empty Arms" in tribute to her. The poem referred to the old arm chair, with empty arms, which stood in Edith's room. Dr. Cooper included this verse in his daughter's book of poetry.

Dr. W. C. Cooper died in 1913; he was buried at Maple Grove Cemetery. Of Cooper, Mr. J. O. Speed, a former resident of Cleves, had the following words to say:

"Dr. W. C. Cooper was a close friend and follower of James Whitcomb Riley and was instrumental in obtaining recognition of Riley as a real poet--as he surely was. Dr. Cooper spent years in Cleves, as he loved the little country town where he practiced his profession successfully--from his patients' standpoint. He was kind-hearted, his fees modest, and he was a poor collector. Elizabeth Bogart and Emma Speed were among his many admirers, as well as friends of his wife and brilliant daughter, Edith, who died in 1901. The latter, too, was a writer of poetry."

Two of Dr. Cooper's own poems may be found elsewhere in this volume, in the chapters "Miami and Whitewater Valley Pioneer Association" and "Railroads Come to Miami Township."

(The subject "Physicians of Miami Township and Its Borders" would be an interesting topic for someone to pursue. Known doctors of the area have included: (Miami and Whitewater Townships) Drs. Stephen Wood, J. H. Thornton, Abel Whipple, John Hughes, Jeremiah Brower, A. L. Bushnell, Wm. Goshorn, Richard H. Ewing, Hiram Rulison, John A. Warder, John King, John M. Diller, George Cassady, Jacob H. Hunt, Royal Struble, Wm. C. Cooper, Marcus Brawley, Wm. C. Hughes, Edw. W. Davis, O. J. Wood, F. I. Black, J. B. Hanna and Chas. F. Culley; Dr. Lee Keidel has continuously served the area for nearly 40 years; (Delhi Township) Drs. John H. MacKenzie, John Campbell, D. D. Barr, C. W. Tangeman, J. H. Haire, C. H. Rosenthal (dentist), Luther B. Terrill, ___Damerow, B. F. Lehman, J. H. Walton, ___Schoenling, Oliver G. Chance and Wm. N. Gracely, who doctored in the community for 50 years, delivering over 4,000 babies. There were no doubt many others.)

****

Physicians of Whitewater Township in 1850 included: C.C. Little, Thomas Francis, John Hughes and Walter Clark.

****

Clark's Store

The first store in Whitewater Township was opened in 1805 by William Clark. Bartering was the method of transacting business and the merchant often found it difficult to make both ends meet. Nevertheless, Clark's Store seems to have survived for at least 40 years. An early post office was established here May 22, 1827, with Wm. Clark as first postmaster. In 1832 Walter Clark succeeded him. Luther Hopping was a bondsman for the station. Clark's Store possibly was located along old Harrison Pike, somewhere between Miamitown and Harrison. (Can a reader give the location?) The post office was discontinued May 10, 1842. Walter Clark, also a physician, soon after opened a hotel and tavern at Elizabethtown. The Clark family was among the first pioneers in Whitewater Township. Dr. Clark later resided at Harrison and was an active member of The Pioneer Association.

Chapter 31

The Legend Of The Wamsley Mad Stone

Mad stone, as defined by Webster, is a stone popularly supposed to counteract the poison from the bite of an animal.

Some of the most interesting of "old wives tales" have to do with the magic powers of stones. Many of the best known stones were given to white folks by grateful Indians to be used as cure-alls, but more specifically for mad dog and snake bites. The technic of application differs, but in general the stone is heated or boiled in water or milk and applied again and again on the victim's body near the place of the bite.

This Miami Township locale is on record as having once had a mad stone within its borders. Tales of the stone's healing powers are yet recalled by old-timers. It was brought to the region by the Wamsley family many years ago. They had obtained the piece of stone, a chip from a larger one, from a gentleman in northern Kentucky, who had acquired it from Indians. (It is thought possible that the parent stone is the "Boone County Mad Stone," kept in a vault at Burlington, Ky.) The Wamsley stone is clear, like crystal quartz, and is very hard.

The earliest Wamsley to settle in the region was William Wamsley (1785-1837), a native of Virginia, who had lived for a time in Boone County where he had married Nancy Bussell. The Wamsleys crossed the river in 1815, to reside near Pike's Landing on Harrison--and later Short--property. The old Wamsley homestead was a familiar landmark along the river, between North Bend and The Point. William Wamsley may have been the one who first acquired the mad stone, although this is not known.

In 1871, (possibly much sooner), the mad stone was in the hands of Moses B. "Doc" Wamsley, son of William, who resided near the old grist mill along the Great Miami River, between Cleves and Lost Bridge. From the Lawrenceburg Press, of that year, comes the following pertinent item:

"There are now at Mr. M. B. Wamsley's three young ladies from Hamilton, Ohio, trying what virtue there is in the mad stone. These make 10 persons that have been there in the last week, all bitten by the same dog. It never fails to cure."

Another interesting account of the Wamsley family appeared in the Commercial Gazette, April 8, 1894:
"Mrs. Moses B. (Eunice Hayes) Wamsley celebrated her 75th birthday at her home below Cleves. Many persons were present for the occasion. The Wamsleys are well known throughout the city for having possession of the celebrated mad stone. Mrs. Wamsley had on exhibition 55 quilts she had pieced herself. The quilts bear names of different U.S. Presidents. Many have taken prizes. Some of the patterns include: Star of the East, Star of the West, Flying Star, Wabash Loaf, Oak Loaf, Poplar Leaf and Log Cabin."

The mad stone was handed down through several generations. In 1940, Clyde Wamsley, then of Cleves, was the possessor of the stone. In that year a Cincinnati dermatologist, Dr. Leon Goldman, for the purpose of writing a medical paper, interviewed Clyde Wamsley and photographed the stone. From the Goldman report* the following notes have been extracted:
According to Clyde Wamsley, his family's technic was to place the stone on the back of the hand, regardless of where the bite. Treatment was delayed for three days to allow the stone "to get all the poison from the system." A small nick was made in the skin and the stone was applied and left to remain in contact for several hours. The hand could be moved in all directions and the stone would adhere. When it fell off it was boiled again before reapplying. So as not to risk losing the stone, patients were kept at the Wamsley farmhouse and charged about five dollars a day. Accounts of many cures, both of dog and snake bite, were vouched by the owners. The Wamsley mad stone was last used around 1905 or 1910.

The Hafner family of Cleves has passed down a favorable report on the mad stone. Edward Hafner, born 1876, son of Joseph Hafner, was bitten by a water moccasin along the rock dam at the family's grist mill, situated in that day along the Great Miami. The young lad, around four years old, was desperately sick. He was treated by "Doc" Wamsley's mad stone and cured, according to the story handed down by the family. The Hafners, at that time, lived near to Moses B. Wamsley. Edward Hafner's cousin, William "Skeeter" Engelbrecht, was also treated for mad dog bite and cured through the use of the mad stone.

Upon the death of Clyde Wamsley in 1966, the famous mad stone, with pertinent records, fell to his daughter, Essie Wamsley Brater of Sayler Park, now of Harrison.

* "The Charm of the Mad Stone with Special Reference to the Famous Stone of Cleves," by Leon Goldman, M. D., Cincinnati, Ohio. Reprint from Ohio State Medical Journal, Vol. 36, Oct. 1940, No. 10. This article may be seen at CHS Library.

Kentucky Post, Sept. 1, 1939; article concerning Boone County mad stone at Burlington, Ky.

**
Dr. Goldman believed that the Cleves mad stone may have been the one used many years before on his father, who was treated with such a stone for dog bite on the leg.

****

Streets of Fernbank, Home City and Delhi

Before the villages of Fernbank, Home City and Delhi were annexed to Cincinnati, they operated independently and each had its own street names. These were all changed after annexation. For example, the street running through all the villages now known as Gracely Drive bore a different name in each area. In Fernbank it was Short, in Home City it was Independence, in Delhi it was Lincoln, and in Industry it was Main. The village of Industry, little of it in evidence, lay from about Huey Avenue on the west to about the brick yards on the east; it lay up beyond Hillside Avenue on the north and down to the river on the south. Streets of Industry bore such names as: Jackson, Adams, Monroe, Polk, Harrison, Jefferson, Washington and Union. St. Aloysius Church then stood on 3rd Street. Hillside Avenue in that day was North Bend Street. Many aristocratic families resided in the Delhi neighborhood. Their large homes, once most elegant, are yet in evidence. Mackenzie Street, named for an early physician, yet bears the name. Names of some of the present day streets and their counterparts of yesteryear are as follows: Fernbank (Chestnut); Overcliff (School Lane); River Road (Commercial, Lower River Road and Nokomis); Gracely (Short, Independence, Lincoln and Main); Elco (Washington); Cherokee (Mound); Home City (Western Row); Thelma (Park); Parkland (Liberty); Monitor (Main); Twain (Center); Lower Ivanhoe (Lafayette); Upper Ivanhoe (Franklin); Revere (Shady and Washington); Zinn (Wesley).

Chapter 32

CLEVES: A PAGE FROM THE PAST

Although the Cleves Area Sesquicentennial Book, edited by Walter W. Harrell, presented a most complete history of Cleves, the following account written by J. O. Speed is a worthy addition for the village annals. Entitled "A Page From the Past," it appeared in The Valley Journal, July, 1953, and paints a vivid picture of the town at the turn of the century.

"Though not a native of Cleves, I feel that I can qualify as one of her elder citizens; and, as such, I may contribute a few items to The Valley Journal.

"My first glimpse of Cleves was from a window of a Big Four railway car on a Cincinnati-bound train from St. Louis, running behind time, in July, 1894. We had been delayed by a wreck of a commuter train near Cleves in which some coaches were derailed and splintered and a number of people were injured. Both sides of the track were lined with people viewing the wreckage, and I then saw a large segment of the Cleves citizenry in their before-breakfast habiliments some of whom, in their excitement, almost completely disregarded the custom of donning day raiment before appearing in public.

"My first visit to Cleves, one that proved to be a crossroad in my life journey, was on a sizzling day in August, 1897. I was spending Sunday with one of my associates of the Big Four general accounting department, who resided here and at whose home I became acquainted with a young lady school-teacher. Two years later we were honey-mooning in Niagara Falls. In due course we were in our new home. Largely through my wife, I soon became acquainted with most of the Cleves residents. Time has wrought many changes since that far-off period--in our means of transportation, our forms of amusements and recreational habits, our styles in dress, even our foods, yes in our salaries and wages and the cost of living as well.

"At that time, Cleves people were solely dependent on the Big Four Railroad for transportation to Cincinnati, where many of its citizens were employed, as now, and to more distant points. But the cost was only about one-third of the present bus fares. Suburban trains ran frequently, the service was good and passengers to the city were discharged at old Union Station, Third St. and Central Ave. There were comfortable, all-season waiting rooms at both ends of the journey. No tiresome, uncomfortable street-corner waits followed by a mad scramble for a seat, as now.

"In those pre-auto days, people were thrown on their own resources for amusement. They had parties and picnics, home talent entertainments, church suppers, hay rides, medicine shows, etc. for diversion. Conspicuous among the home talent entertainers were Pete Keller and Mrs. Nina Hearn, who had good voices, and Genevieve Bernhardt, a talented young elocutionist. Church services and entertainments were well attended and the people went to and from them on their own power. On a Sunday following payday, some local dude with his best girl might be seen as far from home as Miamitown or Cheviot in a livery-stable buggy, but most young couples were content with Sunday afternoon hikes to Harrison's tomb, the Lost Bridge, or the Big Four station to see the 5 p.m. "Cannon Ball."

"We had no chain or self-service stores in those days and very little package goods. Sugar, coffee, salt, molasses, cereals, crackers etc. came to the retail merchant in bulk and he weighed and sacked them as sold to the consumer.

"The grocers of Cleves, John Ingram, George Welch, Dave Chambers and Charles Caine, sent their employees over town in the forenoon to "take orders," and free delivery of goods ordered was made by 10 a.m. Prevailing prices were: sugar, 5¢ per pound; butter 25¢; eggs 15¢; potatoes 40¢ per bushel; and most other items in proportion.

"John Minges, assisted by George Lohe, ran the meat shop, selling tender steaks, roasts and chops from 10¢ to 25¢ per pound. Benjamin Chidlaw, succeeded by Suit Bros., operated the coal and lumber yard. Good lump coal brought $3.50 per ton. Lumber was cheap, clear and well seasoned. Prices $20 per thousand for white pine or poplar siding, $18 for framing lumber.

"A good 50 x 150 building lot could be bought for $100 and $2500 would build a nice five-room residence. The leading carpenters and building contractors were Sam Camira, Albert Heap, Harry Balsley and Wm. Buckwald. John Sonnenday and a Mr. Scoggins were painting contractors; William Spinning, plastering; William Hughes, paper hanging; and Joseph Ingersoll, hardware.

"At that time our Village Mayor was Arthur Moak. John Miller, Peter Keller and Fred Grossman were three of the five councilmen. The school board members were Oliver Smith, Thomas Cassidy, David Hopkins, Frank Blocker and Charles Wood. William Harrell was school principal; the faculty members were Misses Helen Guard, Lizzie Bogart, Emma Stumpp, Marcia Cassidy, Rose Struble, Lida Meyers and Anna Chrisman.

"Some of the teen-agers were attending high schools in Cincinnati; among them were Charles Young, our popular and successful township School Superintendent and Mrs. Mary Dick, our polite and efficient postmistress.

"Prominent educators residing in Cleves then in charge of schools in neighboring communities were Morgan Wamsley, Virgil Henderson, William Chidlaw and William Flinchpaugh.

"Mrs. Melissa Argo, postmistress, and Will Gleason, station agent, filled their rather trying positions most capably. Reverends La Bach and English were the respective ministers of the two Cleves Churches, Presbyterian and Methodist. Doctors Cooper, Wood and Hughes looked after the health of the Cleveites and did a good job of it with the aid of Fred Grossman, druggist and his popular assistant, "Miss Jo" Spinning.

"Our local political leaders were Stanley Struble, Republican, subsequently and for many years a common pleas judge, now living in retirement; and on the Democratic side, August Hildebrand and Wm. Glazier. A.E.B. (Buz) Stephens, an unusually popular and widely-known citizen, who moved from Cleves to North Bend, became a Republican leader in the latter place. After serving as County Clerk he was elected and re-elected to the national Congress from the Second Ohio district, serving until his death.

"Our leading dry goods stores were operated by Edwin Wilke and Wm. Stewart with the assistance of their good wives. They were quite successful, having patrons from many neighboring towns and from people across the river in Kentucky. Hair ribbons and high-button shoes along with woolen stockings, ear-muffs, red shawls and bolts of calicoes and red flannel were much in evidence at the two dry goods emporiums.

"The village boasted of two livery stables of which the respective proprietors were Edw. Argo and Thos. Cassidy. Our hardware store, owned and operated by that fine old citizen, Jos. Ingersoll, was a favorite rendezvous of prominent villagers and such well known farmers as John Chidlaw, Erastus Hayes, Rans Markland, John Flinchpaugh, Jos. Sykes, Ezra Guard, Job and Enos Hayes and Peter Minges.

"Many sons, daughters and grandchildren of Cleves have distinguished themselves in "far-away places" and various fields. Among them may be instanced: Lieut. General Benjamin Chidlaw, U.S. Air Force; Harry Vangorder of the C.N.W. Railway, and his daughter, Nellie Blackford, president, St. Louis Envelope and Printing Co.; Frank Myers, the renowned artist; William Wright, of Hollywood, the theatrical producer and short-story writer, son of Kate Jessup Wright; Richard Stewart, of National Biscuit Co.; and Miss Dora Sonnenday, physician of Norwood.

"Nearly all of the Cleveites herein named have passed to their rewards. But the old town is doing pretty well in the hands of later generations."

(* This article, along with several other articles and poems of Mr. Speed and his wife, Emma Stumpp Speed, were sent to me in 1966 by the author, who then resided in Madisonville, Ky. See account elsewhere of the Speeds.)

****

1969, Feb. 25. "Cleves mayor Tom North speaks. He hopes for new industry, new business and remodeling of old structures. Population of the village stands at 2075 and is not expected to increase substantially."

(Note: For those interested in a complete history of Cleves, copies of the Cleves Area Sesquicentennial Book are yet available from Three Rivers Historical Society, Milton Thompson, Jr., Cleves, Ohio, 45002.)

★★★★★★★★★★

Pioneer Churches

A pioneer Presbyterian congregation was brought together in the Delhi area as early as 1831 by Horace Bushnell. A church at Cleves was also organized in this period. In 1838 Bushnell was pastor of the Delhi and Cleves charge with a total of 41 members. The historic Cleves Presbyterian Church has been in continuous existence since its founding but the early Delhi charge ceased to exist around 1840. No records remain of this latter church. First Presbyterian Church of Delhi was organized in 1866 and held its first services at the I&C railroad depot. A Lutheran Church also existed at Industry in the 1860 era. Another church, denomination unknown, stood near the corner of what is now Cleves-Warsaw Pike and VanBlaricum Road during this same period. Delhi Methodist Church had its beginnings in a Union Sunday School established around 1869. This church was officially organized in 1877 and its church building dedicated in Jan. 1878. St. Aloysius Catholic Church was built in Delhi (Industry) in 1873, opposite a school building which Catholic laymen had erected in 1860. A fine history was compiled by the congregation of Cleves Methodist Church on the occasion of their 75th anniversary. An account of all the local churches, together with stories of pioneer preachers, would present a good history of religion in the community at large.

The Gibson family, lithographers and art publishers, who founded Gibson Art Company, were early day residents of Delhi. The Kites, also prominent in Delhi, operated a large china or queensware store (Dean & Kite) in the city, importing much of their goods from England.

Chapter 33

John O. And Emma Stumpp Speed, Poets

John Orville Speed (1871-   ) and his wife, Emma Stumpp Speed (1871-1960), a native of Cleves, were prolific writers of verse. The Speeds will never become famous but their poems, of familiar, everyday subjects, hold rare meaning and charm for those who recall home and small-town life of yesteryear.

J. O. Speed, born in 1871 in Hopkins County, Kentucky, the region where the pennyroyal plant flourishes, calls himself "The Pennyrile Poet." His little book, Anecdotes and Tall Tales in Rhyme, published in 1962 by Vantage Press, was dedicated to the memory of his wife, a wonderful Ohio schoolteacher.

The father of Emma Stumpp Speed, Fred Stumpp, worked on the farm of John Scott Harrison at Fort Hill, where he met and married Harriet Bevens, one of several sisters who resided on a neighboring farm. After the birth of the Stumpps' first child, Annie, they moved to Cleves where their other five children, William, Louise, Charles, Emma and John were born. The mother died soon afterward, leaving the six young children. Annie took the responsibility for mothering the little Stumpps.

Emma Stumpp attended Cleves Public School and at the age of eighteen secured her teacher's certificate. For nine years, from 1890 to 1899, she taught at Cleves, until she married J. O. Speed. When the Cleves Woman's Club was founded in 1904, Mrs. Speed became a charter member.

In 1906, the couple found themselves living in Washington, D. C., where Mr. Speed was employed. During the period of their residence in that city, Emma Speed was honored in a very special way. It happened that when President Theodore Roosevelt initiated the National Conservation Congress, Mrs. Speed was selected because of her beautiful penmanship to address the several hundred engraved invitations on White House stationery, and to write the identification cards sent to all the state governors, prominent members of both branches of Congress, and national leaders in various fields of activity and many distinguished private citizens.

At the death of Emma Speed in 1960, Mr. Speed returned to his native home in Madisonville, Ky., where he resides today.

Several poems of the Speeds, the first two by Emma Speed and the third by J. O. Speed, selected for their down-to-earth subject matter, are copied here:

PORCH PLEASURE

A house is incomplete to me
   Without a porch, where I can be
To rest myself at close of day,
   When work and cares are put away;
Where Heaven's balmy breezes blow,
   And sunset sky is all aglow
'Tis joy to look at grass and trees,
   And other out-door things like these.

The folks I know pass by and smile,
   And some come in to sit awhile.
The birds' sweet notes and insects' hum
   Are softly heard ere night has come.
From flower to vine they flit about,
   As if they're pleased to see me out.
A porch and chairs I need to own
   To make my house the perfect home.

A LESSON

The birds are very busy now,
For Spring is drawing near,
Their songs are merry tuneful ones,
No jarring jazz I hear.

They scan the premises all o'er,
Appraising bush and tree,
And all the while they're keeping up
Their songs of melody.

Their wise philosophy of life
We well might imitate:
Just try our best to keep in song,
This rule I advocate.

THE OLD COFFEE MILL

The old coffee mill was screwed to the wall,
Too high for the short, just right for the tall;
But music it gave to my welcome young ear,
For its loud, crunching sound meant that meal-time was near.

How often I ended a wearisome day
From a hike through the woods, berry-picking, or play;
Hungry, I lolled in the apple-tree's shade,
Awaiting that signal that supper was made.

The violin's strains soothe my frame to the core;
The harp, the guitar, and the rest I adore;
But nothing, to me, ever sounded so sweet
As the old coffee mill, just before time to eat.

When Fancy the pages of time backward turn,
A picture unfolds for which our hearts yearn--
The joys, the loved ones, of the long-ago past,
Like the old coffee mill, leave memories that last.

*Note: J. O. Speed died July 9, 1970; interred at Maple Grove.

★★★★★★★★★★★★

Burials in VanBlaricum Cemetery

David Kirgan, early land holder in Miami Township in the Home City locale (in the general region where Miami, Delhi and Green Townships meet), is buried in the old Van Blaricum Cemetery off of VanBlaricum Road in Green Township. Kirgan was born July 4, 1770 and had reached the age of 109 years and 11 months when he died June 7, 1879. Other families represented in this old burying ground include the Van Blaricums, Marklands, Orman Manns, Wyatts, Taylors and Reddings, all of whom settled in the Miami and Green Township region in the early part of the 19th century.

★★★★★★★★★★★★★★★★★★★★★★★★★★

Queen of the Cleves Area Sesqui-Centennial

It was appropriate that Miss Linda Lacey should be crowned Queen of the Cleves Area Sesqui-Centennial, 1818-1968. Her ancestor Stephen Lacey settled in the Miami Township region soon after 1800.

Chapter 34

DOWNRIVER COMMUNITIES

The villages bordering the Ohio along the route of old River Road below Anderson Ferry out to North Bend have long been referred to as the downriver communities, or the Lower River Road neighborhood. They include Fernbank, Sayler Park (once Home City) and Delhi (of which the ill fated village of Industry was once a part). These three lay within Delhi Township, with the exception of a part of Fernbank which was situated in the eastern most section of Miami Township. Located along two railroads, the villages literally date their beginnings with the coming of trains.

Fernbank was laid out about 1875 by Charles W. Short, proprietor of the land. At that time it bordered the large corporation of North Bend, which then encompassed the area from Elizabethtown up and along the Ohio to Short's Station. (See "Short's Station, Sekitan and Addyston") Fernbank was designed as a settlement of beautiful suburban residences, located between what was then expected to become industrial towns at its borders. The nearby village of Industry (now within Delhi), dedicated in 1847, had then a promising future as a manufacturing and commercial center. Sekitan and Coal City, within the territory of North Bend on the west, showed signs of becoming a prosperous community in the coal trade and in brick and tile manufacturing.

Charles W. Short (1851-1926), who had wed Mary Dudley in 1872, resided at the ancestral home, "Short Hill," built about 1817 by his father, Judge John C. Short (1792-1864), on ground given to the latter's first wife, Betsy Harrison Short, by her father, General Wm. H. Harrison. After Betsy Short's death in 1846, Judge Short remarried, in 1849, Mary Ann Goodrich Mitchell. To them were born two sons, John Cleves Short and Charles W. Short. The former died in 1880. Charles W. Short fell heir to hundreds of acres of land in the wide territory of North Bend and down around The Point. The bulk of the vast farmlands in the region of old Fort Finney and Fort Hill were sold, in time, to Abram Brower. (See "New Life at The Point.")

In 1877, the Short brothers erected, to the memory of their parents, John Cleves and Mary Ann Short, the beautiful Episcopal Church of the Resurrection in the new little village of Fernbank.

The history of the Fernbank Episcopal Church is closely aligned with the Episcopal Sunday School which had its beginnings at North Bend around 1868. Dr. Hiram Rulison and the Warder family were active in this community Sabbath school program. The first Episcopal Church service was held in 1874 in the home of Judge John S. Conner at North Bend. Conner was then living in the residence of William Mitchell (half-brother of C. W. Short) on Harrison Avenue. Soon after that, the Shorts gave the use of a cottage on Taylor Avenue, just west of what became St. Joseph Church. Here Episcopal services were held, conducted by lay leaders. The Warders conducted a Sunday School at North Bend and later at Fernbank. After the church was built in 1877, Judge Conner was among its first lay leaders. In 1879, North Bend Sunday School and Fernbank Church were one parish, with Rev. Charles Sturgis as pastor. Appointed as rector of the church in 1884 was Rev. Charles D. Williams.

An article that appeared in the Cincinnati Daily Gazette, Jan. 1, 1881, told something of the nature of Fernbank:

"The young settlement at Fern Bank is a great attraction to the businessman who seeks relaxation. The village forms part and parcel of the great manor of Short Hill extending over several thousand acres on which the game is strictly protected for the benefit of the proprietor, his friends and his Fern Bank tenants."

Mention was also made, in the foregoing article, of the wild life, the flora and fauna, that was to be found in the environs. Streets were given such names as Dahlia, Catalpa, Birch, Chestnut and Topinabee.

The village began to grow and by 1887 there was a population of 200. In 1888, Fernbank was incorporated as a village. Its first officers were:

Mayor, Wm. G. Miner; Clerk, Wm. A. White; Treasurer, Perrin G. March; Marshal, John Wyatt; Council, R. B. Beeson, Geo. A. Fitch, Charles W. Short, J. F. Thornton, Geo. Tozzer.

During this era, Short built a fine home (now the March residence) next to the Episcopal Church and vacated the ancestral estate. "Short Hill" and a great parcel of land around it he sold, about 1888, to Matthew Addy, who founded Addyston and established an immense pipe foundry on the site. (See "Short's Station, Sekitan and Addyston") The street running past the new Short residence was called Short Avenue. (Today this is Gracely Drive, named for the beloved physician, William Nast Gracely, who gave over fifty years of devoted service to the downriver community, during which time he delivered over 4,000 babies.) It was also around 1888 that an impressive train depot was erected at Fernbank, through Short's influence, another convenience established to attract new life to the village.

The pipe foundry not only brought about an overnight growth of Addyston but stimulated the settlement of Fernbank, as well. Prominent officials of the pipe company, and other related industries, located here. The village attracted families of means and culture who engaged in a variety of social, civic and educational pursuits.

Around 1880, a one-floor schoolhouse was built at the end of what was then Chestnut Avenue and School Lane. Some years later, the floor of the school was raised and an additional floor built under it, making it a two-storied building. The old schoolhouse is now the Masonic Lodge Hall. Chestnut Avenue (now Fernbank Avenue) was once lined with lovely chestnut trees but these were destroyed by a blight.

John M. Grimsley was an early schoolmaster at Fernbank. He had previously taught at Cleves and was considered a fine teacher. Other known teachers here in the 1880-1910 era included:

Helen Cunningham, Carrie Conklin, Mrs. Pinkerton, Mrs. Mary Morton, Charles P. Loth, Edith M. Converse, Nannie A. Lord, Amy Merrel, Elwinna Stewart, Elsic Tangeman and Miss King. Mrs. Hermione Flagler was an early music teacher in the Fernbank community, and Mrs. Margaret Sweeney Mobberley also became a piano teacher of note.

A high school was also once conducted at Fernbank. About the time when the villages were annexed to the city, pupils from Fernbank, Sayler Park and Delhi began to attend classes together at the Home City Schools, grade and high school, which were located on the lot opposite where the Sayler Park theater now stands.

Mayors of Fernbank included: Wm. A. White, 1891; C. W. Short, 1893; and D. W. McClung, 1899-1901. Postmaster of the village during this period was A. S. Forman.

Telephone service was introduced to the area in February, 1902, the first exchange being located in Delhi.

It was during the 1890 era that the neighboring downriver communities were also experiencing rapid growth. The villages of Fernbank, Home City and Delhi became so interrelated and so inter-dependent in economic, civic, social, school and church affairs that it soon became difficult to separate one place from another. Back in 1879, there had been strong talk of incorporating the Delhi Township villages of Home City, Delhi and Industry under the name Delhi. Petitions were circulated promoting this plan without success. Each village operated its own grade schools and elected its own officers. Each continued to maintain separate existences until annexed to Cincinnati.

Lower River Road was first to be annexed to the city on May 20, 1909. Prior to that time this roadway below Anderson Ferry had been operated under a toll road company. In order to secure city water service, the down river villages chose to annex to Cincinnati, Delhi on June 23, 1910, Sayler Park on June 3, 1911, and Fernbank on Nov. 12, 1912. It was also after this time that the original street names of the villages were changed.

A complete and detailed history of these downriver communities is yet to be written. The region merits an account of its own.

(A brief sketch of the village of Industry, from S. B. Nelson's History of Cincinnati and Hamilton County, follows:

Industry, lying within the present village of Delhi, was platted by James Cooper, county surveyor, for James and Samuel Goodin. The town was dedicated as Industry in 1847. Its early industries included a flour mill, match factory, cotton mill, foundry. With signs of progress, some modest homes were built and a few families located at Industry. But the match factory soon burned; the flour mill was undermined by a spring flood; the proprietors of the cotton mill became financially embarrassed; the foundry ceased operating because of embezzling by the manager; all causing the village of Industry, which early gave such bright promise, to relapse into decadence. St. Aloysius Church and a public school, as well as an orphanage, were located at Industry.)

The old "Short" house was built—as far as known—before 1847 by Judge John C. Short. It stands in Fernbank, just inside the Cincinnati corporation, near Route 50.

Chapter 35

FERNBANK'S POINTS OF INTEREST

Fernbank is, or has been, the site of several unique places of local interest. These include an Indian statue, a nine hole golf course, a river park, and an Ohio River lock.

The Fernbank Indian has received more than its share of publicity. This cast iron statue was placed in the community in 1912 by Eliza Morgan Thornton in memory of her husband, J. Fitzhugh Thornton, called "General" by his neighbors. This particular memorial was selected to call attention to the fact that the region was once "the happy hunting ground" of the Red Man. (Eliza M. Thornton, herself, was a descendant of Dr. Stephen Wood, pioneer physician who came to North Bend with Judge John Cleves Symmes when the land was yet occupied by the Indians. J. Fitzhugh Thornton was a son of Dr. J. H. F. Thornton of Cleves, whose first wife had been a daughter of General Wm. H. Harrison.) In 1940, the Fernbank Indian was hit by an automobile and knocked from its pedestal. The statue was subsequently hauled away and sold to an antique dealer for junk. When Fernbank residents learned of its "capture" they went on the war path. After many moons the Indian was finally located and remounted in its rightful spot at Thornton Place. Several times since, the statue has been struck and damaged, but each time--at the insistence of Fernbank "warriors"--their chief has been repaired and restored to his position as lookout over the village.

Short's Woods, named for its founder, C. Wilkins Short, (son of Charles W. Short), is the site of a privately operated nine hole golf course (Fernbank Golf and Tennis Club). The place was once known, in earlier days, as Wyatt's Woods. Here church camp meetings and picnics were held back before the turn of the century. Arthur Colburn, Sr., born at Home City in 1880, recalls that steamboat loads of people were brought to Fernbank to attend the outdoor gatherings at Wyatt's Woods. (Thomas Wyatt was among the earliest settlers, having arrived in 1843. He lived on property first owned by Judge Matson, and later by C. W. Short.) Mr. Colburn recalls one particular camp meeting he attended as a lad, around 1890. On this occasion the preacher, who had been delivering a lengthy address, suddenly interrupted his discourse to tell the audience that he could see, in the distance, several boys stealing watermelons from a farmer's garden patch. Volunteers immediately went forth from the gathering to apprehend the young culprits. The mission accomplished, the preacher resumed his sermon, so Mr. Colburn humorously recalls.

Another park that existed in the down river region back before the turn of the century was Cross Farm Lake. Although not situated in the immediate Fernbank locale, it attracted people from all around the community. Cross Farm was the home of Peter H. Cross, brick maker, who had settled in Delhi in 1852. His brickyard was located at Industry where the Delhi brickyard stands today. A small lake on the Cross farm was enjoyed by all the neighborhood, ice skating being its chief attraction in winter. An item from the Commercial Gazette tells more of this place:

Jan. 7, 1883. "Several of our wealthy citizens are making arrangements to beautify Cross Farm Lake and will place seats amidst the elms."

River Park, located at Fernbank, is a 15 acre tract operated by the Cincinnati Park Board. When Fernbank was annexed to the city, this parcel was under lease by the village with a purchase option. The city took up the option. Outdoor fireplaces, a shelterhouse of stone and a concrete dance floor were built here. The park commands a lovely view of the river. This site is likely the same place once known as "Short's Grove," a picnic ground along the I&C Railroad which came into being during the 1860's.

Robins Nest Resort and Bathing Beach was once a Fernbank attraction of the 1920's. In the same general location of the old beach, today, is an enjoyable floating restaurant called "Sycamore Shores."

"Forest of Arden," the estate of the Sayler family, may yet be seen standing between River Road and Gracely Drive at Laura Lane. A train stop, once situated along the railroad and what was then Commercial Avenue, at this point, bore the name Arden Station. The general locale, between Fernbank and Home City, was known as Arden. Builder of the impressive house was Nelson Sayler, who served as first mayor of Home City from 1879 to 1889. Near to the Sayler residence, in those days, were the homes of Rees B. Price and Abram Brower.

The Saylers were among the many prominent families who settled in the new down river community. Nelson Sayler, who had been a classmate of Benjamin Harrison at Miami University, Oxford, was a son of Milton Sayler, one-time Ohio Congressman and Acting Speaker of the U.S. House of Representatives (1873-1879 era). John R. Sayler, another son of Milton, became a Judge in Hamilton County Common Pleas Court and President of Southern Railway. Nelson Sayler, himself, was a successful attorney and had served three terms (ca. 1860) as a chemistry professor at Cincinnati's Medical College of Ohio.

It was around 1909 that Home City was officially renamed Sayler Park in honor of its first mayor, Nelson Sayler. The Sayler family erected a beautiful bronze fountain in his memory at the village park in that year.

The Sayler home, "Forest of Arden," a well known landmark, was so named because of its owner's love of Shakespeare. Around the turn of the century this grand place was the scene of frequent Sunday afternoon community concerts.

Fernbank was once the site of a large U.S. Army Corps of Engineers Depot and Marine Ways, situated next to an equally noted landmark, the Ohio River Lock and Dam #37. These are now gone. Fernbank Dam, the construction of which was begun in 1907, was one of the first in the Ohio's long system of 50 locks and dams, which were established to create a navigable depth of nine feet throughout the entire Ohio channel.

The historic completion of Fernbank Dam in 1911 was marked by a grand celebration, worthy of recall. The program of events lasted from September 5th to the 9th. It was a great occasion for the down river residents.

The celebration was begun with a spectacular steamboat parade. Capt. Charles Menges led the line with the flagship PRINCESS, followed by the ISLAND QUEEN (No. 1), U.S. snagboat E.A. WOODRUFF, GOLDENROD, GREENWOOD, TACOMA, RANGER and dozens of other large and small boats. Gen. Wm. H. Bixby, chief of U.S. Army Corps of Engineers, was among the speakers.

On another day a band contest, arranged by A. W. McBrair, was featured. Twenty-two bands participated in this event on Government Square. The Classic Ohio Valley Band from Addyston, directed by O. F. Hubbard, competed.

A colorful pageant of floats was staged in the city. A replica of the first steamboat to navigate on western waters, the NEW ORLEANS, which had made its historic journey downbound in 1811--exactly 100 years earlier, was christened by Mrs.

Alice Roosevelt Longworth. Mrs. Longworth's husband was a descendant of the builder and captain of that legendary NEW ORLEANS of 1811, Capt. Nicholas Longworth.

A "Union of Waters" ceremony was a gala spectacle of another day. Jars of water from the Golden Gate, Boston harbor, Duluth on Lake Superior, New Orleans and the Gulf of Mexico were united with waters of the Ohio at Fernbank to create the greatest mixture ever made, the "Fernbank Cocktail."

Col. John L. Vance, President of the Ohio Valley Improvement Association, addressed a gathering at Music Hall, Sept. 4, 1911. His topic was "The Fernbank Dam and What Its Completion Means to the City of Cincinnati and the Ohio Valley." (History of Fernbank Dam, by Marie P. Dickore, Cincinnati Times-Star.)

Several boats lay claim to having been the first to pass through the new lock. However, the Steamer RAMONA (1902-1932) seems to hold the record, having made the first trip through July 22, 1911. Others which have the distinction of being among the first vessels to lock through the new dam were the DIXIE, on July 23, 1911, and the J.M. GRUBBS, on July 25, 1911. (More may be found on the J.M. GRUBBS in "Legend of a River Lady.")

Charles Siper had the honor of serving as the first lockmaster at Dam 37, where he remained until about 1917.

Another exciting event in the history of Fernbank Dam took place Oct. 22, 1929, when President Herbert Hoover passed through the city to dedicate the completion of the canalization project on the Ohio. As the flagship, CINCINNATI, carrying the President and other notables locked through Fernbank Dam, many local residents and school children were present to pay tribute.

When completed and opened back in 1911, Fernbank Dam #37 and the grounds surrounding it were lovely to see. A row of identical yellow-brick houses, dwellings of the #37 lockmen, commanded the river from a queenly setting. In springtime the grounds were flanked by row upon row of peonies, iris and hardy amaryllis, blooming in stately attention. This for thirty-five years was the home of the James Stutzmans. As lockmaster, Jim was typical of the superior character of all lockmen known to thousands of boatmen plying the stream. When Lock #37 was retired (dynamited) in 1962, in order to make way for the new higher level dams, the Stutzmans retired, too.

The fall of Lock #37 was viewed in an aura of reflection by Mr. and Mrs. T. Clifford Mobberley, who have spent their entire lifetime within sight of the river at Fernbank. While the lock was under construction, beginning in 1907, Margaret Sweeney and Clifford Mobberley, as young people, had ice skated in the cofferdam. For them the year 1911 was doubly eventful because it marked the beginning of their wedded life. As a team they made fruitful contributions to the down river community, he as a school teacher and she as a church organist for nearly fifty years. Dam #37, closeby, held fond memories for the Mobberleys. In the spring of their lives they saw it rise; in their autumn years they saw it fall, paving the way for progress.

The site of the old dam is presently slated to become a public park and recreation ground.

Chapter 36

Women and Their Activities in the Community: The Women's Fortnightly Reading Club

Honor to women! to them it is given
To garden the earth with the roses of heaven.
                                            Shakespeare

During the era following the Civil War, women became interested in improving their lot and in having themselves heard. They sought to elevate the position of women in the home and community, and to gain incentive and direction for their lives. Although many women were actively engaged in the work of their churches, they felt a need for broader associations and pursuits. They soon learned that by banding together in clubs and societies, working for civic, patriotic, moral, health and educational causes and improvements, there was no end to what they could accomplish. Among the national organizations prompted by womens' movements of this era were the D.A.R., organized in 1890, and the P.T.A., founded in 1895.

Women of Miami Township and its borders were also caught up in this national spirit of reform and education. Temperance societies were begun, "whiskey wars" were conducted and saloons closed. Schools were improved. Sewing, painting and elocution classes were launched. Community lectures were provided at town halls. Literary, music and dramatic societies sprang up in every local village.

Not to be outdone by Cincinnati, the Delhi-Home City community organized a May Music Festival all its own, the outstanding success of which must be credited, in a large part, to the role played by women of the villages.

The following news items from the Commercial Gazette tell something of the activities initiated and promoted by women in the down river community:

Dec. 19, 1877. "Delhi has a Literary and Dramatic Club which gives public readings and exhibits. Rev. H.B. Ridgeway's lecture on 'Egypt' last week was appreciated."

Feb. 3, 1879. "The parlors of the C. F. Vent residence were filled to overflowing to witness the initial meeting of the Fernbank Literary and Dramatic Club."

Dec. 31, 1879. A list was published in the Daily Gazette naming the ladies who were prepared to receive New Year's Day calls, a popular social custom of the Fernbank, Home City and Delhi community.

April 18, 1883. "The Literary Club held its meeting at the Presbyterian Church. Miss Chidlaw read a paper on the country of Wales, where she recently visited."

April 18, 1883. "One of the popular afternoon coffees will be held at the residence of Mrs. S. D. Patterson."

May 26, 1883. " 'The Delhi,' a society of ladies with a charitable object, held a meeting at the home of Mrs. J. D. Parker."

July 15, 1883. " 'The Hornets,' a club for literary and social improvement, was organized at the residence of Mrs. Twitchell."

These early coffees and tea parties, with literary programs and readings added to lend flavor and stimulus, gave impetus to the organization of a women's club, in 1890, which is in existence yet today. Something of its history must be told. It is a representative example of a small town women's club of the mid-west. Called "Woman's Fortnightly Reading Club" by its founders, the society has come to be recognized simply as "Fortnightly."

As it happened, a group of mentally alert ladies of Home City, Delhi and Fernbank organized a reading and study club. They set for themselves rules of high purpose and aimed at mental growth and self-improvement. In order to justify their time spent on "self," the ladies usually came laden with sewing baskets, and they darned and mended while they grew and improved mentally. Seeds were carefully sown by the organizers, and the Woman's Fortnightly Reading Club (W.F.R.C.) burst into bloom. Little did they dream that their society would grow to hold a legendary place in the annals of village history.

Most scholarly themes of study were pursued by the club, and it was quite in order for six or seven ladies to contribute to an afternoon's program, each being limited to ten minutes presentation time. Fines were levied for tardiness, unexcused absences and failure to provide program assignments. Roll calls were answered with current topics. According to the earliest constitution, a member who failed to have his quotation for roll call was also fined five cents. Minutes of 1913 reveal that "the club collected quite a nice amount in fines" that year.

A strict order of parliamentary procedure was followed and a critic was elected, along with the other club officers. The bounden duty of the respected critic was to point out mistakes made by members and "to give a rub where needed." A quote of 1897: "The critic, Mrs. Early, reported a few lapses from the Queen's English at the last meeting." An 1898 quote: "Our attention was drawn to the fact that we should be more careful to hand in mispronounced words to the critic." Another quote from minutes of 1901: "The critic had to call two members to order for breach of parliamentary etiquette." A 1915 account in an old treasurer's book shows "purchase of a pronouncing dictionary for the critic." Since self-improvement was the club's purpose, criticism was accepted in the proper spirit--that is until the 1920's era. Then the office of critic was, of necessity, abolished.

Membership at first was limited to fifteen. However, this number quickly was increased. The roster came to include associate members, as well, and during the 1910-1920 era, the total membership, at one time, reached 78. Names on the roll changed continually; minutes show frequent leaves of absence and resignations, often temporary.

Secretarial reports were composed in perfect grammar and fluently classical language, and the handwriting was often exquisitely beautiful. Minutes of Mrs. Winifred Wrampelmeier, Mrs. Nannie Early and Mrs. Howard Beidler are worthy of note.

The women "grappled" with program-subjects, many of which are yet to be solved today. On one occasion, Mrs. Sarah B. Hornaday discussed "The Influence of Fairy Tales on the Child Mind."

One quotation, which appeared in an early program booklet, timely today, stated: "The true test of civilization is not the census, the size of the cities, nor the crops . . . no, but the kind of man the country turns out."

Minutes of December, 1895, also include notations of the club's New Year's Eve reception, which was "complete with readings, vocal and instrumental music, refreshments, more music, Virginia reel, and Happy New Years."

In direct contrast to this dignified New Year party, a Leap Year party was given Feb. 29, 1928, which bears recall. It would no doubt have shocked some of the founders of 1890. Recorded as a "frolic," it must have been just that, according to the minutes as follows:

"On gathering at the home of the hostess, members were amused to learn that in order to participate in the gala affair all must leap over boards that had been fastened across the door ways. Club business was postponed. All joined in games of consequence. The ladies were invited to the dining room for a progressive dinner. The table was covered with an old red cloth. Corn bread, baked beans and peas were to be eaten with a knife and all were forced to drink coffee from a saucer. The meal progressed rapidly from the primitive style to the untramodern, as dessert consisted of Eskimo-pie served in lolly-pop fashion." (Author's note: The reader will recall that this was the era of "The Roaring Twenties" and the period of "Anything Goes.")

Back in May, 1907, "Fortnightly" held a regular meeting, with 40 in attendance, at Clovernook Home for the Blind. The home, opened in 1903, was located on the property of the former Ohio poets, Alice and Phoebe Cary. (Phoebe Cary's best known poem, "One Sweetly Solemn Thought," was a favorite of the ladies.) On this memorable occasion in May, 1907, the question "Is Cartooning Carried to Excess?" was discussed by Mrs. Annie B. Calloway "in a masterly manner." (Parents today are still probing the same question.) On that same day, Mrs. Sarah B. Hornaday read a "spicy" paper entitled "How Shall a Maiden Know Whom to Choose." This same Mrs. Hornaday made a trip to Alaska in 1910, a feat of accomplishment in that time.

Mrs. A. E. (Cora) Patterson, Mrs. Hornaday and Mrs. Calloway were among the first ladies of "Fortnightly," those who sowed the seeds that set the club to blooming. Mrs. Patterson, affectionately known as "Patty," remained a member all her life, cultivating and plucking the blooms of her endeavors for 62 full years, until her death in 1953. Born in Cleves about 1866, Cora Patterson was the daughter of D. W. Gibson, a wholesale hatter.

Mrs. Sarah Hornaday was a tireless worker in her church as well as in the community. In her "Fortnightly" presidential inaugural address in 1898, she urged that the "club program might be given wholly to work and study, unimpeded by socialities." Mrs. Hornaday's daughter-in-law, Mrs. Howard Beidler, followed in her footsteps and proved just as faithful a club member as she.

The club's colors were designated in 1896 as white and heliotrope (purple), so early program booklets were tied with cords of these colors. The fee for printing the club program book in 1895 was $8. Today the cost is around $40. During the World War I years, the ladies hand-printed several of their programs, and an artistically talented member, Mrs. William Hall, decorated the covers with irises.

In early years, the organization scheduled numerous public programs at the Presbyterian Church assembly room. Lectures, often coupled with stereopticon slides, and presented by outstanding speakers, were given for the entire community and these were well attended.

Minutes of a meeting in the spring of 1896 note that "spring housecleaning had a visible effect on attendance."

A report of one particular Christmas program stated that "Mrs. Calloway charmed us with the delightful way she got the little Ruggleses ready for the dinner party." This quote recalls to the mind of this writer that in 1962, the late Miss Greta Spencer, life long Sayler Park teacher, charmed the club with her reading of "A Pint of Judgment," a Christmas story by Elizabeth Morrow, equally as delightful as "The

Bird's Christmas Carol."

Mrs. Thomas (Anna Bowles) Calloway was among the club's earliest members. Her ancestors were also among the earliest settlers of Whitewater and Crosby Townships. She was a fine artist and taught china and landscape painting in her studio, which now houses the Sayler Park Post Office. Many examples of her china painting yet grace the homes of residents in the down river community. Anna Calloway also sold notions and dry goods in her art shop. Through her efforts, Home City had its first branch of the Cincinnati Public Library, also in her charge. Once when Mrs. Calloway had sprained her ankle so severely that she was unable to travel about, "Fortnightly" voted to meet regularly at her home until she was fully recovered. The members held her in such high esteem that at her death her family provided a special traction car to Harrison, Ohio, so that the entire club could attend the funeral. Each lady placed a purple iris, symbolic of the club's colors, on her casket.

A report of a "Thanksgiving recollections" program in 1897, ended with this line, written by the secretary: "Our topic led to comparison with the present, that the day originally set apart for Thanksgiving and prayer, and made sacred for family reunions, is to so great an extent devoted to the most uncivilized of modern (1897) athletic games!" (We see that they, too, had Thanksgiving Day football and dinner schedule complications back in 1897.)

Reflect now on this quote from an 1897 club discussion on the Elizabethan Era: "Its social excesses and increasing luxury of the age, proved in after years the truth of the quaint saying:

'When houses were nillen, Englishmen were oaken;
Now houses are oaken, Englishmen are straw.'

The Young Ladies Literary Society of Delhi joined into membership with the W.F.R.C. in 1903.

(Another women's club, also among the oldest in the region, was organized at Cleves in October, 1904. Founder and first president of Cleves Women's Club was Grace Schiele Walker. Her successor as president was Alice Argo Struble, yet living, who has retained membership in that association all 65 years.)

It was in 1906 that Mrs. William (Grace) Gracely's name first appeared in "Fortnightly" annals. At that time, she was a young wife of a busy physician. Her home role, which often required that she assist her husband, prevented Grace Gracely's continuous membership, but she was associated, off and on, with the club until her death in 1969. Although blind for many years, her unique sense of humor was an inspiration to others.

One day in 1909, a number of "earth-shaking" topics headed the agenda of the Woman's Fortnightly Reading Club program. These included: "The Moral Value of Clothes," and "Why Men Object to Business Dealings With Women."

The minutes of May 24, 1911, written by the secretary, Georgia Avey Hey, tell of a delightful meeting:

"Thirty-five members embarked on the 'Little Boone' for the picnic ground near the home of Mrs. Vincent (Joanna) Pickelheimer (cross river at Taylorsport, Ky.) There we were met by the hostess and her mother, Mrs. Grubbs. The day was perfect and our hostess had transformed the grove into a bower of rustic beauty. Under one tree was a stone furnace with the tea-kettle singing merrily. Nearby was a long table in white with decorations of fern and roses. Never shall we forget our delightful dinner under those shady trees with such beautiful scenery all around us. A business session followed. Mrs. Greaves moved that our music for next year be left in the hands of a committee of three. They are to have the power to ask anyone suitable to take part, and these are to be called "complimentary" members. Mrs. Early read a letter from the Presbyterian session granting use of the lecture room for next year's meetings. Miss Macbrair moved we accept the invitation and donate $15 to the church, and $5 to the janitor. The remainder of the afternoon was spent in the house of Mrs. Pickelheimer, where we greatly enjoyed her songs and those of her brother, Mr. Grubbs. We left on the ferry for home with the opinion that this last club meeting of the year had been a 'red letter day in our lives.' " (More of Mrs. Pickelheimer may be found in "Legend of a Riverlady.")

That music committee, appointed at the May, 1911, picnic meeting, lost no time in recruiting its first "complimentary" member, Mrs. Clifford (Margaret) Mobberley. In fact they recruited so well she is yet a member of the club. As Margaret Sweeney, she performed her first "Fortnightly" solo in 1909. From that day forth she continually played piano, accompanying singers or instrumental performers. She served as organist for 50 years at Delhi Methodist Church. Several years ago Margaret Mobberley found it necessary to turn the keyboard over to "fledgling" Esther Kamphaus Fleming, who had been under her musical wing since childhood.

A quote from the club minutes of 1897 stated: "Mrs. R. W. Wise's current topic was a review of the marvelous strides in all branches of science, filling thoughtful minds, even with a wonder, whether much else is left to be discovered."

What changes have been wrought! On turning back to a club meeting of Oct. 13, 1912, we find that Miss Ruth Van Tyne read a paper on "The Moving Picture Show," which commanded attention and provoked comment. Miss Van Tyne fully described this popular new amusement, and said it was making history. She stated that it should be a refined and clean form of entertainment, and an incentive for education. She predicted it would be a future method of lecturing.

"Fortnightly," in early years, occasionally met with, or entertained, other women's clubs. In 1896, Riverside Culture Club rode the train to Home City to be guests of the club. The visitors were met at the train station by an appointed delegation and escorted to the meeting at the impressive home of Mrs. W. L. Kayser. (Mrs. Kayser was the former Miss Jessie Hunt of Valley Junction.) The address of the Kayser home in that day was Liberty Street (now Parkland Avenue, where the Childresses until recently lived.) On another occasion, around 1898, "Fortnightly" visited Westwood Women's Club, traveling by way of "waggonette," which was provided by the livery stable of Clifford Mobberley's father. On still another occasion, in 1916, the ladies attended a meeting of Harrison, Ohio, Advance Club, going by traction car.

From foregoing records, it is easy to see that "neither snow, nor rain, nor heat, nor gloom of night" stayed those grand club ladies from the completion of their appointed rounds to "Fortnightly" affairs, whether by "waggonette," train, ferry, street car, skiff, automobile or on foot.

The club participated in early years in many forms of civic and philanthropic work. Notes of appreciation appear in the minutes from Prof. J. O. Falkinburg, on behalf of Home City School children, for "a painting of Betsy Ross and her flag," and for a "book shower" given, in 1907, by the club to benefit Home City High School library. Club records reveal that the women frequently gave financial assistance to the nursing program at Addyston Episcopal Mission. On Nov. 7, 1911, the ladies observed the Anti-Tuberculosis League flag day. A flag sale was conducted by the members throughout the down river community. Contributions were frequently made to Ohio Federation of Women's Club projects. Members themselves engaged in church work and civic undertakings of their own. Mrs. Joseph (Elizabeth) Burger, present day member, has been a volunteer worker in the sewing department of the American Red Cross for over 35 years.

Elizabeth Burger, who first joined the club back around 1914 as an associate member, when she came to Sayler Park as a bride, has stated that her childhood was spent in a rural area where she had little opportunity for furthering her education. Affiliation with "Fortnightly" opened a whole new world to her. She eagerly adopted the society's purpose of mental growth and mutual improvement as her own personal aim. She has missed few meetings in her long years of club association. Membership in the reading club still remains a challenge to Elizabeth Burger, and she views each new program assignment with enthusiasm.

Mrs. Arthur (Grace) Colburn, Sr., is another who has enjoyed long years of "Fortnightly" association. She, too, joined as an associate, around 1914, in those days when the roster included nearly 75 members and meetings were conducted at the Presbyterian Church lecture room. Like Elizabeth Burger, Grace Colburn was a newcomer to Sayler Park, settling here as a bride. The Colburn home for many years was situated on Nokomis Avenue (now River Road.) Hospitality and pumpkin pie are Grace Colburn's specialities. Her southern background has given her refinement and graciousness, qualities still admired in ladies today.

Another member who dates her affiliation with the club back to 1914, during the same era when Margaret Mobberley's, Grace Colburn's and Elizabeth Burger's names first appeared on the rolls, was Mrs. L. Arthur (Ethel) Perkins. Several years after Ethel Perkins' initial introduction to the club, she moved with her young family to Bessemer, Alabama. However, she continued her club association as a corresponding member, one of several who prepared and mailed their program assignments for presentation on the appointed dates. She kept her membership in good standing by this mode until 1922. In that year, club chronicles inform the reader that "Ethel was back in town!" No member was ever more enthusiastic than this one.

In 1929, Ethel Perkins reported: "The club conservation committee has taken up the problem of purification of Muddy Creek, which is contaminated with sewage." Mrs. Perkins, to this day, continues to take on projects every bit as big as "the problem of purification of Muddy Creek." She has had much to offer the club with her amazing knowledge of geography, history, literature, Early American glass, antiques, botany and wildlife. Back in 1929 and 1930, she held the chair of president--but not before she was installed with pomp in a unique ritual conducted in musical rhyme to the tune of "We'll Be Loving You, Ethel." Joanna Pickelheimer, from over the river, was inducted as vice-president to the strains of "Down on the Levee, Waiting for the ROBERT E. LEE." (Again we note the gay atmosphere of "Fortnightly" during the "Roaring Twenties.")

For a number of years, Mrs. Perkins found it necessary to withdraw from active participation in the club while she was teaching school. The group welcomed her back when she was able to return. In 1968-1969, she served again as club president, after having been president almost 40 years earlier. The ladies of "Fortnightly" have enjoyed many wonderful picnics at the Perkins home in North Bend.

The club gavel, now being used by Mrs. Alfred Stuewe, was carved by Bob Lowe expressly for his mother, Mrs. Howard (Belle) Lowe, when she was "Fortnightly" president in 1939-1941. Belle Lowe's book reviews have been judged "superior" by women throughout the down river area, as well as in Lawrenceburg, where she now resides.

Over the years the club has met in the homes of its members. At times, however, when membership was large the group assembled at the Presbyterian Church, the American Legion Hall and Sayler Park School. Once, after a fire in the club's meeting place, "Fortnightly" gathered in a room above what is now Sayler Park show. Mrs. Walter (Bessie) Noe, a fine member of that era, not too proud to get her hands dirty, always built the fire in the stove at that particular meeting place. Mrs. Noe was a lady. She was most active in the local club as well as in the Federation of Women's Clubs. It is said that she should be credited with initiating, in this district, the first campaign against obscene literature in in 1920's. Good books were vital to her.

Fortnightly came to mean much to its members. None cherished it more than Mrs. H.D. Haynes and Mrs. E. Trisler.

Mrs. Haynes put much of herself into the club and its program. She studiously prepared her papers and book reviews. In late life, Mrs. Haynes chugged around the village in her early vintage car and got far better mileage out of herself, as well as her car, than most women half her age. Anna Trisler, president of the club back in 1904, was another who held dear her affiliation in "Fortnightly." Her home on Center Street (now the Sweeder home on Twain Avenue) always stood ready to welcome the club. In fact, during one entire club year, 1931-1932, when public meeting places were hard to find, Mrs. Trisler invited the ladies to meet regularly with her. Such was her love for her home town, where she had in early days taught school, that at her death in 1965, she bequeathed gifts of money to four churches of the community for the benefit of her friends.

"Fortnightly" today owes much to its older ladies, those who joined in 1911 and 1914, when the club was young. Nevertheless, the membership rolls include a number of women with 30 to 40 year affiliations who have also contributed immeasurably by nurturing the organization and keeping it alive and blooming. The 1930's saw the initiation of Mrs. Howard Lowe, Mrs. L. C. (Edna) Greiser, Mrs. Arch (Helen) Long, Mrs. Earl (Kyle) Dickerson, Mrs. Edward (Emma) Zind and Mrs. Frank (Mabel) Herbert, all of whom have retained membership. Each one has made valuable contributions, each in her own way, to the program of "Fortnightly." Through the years countless women have come and gone, sowing and reaping the rewards of association in this legendary organization. The club can surely be said to have left a mark for good in the pages of history of the down river community, that is, if Shakespeare was right when he wrote:

Honor to women! to them it is given
To garden the earth with the roses of heaven.

Since 1938, a prayer, "Collect for Club Women," written by Mary Stewart, has had a place in all program booklets and is read regularly. It is the ultimate desire of all women to live up to the meaning of this prayer:

"Keep us, oh God, from pettiness; let us be large in thought, in word, in deed. Let us be done with fault-finding and leave off self-seeking. May we put away all pretense and meet each other face to face--without self pity, and without prejudice. May we never be hasty in judgment, and always generous. Let us take time for all things. Make us to grow calm, serene, and gentle. Teach us to put into action our better impulses, straight-forward and unafraid. Grant that we may realize it is the little things that create differences, that in the big things we are as one, and may we strive to touch and to know the great common woman's heart of us all, and, oh Lord God, let us not forget to be kind."

Chapter 37

LEGEND OF THE RIVER LADY

River annals are brimming over with legends of river men; for a change here is a story of a river lady. It is introduced to tell something of the role the river played in the lives of the citizens of the down river neighborhood and to point out little known events that took place in and around the ports of North Bend and Delhi at the turn of the century. It tells particularly of the life of Joanna Grubbs Pickelheimer, who lived cross river from Delhi at Taylorsport in Boone County.

Taylorsport, named for Gen. James Taylor--founder of Newport, Ky., was situated in a rural locale in a region of sparse settlement, a direct contrast to the rapidly growing communities of Delhi, Home City and Fernbank across the Ohio. The truth of this fact was brought out in an account, On the Storied Ohio, by Reuben Gold Thwaites. Led by his interest in history and the river, Thwaites floated down the Ohio in a skiff in 1894. He camped along shore each night and kept a daily log of the journey. From his book the following paragraph, applicable to this account, is copied:

Friday, May 25th, 1894. Written near Petersburg, Ky. (Petersburg was cross river from Tanner's Creek at Lawrenceburg, Ind.)

"The Kentucky side, today, from Covington out, has been thoroughly rustic, seldom broken by settlement; while Ohio has given a succession of suburban towns all the way out to North Bend, which is a small manufacturing place, lying on a narrow bottom at the base of a convolution of gentle wooded hills. One sees that Cincinnati had a better and broader base; North Bend was handicapped by nature in its early race."

In this rustic setting along the Kentucky shore at Taylorsport lived the Grubbs family. They had occupied the land for a number of decades. Here was where Joanna Mundane Grubbs (called Jo) had been born in the family homestead in 1873. Both her father, W. Bruce Grubbs (1835-1897), and her grandfather, James T. Grubbs (1794-1884), were respected doctors in the rural community.

James T. Grubbs was a member of the very first graduating class, in 1821, of the Medical College of Ohio, founded by Daniel Drake. Dr. Grubbs immediately began his practice of medicine in Boone County, where he remained all his life. In 1875, fifty-four years after his graduation, he had the distinction of presiding over a meeting of the alumni of the Medical College. His son, W. Bruce Grubbs, followed his example and likewise studied medicine.

The Grubbs family was talented musically. Many happy hours were spent singing and fiddling around the comfortable parlor of their home. It was Joanna's pleasure to assist in caring for the homestead, wherein were harbored the treasured furnishings and heirlooms of her forefathers. The river-bottom farm, situated in a peaceful but rather isolated region, yielded crops of grain and fruit.

From this vantage point along the Kentucky shore, Jo--since childhood--had watched the paddlewheels of the steamers whip and churn the water into spreading patches of thick, white foam. From there she had listened to the engines and boilers, panting and laboring under their loads, as the steamboats shoved upstream. She grew to recognize the sound of each bell and to know the owner of each whistle. She learned readily to row a skiff.

Since this Kentucky side of the river, as stated by historian Thwaites in 1894, was "rustic and seldom broken by settlement," in contrast to the Ohio side, life for the Grubbs family might easily have been lonely. However, this was not the case. Dr. and Mrs. W. Bruce Grubbs and their family joined, about 1878, the new Delhi Methodist Church, a short row across the river. Dr. Grubbs sang in the choir and frequently took leading roles in the cantatas and May Music Festivals sponsored by the church. He occasionally played baseball and acted as umpire, back in the days when this sport was in its infancy. The following item from the Lawrenceburg Press tells of his activity:

July 29, 1869. "The Lawrenceburg B B (baseball) Club visited Cleves and played a game with the Blue Stockings of that place. At the end of the ninth inning, the score stood at 29 to 18 in favor of the Blue Stockings. Dr. Grubbs of the Parlor Grove Club acted as umpire."

When Jo and her brother, Pericles, were old enough, they, too, joined the Delhi Methodist Church choir. Pericles Grubbs became an accomplished violinist and he later served, for some years, as choir director, often crossing the river in ice and flood in order to attend practices.

Living nearby in Taylorsport was young Vincent Pickelheimer. Vincent's father, Moses Pickelheimer, was a steamboatman. Born in 1833, Moses Pickelheimer obtained his first issue of pilot license in 1862. He steered all his life in stretches above Cincinnati and down to Louisville. In the year 1912, when he was 79 years old, he received his last pilot's license renewal. This fact serves to point out that once a man cast his lot with the river he was snagged for life. Steamboating was not always an easy way of life, as seen in the following item from the Cincinnati Commercial:

Feb. 26, 1870. "The towboat NEVILLE, in command of Capt. Moses Pickelheimer, formerly on the Str. CHAMPION, exploded her boilers opposite North Bend. The captain was asleep in his room when the explosion occurred but he escaped, although his room was blown to pieces. The pilot, James Prater, was blown high in the air, still retaining hold upon the wheel, but he fell into the wreck and was killed along with two others of the crew. The vessel was overtaken by the U.S. mail boat General Buell and the dead and wounded carried to Lawrenceburg."

Being so close to the river at Taylorsport, it was inevitable that Moses' son, Vincent, would also join the ranks of steamboating men. Born in 1867, Vincent was granted his first pilot license in 1889; he too held engineer license, dating from 1893. In addition to operating towing steamers, the Pickelheimer men built boats along the river near their home. They also ran a ferry, off and on, sometimes no more than a skiff, between Delhi and Taylorsport, and possibly up to Parlor Grove amusement park.

Joanna Grubbs and Vincent Pickelheimer married. Their common interest in the river was likely the force that drew them together, for in many respects they were quite different. Jo learned to steer the boats and operate the engines for her boat-building, engineering, captain-husband. Contrary to legend, however, she did not have a pilot's license.

Among the boats built at Delhi and Taylorsport by Vincent Pickelheimer were the LEADER, built in 1907, the ALICE BARR, named for Vincent's sister, and the J. M. GRUBBS.

The Steamer J. M. GRUBBS, built in 1898 at Delhi, was named for Joanna Grubbs Pickelheimer. A small vessel, she had a wooden hull, single deck and sternwheel. Later a cabin was added, converting her to a pool style boat. On July 25, 1911, the J. M. GRUBBS locked through the new Fernbank Dam #37, one of the first steamers to do so. During her thirty years of operation between the Big Sandy River and Louisville area, where her ownership changed frequently, the GRUBBS did general hauling, sometimes towing showboats. An item from The Waterways Journal tells of her work:

Oct. 24, 1925. "The J. M. GRUBBS and showboat COLumbia departed for the Green River to go into winterquarters."

The J. M. GRUBBS is credited with being the last steam towboat to navigate up Salt River (Ky.), her one minor claim to fame. She bore the name J. M. GRUBBS until 1929, when she was sold and her name changed.

What a thrill it must have given Jo to see a boat bearing her name paddling industriously past Taylorsport, carrying cargo for delivery to ports up and down the Ohio!

Since Taylorsport was located in a relatively isolated locale, Jo Pickelheimer began to feel the need for broader associations and pursuits, as did the women living in the villages across the river. The rural Boone County community had few cultural advantages to offer its women at the turn of the century. By nature, Jo was a warm, friendly, industrious person, an intelligent and talented woman. She and her husband had not been blessed with children, so, in spite of her industriousness, she soon faced a void in her life. She sought to fill this void with self-improvement. The river, with its restorative powers, became her partner in the venture.

Delhi and Home City, across the river, beckoned Jo. Over she rowed, or ferried, to participate in the activities of those villages. She joined the D.A.R. and became a dedicated member. She also joined the Woman's Fortnightly Reading Club. Founded in 1890, as was the D.A.R., the club's purpose was mental growth and self-improvement. This association was made-to-order for Jo Pickelheimer; it was, in every respect, her cup of tea.

Participation in "Fortnightly" added scope to Jo's life. She also had much to offer the club. She frequently entertained with music, sometimes accompanying herself on a guitar. For a grand association banquet in 1913, Jo composed a club song for all to sing. Throughout her many years of membership she often served as an officer or program chairman. Her secretarial reports appear again and again within the pages of the old record books. She was clever at rhyming and occasionally penned her minutes in verse. It was likely Jo's husband who ferried the club over to Taylorsport on the "Little 'Boone," as recorded in the minutes of May, 1911, for a memorable picnic at her home.

For a time around 1915, Ethel Perkins lived in a big house in Delhi which faced the Ohio River. From here could be seen the Grubbs and Pickelheimer home over in Taylorsport. Legend tells that each evening at lamplighting time, Ethel and Jo used to exchange lantern signals with each other over the river. That was before the advent of electricity in the community, and the gesture created a warm feeling of neighborliness for both. "Fortnightly" never had more enthusiastic members than these two.

To Joanna Pickelheimer the river was never a barrier. She seldom missed a scheduled meeting, whether church, D.A.R. or "Fortnightly" affairs. Records state that "she often came across with chunks of ice bumping at the boat." When it was cold and muddy she had to wear high boots. However, she always carried along her best slippers to don when she reached Delhi, so as to be properly dressed for "Fortnightly." She continued her affiliation with the club until her death in 1936.

The river, which might have proven an obstacle to another, added new dimensions to the life of Joanna Grubbs Pickelheimer. She surely earned the title "River Lady." For her time and place she was unique.

Chapter 38

U.S. CENSUS RECORDS

Miami Township, 1820 Census; Heads of Families.

(Note: Spellings very poor; difficult to read; many errors. Copied from micro-film as they appeared to be. (MBB)

Adams, Caleb
Aims, Austin
Akins, Jess (Akers?)
Akins, Levi (Akers?)
Anderson, Francis
Anthony, Whinny
Argo, Moses
Armstrong, Ruth
Athens, Fairfan
Avery, Isaac

Baily, Daniel
Baily, Mark
Baker, Earnest
Bannister, John
Batteman, Aron (sp.?)
Beck, Eliza
Berton, Eliza (sp.?)
Bevans, Peter
Bevans, William
Broderick, Anth
Brogart, John (sp.?)
Brooks, Josiah
Brown, Robert
Buck, Harman
Buck, William L (or S.)
Bump, Ansel
Bump, Lawson
Burr, Samuel
Bussel, Moses

Cady, Joseph
Carson, David
Chambers, Benjamin
Cheek, George
Chew, William
Clawson, Nathan
Coleman, Jacob
Colkins, James
Columba, Willie (sp.?)
Columba, John (sp.?)
Cooper, Isaac
Coovert, Jeremiah
Copetu, Abraham (sp.?)
Corwin, J. Sam
Cowin, Moses
Cowin, Simmons (sp. Coinin?)
Craig, John
Craig, John
Crawford, Urah
Creech, Elpha
Creech, Isaac
Crowder, James
Crowder, Willie
Cuningham, John

Dains, Joseph
David, Lewis
Davis, Ely
Davis, John
Davis, Stephen
Denneson, Daniel
Doge, Amasa
Doty, John

Dugan, Henry
Dunn, John

Ellis, Moses

Fairfield, John
Farmer, John
Fauver, John
Ferril, John
Fisk, Nathan
Flora, George
Flinchpaugh, Henry
Ford, Perly
Francis, Samuel
Frasher, Mary
French, John
Fulsher, George

Gilbert, Nathan
Glass, Robert
Golshorn, Peter
Goodrich, Jeremiah
Grian, John
Grian, Noah
Gruem, Jeremiah (Grium?)
Gustus, Abra

Haid, Richard
Harper, Med
Harrell, William
Harris, Charles
Harrison, William H.
Hart, John
Hatton, Harris
Haven, Jason
Henman, Arnold
Herndly, John
Herrand, Jesse (sp.? Hearn)
Hodges, Matthew
Hogan, Philip
Howard, Philip H.
Howell, Daniel
Howerton, Obidiah
Hutchison, Sam
Hutson, Georby

Ingersole, Able
Ingersole, Jami

Jackson, Robert
Jackson, Robert

Ketcham, James
Kimball, Edmond
Kincaide, Thom
Kincaide, Vina

Lacy, Stephen
Lambert, Jesse
Lamdisi, John (sp.?)
Lasly, Abigail (sp.?)
Lawyer, Cyrus
Lawyer, Jona
Leffler, John, Jr.

Lefler, Henry
Lefler, John
Lefler, ___?___zll
Lownsburgh, Joseph (sp.?)

Mann, John
Martin, James
Martin, James, Sr.
Martin William
Malston, Francis
Malston, John
Matson, John (over 45)
Matson, John
Matson, James (over 45)
Matson, Joanha (over 45)
Matson, John (over 45)
Mattews, George
McCoy, John
McDaniel, Andrew
McDaniel, Joseph
McDaniel, Maj. (?)
McKennon, John
Moke, Christian (Moak)
Moreland, Brison
Morgan, Jacob
Morly, Rilborn
Morrol, Henry
Miller, David
Miller, George
Miller, Henry
Miller, Jacob

Ogden, Hiram
Osburn, Caleb
Osburn, John

Palmer, Henry
Palmer, Hiram
Parvin, William
Patterson, Jayn
Patterson, Mra (sp.?)
Patterson, Peter
Phelps, John
Piatt, William
Plew, Jeremiah
Plow, Henry
Plow, Philip
Poke, Isaac
Pratt, Daniel
Prespon, Abra (sp.?)

Quick, Elza
Quik, Richard

Racely, George (sp.?)
Reding, Eliza (Redding)
Riely, Dickerson
Rino, George
Rittenhouse, William
Robison, John

Rolison, Robert (Rulison?)
Rudisole, Jacob (Rudisell)
Rudisole, Philip
Rumburgh, Eliza

Scogden, Benjamin (Scoggins?)
Scott, Owen
Searham, Richard
Short, John C.
Shotts, Henry
Shotts, John
Simmons, Isaac
Silvers, James
Skule, John (? Scull or Skull)
Smith, Collins
Smith, Henry
Smith, Isaia
Smith, James F.
Smith, Michel
Smith, Press
Smith, Trak (sp.?)
Smithlap, David
Stephenson, John
Stewart, Isaac
Stidwell, David
Strong, Barny
Strong, James

Tallman, John
Thuston, Serias
Towner, Daniel
Twillegar, Mary

Van Curin, Gilbert (sp.?)
Vangorder, Abra
Vangorder, Eliza
Van Winkle, Noah
Van Winkle, William

Wade, Benjamin
Wadly, Tho (sp.?)
Wallace, Nathan
West, James H.
Westcott, Davie
Westcott, James
Whietecotton, Moses (sp.)
White, Jani
Williams, Ben
Williams, John
Willis, John
Willyard, Henry
Wilson, John
Wolemsly, Wm. (sp. Wamsley)
Wood, Ebenezer
Wood, John
Wood, Molly
Wood, Dr. Stephen

Yanly, Francis (sp.)

Total of 226 names recorded by census taker in 1820.
(Foregoing names should be compared with later census readings to determine correct spellings.)
(Marjorie Byrnside Burress, 1968)

U.S. Census Records, Copied from micro-film.
MIAMI TOWNSHIP 1830, Heads of Families;
Cleves, at end.

Acers, Levi
Akers, Jesse
Akers, John

Alfred, Harrison (Alford)
Alfred, James
Allison, Samuel

Andrews, Isaac
Andrews, Jacob
Andrews, Joseph
Andrews, Samuel
Armstrong, Ruth
Athens, George W.
Athens, Fairfame (sp)
Augusta, Mrs.
Ayres, Moses
Babcock, John
Bannister, John
Bateman, Aron
Bevins, Henry
Bingle, William (sp. Ringle)
Bogart, Helmes
Boothly, James
Bossy, Lyman (sp)
Bowers, David
Bowers, William
Brick, Thomas
Brower, Robert
Brunner, Jacob
Bump, Ansel
Bunnel, Isaac
Bunts, John (Bunce)
Burns, Isaac
Burr, Samuel
Burton, Elizabeth
Bussell, Moses
Cady, Daniel L.
Cail, Eleanor
Carpenter, Abram
Chambers, Benjamin
Chambers, Josiah
Cheek, George
Clemens, Reuben C.
Coleman, Jacob
Conner, James
Cooper, John
Covert, Jeremiah
Cox, Jacob
Crowell, Archibald
Dane, Mary
Davies, Eli
Demoss, Charles
Dennison, Daniel
Disbrow, Isaac
Disbrow, Jesse
Dodge, Amaziah
Dugan, Henry
Esex, Benjamin
Evenger, Thomas
Fagaly, John
Fagaly, Sarah
Fauris, John
Flinchbaugh, Henry
Flinchbaugh, Christopher
Frazee, Jonas (age 70-80)
Frazee, Jonas
Frazee, Reeder
French, John
Gardner, Reuben
Garrison, Joseph
Gibson, Joshua
Gilbert, Oramel
Gilland, John
Goodrich, Jeremiah
Guller, John (sp.)
Hager, Ephraim
Hammet, Christopher
Harbaugh, Jacob
Harcourt, E. L.
Harper, Middleton

Harrid, William
Harrison, Gen'l Wm. H.
Harrison, Wm. H., Jr.
Hart, Jacob
Hartman, Moses
Hayes, James
Hayes, Job
Hayes, Josiah
Herring, Jesse (sp)
Hoatz, Benjamin
Hodge, Adam
Hogan, Philip
Holmes, Reuben
Howard, Philip
Hudson, Corbly
Hull, John
Hunter, John
Hurd, Adam
Hutchinson, Randolph
Iliff, Samuel
Ingersol, Abel
Jones, Moses
Kelly, Joseph
Kelsey, William
Kiger, Samuel
Kincaid, James
Kincaid, Viney
Lacy, Stephen
Ladd, Ira D.
Lambert, Jesse
Lawrence, Isaac
Leg, John
Leiper, W. M.
Lewis, Dyer (or Lewis Dyer)
Lind, Andrew
Lind, George
Lind, Isaac Z.
Malston, Frank
Malston, Sedam
Malston, Polly
Markland, Bryson
Markland, William
Mason, Jacob
Mathers, Levi
Matson, James
Matson, John
Matson, John, Jr.
McCorkle, Brice
McGee, John
McIlroy, James
McKinny, Andrew
McKinny, Anthony
McKinny, Micah
McKinny, Moses
Miller, John
Millers, Daniel
Millers, Ludlow
Moak, Christian
Moak, John
Moore, Asher
Moore, John L.
Morgan, Isaac
Morgan, Jacob
Morgan, Lewis
Morgan, Proctor
Neal, John
Ogden, James L.
Osborn, John
Ottman, Dick
Parks, Jonathan
Patterson, Abram
Patton, John
Payne, Abraham

Pendergrass, John
Quigley, John
Redding, Elijah
Redding, James
Reeves, Daniel
Riddle, Benjamin
Rittenhouse, Hiram H.
Rittenhouse, William
Rittenhouse, William, Jr.
Robinson, John
Rudisell, Christopher
Rudison, John
Rudison, Willa
Rudison, William
Rynegar, Casper (Rininger)
Salmons, William
Sammons, Isaac
Schmidlap, Christian
Schumway, David (sp)
Scull, Joseph
Short, John Cleves
Shots, Levina
Shotts, John
Silvers, Betsy
Smith, George
Smith, Henley
Smith, James
Smith, James
Smith, Patrick
Spence, Joseph
Spence, Robert
Stalkner, Jacob
Stalkner, John
Standiford, James
Stewart, Isaac
Stillwell, David

Stone, William L.
Storms, Jacob
Storms, William
Story, James
Stuart, William
Taylor, William L.
Thurston, Cyrus
Towner, Abigail
Trigner, Richard
Tully, David
Turner, George
Tyler, Heman
Vangorder, Abram
Vangorder, Elijah
Vanvormer, Fields
VanWinkle, Noah
Wallace, William
Ward, Stephen
Warren, Benjamin
Watkins, John
Westcott, Ebenezer
Westcott, James
Westcott, John D.
Williams, Enoch
Williams, John
Wilson, Ann
Wiseman, Isaac
Wood, John
Wood, Jonathan
Wood, Stephen (age 60-70)
Wood, Hiram
Wood, Theodore
Wright, Hiram
Wright, John
Yoder, Henry
Young, Samuel

Miami Township, 1830, Heads of Families in Cleves

Armstrong, Cyrus
Barker, Hiram
Clendennin, J.
Collins, Thomas
Eckman, Jacob
Edmunds, Samuel
Eisentrig, Peter (sp)
Howell, Dan
Hurrin, William
Linn, Joseph (?Lind)
Porter, Andrew

Richards, Chester
Rittenhouse, George F.
Runyan, Joseph M.
Shepherd, Charles G.
Simpson, Oliver
Smith, Randolph
Smith, Sarah
Strong, Freeman
Taylor, Ulysses
Weaver, J.
Young, Henry

(Names of the 1830 census were copied as they appeared to be, although there are no doubt many errors. MBB, 1968.)

Representative list of occupations and professions found in Miami Township and Cleves, in 1850, listed below:

Miami Township:
Boarding House, James Farrell; Blacksmiths, Seth Allen, Joseph Bussell; Carpenters, Asa D. Ladd, Roswell Reed, Stephen Wilkenson, W. K. Elliott; Cooper, Henry Gridley, Bateman; Cook at Boarding House, Geo. Sidemore; Gunsmith, Blemus Hayden; Innkeeper, Moses Bussell; Merchants, Chas. H. Gardner, Ephraim Morgan; Mason, Andrew Douglass; Millwright, David Smith; Minister, Methodist, Wm. H. Biddle; Physician, J. H. F. Thornton; Shoemakers, Wm. Baker, Michael Coleman, Thos Folz; Speculators, A. T. Bussell, George W. Balsley, George Balsley, Jr.; Stonemason, John Creech; Tanner, J. O. Howell, James Love.

Cleves: 1850
Blacksmiths, John Cheek, David Myers, Sam Wamsley, Jacob and Geo. W. Eckman; Bricklayer, Sam Carr; Butcher, John Moore; Carpenters, Wm. B. Wamsley, Alfred Evans, Richard Simpers; Cooper, James Herron; Merchants, David J. Brown, Stephen Cooper, Joseph Runyan; Ministers, Methodist, John W. Riely, United Brethren, Harrison Harrell; Physicians, R. C. Ewing, Wm. Goshorn; Shoemakers, Ebenezer Argo, Chas. Denny, Wm. Finkbine, Wm. & James Kinder; Speculator, Isaac Harrell; Surveyor-Engineer, Andrew Porter, Wm. Porter; Tailor, Henry Kinder, Chas. Purdy; Tavern keeper, J. L. Watkins; Wagon Maker, John Laird.

(Note: The majority of residents of Miami Township were listed in 1850 as farmers or laborers.)

****

Home City High School graduating class of 1904-05. Students from Elizabethtown up to Delhi attended here. Pictured are, left to right, bottom row: Mary Halliday, Myla Wood, Jennie Sweeney Crawford, Ella Wilson Johnson, Janet March Drewry, and Virginia Schroyer Elrod. Second row: Elsie Tangeman, Martha Law, Margaret Sweeney Mobberley, Alta McKinney Baker, Ida Gottschalk Beach, Cora McKinney Hearn, Olive Begley Breining. Third row: John Wentzel, Gus Hey, Perrin March, William Kite, Harry Robinson and Miss Amy Merrel, teacher (Picture ocurtesy of Mrs. Milton Breining.)

BIBLIOGRAPHY

In many instances sources of information are given with each account. Chief sources, only, are listed below.

Bond, Beverley W., Jr., The Correspondence of John Cleves Symmes, 1926.
Bond, Beverley W., Jr., The Intimate Letters of John Cleves Symmes and His Family, 1956.
Cist, Charles, Cincinnati in 1841; Cincinnati Miscellany, 1844-1845; Sketches & Statistics of Cincinnati in 1851.
Cleves Area Sesquicentennial Book, edited by Walter W. Harrell, with Dennis W. Collins as historian, 1968.
Cotton, Alfred J., Cotton's Keepsakes, 1858, Dearborn County.
Flint, Timothy, Recollections of the Last Ten Years in the Valley of the Mississippi, 1826.
Green, James Albert, William Henry Harrison: His Life and Times, 1941.
Greve, Charles T., Centennial History of Cincinnati, 1904.
Hale, Harry, "Suburbs of Cincinnati," Cincinnati Enquirer.
Hamilton County, Ohio, Court and Other Records, Vol. I, by Virginia Raymond Cummins.

Hamilton, Jonathan Newman, "A Storeboat on the Ohio River," journal at Cincinnati Public Library.
Harlow, Alvin F., Old Towpaths, 1926.
Hayes, Royal S., The Hayes Family.
Heiser, Alta Harvey, West to Ohio, 1954.
Historical Collections of Ohio, Vol. I, by Henry Howe, 1847 and 1888.
History of Cincinnati and Hamilton County, by S. B. Nelson, 1894.
History of Dearborn and Ohio Counties, Indiana, by F. E. Weakley, 1885.
History of Hamilton County, Ohio, by Henry A. Ford, and Mrs. Kate B. Ford, 1881.
Juettner, Otto, Daniel Drake and His Followers, 1909.
Mt. Nebo Society papers, found at Taylor High School, North Bend, Ohio.
North Bend, Ohio, Souvenir Book of U. B. Church, 1916.
Ogden Store Ledger, owned by Dennis W. Collins, North Bend.
Piatt, John James, The Hesperian Tree, Vol. I, ed. 2, 1900.
Pioneer Annals of Green Township, by Reese P. Kendall, 1905.
Parkhurst, Jacob, Sketches of Parkhurst, 1772-1863, by himself; Published in 1963 by Eastern Indiana Publishing Co., Knightstown, Indiana.
Sievers, Harry J., S. J., Benjamin Harrison: Hoosier Warrior.
Smith, Robert F., The Ohio and Mississippi Railroad.
Starr, S. F., The Archaeology of Hamilton County, Ohio, 1960.
The Cincinnati Guide, Ohio Writer's Project, 1943.
Wesler, C. H., "The Old Whitewater Canal," a manuscript at CHS Library.
Williams, Stephen R., The Saga of Paddy's Run.

Chief Additional Sources

Cincinnati and Hamilton County Directories, published by Williams Directory Company.
Cincinnati and Hamilton County Public Library
Cincinnati Enquirer
Cincinnati Gas and Electric Company, "A Guide to Miami Fort;" "The C.G.&E. Story," 1959
Cincinnati Historical Society Library
Cincinnati Post & Times-Star
Hayes, Edna Truitt; reminiscences and school programs.
Lawrenceburg Public Library; early Lawrenceburg newspapers found there.
Maps of Hamilton County found at CHS Library and Hamilton County Engineer's Office, Court House.
Matson diary, owned by Mrs. John B. Bonham
Rittenhouse, Cora; family papers, diaries and Mt. Nebo Society and school records.
Steele, Eunice Guard; reminiscences.
Struble, Alice Argo; reminiscences.
U.S. Census Records, copied from micro-film at CHS Library.
U.S. Post Office Department, Washington, D.C.
Woman's Fortnightly Reading Club records.

★★★★★★★★★★★

INDEX

Indexed by chapter

Addy, Matthew 19
Addyston 19
Addyston schools 19, 20
Anderson's Ferry 11
Argo, Wm. 2
Baker, Alta McKinney 5, 24
Bateman, Aaron 4
Bebb, William 23
Beecher, Henry Ward 21
Berea 15, 24
Bevens family 4
Big Bone Lick, Ky. 4
Big Oak 16
Bingle family 4
Blackford, Nellie V. 4, 22
boats 9
Bogart, Elbert 23
Bogart, Elizabeth 30
Bogart family 23, 30
Bollinger, Albert E. 23
Bonham, Charles B. 20
Bonham, Minnie Matson 14, 24
Bonham's schoolhouse 22
Boxwell examination 24
Braam, Max 2, 23
Brannon, John E. 23
Brater, Bertha 20, 23
Breining, Martin 17
brick making 12
bridges 13, 14
Brower, Abram 14, 21
Brower, Dr. Abram 21
Brower, Dr. Jeremiah 21
Brower Road 21
Brown, Capt. John 9
Bump family 4, 18
Burger, Elizabeth F. 36
Burr School 23
Burr Oak School 19, 20
buses 15
Bussell's Tavern 17

Cady family 4, 22
Caine, Charles W. 16
Caine, Hallie S. 16, 23
Calloway, Anna Bowles 36
Calloway, Elmer 16
Calvert, John 19
canal boat 12
canals 12
Carlin, Mollie 23, 30
Cary's Academy 4
Census records 38
Chamberlain, John V. 14
Chance, S. G. 24
Chidlaw, Wm. Matson 23
Chidlaw, B. W. 7, 8, 12, 14, 23
Chidlaw, Mattie Irene 5
Cin'ti. Gas & Electric Co. 21
Cin'ti.-Whitewater Canal 12
Cincinnatus 1
CL&A Traction Co. 15
Clark, Noah 14
Cleves 1, 32
Cleves Bridge Co. 10, 14
Cleves Horticultural Soc. 17
Cleves Literary Soc. 17
Cleves P.O. 1
Cleves schools 23
Cleves Women's Club 36
Coal City 19
Colburn, A. G., Sr. 9, 35
Colburn, Grace 36
Cold Spring 16, 19
Cold Spring House 16
Columbia Park 21
Columbia Power Station 21
Congress Green Cem. 2, 4, 5
Conner, John S. 17, 23
Cooper, Harry L. 4
Cooper, Dr. W. C. 7, 30
Cooper's Tavern 17
Coulthard, Charles R. 23
covered bridge 10
Creemer, Lucy H. 16
creosoting plant 21
Crisler, Richard C. 17
Cross Farm Lake 35

Darby, Henry 11
Davidson, W. A. 17
Delhi 34
Devin, Amanda B. 19
Devin, Augustus 4, 19
Devin's Station 17, 19
Dick, Harry C. 19
Dockweiler, Milton H. 23
downriver communities 10, 27, 34
Dugan's Gap 21, 24
Dunn, John Wesley 23
Dunn, Hugh 21

Eaton, Bettie H. 16, 28
Eaton George 17
electricity 17, 21
Elizabethtown 21, 23
E-town Female Institute 23
E-town High School 23
Elizabethtown P.O. 21
Ervina 10, 19
Ewing's private school 23

Fagaly School 23
ferries 11
Fernbank 19, 34, 35, 36
Fernbank Epis. Church 34
Ferris, Dr. Ezra 4
Fiddler's Green 19
Finney 21
Finney, Fort 1, 8
Finney schools 21, 22
Fischer, Fred W. 21
Fisher, Raymond A. 21, 22
flatboats 9
floods 6, 14
Forest of Arden 35
Fort Hill 4, 21

Gaff, J. W. 9
Garrison, Abraham 4
Garrison, Joseph D. 4, 10
Garrison, Joseph W. 2
Garrison, Nell Morgan 17
Garrison, Sarah 17
Glatting, Jessie M. 21
Goodrich, Jeremiah 19
Goose Pond 4
Gracely, Grace 36
Gracely, Dr. Wm. N. 34
Gravel Pit 13, 17, 21
Great Miami River 14
Griffith Samuel 17
Griffith's Station 17
grist mills 6
Grouseland 9
Grubbs, Dr. James 37
Grubbs, Dr. W. B. 37
Guard, Alexander 4, 5, 7, 8,
Guard, Bailey 4, 8
Guard, Chalon G. 4, 14
Guard, David 4
Guard, Ezra 4
Guard, Ezra G. 14, 22, 24
Guard, Helen E. 23

Guard's Island 4
Gwaltney, David W. 23, 24

Hafner, Joseph 6, 31
Halliday, Geo. V. 17
"Hamburg" 17
Hamilton County Parks 21
Harding, Wm. H. 16
Harrell, Will 23
Harrison, Anna Symmes 16
Harrison, Benjamin 4, 21
Harrison, Carter B. 4, 9
Harrison Clarissa Pike 9
Harrison family 2, 16, 28
Harrison, J. C. Symmes 9
Harrison, J. Scott 4, 7, 12, 21
Harrison Memorial Park 2
Harrison, Wm. H. 2, 9, 16, 18
Harrison, Ohio 13, 14
Harrison Junction 13, 25
Harrison Pike 10
Hayes, Charles S. 7
Hayes, Edna T. 17, 20, 24
Hayes, Enos 14
Hayes, Erastus B. 12, 17
Hayes, Ezra G. 4, 14
Hayes, Jarvis 14
Hayes, Job C. 24
Hayes, Capt. Jos. 7
Hayes, Robert T. 24
Hayes, Royal S. 23
Hayhurst, Fannie W. 15
Haynes, Mrs. H. D. 36
Heimbrock, Joseph 5, 21
Hempfling family 11
Henderson, Edwin 13
Henderson, Virgil 20, 23
Hendryx, James B. 16
Herbert, Mabel L. 14, 19
high schools 23
Hitchens, Meredith 20, 23
Home City 10, 27, 34
Hooven, Ohio 15, 23
Hornaday, Sarah B. 36
horse cars 15
Horton, Henry V. 17
Howell, Daniel G. 3
Howell, Eunice Keen 3, 5
Hughes, Ezekiel 24
Hunt's Grove 7

ice cutting 18
Indian Creek 17, 18
Indian mound 10, 21
Indian statue 35
Industry 34
inns 10, 17

Jackson, Andrew (house) 24
Jackson, Waldo 5
Jenkins, Earl J. 23
Johnson, Cave 1, 2, 17
Jones, W. Bracken 23, 24
Jordan School 23

Karr, Charles W. 17, 29
Keen, Capt. James 3
Keller, Daniel 6
King, Dr. John 17, 29
Kottmyer family 11

Lake Edward 18

Laird school 23
Landon, Hallie M. 24
Lind, Andrew R. 4
Lind, Thomas N. 4, 5
Lind, Whipple 5, 14
Lloyd, John Uri 19, 29
Long Island Park 7
Looker, Othniel 23
Lost Bridge 14, 15
Luce, Francis 1

McClung, D. W. 17
McDonald, Edward 14, 23
McGuffey, Wm. H. 23
McIntyre, Arthur 6, 16
McIntyre, George T. 10
madstone 31
Maple Grove Cemetery 2
Maple Grove School 23
Matson family 1, 6, 10, 22, 23
Maurer, Joseph 17
Maurer, William 15
Mechanics Row 17
Miami Fort 4, 21
Miami Fort Station 21
Miami Point 4
Miami Purchase 1
Miami Township B&L 17
Miami Township Hall 7
Miami Township schools 20, 22, 23, 24
Miami-Whitewater Pioneer Association 7
Miamitown Bridge 14
mills 11
mills 6
Mills, Isaac 21
Mobberley, T. C. 35
Mobberley, Margaret 35, 36
Moreland, Manning R. 17
Morgan's Raiders 14
Morris, Howard 17
Morton, John H. 17
Mt. Nebo 5, 24
Mt. Nebo M. E. Church 5
Mt. Nebo schools 5, 24
Mt. Nebo Society 5
Myers, John 4, 9

Noe, Bessie 36
North Bend 1, 16, 17
North Bend Lit. Soc. 17
North Bend Masonic Lodge 17
North Bend P.O. 17
North Bend Road 10
North Bend schools 22, 23
North Bend United Methodist Church (E.U.B.) 17
North, Thomas 32

occupations in 1850 38
Ogden's Store 9, 17
Ohio R. Lock #37 35
omnibus 10, 15
Oyler Institute 24

Parker, Capt. J. D. 9
Parkhurst, Jacob 3
Parlor Grove 11
Patterson, Cora Gibson 36
Patterson examination 24
Perkins, Ethel 10, 36, 37

Perkins, L. Arthur 25
physicians 30
Piatt, John J. 19, 26, 27, 28
Piatt, Sarah M. B. 26
Pickelheimer, Joanna G. 36
"Pig's Ankle" 17
Pike, Clara 9
Pike, Zebulon 9
Pioneer Society 7
pipe foundry 19
plank roads 10
Point, The 4, 14, 21
postal service 1, 9, 17, 21
Price, Rees E. 10
punch bowl legend 16

railroads 13, 14
race tracks 10
Reynolds Ice Company 18
river 9, 14, 37
River Park 35
River Road 10, 11, 15
Riverside 21
roads 10
Rittenhouse, Cora 3, 5
Rittenhouse, Herbert 24
Rittenhouse Hill 5
Rittenhouse, Capt. Wm. 3, 5
Riverdale P.O. 21
Robin's Nest Resort 35
Rulison, Dr. Hiram M. 17
rural schools 24

saw mills 6
Sayler family 35
Sayler Park 10, 34
St. Joseph Church 17
Schardine, Ruth 23
Schmaltz, Burkhardt 19
schools 20, 22, 23, 24
Sekitan 19
Seven Mile House 10
Shady Lane 17
Shawnee Lookout 21
Short, Charles W. 19, 34
Short Hill 19
Short Judge John C. 19, 27
Short's Grove 19
Short's Station 17, 19
Short's Woods 35
Silver, James 19
Sizemore, Betty Creemer 16
Smith, Curtis Jr. 17
Smorzka's Tavern 17
Sons of Temperance 17
South Bend 10, 11
Speed, Emma Stumpp 17, 25, 33
Speed, John O. 32, 33
Spencer Platt 23
Spraul, Joseph 17
stage coach lines 10
State Line Road 10
steamboats 9
Str. Forest Queen 9
Str. General Pike 4
Str. J. M. Grubbs 35, 37
Str. J. R. Ware 14
Str. Moselle 12
Str. New Orleans 9
Steele, Eunice Guard 16
Stephens, A.E.B. 23

Stephens, Sylvia W. 20, 23
Stone Lake Ice Co. 18
Stone family 17
storeboat 9
street cars 15
Strong, Barnabas 4
Struble, Alice Argo 16
Struble, Stanley 5, 14, 23
Stutzman, James 35
Sullivan, Edward 18
Swisher, Oliver 23
Symmes, Capt. John C. 1
Symmes, Judge John C. 1, 6
Symmes' home in Cleves 1

taverns 10, 17
Taylor, Anna Harrison 16
Taylor High School 23
Taylor, Col. W.H.H. 16
Taylor, W.W. 17, 23
Taylorsport, Ky. 37
telephones 17
The Point 4, 12, 21
Thornton, J. F. 35
Three Rivers Hist. Soc. 7
toll gates 10
toll roads 10
trains 13
Trautman 11, 27
Trisler, Anna H. 36
trolleys 15
Truitt, Thomas 2, 17, 23
tunnel 12, 13
turnpikes 10

U.S. Army Eng. Depot 35

Valley Junction 13, 25
Vangorder family 4, 22
Virgin, Brice 1, 3
Volz, E. W. 7, 17

Wamsley, Charles 14
Wamsley family 31
Wamsley, Morgan 22, 23
Warder, Dr. John A. 17, 25
Warder, Reuben H. 25
Warder, Robert 25
Washington, Geo. (statue) 16
Watkins, J. L. 10
Welsh, George 16
Welsh, Wm. B. 23, 24
Western Female Seminary 23
Whitewater Canal 12
Whitewater Park 7
Whitewater Valley R.R. 13
Winter, Charles B. 21, 22
Wise, Capt. R. W. 9
Woman's Fortnightly Reading Club 36, 37
Wood, Charles Albert 3
Wood, Dr. Stephen 1, 3, 17
Wyatt's Woods 35

Yanney, Fern 22
Young, Charles T. 20, 23
Young, Jacob M. 16
Young, Wm. T. 16
Yunker, Benedict 10

Zinn, Peter 4, 10
Zondler, Jacob 7

www.ingramcontent.com/pod-product-compliance
Lightning Source LLC
Chambersburg PA
CBHW051805100526
44592CB00016B/2570